EXPLORING THE FUTURE

Exploring the Future

John Phillips

LOIZEAUX BROTHERS

Neptune, New Jersey

First edition copyright 1983 by John Phillips.
Revised edition copyright 1992 by John Phillips.

A Publication of Loizeaux Brothers, Inc.,
a Nonprofit Organization Devoted to the Lord's Work
and to the Spread of His Truth.

Previously published by Thomas Nelson, Inc., Nashville, Tennessee.
The current edition has been substantially revised and updated.

Unless otherwise indicated,
Scripture quotations in this book are from
the King James version of the Bible.

Scripture references noted NIV are from the Holy Bible:
New International Version.
Copyright © 1973, 1978, 1984
International Bible Society.
Used by permission of Zondervan Bible Publishers.

Library of Congress Cataloging-in-Publication Data
Phillips, John, 1927-
Exploring the future / John Phillips. — Rev. ed.
Includes bibliographical references.
ISBN 0-87213-625-6 (pbk.)
1. Bible—Prophecies. I. Title.
BS647.2.P47 1992
220.1'5—dc20   91-39048

Printed in the United States of America.

10   9   8   7   6   5   4   3   2   1

Contents

Foreword

From the prolific pen of John Phillips comes this volume on Biblical prophecy. Seldom, if ever, have I read a more thorough survey of the great prophetic themes. With unusual clarity and refreshing alliterative arrangement the author traces God's plan for the ages culminating in the rapture of the church, the regathering of Israel, the realignment of the nations, and the return of Christ.

His is an evident confidence in the inerrancy of the inspired Scriptures. Undergirding this excellent exegesis of the prophetic Word runs the dominant chord that "the testimony of Jesus is the spirit of prophecy." Central in the prophecies of the Bible, as in all the canon, is the person of God's Son, the Lord Jesus Christ. This book honors Him.

It is a distinct privilege to commend *Exploring the Future* to the Christian public. John Phillips's ministry of prophetic truth is not shadowed by cheap sensationalism, but rather characterized by a sane, sensible correlation of history, current events, and unchanging Bible truth.

May this exceptional work on the prophetic Scriptures be used of God to quicken the hope of believers and awaken a new interest in those who have been "slow of heart to believe all that the prophets have spoken."

Paul R. Van Gorder
Associate Teacher Emeritus
Radio Bible Class

Preface

The countdown seems to have begun.

When we launch a satellite into space, NASA has an impressive checklist of things to be tested before the vehicle finally lifts off from its pad. There are sometimes delays in checking off the items on the list, but once the countdown has begun, it usually continues to the end. It is only a matter of time. We are all familiar with the impressive final seconds—ten, nine, eight . . . three, two, one, blastoff!

As we look at today's world and then look at the variety of Scriptures that focus on the endtimes, it seems that the countdown to the coming of Christ has begun. Neither the "day nor the hour," the "times or the seasons" are ours to know (Matthew 25:13; Acts 1:7). But everywhere today there seems to be a rapid movement of events to the final seconds before the church is launched into space—and the subsequent judgments descend on the world.

All Bible prophecy relates to four great themes—the rebirth of Israel, the realignment of nations, the rapture of the church, and the return of Christ. There are increasing indications in all four areas that the endtimes are closing in.

That is what this book is about. I have brought together a number of major Bible segments that bear on the endtimes. I have summarized the prophetic teaching of Daniel and the apocalyptic visions of Revelation. I have examined a number of Old Testament prophecies that deal with the end-time rebirth of the state of Israel and with the future destiny of the Jewish people. I have looked at Bible prophecies that have to do with the future of the nations and also at prophecies relating to the church age and its approaching end. Attention has been paid to the prophetic teaching of the Lord

Jesus, especially to His Olivet discourse. The prophetic teachings of Peter and Paul have also been examined.

To help us appreciate how things are unfolding in accordance with the divine blueprint, I have included a section on modern Israel and one on the rise and significance of Russia and its satellites.

Because a study of prophecy ought always to have practical significance, I have included a section dealing with personal issues. Each of us has to face a personal countdown to eternity. That countdown has already begun for each person alive on the earth today.

Let us satisfy ourselves that the Bible *does* foretell the future. Then come, explore the future with me.

1

The Bible and Fulfilled Prophecy

F oretelling the future is a risky business. Just prior to the 1980 presidential election in the United States, the *Saturday Evening Post* interviewed five leading astrologers in the country and asked them to predict the outcome of the party conventions and also of the November election.

Five candidates were in the running at the time—President Jimmy Carter, Senator Edward Kennedy, former Governor Ronald Reagan, former Governor John Connally, and Senator Howard Baker. As we know, the Democrats nominated Jimmy Carter to run for the presidency, and the Republicans nominated Ronald Reagan.

In light of Reagan's landslide victory both in the party convention and in the number of electoral college votes, the *Post* article makes very interesting reading. Some of the prophecies were extraordinarily ambiguous. One astrologer said that Carter's chart indicated he would be facing a new beginning of some sort in November. Brilliant. Anyone could have made a guess like that. Another astrologer said that with so many unknowns there was no positive way to predict a winner. At least that was honest. Another thought that "a dark horse" might perhaps enter the race and change the election picture. There was no hint as to who this mysterious dark horse might be, though even a wild guess would have been more to the seer's credit than such cautious ambiguity.

More interesting than the obvious hedging were the bold plunges taken by some of the astrologers. One thought that Carter could not win by a landslide. Since he lost by a landslide, that was some prediction. The same astrologer also predicted that the outcome of the election would either be very close or Carter would lose. One wonders why he could not have foretold Reagan's overwhelming victory. Another false prophet looked at Connally's transits for the time of the election and said that they were excellent and that he could be the winner. We now know that Connally never even made it as a candidate to the party convention. Another prognosticator declared that the final race would be between Connally and Kennedy, neither of whom even won their party's nomination.[1] All of which shows what a precarious business prophecy is.

Secular historians who venture into prophecy do no better than the soothsayers, psychics, and stargazers who are popular in our society. H. G. Wells was a well-known futurist novelist in his day and the author of a best-selling book on world history. He once tried his hand at foretelling the future of the Jewish people. Wells was an avowed enemy of the Bible and the Christian faith, and his ignorance of the Bible did not help him much with his prophetic vision. Writing from an imaginary point in the distant future, he said:

> Between 1940 and 2059, in a little more than a century, this antiquated obdurate culture [Jewish] disappeared. It and its Zionist state, its kosher food, the Law, and all the rest of its paraphernalia were completely merged in the human community. . . . Their attention was distracted from Moses and the promise of Abraham, and the delusion that God made His creation for them alone, and they were taught the truth about their race.[2]

Zionism, of course, was a growing voice in world affairs when H. G. Wells wrote that. What he did not foresee was the triumph of Zionism in the rebirth of the present state of Israel in 1948, nor did he have any comprehension of the place the Jewish people have in the plan of God.

The historian Lord Bryce, in the second volume of his work *Modern Democracies* (pp. 657-658), made an interesting observation about the inability of men of genius and of great intellect to foresee the future. He wrote:

> We cannot refrain from conjecture. Yet to realize how vain conjectures are, let us imagine ourselves to be in the place of those who, only three or four generations ago, failed to forecast what the next generation would see. Let us suppose Burke, Johnson, and Gibbon sitting together at a dinner of the club in 1769, the year when Napoleon and Wellington were born, and talking on the politics of the European continent. Did they have any presage of the future? The causes whence the American Revolution and the French Revolution were to spring, and which would break the sleep of the peoples in Germany and Italy might, one would think, have already been discerned by three such penetrating observers, but the only remarks most of us recall as made then and for some years afterward to note the symptoms of coming dangers were made by a French traveler, who said that the extinction of French power in Canada had weakened the tie between the American colonies and Britain; and by an English traveler who saw signs of rottenness in the French monarchy. Men stood at the edge of stupendous changes, and had not a glimpse of even the outlines of those changes, not discerning the causes that were already in embryo beneath their feet like seeds hidden under the snow of winter, which will shoot up under the April sunlight.[3]

John Parker, the hymnwriter, summed it up for us:

> God holds the key of all unknown,
> And I am glad;
> If other hands should hold that key
> Or if He trusted it to me,
> I might be sad.

In contrast with the vagaries, inaccuracies, and ambiguities of secular prophets, the Bible boldly stakes its claim to credibility as the inspired Word of God on the accuracy of its prophecies. God claims to be the only one able to foretell the future. He says, "I am God, and there is none like me, Declaring the end from the beginning, and from ancient times the things that are not yet done" (Isaiah 46:9-10). He challenges others to foretell the future: "Who, as I . . . shall declare . . . the things that are coming, and shall come, let them shew unto them" (Isaiah 44:7). He throws down the gauntlet to unbelievers: "Produce your cause, saith the Lord; bring forth your strong reasons. . . . shew us what shall happen . . . declare us things for to come. Shew the things that are to come hereafter, that we may know that ye are gods" (Isaiah 41:21-23).

The Bible not only foretells the future; it boldly piles up scores of specific details—unlike the Delphic oracle when it was consulted by the fabulously rich Croesus, the last king of Lydia, as to whether or not he should attack the Persians. The oracle assured him that if he attacked the Persians he would destroy a mighty kingdom. Accordingly, Croesus joined forces with Babylonia and Egypt and, expecting help from his allies, attacked Persia in 546 B.C. But the help was not forthcoming, and as a result his kingdom was overthrown by Cyrus the Persian. Thus the ambiguous oracle spoke truly. Croesus destroyed a mighty kingdom—his own.

Of the hundreds of specific and detailed prophecies in the Bible we could examine, we shall concentrate here on one of the most famous: the body of prophecy concerning the destruction of Tyre. That magnificent Phoenician city on the coast of Palestine was leveled to the dust by Alexander the Great in 332 B.C. in one of history's most spectacular battles. To accomplish his goal, Alexander employed military tactics, engineering genius, and innovative methods never before seen.

The story of Tyre's doom originated several centuries earlier when the prophet Ezekiel pronounced the city's destruction because of its traffic in slaves and its vile, cruel religion. In foretelling Tyre's overthrow, the prophet added detail after detail (Ezekiel 26). He said that the invader would first take the suburbs of the city (the "daughter" cities of Tyre) and then he would take Tyre itself (26:6-11); that many nations would come against the city (26:3); that Tyre itself would be thrown into the sea (26:12); that the actual site of the city would be left flat and scraped as clean as a rock; that where Tyre once had stood fishermen would spread their nets; and

12

finally, for good measure, the city known to Ezekiel would never again be rebuilt (26:14).

In Ezekiel's day such predictions as those must have sounded ridiculous. Tyre was mistress of the seas, the seaport of the world. Even mighty Carthage, whose troops under Hannibal almost conquered Rome, was a mere colony of Tyre. Tyre enjoyed its greatest prosperity between 1100 and 573 B.C. Its location enabled it to resist capture for centuries. Its walls defied even the siege-wise troops of Assyria. Tyre was the proudest and most prosperous city on earth when Ezekiel wrote—the emporium of the world, its markets bulging with gold and precious stones from Ethiopia and Arabia, silver from Spain, tin from Britain, emeralds from Damascus, ivory from the East, and wheat, honey, and oil from Palestine.

By the time Nebuchadnezzar's troops came hammering at its gates, Tyre was riding the crest of imperial might and power, secure in the belief that, having defied the Assyrians for five years, its defenders could certainly sneer down from its walls and fortresses at the Babylonians. But Tyre's hour had come, although none of its citizenry knew it.

First, Nebuchadnezzar's armies took the daughter cities of Tyre on the mainland as foretold; then, in 585 B.C., he brought the full weight of arms to bear on the main prize itself. For months he battered away at the city's defenses until at last he broke through, sacked the town, burned the city to the ground, and left it a heap of rubble littering the landscape.

The people of Tyre, however, escaped to an island lying half a mile offshore, and from there they continued to defy the Babylonians. Nebuchadnezzar had neither the fleet nor the resources for an amphibious assault on the new Tyre. He continued his siege for another thirteen years and then gave up. Both sides acknowledged that the situation was a stalemate, and they signed a truce in 572 B.C.

Tyre had won a moral victory over Nebuchadnezzar, but part of Ezekiel's prophecy had been fulfilled. The Tyre known by the prophet was no more, and its ruins testified to the partial fulfillment of prophecy. But it seemed it must remain just a partial fulfillment, for Nebuchadnezzar had more important matters on his mind than tossing the rubble of Tyre into the sea merely to fulfill the oracles of a Hebrew prophet whose name he likely did not even know.

13

Meanwhile, the people of the new island Tyre set about fortifying their city against further would-be conquerors. They built mighty walls 150 feet high all around the coastline of their city. They mined the channel to the mainland with underwater obstacles to sink unwary enemy ships, and they built a first-class navy. For two and a half centuries they continued to live on in security while Ezekiel's prophecies slumbered in the womb of time. Then, in 332 B.C., Alexander the Great came hammering at their walls, and Alexander was a far more brilliant tactician than Nebuchadnezzar.

The Macedonians had just won a tremendous victory over the Persian army in 333 B.C. Flushed with victory, they were marching south to take Egypt. Alexander had no intention of leaving a powerful city-state like Tyre standing astride his lines of communication, and since his navy was no match for Tyre's, he decided to build a causeway from the mainland to the island. To get the materials he needed for that mammoth project he used the rubble of old Tyre, left behind centuries before by Nebuchadnezzar. Before the causeway was finished, his engineers and sappers had scraped up the very dust of the old ruins and thrown it into the sea.

The people of the island fought back desperately to halt the building of that causeway of doom, but God's clock had struck the hour. Nothing now could prevent Tyre's full and final fall. Alexander's men made giant shields for shelter from the arrows and missiles of the foe as the mole they were building crept relentlessly on. Then his engineers built mobile towers, twenty stories high, with an upper platform that towered 160 feet above the ground. These towers were dragged along the causeway and from them Alexander's troops could look right down into stricken Tyre. Drawbridges on the front of the towers enabled the Macedonians to leap at last over the massive walls and take the city. So Tyre fell and Alexander had unwittingly fulfilled Ezekiel's ancient prophecy. As the centuries came and went, drifting sand from the sea converted Alexander's causeway into a peninsula on which fishermen now spread their nets.

Peter Stoner, a mathematician, once applied the law of compound probabilities to seven Biblical prophecies concerning Tyre. He assigned conservative estimates of probability to each of the seven statements to see if Ezekiel's prophecy could have been fulfilled by chance. He concluded that Ezekiel's chances of writing this prophecy and having it come true by luck amounted to one chance in seventy-five thousand. Yet everything came true to the minutest detail.

If this were the only such prophecy in the Bible one could concede that a fortuitous series of coincidences might have brought about the fulfillment. But there are scores of other such prophecies in the Old Testament dealing with the fate of cities and nations.

Following the same ground rules, Dr. Stoner applied the law of probabilities to Bible prophecies concerning (1) Samaria, (2) Gaza and Ashkelon, (3) Jericho, (4) the golden gate in Jerusalem, (5) the plowing of Zion, (6) the enlargement of Jerusalem, (7) Palestine, (8) Moab and Ammon, (9) Edom, and (10) Babylon. He worked out the probabilities for the various prophecies connected with those places and came to the astonishing conclusion that the chances of the accumulated predictions all coming true were one in 5.76 X 10^{59}—that is, one chance in 5.76 multiplied by 10 and followed by 59 zeros.

Such a figure is beyond our power to comprehend when thus stated; it is astronomical. Dr. Stoner, therefore, illustrated what such a figure means. He suggested we make 5.76 X 10^{59} silver dollars. That many silver dollars, he said, would be sufficient for us to make 10^{28} solid silver balls each the size of our sun. Or, to put it another way, from our pile of silver dollars we could make the equivalent of all the stars in all the galaxies of space two million times over. Now let us suppose that *one* of those 5.76 X 10^{59} silver dollars was marked. The chance that these accumulated prophecies could all come true would be the same chance of a blind man finding that marked silver dollar the first time he tried.[4]

The Bible contains far more than the eleven groupings of prophecy treated by Dr. Stoner. Thirty-three prophecies were fulfilled in a *single day* when the Lord Jesus died. Those prophesies included details of His betrayal (Psalm 41:9; Mark 14:10), His being forsaken by His disciples (Zechariah 13:7; Mark 14:50), the actual price of His betrayal (Zechariah 11:12; Matthew 26:15), what would be done with the betrayal money (Zechariah 11:13; Matthew 27:3-7), His scourging (Isaiah 50:6; Matthew 27:26,30), His trial being furthered by false witnesses (Psalm 35:11; Mark 14:56), what would be done with His garments (Psalm 22:18; John 19:24), His death by crucifixion contrary to the normal Jewish method of execution by stoning (Psalm 22:16; John 19:16), His thirst (Psalm 69:3; John

19:28), His being given vinegar to drink (Psalm 69:21; John 19:29), the piercing of His side (Zechariah 12:10; John 19:34), the mockery of the people (Psalm 22:7-8; Matthew 27:40), no bone being broken in His body (Exodus 12:46; John 19:33,36), and His place of burial (Isaiah 53:9; Matthew 27:57-60).

These were by no means all the prophecies fulfilled in the life and death of Jesus, but these were all fulfilled in a single day. Some of these prophecies depended for their fulfillment on the actions of His enemies, people who knew well the prophetic Scriptures and who certainly had no interest in seeing any of them fulfilled in the person of Jesus of Nazareth. Then, too, some of the prophecies depended on the actions of His executioners, the Roman soldiers who crucified Him, men who did not have the remotest idea that they were fulfilling prophecy.

Now let us consider the remarkable case of the Roman emperor Julian (A.D. 331-363). He is often called Julian the Apostate because, although he was raised by Eusebius, bishop of Nicomedia (a relative of Julian on his mother's side) and received a thorough education in the things of God, he revolted against the strict requirements of Christianity as mandated by his teachers. He secretly gave himself to the service of the pagan gods of his forefathers and in due time was clandestinely initiated into the heathen religion at Ephesus. His dissimulation lasted for ten years until he felt secure enough to throw off pretense and openly declare himself the foe of Christianity.

As soon as Julian became the caesar he ordered all pagan temples to be reopened, and he dedicated himself zealously to the service of his tutelar deity, the sun. To show his devotion to the gods, he would visit the temple of whatever god or goddess happened to be on the calendar for a particular day and would bring the wood, blow the fire, slay the sacrifice, draw forth the entrails, and read the day's auguries.

He knew all about Christianity and all about the words of Jesus foretelling the doom of Jerusalem and the temple. The temple was to be thrown down until not a stone remained standing on another, and Jerusalem was to be "trodden down of the Gentiles, until the times of the Gentiles be fulfilled" (Luke 21:24). Julian knew, too, how literally the words of Jesus had been fulfilled by the armies of Titus in A.D. 70 and how, later, Hadrian had commanded a plow-share to be drawn over the consecrated temple site as a sign of perpetual interdiction. Julian knew that Zion had been abandoned and that pagan buildings had filled the lower valley of Jerusalem and the adjacent hill of Calvary. The holy places had been polluted with idolatrous monuments. A chapel dedicated to Venus had been erected on the spot once sanctified by the death and resurrection of Christ. Julian also knew how, over a hundred years later, the chapel of Venus had been demolished by Constantine, the site of the holy sepulcher cleared for people to see, and a Christian church erected there. Julian decided to turn back the clock, to defy God in Heaven, to rebuild the Jewish temple as an act of defiance and as a challenge to the detested Galilean.

We are indebted to historian Edward Gibbon for an account of what actually happened. Gibbon's testimony can be taken as unbiased, since he himself was an infidel and no friend to either Christianity or the Bible. We shall not reproduce here the somewhat verbose and pompous style of Gibbon. Those who wish to read his account for themselves can do so; his words are readily available today.[5]

Julian undertook to rebuild the Jewish temple in Jerusalem, Gibbon told us, because the Christians of his day believed that a sentence of perpetual destruction had been leveled against Judaism. Julian believed that the success of his project would be a telling argument against belief in prophecy and the Bible.

Gibbon told how Jews from all over the Roman empire hurried to mount Moriah in answer to the emperor's summons. Money poured in; the rich even gave spades of silver and mantles of silk and purple to use for carrying off the rubbish cluttering the temple site. The actual undertaking was entrusted by the emperor to his friend Alypius, who at once enlisted the support of the governor of Palestine.

So work began amid the jubilation of the Jews and the consternation of the Christians, who confidently expected that a miracle would vindicate them and their God. Nor were they disappointed. Gibbon told how an earthquake, a whirlwind, and a strange fiery eruption overturned and scattered the new foundations of the temple. He cited contemporary witnesses, with special attention to the testimony of Roman historian Ammianus Marcellinus, whose unimpeachable character and testimony Gibbon conceded. This witness graphically told of "horrible balls of fire" erupting near the foundations, so that the workmen were scorched, blasted, and driven away. The supernatural phenomena continued, Gibbon wrote, until the whole project was abandoned.

The facts are evident. First, Julian was determined to disprove Bible prophecy by attempting to rebuild the temple before its time as an outright challenge to God. Second, with all the wealth and power of the world at his command, he failed. Nor has anyone since Julian's day made a similar experiment.

The Jewish temple in Jerusalem *will* be rebuilt, as we learn from other prophecies, but not until "the times of the Gentiles" have almost run their course. The temple will be rebuilt under the sponsorship of the antichrist for his own sinister purposes. To this present time devout Jews gather at the Wailing Wall, what's left of Solomon's temple, to pray for the speedy rebuilding of their temple.

As we have seen, Bible prophecies are far-reaching, intricate, and detailed. They deal with empires, nations, cities, people, and events. They speak of things to take place within the prophets' own times and in times far distant from the days of those who foretold them. Many Bible prophecies have already been fulfilled to the letter, and can be checked as a matter of history. Some of them have had a partial fulfillment and await more complete fulfillment in days ahead. Some of them concentrate entirely on events still to come, the shadows of which are beginning to lie heavily on our own age.

For those who would like to pursue the subject further, I provide in the Appendix a list (by no means complete) of some of the prophecies of the Word of God. These prophecies concern empires, nations, cities, individuals, events, the first coming of Christ, and His second coming. Research these prophecies. Mark those that have already been fulfilled, those that have been partially fulfilled, and those that still slumber patiently awaiting the coming of the hour when they will awake to completion.

No wonder the Bible stands apart from all other books, religious or otherwise. It is supernatural in its origin and nature, the living Word of the living God, who sees the end from the beginning and from whom nothing can be hidden.

The prophecies that have already been fulfilled lead us to the confident expectation that every prophecy still awaiting fulfillment will in due course come to pass exactly as written.

1. Eugene Moore, "Polling the Stars," *The Saturday Evening Post* (March 1980), pp. 58-63, 90.
2. H. G. Wells, *The Shape of Things to Come* (1933), pp. 383-384.
3. Cited by Wilbur M. Smith, "In the Study," *Moody Monthly* (February 1953).
4. See Peter W. Stoner, *Science Speaks*, 3rd rev. ed. (Chicago: Moody Press, 1969), pp. 68-69.
5. See Edward Gibbon, *Decline and Fall of the Roman Empire*, vol. 1 (New York: Random House, n.d.), pp. 778-781.

2
God's Plan of the Ages

G od has dealt with the human race in different ways at different times. He has tested mankind under a variety of conditions and for varying lengths of time. Some knowledge of these periods, or "dispensations," is necessary if we are to have a comprehensive understanding of God's dealings with mankind.[1]

The Lord Himself recognized the dispensational principle in God's administration of human affairs. In the Nazareth synagogue He stood up to read the Scriptures and turned to Isaiah 61:1-2. He read all of the first verse and part of the second verse, but stopped short in the middle of a sentence. Then He deliberately closed the book, turned to the congregation, and said, "This day is this scripture fulfilled in your ears" (Luke 4:16-21). But why stop in the middle of a sentence? There is no mark in the Hebrew text to indicate a break. The Lord finished His reading with the words "to proclaim the acceptable year of the Lord," omitting the next statement, "and the day of vengeance of our God." The reason for the break is not contextual, but dispensational. The acceptable year of the Lord had come; the day of the vengeance of our God had not come. We now know that the nearly two-thousand-year-long age of grace comes between the two expressions. Jesus understood that; hence He closed the book in the middle of a sentence.

We are going to look at nine clearly defined changes in the overall way God has handled human affairs. A grasp of these administrative changes is the foundation on which understanding of the prophetic Scriptures rests. Ignore them and all is confusion. Instead of obvious differences between the nation of Israel and the church of Christ, we have a muddled mixing of the two. And instead of Christ coming to reign in millennial glory, we have whole sections of prophetic truth explained away by misty spiritualizings.

The first age was *the age of innocence*. It was characterized by *perfection,* and it stretched from the creation to the fall and consequent expulsion of Adam and Eve from the garden of Eden. Man was created a perfect, rational, moral, and spiritual being. He was placed in a pristine environment, given congenial employment, and blessed with a "help meet" created just for him. He ruled over the works of God's hands. He was crowned with glory and honor, and he enjoyed daily God's fellowship. He was given all things richly to enjoy. There was no sin, no curse—nothing to mar his joy. The only restraint placed on him was that he must not eat of the tree of the knowledge of good and evil upon pain of death.

We do not know how long Adam and Eve enjoyed their innocence in that glorious garden, but we do know that Satan entered the garden in the guise of a serpent and persuaded Eve to eat the forbidden fruit. She did so and tempted her husband to do the same. Thus "sin entered . . . and death by sin" (Romans 5:12). Adam and his wife were driven out of the garden, and cherubim with a flaming sword mounted guard at the gate to prevent them from perpetuating their lost condition by eating of the now-forbidden fruit of the tree of life.

The second age was *the age of conscience*, since a conscience (knowledge of right and wrong) was the only legacy Adam and Eve brought with them from the garden of Eden. The lengthy period of time covered by this age was characterized by *permissiveness*. No restraints were imposed on society, since every man's conscience was his sole guide. With such dangerous freedoms it did not take long for a pornographic culture to develop, a culture so violent and vile that God had to intervene in judgment. The age ran for some fifteen hundred years, ample time for the patience of God to be displayed and ample time, too, for lawlessness to come to full fruition. Art, science, and industry coexisted with moral depravity and occult wickedness. The age of conscience ended with the flood.

Next came *the age of human government*. This age was marked by *protection*. The individual's right to "do his own thing" was subordinated to the general good of society as a whole. The sword of the magistrate was entrusted to Noah, and instructions were given to ensure that the lawlessness of the past age was not repeated. The death penalty was imposed for murder (Genesis 9:6). No doubt the greater included the lesser, and capital punishment for capital crime included lesser punishment for lesser crime. The individual was made answerable to society. Capital punishment for murder is taught throughout the Scriptures (e.g., Romans 13:1-4) and is based on the sacredness of human life in God's sight. The Bible advocates the appropriate use of capital punishment. It avoids the extreme of capriciously imposing the death penalty for all sorts of minor offenses, and it avoids the opposite extreme of letting murderers escape with a lesser punishment than their crime deserves.

It was not long, however, before the sword of the magistrate was converted into the sword of the conqueror by Nimrod (his name means "we will rebel"), who set out to unite the world under a godless central government. Plans for political unity were symbolized by a city to be built at Babel; plans for religious unity were symbolized by a sky-scraping tower; plans for cultural unity were based on a universal language. The repeated expression "let us" shows that a secular man-centered society was the goal. Their materials, methods, and motives make it clear that this first "united nations organization" was planned in opposition to God and was intended to glorify the human race. This ambitious scheme bears the marks of the last federation of nations to be organized by the beast, the final lawless one. He, too, will seek to unify the human race in defiance of God, and the center of human interest will again be Babylon (Revelation 18). Before the lawless plans of Nimrod could be consummated, God came down and overthrew the entire project by confounding human speech and scattering the nations.

The next age was *the age of the patriarchs*, characterized by *promise*. Having scattered the nations, God selected an individual named Abraham, made certain promises to him, and purposed to make of him a great nation. He deeded to Abraham a strategically important country in the Middle East, stretching from "the river of Egypt" (possibly the Nile) to the Euphrates. Along with the promise of the land was the promise that the "seed" (Christ) would come from among Abraham's descendants. The promise to Abraham was confirmed to his son Isaac and then to Jacob. With Jacob began the formation of the tribes (the children of Israel), each tribe headed by one of his sons.

None of the three patriarchs actually received the promised land (Abraham was told that some four hundred years at least must lapse before title would be made good), but they believed in the promise. In the providence of God the patriarchal family settled for several centuries in Egypt. There the children of Israel multiplied and became a populous people while events in Canaan moved toward judgment. In Egypt the Hebrews lost sight of the promises of God, learned idolatrous ways, and sank into slavery. Egyptian oppression ripened into active persecution and persecution into planned extermination. It seemed that the age of promise was an illusion after all.

But then came *the age of Law*, the age of *precept*, ushered in by Moses, the liberator and lawgiver of the Hebrew people. By this time the patriarchal family numbered some three million people in Egypt. Moses, first adopted into the pharaonic family, then exiled in Sinai, was brought back by divine mandate to be the emancipator of the Hebrew people. God used him to humble Egypt and to guide the fledgling nation into the wilderness and on to the borders of Canaan.

Moses' greatest work was to give the law to Israel. This law, summarized in the Decalogue, comprised two major segments— one moral, the other ceremonial. In all, the law contained 613 separate commandments embracing every facet of life. Failures under the moral law were met by appropriate punishments (capital punishment was extended to a number of offenses besides murder, including adultery, bestiality, sodomy, witchcraft, kidnapping, sacrilege, and defiance of parents). The ceremonial law embraced matters of religion and made temporary provision for covering sin until such time as proper provision could be made for all human sin at Calvary. The basic emphasis of the Mosaic law was "This do and thou shalt live."

The period of the law was extensive, running for some fifteen hundred years from Moses to Christ. The law was given to Israel as a nation; its sabbath provision was national; its blessings and curses were categorical and comprehensive; its mandates were upheld by a succession of prophets who were raised up by God to bring the nation back to its founding charter. It is described as "holy, and just, and good" (Romans 7:12), but keeping it was an intolerable burden (Acts 15:10).

The Mosaic law set Israel apart from other nations, even though its jurisprudence has become the basis of law in the western world. Many Gentiles did find the majesty of the law attractive, but the demand for circumcision as an initiatory rite into the Jewish faith and covenant was a deterrent to large-scale conversion.

By the time of Christ, the Jews had loaded the law with traditions and with a growing accumulation of oral rabbinical pronouncements, which were considered as authoritative as the original law itself. Because of their bigotry, racism, pride, and ignorance, the Jews in Christ's day soon resented His incisive interpretation of their Scriptures. They saw Him as a dangerous reactionary and plotted His death. The age of the law ended with the withdrawal of God's blessing on the nation of Israel, the Jews' invocation of a fearful curse upon themselves (Matthew 27:25), and the subsequent scattering of the Jewish people to the ends of the earth.

The next age is *the age of grace*, the age in which we live, sometimes called "the church age" or "the age of the Holy Spirit." It is an age marked by *patience*, during which God is visiting "the Gentiles, to take out of them a people for his name" (Acts 15:14). The feature of this age is the baptizing work of the Holy Spirit: the Spirit of God takes individual believers in the Lord Jesus, whether they be Jew or Gentile, and baptizes them into the mystical body of Christ, the church (1 Corinthians 12:13).

This is something unique to this age. The church was supernaturally injected into history on the day of Pentecost and is made up of people supernaturally regenerated by the Holy Spirit. It will be supernaturally ejected back out of history at the rapture. For the duration of this age, God's national purposes with the Jewish people and with the nation of Israel have been set aside temporarily, although, as we will see elsewhere, the return of the Jews to the promised land heralds a soon-coming end to this present age of grace.

This age of grace is to be followed by *the age of judgment*, the characteristic feature of which will be *punishment*. The Lord will allow the developing wickedness in the world to come to a head as it did in the days of Noah and of Nimrod. Satan will produce his masterpiece of deception, the beast, who will unite the world, enthrone himself as messiah and god, and lead mankind in the worship of Satan. The Holy Spirit will revert to His Old Testament ways in dealing with mankind. The coming age will be one of fearful persecution of God's people. It will also be a time when God will pour out catastrophic judgments on this planet, climaxing in the outpouring of the vials of His wrath in the battle of Armageddon. The Lord's return will put an end to man's mismanagement of the planet and will climax in the judgment of the nations in the valley of Jehoshaphat.

Then will follow *the age of the millennium*, an age of *power* during which the Lord Jesus will rule this planet with a rod of iron as King of kings and Lord of lords. It will be an age of peace and prosperity foreseen in many an Old Testament prophecy. The promises made to Abraham, Isaac, Jacob, and David will be kept to the letter. The age will last for a thousand years, as the name "millennium" implies. It, too, will end in rebellion when Satan, who has been bound in the abyss throughout the period, will be released. He will rally the unregenerate to himself and march on Jerusalem. The Lord will explode the universe and hurl people headlong into eternity to stand naked and shivering before the great white throne.

Last of all, we have *the eternal age*, an age of *permanence* of which very little is said in Scripture. The Lord Jesus will deliver up the kingdom to His Father (1 Corinthians 15:24), and the endless ages will roll their waters into the shoreless ocean of eternity. The lost will spend those ages in eternal anguish, the redeemed in bliss beyond words to describe. The book of Revelation points repeatedly toward eternity with its recurring refrain, "forever and ever, forever and ever." The best-kept secret in the universe is what God has in store for us in that new heaven and new earth He plans to create. Peter told us that we have "an inheritance incorruptible, and undefiled, and that fadeth not away, reserved in heaven." We can savor it now in that "joy unspeakable and full of glory" that is ours in Christ (1 Peter 1:4,8).

---

1. For a scholarly vindication of the maligned dispensational approach to the Scriptures see: C. Ryrie, *Dispensationalism Today* (Chicago: Moody Press, 1965).

GOD'S PLAN OF THE AGES

	AGE	CHARACTERISTIC	SYMBOL	END	DURATION
1.	Innocence	Perfection	A Garden	Expulsion from Eden	Creation to the Fall
2.	Conscience	Permissiveness	The Mark of Cain	The Flood	The Fall to the Flood
3.	Human Government	Protection	The Sword	Babel	The Flood to the Tower of Babel
4.	Patriarchs	Promise	A Tent and Altar	Bondage	Abraham to the Bondage in Egypt
5.	Law	Precept	The Tables of Stone	Israel Rejected	Moses to Christ
6.	Grace	Patience	The Cross	Rapture of the Church	Pentecost to the Rapture
7.	Judgment	Punishment	The Mark of the Beast	Armageddon	The Rapture to the Return of Christ
8.	Millennium	Power	A Rod of Iron	Great White Throne	The Return of Christ to the Last Judgment
9.	Eternity	Permanence	New Jerusalem	No End	From the Creation of the New Heaven and Earth and Forever

3

The Prophecies of Daniel

D aniel was a young man of royal blood, of the tribe of Judah, who was deported to Babylon by Nebuchadnezzar. He lived in exile through the reigns of a half-dozen Babylonian kings (Nebuchadnezzar, Evil-merodach, Neriglassar, Labash Marduk, Nabonidus, and Belshazzar) and two Medo-Persian kings (Darius and Cyrus). In other words, he lived in Babylon throughout the entire period of the captivity.

Daniel was probably in his teens when he began his exile and in his nineties when he recorded his last prophetic vision. One timeline for the events in his life suggests that he was about nineteen at the time of his deportation, twenty-two when Nebuchadnezzar had his dream, eighty-seven when summoned by Belshazzar to explain the writing on the wall, eighty-eight when cast into the den of lions, and ninety-two when he wrote the closing visions of his book.

The prophecies of Daniel are in such detail, and so many of them have already been so meticulously fulfilled in history, that unbelieving critics have resorted to suggesting a late date for the book. According to them the book of Daniel was written *after* the prophecies it records took place. That would make the book a forgery, the author a fraud, and its divine inspiration a farce.

There are sound reasons for accepting the traditional early date for Daniel. In the first place, the Lord Jesus appealed to this book, accepted it as authentic, and based some of His own prophetic teaching on it. He spoke of "Daniel the prophet" (Matthew 24:15) and thus put His imprimatur on the book. That is enough for the devout believer. While the Lord accused the Jews of many sins, never once did He accuse them of tampering with their holy writings.

Indeed, the Jews went to extraordinary lengths to preserve inviolate the integrity of their Scriptures. The Masoretes, for instance, devised complicated safeguards against even scribal slips. They counted how many times each letter of the alphabet occurred in a given book. They could point out the middle letter of the Pentateuch, the middle letter of the whole Bible, and made even more complicated calculations. They reverently interred copies of the Scripture too old for further use. No wonder Christ accepted the Scriptures as being accurate.[1]

Dr. Robert Dick Wilson demonstrated that the text of Daniel belongs to the period between 600 and 500 B.C. His proof centered on the vocabulary of the book. To prepare himself for his task, Professor Wilson studied all the cognate languages of the Bible, all the Aramaic dialects, and all the modern European languages in which the critics had written attacking the Scriptures. His linguistic explorations extended over some forty-five languages.

Wilson maintained that a document could be accurately dated by its vocabulary, especially by the foreign words embedded in it.[2] For example, if we were to find a piece of writing containing the word *Sputnik* we would be able to place it with fair accuracy. We would know that the writing could not have been penned prior to 1957, because it was not until October 4, 1957, that the word leaped suddenly into our vocabulary as a result of the spectacular Russian space launch. After holding the spotlight for a few years, the word gradually fell into disuse as other Russian and American space spectaculars introduced new terms. Using this phenomenon of language, Professor Wilson established impressive proof that the book of Daniel must have been written by a Jew, in Babylon, during the period of the Babylonian captivity of the Jews, and in the days that marked its close.

In this synopsis of the book of Daniel we are not studying the historical sections of the book. However, in order to keep our perspective, here is a general outline of the book:

I. Daniel and His Personal Friends (chapters 1–6)
   A. Tests (1–3)
      1. The Word of God and the king's meat (1)
      2. The wisdom of God and the king's dream (2)
      3. The worship of God and the king's image (3)
   B. Triumphs (4–6)
      1. A king's dream (Nebuchadnezzar) (4)
      2. A king's dread (Belshazzar) (5)
      3. A king's decree (Darius) (6)
II. Daniel and His People's Future (chapters 7–12)
   A. The character of the future (7–8)
      1. Bestial (7)
      2. Belligerent (8)
   B. The control of the future (9–10)
      1. A glimpse of the ages (9)
      2. A glimpse of the angels (10)
   C. The course of the future (11)
      1. The coming of Antiochus (11:1-35)
      2. The coming of antichrist (11:36-45)
   D. The climax of the future (12)

Before beginning our examination of the various prophecies of Daniel, let's visualize in which reigns the various events occurred.

HISTORY	KING	PROPHECY
Chapter 1 – 4	Nebuchadnezzar	Chapter
5	Belshazzar	7 – 8
6	Darius	9
	Cyrus	10 – 12

NEBUCHADNEZZAR'S DREAM (DANIEL 2)

The first major prophecy in Daniel was given by God to the heathen king Nebuchadnezzar, ruler of Babylon and its empire in the Middle East. Nebuchadnezzar had been given a dream, and it had disturbed him greatly. The next morning he summoned his dream specialists. He told them he had been given this dream but claimed he had forgotten its details. Nevertheless, he demanded that his magicians and soothsayers recall the dream for him and then, having given this proof of their ability, expound to him its meaning. He shrewdly reasoned that it should be no more difficult for a true psychic to do one than the other. Indeed, if a man could recall the king's dream for him, the king could have confidence in that man's subsequent explanation of its significance.

The rank and file of the college of magicians threw up their hands in horror, but Daniel sent word to the king that he could do what Nebuchadnezzar asked. Accordingly, the youthful prophet was summoned into the royal presence and promptly did all that the king required.

In his dream the king had seen an impressive image. Its head was of gold, its breast and arms were of silver, its belly was of brass, its legs were of iron, and its feet were of iron and clay. The king had dreamed of a Gentile world empire in general. Its various details were really a summary of a significant period of time, afterward called by the Lord Jesus "the times of the Gentiles," the times during which the right to world dominion was officially placed in Gentile hands by God. The period commenced with Nebuchadnezzar and runs down all the long ages since; it will continue until the second coming of Christ in the closing days of the empire of antichrist. During this period, as Jesus declared, Jerusalem will be largely in heathen hands. The fact that the Jews have retaken Jerusalem heralds the approaching end of this period of time.

Gentile world rule was to be marked by deterioration, as was evident from a number of things about the image. The metals of which it was composed, for instance, decreased in value from gold to silver, from silver to brass (copper), from brass to iron, and from iron to clay. The parts of the image are likewise mentioned in a descending scale. The description begins with the head (the intellect). It moves down to the breast (the emotions), then to the belly (the digestion), and ends with the feet that walk in the dust.

The specific gravity of the various materials in the image are similarly marked by a scale of declension. The specific gravity of gold is 19.3, that of silver is 10.51, that of copper is 8.5, that of iron is 7.6, and that of clay is 1.9. The image had all the weight at the top and was balanced on light, brittle, unsubstantial clay. The whole thing was top-heavy, erected as it was on clay, a Biblical symbol of unredeemed humanity. The lesson of the image was that it would never survive a fatal blow. In the end such a blow was administered to the feet of the image by a descending stone. The whole thing collapsed in ruins, and the stone itself grew until it became a mountain that filled the earth.

Nebuchadnezzar was the head of gold—he and the empire over which he ruled. He was an absolute monarch and one to whom God expressly gave the right to rule the world. The Babylonian empire, of course, did not embrace the whole world. Indeed, it was one of the smallest of the world empires of prophecy. Nevertheless, Nebuchadnezzar could have ruled the world; the right to do so was given to him. Moreover, the Babylonian empire *was* Nebuchadnezzar. He it was who really brought it into being, and none of the kings who followed him on the throne amounted to much. The first empire, then, was that of *Babylon*, particularly Nebuchadnezzar's Babylon.

The silver in the image represented the next world empire, *Medo-Persia*. The two arms of the image symbolized the dual character of that empire, with the left arm representing the weaker Median element in the partnership. The Persian kings did not exercise the same autocratic power enjoyed by the Babylonian kings. Once a Persian king passed a law, he was bound by it and could not change it. This limitation to the power of a Medo-Persian king worked to the detriment of Daniel (Daniel 6:8-9), but it worked in favor of the repatriated Jews in the days of Zerubbabel (Ezra 5:7–6:12).

The brass, or copper, in the image symbolized the *Greek* empire. Little is said in this particular prophecy about Greece; but in later revelations (notably Daniel 7–8 and 11) considerable details would be added. The inferiority of brass to silver is a symbolic way of telling us, perhaps, that Alexander's brilliant conquests did not profit him much.

The iron legs of the image stood for the *Roman* empire although, strange to say, it is not actually mentioned by name in Daniel. The mighty power of Rome, however, is clearly foreshadowed in this prophecy as it is in several later ones in Daniel. The iron legs of the image symbolized Rome's relentless rule. The division of the image into two legs foreshadowed the ultimate division of the Roman empire into two empires. History books tell us how for many centuries two Roman empires flourished—one in the West ruled, as always, from Rome; the other in the East ruled from Constantinople.

The feet and toes of the image anticipate the endtimes. They were comprised partly of iron and partly of clay, substances that do not mix or cohere. The iron and clay depict the inherent strength and weakness of the democratic form of government. The ten toes anticipate the final form of Gentile world rule, one that has not yet materialized. There will ultimately emerge a ten-nation confederation of European powers, a "revived Roman empire" as some have called it. The Roman empire has actually lived on down through the centuries in the languages and laws of the West. Attempts have been made by such men as Charlemagne, Napoleon, and Mussolini to revive the Roman empire, but the time was not ripe for these men to bring it back on stage.

The European common market today foreshadows the impending revival of this empire. The common market was created by the Treaty of *Rome* in 1957. Membership in this potentially powerful European trading community continues to fluctuate. It will probably continue to do so, despite recent attempts to create a European parliament, until such times as the beast (i.e., the antichrist) comes (Revelation 13). He is the one who will finally bring these prophecies of Daniel to complete fulfillment.

At this stage in Daniel's prophecies little is said about the coming empire of the beast, the devil's messiah. Later on, fresh revelations will be given to the prophet (Daniel 7,11) and the picture will be clearer. But in chapter 2 Daniel simply stated that the final form of Gentile world government will be swept away by divine intervention.

Nebuchadnezzar's dream ended when a stone "cut without hands" smote the feet of the image, breaking the whole thing in pieces so that it was blown into oblivion. The stone itself became a mountain to fill the earth, a symbolic reference to the coming millennial kingdom of the Lord Jesus Christ.

THE VISION OF THE FOUR BEASTS (DANIEL 7)

This vision covers much the same ground as the one in Daniel 2 but with certain basic differences. Nebuchadnezzar's view of human world government was seen in a dream; Daniel's was communicated in a vision. One was given to a heathen king, the other to one of God's choicest saints. One envisioned a Gentile world empire as something magnificent, something to be put on a pedestal and worshiped (Daniel 2:31; 3:1); the other saw it as something diabolical and dreadful, something bestial and brutal (Daniel 7:15).

Daniel first saw a lion, but a lion with an eagle's wings. The lion depicted the Babylonian empire (then soon to end), especially the victorious conquests of Nebuchadnezzar. The eagle's wings portrayed the swiftness of the Babylonian monarch's rise to power. In the vision, Daniel saw the wings plucked and the beast erected on its feet so that it walked like a man. Moreover, it was given a human heart. Much of this had already been fulfilled in the story of Nebuchadnezzar. Soon after consolidating his empire, he lost his lust for conquest, became a humane ruler, and was apparently even converted to belief in Daniel's God (Daniel 4).

The prophet next saw a bear which raised itself up on one side. The bear symbolized the Medo-Persian empire and the supremacy of Persia over Media in the alliance. The Persian conquests were likened to the lumbering but dangerous movements of a bear, for the Persians deployed ponderous, laborious, massive armies in the field. The bear had three ribs in its mouth, symbolizing the three kingdoms of Lydia, Babylon, and Egypt, which formed a futile triple alliance to oppose expanding Medo-Persian power in the world.

The third beast, a leopard, stood for the empire of Greece. The leopard had "four wings of a fowl" and also four heads. The wings symbolized the swiftness of Macedonian conquest. The four heads represented the four kingdoms into which Alexander's empire was divided after his death: Thrace, Macedonia, Syria, and Egypt. Two years later Daniel was given a further vision that elaborated on this aspect of Gentile world power (Daniel 8).

The fourth beast was unlike any ever seen on earth. It was a monster, ferocious and terrible, and it represented the empire of Rome. It had iron teeth suggesting the tenacity of Roman conquest and ten horns symbolizing the Roman empire as it will be in its final form, the ten-nation confederacy of European powers.

As Daniel watched he saw a "little horn" spring up in the midst of the other ten. This strange horn had eyes like a man and "a mouth speaking great things." The little horn tore up three of the original horns by the roots. Daniel watched until he saw the thrones of all these kings thrown down and their place taken by an everlasting kingdom established by "the Ancient of days" (Daniel 7:13) and administered by the saints.

The little horn was a symbol for the coming antichrist, who will rise to power in the Roman world in a day to come. He will not be deemed significant at first; but when he overthrows three of his confederates, he will suddenly emerge as a power to be reckoned with. He will unite the West and ultimately extend his rule over the whole earth, as we learn from Revelation 13. The right to rule the world, granted by God to Nebuchadnezzar (the first Gentile world ruler) but never attained by him, will be attained by the antichrist, the last of the line.

Once he has the world in his grasp, the antichrist will lead the world in a Satan-inspired attack on God and His people. It is in this prophecy that we learn for the first time that the coming great tribulation period will last for three and a half years ("a time, and times, and half a time," Revelation 12:14). The antichrist's empire will not last long, and his end will be swift. His bestial empire will be replaced by the beneficial world empire of the Lord Jesus, an empire that will last for a thousand years.

THE RAM AND THE HE- GOAT (DANIEL 8)

The visions of Daniel 2 and 7 outline the overall facts of Gentile world dominion. In chapter 8 the arena is narrowed, and the prophet's attention is focused on the two middle phases of Gentile world empire, the Persian and Greek periods. The Persian empire was the last of the eastern, Asiatic empires; the Greek empire was the first of the western, European empires. This vision concentrates on the passing of world dominion into the hands of the western powers.

In chapter 7 the empires of Persia and Greece were depicted under the symbolism of a bear and a leopard. Here in chapter 8 they are seen in the figures of a ram and a he-goat.

The vision of Daniel 8 was given to the prophet in the third year of the Babylonian king Belshazzar, the year of the fall of Babylon.

This explains why the aged prophet was so disdainful of Belshazzar's offer to make him "third ruler in the kingdom" if he would explain to him the mysterious writing on the wall (Daniel 5:16-17). Even before reading the writing, Daniel knew that Babylon's last hour had come and there was no kingdom to divide.

Let us visualize the main points of Daniel 7 and 8 so we can compare and contrast the two visions.

MEDO-PERSIA		
Chapter 7	**Chapter 8**	**Significance**
A bear	A ram	Medo-Persia
Two sides	Two horns	A dual alliance
Raised on one side	One horn higher than the other	Persia predominant over Media
	The higher horn comes up after the other	Persia raised up after Media
Three ribs in its mouth	Pushed west, north, and east	Medo-Persian conquests

GREECE		
Chapter 7	**Chapter 8**	**Significance**
A leopard	A he-goat	Greece
	Came from the west	A western power
Given dominion	Conquers the earth	Extent of conquests
Four wings of a bird	Touched not the ground	Swiftness of conquest
	A notable horn	Alexander the Great
Four heads	Four horns	Division of Alexander's empire
	A "little horn"	Antiochus Epiphanes

In his vision Daniel saw a ram with two horns, one higher than the other. The ram was a well-known emblem of Persia, so we easily recognize the Persian empire in this ram. In any case, Daniel was expressly told, "The ram which thou sawest having two horns are the kings of Media and Persia" (Daniel 8:20). (The dominance of Persia over Media in the alliance is again clearly symbolized in the two horns.) The ram pushed westward, northward, and southward, indicating Medo-Persian conquests against Lydia in the north, Babylon in the west, and Egypt in the south.

Suddenly a he-goat moving with incredible speed appeared from the west, a he-goat with "a notable horn" between its eyes. The goat represented Greece and the prominent horn, Alexander the Great. History tells us how Alexander came thundering out of the west, demolished the vast but ponderous Persian army at Issus in 333 B.C., went on to defeat an even greater Persian army at Arbela in 331 B.C., and in very short order made himself master of the world.

Daniel saw that the "notable horn" was broken when it was in its prime; and four other horns came up in its place, horns that pointed "toward the four winds of heaven." Alexander died prematurely at the height of his power in 323 B.C., and his vast empire was seized by four of his generals—Cassander, Lysimachus, Seleucus, and Ptolemy—who carved the world up among themselves.

As Daniel continued to watch he saw that "a little horn" came up on the head of the goat. We must not confuse the little horn of Daniel 7 with the little horn of Daniel 8. The one in Daniel 7 is associated with the *Roman* world; this one in Daniel 8 is tied to the *Grecian* world. That one symbolized the antichrist; this one symbolized Antiochus Epiphanes, one of history's most remarkable types of antichrist.

Antiochus Epiphanes (Antiochus the Illustrious) was a younger son of Antiochus the Great. He became the eighth king of Syria and was nicknamed Antiochus Epimanes (Antiochus the Mad) by his contemporaries. One of his ambitions was to convert all his subjects to the worship of Olympian Zeus, and he especially wanted to force his Jewish subjects into this form of worship. To that end he invaded Jerusalem, defiled the temple of Jehovah, and persecuted all who would not bend to his will. The prophetic history of this odious person was detailed further for Daniel at a later date in the visions of chapter 11.

Some of the details of this vision of the ram and he-goat were interpreted for Daniel. The chief actors were identified as Persia and Greece, and special emphasis was placed on the significance of the "little horn." Daniel was told that this horn represented a coming ruler, that he would be "a king of fierce countenance," that he would be adept at "understanding dark sentences," and that he would make "craft to prosper" (Daniel 8:23,25). All in all he was to be a very nasty proposition.

It is not easy to decide which details in this prophecy apply to Antiochus Epiphanes, which ones apply to the coming antichrist, and which apply more or less to both. It is a common feature of Bible prophecy that certain statements have a double fulfillment. This feature of prophecy is evident here in Daniel 8 and also in Daniel 11. Some of the predictions in both these chapters have been fulfilled in the history of Antiochus, others have been partially fulfilled, others await reenactment on a grander scale when antichrist comes, and still others have had no fulfillment at all but will come into their own at the time of the end. One thing is clear, however. The antichrist, when he comes, will be marked for his subtlety and savagery. Also, his fall will be swift and sure; like Antiochus Epiphanes, he will be broken by God when his blasphemies overflow even those wide banks set by the marvelous patience of God.

The Vision of the Seventy Weeks (Daniel 9)

Daniel was an old man when the visions of this chapter were given to him. He knew from such Scriptures as Jeremiah 25:11 and 29:4-10 that the time had come for God to fulfill His promises concerning the ending of the captivity by clearing the way for the Jews to return to the promised land. Daniel had no doubt at all that those prophecies were to be taken literally; confident that great changes were about to take place, he gave himself earnestly to prayer. Already the Persian era had dawned, and Darius the Mede was installed in Babylon. But so far God had not acted—hence the deep spiritual exercise of this godly man.

In response to Daniel's prayer God gave him a startling revelation. The seventy-year captivity of the Jews in Babylon was only one of the time periods in the mind of God in connection with Israel.

There was another and a far more comprehensive time period about which Daniel should be informed. The period of seventy years about to end, was to be followed by a further period of seventy "weeks" of years.

The new prophecy entrusted to Daniel has to do primarily with the period during which the Jewish people were actually living in the land of promise. That is an important clue to understanding the prophecy. Moreover, the word translated "weeks" really means "sevens" and in this particular prophecy has to do with "sevens" of years. The prophecy embraces a period of 70 times 7 years; that is, it deals with a specific time period of 490 years.

This significant period was to begin with a specific date. It was to run from "the going forth of the commandment to restore and to build Jerusalem" (Daniel 9:25). Four Persian decrees connected with the Jewish period are recorded in Scripture, and all of them have been considered as suitable starting points for this prophecy. There is the decree of Cyrus (538 B.C.) authorizing the building of the temple (Ezra 1:1-4). There is the decree of Darius Hystapses (519 B.C.) that reaffirmed the right of the Jews to rebuild their temple. And there is the decree of Artaxerxes (456 B.C.) that authorized Ezra to take some priests and Levites with him to Jerusalem to participate in religious services at treasury expense (Ezra 7:11-22). None of these three official edicts is an adequate starting point for this prophecy.

The prophecy really begins with another decree of Artaxerxes (445 B.C.) given in the twentieth year of his reign, which authorized Nehemiah to go to Jerusalem and rebuild its walls (Nehemiah 2:1-8). The other three decrees were of a religious nature; this one was political. In executing the provisions of this decree Nehemiah ran into serious opposition, just as the prophecy of Daniel 9 predicts.

We start, then, with the year 445 B.C. The prophecy divides the 70 "weeks" which run on from that date into three units: 7 + 62 + 1. Or, to express the period in years rather than "weeks" or "sevens": 49 + 434 + 7 gives a total of 490 years. It is not clear why the first 7 "weeks" (49 years) should be set off by itself at the beginning of the period. No less an authority than Sir Robert Anderson suggested that this initial period of 49 years takes us down to the time of the prophet Malachi, with whom the Old Testament canon of Scripture closed.[3] After Malachi's day God had no more to say to men until the coming of Christ.

To this period of 49 years we add the second period of 62 "weeks" (434 years), at the close of which period the Messiah would be "cut off." Obviously the closing date of the 69 (7 + 62) "weeks" (483 years) is of great significance. The calculations in unraveling this prophecy are complex because of differences between the Hebrew 360-day calendar and the calendar we use today. However, we start with the political decree of Artaxerxes in 445 B.C. and end with Christ's triumphal entry into Jerusalem. Then, indeed, Messiah *was* "cut off" by crucifixion.[4]

The *seventieth* week is dealt with separately in the prophecy. Evidently there was to be a gap between the sixty-ninth and the seventieth weeks, between the cutting off of the Messiah and the fulfillment of the rest of the prophecy. An event so horrendous, criminal, and high-handed as the murder of the Messiah must inevitably bring its own train of consequences. We now know that the entire church age has intervened between the sixty-ninth and seventieth weeks of the prophecy. During almost the entire period of this "gap," the Jews have been out of their land, dispersed far and wide throughout the world. The present-day rebirth of the state of Israel heralds the approaching fulfillment of this final "week" of seven years.

This final week coincides with the coming of antichrist. He will sign a seven-year pact with the Jews, called in Scripture an agreement "with hell" (Isaiah 28:15). With the signing of that pact, this final seven-year period will begin to run its course. During the first half of the "week" the Jews will have a powerful protector in the western dictator, but halfway through the period the beast will break his treaty and begin that fearful time of persecution known as the great tribulation.

THE DRAMA OF THE AGES (DANIEL 11)

We sometimes speak of "the silent years" that lie between Malachi and Matthew, the years during which God had nothing to say to mankind. In one sense they were not silent at all, for the broad outline of those years was given in the detailed prophecy of Daniel 11, which we are now going to examine.

This prophecy was given to Daniel in the first year of Darius the Mede. It deals with the rise and fall of empires, with alliances and intrigues, with the marching of armies, with imperial ambitions and palace plots. It covers the turbulent years when Syria and Egypt struggled for supremacy in the Near East and when wretched Palestine was torn first from the grasp of this king and then from that one. The prophecy reaches all the way from the heyday of the Persian empire right down to the days of Antiochus Epiphanes and to the deployment of Roman armies on the stage of the world. Then it takes a giant leap down the centuries to the endtimes to give us details about the coming reign of antichrist.

In this synopsis we are not going to dwell on all the fascinating details of this chapter as those details have been worked out in history. We shall touch lightly on the general flow of events and then concentrate on the verses that tell of the coming of Antiochus Epiphanes and on the verses that speak of the coming antichrist.

First we need to get the overall plan of the chapter before us as we try to unravel the complex prophecies it contains.

I. The Coming of Antiochus (Daniel 11:1-35)
   A. The world of Alexander the Great (11:1-9)
      1. His success (11:1-4)
         a. The concluding period of Persia (11:1-2)
         b. The coming punishment of Persia (11:3-4)
            (1) Alexander's conquests (11:3)
            (2) Alexander's collapse (11:4)
      2. His successors (11:5-9)
         a. The Egyptian prince (11:5)
         b. The Egyptian princess (11:6)
         c. The Egyptian protest (11:7-9)
   B. The wars of Antiochus the Great (11:10-20)
      1. His first campaign (11:10-12)
         a. He is victorious (11:10)
         b. He is vanquished (11:11-12)
      2. His further campaign (11:13-17)
         a. Mobilization (11:13-14)
         b. Molestation (11:15-16)
             (1) Pharaoh defeated (11:15)
            (2) Palestine desolated (11:16)
         c. Manipulation (11:17)
      3. His final campaign (11:18-20)
         a. His vain scheme (11:18-19)

b. His vile son (11:20)
C. The wickedness of Antiochus the God (11:21-35)
    1. His contemptibility (11:21-22)
        a. His coming to power (11:21)
        b. His control of the priesthood (11:22)
    2. His craftiness (11:23-24)
    3. His conquests (11:25-27)
        a. Entering the Egyptian kingdom (11:25)
        b. Entertaining the Egyptian king (11:26-27)
    4. His cruelty (11:28)
    5. His crimes (11:29-35)
        a. His rebuff (11:29-30)
        b. His revenge (11:30-35)
            (1) Invading Jerusalem (11:30)
            (2) Insulting Jehovah (11:31)
            (3) Inflaming Judea (11:32-35)
                (a) Those who deified him (11:32)
                (b) Those who defied him (11:32-35)
II. The Coming of Antichrist (Daniel 11:36-45)
    A. His blasphemies (11:36-38)
        1. His royal pride (11:36)
        2. His religious policy (11:37)
        3. His real purpose (11:38)
    B. His battles (11:39-45)
        1. His great powers (11:39)
        2. His great problems (11:40-45)
            a. His rivals (11:40)
            b. His revenge (11:41-43)
            c. His rage (11:44)
            d. His ruin (11:45)

A clear-cut break in this remarkable prophecy occurs between Daniel 11:35 and 11:36. The prophetic history is continuous right down to the days of Antiochus Epiphanes (the god). Then it leaps over the ages (as does the prophecy of Daniel 9:25-26) and comes back into focus at the time of antichrist, of whom Antiochus was a type.

Before exploring the prophecies of this chapter, note the intricacies of the history to which they refer as diagramed on page 42. You will find it helpful to refer from time to time both to the outline and the diagram.

The Intertestamental Period

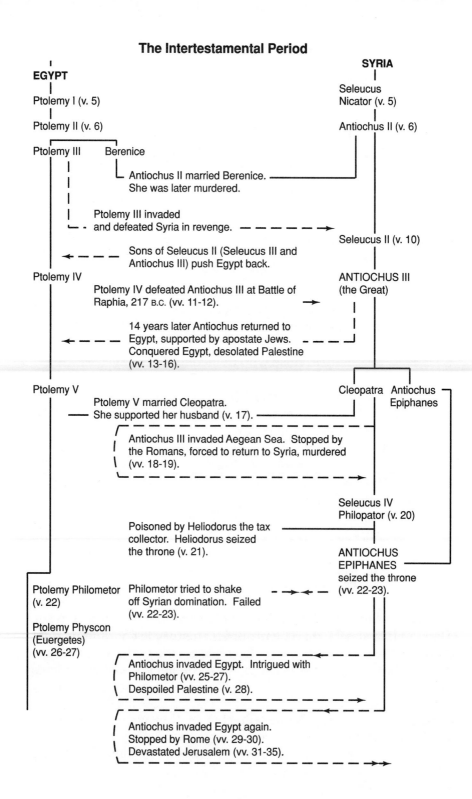

The cold recitation of the facts of history in the diagram should not bore us. They are thrilling if we remember that when Daniel 11 was written these things were not history, they were *prophecy*. We see them as history. Daniel saw them still ahead in the unborn ages. There is no chapter in all the Scripture that gives us such an awesome exhibition of God's power to foretell the future.

> Behold, there shall stand up yet three kings in Persia; and the fourth shall be far richer than they all: and by his strength through his riches he shall stir up all against the realm of Grecia (Daniel 11:2).

The three Persian kings were Cyrus, Cambyses, and Darius Hystapses. They were followed by Xerxes, the most powerful of them all. His invasion of Greece and defeat at Salamis are foreseen.

> And a mighty king shall stand up, that shall rule with great dominion, and do according to his will. And when he shall stand up, his kingdom shall be broken, and shall be divided toward the four winds of heaven; and not to his posterity (Daniel 11:3-4).

The conquests of Alexander the Great are thus foreshadowed, as well as the subsequent division of his kingdom into four parts after his death. His kingdom did not go to his own posterity, but was carved up among four of his generals.

> And the king of the south shall be strong, and one of his princes . . . shall be strong above him (Daniel 11:5).

The geographic references to north and south in the Bible are always in reference to Israel. One division of Alexander's empire went to Ptolemy I. The phrase "one of his princes" refers to Seleucus Nicator, who was originally one of Ptolemy's officers but became king of Syria and the most powerful of Alexander's successors. From here on, the prophecy emphasizes the struggles between Egypt and Syria, in which Palestine, lying between the two countries, was an inevitable pawn.

> And in the end of years they shall join themselves together; for

the king's daughter of the south shall come to the king of the north to make an agreement: but she shall not retain the power of the arm (Daniel 11:6).

In due time Berenice, the daughter of Ptolemy II of Egypt, was given in marriage to Antiochus II or Syria. She was murdered.

But out of a branch of her roots shall one stand up in his estate, which shall come with an army, and shall enter into the fortress of the king of the north, and shall deal against them, and shall prevail (Daniel 11:7).

Ptolemy III, who was the brother of the murdered Berenice, avenged her death by invading and defeating Syria.

But his sons shall be stirred up, and shall assemble a multitude of great forces: and one shall certainly come, and overflow, and pass through: then shall he return, and be stirred up, even to his fortress (Daniel 11:10).

The sons mentioned here were the Syrian princes Seleucus III and Antiochus III (afterward known as Antiochus the Great). The reign of Antiochus was one of war; and at first he was entirely successful in his campaigns against Egypt, as here foretold.

And the king of the south shall be moved with choler, and shall come forth and fight with him, even with the king of the north: and he shall set forth a great multitude; but the multitude shall be given into his hand (Daniel 11:11).

This prediction was fulfilled by Ptolemy IV of Egypt, who defeated Antiochus III in the battle of Raphia near the frontiers of Egypt in 217 B.C. In this battle Antiochus suffered great loss.

For the king of the north shall return, and shall set forth a multitude greater than the former, and shall certainly come after certain years with a great army and with much riches (Daniel 11:13).

Fourteen years later, Antiochus III returned to Egypt with a great army.

And in those times there shall many stand up against the king of the south: also the robbers of thy people shall exalt themselves to establish the vision, but they shall fall (Daniel 11:14).

Antiochus was supported in his campaign against Egypt by apostate Jews, riotous men who defied law and order.

So the king of the north shall come, and cast up a mount, and take the most fenced cities: and the arms of the south shall not withstand (Daniel 11:15).

Antiochus III defeated Egypt.

But he that cometh against him shall do according to his own will, and none shall stand before him: and he shall stand in the glorious land, which by his hand shall be consumed (Daniel 11:16).

Antiochus III invaded, conquered, and desolated Palestine.

He shall also set his face to enter with the strength of his whole kingdom, and upright ones with him; thus shall he do: and he shall give him the daughter of women, corrupting her: but she shall not stand on his side, neither be for him (Daniel 11:17).

Antiochus III gave his own daughter Cleopatra, then only eleven years of age, in a treacherous marriage to Ptolemy V of Egypt, a boy of twelve. He hoped his daughter would help him complete his control over Egypt. However, she sided with her husband and defeated her father's plans.

After this shall he turn his face unto the isles, and shall take many: but a prince for his own behalf shall cause the reproach offered by him to cease. . . . Then he shall turn his face toward the fort of his own land: but he shall stumble and fall, and not be found (Daniel 11:18-19).

Not content with his successes, Antiochus set out to conquer Pergamum, which had been a thorn in his side. Then he tried to conquer Greece, hoping to make himself a second Alexander. He prepared a fleet of three hundred warships and proceeded to create havoc along the Mediterranean coast. He captured Rhodes and a number of islands. This alarmed the Romans who sent the consul Ancilius against him. The Romans met Antiochus at the pass of Thermopylae. They then defeated him at the battle of Magnesia in 190 B.C. His younger son, Antiochus, was carried off to Rome as a hostage. Antiochus III returned to Syria and was slain in an ignominious attempt to plunder a temple.

> Then shall stand up in his estate a raiser of taxes in the glory of the kingdom: but within few days he shall be destroyed, neither in anger, nor in battle (Daniel 11:20).

Antiochus was succeeded by his son Seleucus Philopator, an easygoing, peace-loving man. The Romans had put Syria under heavy tribute, and much of this king's reign was spent in trying to raise taxes to meet this onerous burden. The "raiser of taxes" referred to in the prophecy turned out to be Heliodorus, who was sent throughout Judea by Seleucus to extract money and to plunder the temple. He was hindered in this last objective by a supernatural apparition which faced him as he was about to enter the sacred treasury. When he returned to Syria, he poisoned his royal master the king.

> And in his estate shall stand up a vile person, to whom they shall not give the honor of the kingdom: but he shall come in peaceably, and obtain the kingdom by flatteries (Daniel 11:21).

The rightful heir to the Syrian throne was Demetrius, the son of Seleucus Philopator. However, he was at this time in Rome as a hostage where he had been sent by his father to replace Antiochus (the younger brother of Philopator and soon to be known as Antiochus Epiphanes). Antiochus was on his way home when the tidings reached him of the murder of his brother Seleucus Philopator. He was infuriated by the news that Heliodorus the tax collector had not only murdered his brother, but had seized the kingdom.

> And with the arms of a flood shall they be overflown from before him, and shall be broken; yea, also the prince of the

covenant. And after the league made with him he shall work deceitfully: for he shall come up, and shall become strong with a small people (Daniel 11:22-23).

Antiochus first gained the assistance of the rulers of Pergamum, with whose troops and financial aid he was able to displace the usurper. Then, scornful of the rightful claims to the throne of Demetrius, Antiochus seized it for himself. He swept away all his enemies and put Heliodorus to death. He also deposed the Jewish high priest ("the prince of the covenant"), Onias III, probably because he not only opposed the hellenizing party in Jerusalem but also favored the Ptolemies. His brother Jason paid a large sum for the priesthood.

Antiochus obtained the kingdom by flatteries, as predicted. First he flattered the rulers of Pergamum, then the Syrians with promises of clemency, then the Romans to whom he sent ambassadors with tax arrears and promises of the same treaty arrangements they had made with his father, Antiochus III.

He was a "vile person," too, as the prophecy foretold. He was licentious and dissolute. He often publicly frequented brothels and places of dissipation. His orgies, as much as anything, earned him the title of *Epimanes*, "the mad."

Soon after ascending the Syrian throne he discovered that his nephew, Ptolemy Philometor of Egypt, then a boy of fifteen, had taken advantage of the disturbances in Syria to recover Egyptian territory held by Syria. Antiochus crushed a great Egyptian army assembled to further Ptolemy's ambitions at a battle near Pelusium.

He shall enter peaceably even upon the fattest places of the province; and he shall do that which his fathers have not done, nor his fathers' fathers; he shall scatter among them the prey, and spoil, and riches; yea, and he shall forecast his devices against the strong holds, even for a time (Daniel 11:24).

Unlike his predecessors, Antiochus Epiphanes was prodigal and lavish with his gifts, distributing his spoils among his followers with an open hand. At the same time he studied his plans for taking all of Egypt and subduing her strongholds. Although he failed to take the city of Alexandria, he did take a number of Egyptian cities such as Pelusium, Naucratis, and Memphis.

> And he shall stir up his power and his courage against the king of the south with a great army; and the king of the south shall be stirred up to battle with a very great and mighty army; but he shall not stand: for they shall forecast devices against him. Yea, they that feed of the portion of his meat shall destroy him, and his army shall overflow: and many shall fall down slain (Daniel 11:25-26).

Although Antiochus had already invaded Egypt once, his first formal campaign did not take place until he had made adequate preparations. His enemy, Ptolemy Philometor, however, had assembled an equally large army. The two armies met at a point between Pelusium and mount Casius. The Egyptian army was defeated and Ptolemy was taken captive, having been betrayed by a number of his courtiers who had been corrupted by Antiochus. Antiochus was now master of Egypt, except for Alexandria. The Egyptians by now were disillusioned with Ptolemy Philometor and, abandoning him, made his brother Ptolemy Physcon (Euergetes) king in his place.

> And both these kings' hearts shall be to do mischief, and they shall speak lies at one table; but it shall not prosper: for yet the end shall be at the time appointed (Daniel 11:27).

The crafty Antiochus received the captive Ptolemy Philometor with many professions of friendship and promised to restore him to the throne of Egypt. Uncle and nephew were a pair well met for treachery, each lying to the other without shame. Antiochus left Philometor at Memphis as king and, pretending he was going to support the claims of Philometor to the throne of all Egypt, hurried off to besiege Alexandria. Alexandria, however, held out.

In the meantime, Philometor, suspicious of his uncle's schemes, entered into secret negotiations with his brother Physcon. They agreed to rule Egypt jointly, and Philometor was received into Alexandria where the two brothers joined forces against the common foe. Thus the prophecy of lying and treacherous dealing was fulfilled.

> Then shall he return into his land with great riches; and his heart shall be against the holy covenant; and he shall do exploits, and return to his own land (Daniel 11:28).

Antiochus Epiphanes left Egypt laden down with spoil. On the homeward march he heard that a rumor of his death had been joyfully received in Palestine. Moreover Jason, whom Antiochus had by now deposed from the office of high priest in favor of Menelaus, had hired mercenaries and had taken Jerusalem. Antiochus was enraged and, as the prophecy puts it, his heart was "against the holy covenant," that is, against the Holy Land and its people. He at once attacked Jerusalem with a great army and massacred some forty thousand people and sold a like number into slavery. He then plundered the temple and carried off treasure worth eighteen hundred talents. To the horror of the Jews, he sacrificed a sow on the altar and sprinkled broth made from its carcass all over the temple. Satisfied with his vengeance, he returned to Syria.

> At the time appointed he shall return, and come toward the south; but it shall not be as the former, or as the latter. For the ships of Chittim shall come against him: therefore he shall be grieved, and return, and have indignation against the holy covenant: so shall he do; he shall even return, and have intelligence with them that forsake the holy covenant (Daniel 11:29-30).

In the spring of 168 B.C. Antiochus led another army against Egypt to force the surrender of the joint pharaohs. The Egyptians appealed to Rome, which is referred to here as "Chittim." The name originally referred to the island of Cyprus, but it came to include a number of islands and coastlands of the Mediterranean.

When the armies of Antiochus arrived within four miles of Alexandria, he received a shock. A Roman fleet lay at anchor in the bay; and the Syrian himself was met by Popilius Laenas, the representative of Rome. He ordered Antiochus to evacuate Egypt at once and leave the pharaohs alone. The crafty Antiochus glanced at the document tendered to him and replied that he would consult his advisers. Thereupon the Roman drew a circle in the sand around Antiochus. "Before you step out of that circle," he said, "give me such an answer as I may report to the Senate." The proud Syrian tyrant was cowed. "If it so please the Senate," he said, "we will depart." And depart he did, but with a rage and a fury that knew no bounds.

The only place where he could vent his wrath was in Palestine. He had sympathizers in that unhappy land, Jews who had been recipients of his favors and who, led by Menelaus, sought to hellenize the Jewish people. These are the people referred to in the prophecy as "them that forsake the holy covenant."

> And arms shall stand on his part, and they shall pollute the sanctuary of strength, and shall take away the daily sacrifice, and they shall place the abomination that maketh desolate. And such as do wickedly against the covenant shall he corrupt by flatteries: but the people that do know their God shall be strong, and do exploits (Daniel 11:31-32).

This part of the prophecy brings us to the climax of the evils wrought by Antiochus Epiphanes. He sent the Syrian general Apollonius against Jerusalem, who, knowing the habits of the Jews, attacked on the sabbath day. Thousands were captured, and terrible massacres, persecutions, and outrages followed. Syrian troops were garrisoned in the citadel of David, and Antiochus ordered all Jews to embrace a uniform pagan culture.

He then ordered all Jewish ceremonies and sacrifices to cease. Copies of the Scriptures were confiscated and destroyed. The annual feast of tabernacles was replaced by a feast to Bacchus, and the temple was dedicated to Jupiter Olympus. The youth of the city were corrupted and taught lewd practices. Over the altar of burnt offering Antiochus erected an idol-altar, accompanied, we are told, by an image of Zeus. The Jews contemptuously called it "the abomination of desolation," and many of them resolutely refused to bow to the will of the tyrant.

> And they that understand among the people shall instruct many: yet they shall fall by the sword, and by flame, by captivity, and by spoil, many days. Now when they shall fall, they shall be holpen with a little help: but many shall cleave to them with flatteries. And some of them of understanding shall fall, to try them, and to purge, and to make them white, even to the time of the end: because it is yet for a time appointed (Daniel 11:33-35).

The prophetic expression, "the people that do know their God shall be strong, and do exploits" (Daniel 11:32), is a prophecy concerning Mattathias, the aged high priest, and his five sons. These men became leaders of the dissident Jews, and together with their successors, they became known as the Maccabees. They ruled Palestine from 166 B.C. until 47 B.C., striving to restore the national life of Israel.

The Maccabees revolted against Antiochus, driven to desperation by his cruelties, and formed guerrilla bands in the mountains. Judas, known as "the hammer," routed every Syrian army sent against him. In 165 B.C. he retook Jerusalem, purified the temple, and restored the daily sacrifices.

During the latter period of this epoch, one that ended with the Roman subjugation of Palestine, there arose a new class of spiritual leaders among the Jewish people. These were the *Maschilim* ("the instructed ones"), who sought to keep a knowledge of God alive among the common people.

Beginning at Daniel 11:36 the fulfillment of this long prophecy leaps over the centuries and resumes in the days of the coming antichrist. The remainder of this fascinating chapter, then, still awaits fulfillment. We can be sure that it will be fulfilled as literally as has been the rest of it. If some of the statements seem obscure to us, we can be sure they will be clear to those who read them in the coming days of fulfillment.

> And the king shall do according to his will; and he shall exalt himself, and magnify himself above every god, and shall speak marvellous things against the God of gods, and shall prosper till the indignation be accomplished: for that that is determined shall be done (Daniel 11:36).

The antichrist eventually will rule the world, as we learn from the Apocalypse. In the day of his power he will exhibit a massive and consuming pride. He will seize the temple that the Jews will have rebuilt in Jerusalem (2 Thessalonians; Revelation 13) and will proclaim himself to be God, demanding that the whole world worship him and his father the devil. We can easily identify this "king" here with "the little horn" of Daniel 7, with the "man of sin" of 2 Thessalonians, and with the first beast of Revelation 13 and 17.

We are told that he "shall prosper" and that nothing will stand in his way "till the indignation be accomplished." The "indignation," of course, is God's outrage against the nation of Israel for its persistent, age-long rejection of the Lord Jesus Christ. The same period is called "the great tribulation" (Matthew 24:21) and "the time of Jacob's trouble" (Jeremiah 30:7). It is referred to many times in Scripture. It will last for a period of three and a half years (the last half of Daniel's seventieth "week") and will terminate when the Lord returns to put down all His foes at Megiddo. During the days of antichrist's triumph, it might well be said of him exactly what Jesus said to those who handed Him over to crucifixion: "This is your hour, and the power of darkness" (Luke 22:53).

> Neither shall he regard the God of his fathers, nor the desire of women, nor regard any god: for he shall magnify himself above all (Daniel 11:37).

The phrase "the desire of women" has perplexed many commentators. It is placed between the words "the God of his fathers" and the words "any god," which suggests that the phrase likewise refers to a god. The most likely suggestion is that it refers to a god or goddess especially adored by women. From pagan times right down to the present there has been just such a goddess. She was variously known as the Beltis (Madonna) of the Babylonians, the Ishtar of the Assyrians, the Astarte of the Phoenicians, the Isis of the Egyptians, the Aphrodite of the Greeks, and the Artemis (Diana) of the Ephesians. Isis, for instance, was regarded as both the mother of Horus and the ever-virgin one at the same time.

After Constantine embraced Christianity and made it the state religion of the Roman empire, many pagan rites, holy days, and objects of adoration were "baptized" and incorporated into the Christian calendar under other and more respectable names. In their new guise they continued to hold the affections of their devotees.[5] We would not have to look far for the modern counterpart of the "desire of women" in the world today.

The antichrist will reject all gods: the god his father worshiped, the virgin Mary, and every other deity. In their place he will enthrone himself as god over all. We know from Revelation 17 that the beast (the antichrist) will first be supported by the scarlet woman (the harlot world religious system of Christendom). As soon as he is strong enough, however, he will destroy that system to clear the way for the worship of himself.

But in his estate shall he honor the God of forces: and a god whom his fathers knew not shall he honor with gold, and silver, and with precious stones, and pleasant things (Daniel 11:38).

The antichrist himself will worship Satan. We learn from Revelation 13 that it is Satan (the dragon) who gives him his throne and his authority over the world. When Satan tempted the Lord Jesus in the wilderness he offered Him the kingdoms, the power, and the glory of this world (Luke 4:5-8) in exchange for His worship. This was nothing less than a daring attempt to turn the Christ into the antichrist. What Jesus indignantly refused, the beast will gladly accept. As the Lord Jesus receives our worship and channels it to His Father in Heaven, so the antichrist, the imitator and mimic of Christ, will receive worship and channel it to his father the devil, called here "the God of forces."

Thus shall he do in the most strong holds with a strange god, whom he shall acknowledge and increase with glory: and he shall cause them to rule over many, and shall divide the land for gain (Daniel 11:39).

Those who cooperate with the antichrist will be raised by him to great authority in the world. The prophecy notes the carving up of the state of Israel into administrative districts, each under the control of one of the beast's agents. Thus he will ride the crest of the wave of popularity and power, carrying almost all the world's people with him and promoting Satan worship in all parts of the planet. The modern resurgence of Satanism, spiritism, witchcraft, astrology, and occultism herald the fact that the days are approaching when these sinister forces will triumph on the earth.

And at the time of the end shall the king of the south push at him: and the king of the north shall come against him like a whirlwind, with chariots, and with horsemen, and with many ships; and he shall enter into the countries, and shall overflow and pass over (Daniel 11:40).

In the end the antichrist's worldwide empire will fall apart. In our synopsis of the book of Revelation we shall deal with this further. Here, however, we note that two kings revolt against his rule; one is "the king of the north." Many have linked this coming battle with the Russian invasion of Israel chronicled in Ezekiel 38 and 39. There are good reasons, however, for rejecting this view, reasons we touch on in the chapters on Russia and the Apocalypse.

One of the titles the antichrist will wear is "king of the north," a title he probably assumes after the demise of Russia as a world power. In the context of Daniel 11, the "king of the north" is always Syria; so probably we must interpret the phrase like that here. The king of the north, then, would seem to be one of the antichrist's vassal kings administering Syria and possibly adjacent regions on his behalf.

When this insurrection breaks out, the antichrist himself will probably be at Babylon, his new world capital. Syria and Egypt, together with their allies, will "push at him"; that is, they will take up arms against him and attack him, probably by invading the land of Israel which lies between them. The beast's response will be swift. He will mobilize his forces and march against Egypt like a whirlwind, committing both land and naval forces to the attack.

> He shall enter also into the glorious land, and many countries shall be overthrown: but these shall escape out of his hand, even Edom, and Moab, and the chief of the children of Ammon. He shall stretch forth his hand also upon the countries: and the land of Egypt shall not escape. But he shall have power over the treasures of gold and of silver, and over all the precious things of Egypt: and the Libyans and the Ethiopians shall be at his steps (Daniel 11:41-43).

His line of march will lie through the land of Israel. Probably at this time he makes the assault on Jerusalem mentioned by Zechariah when "half of the city shall go forth into captivity" (Zechariah 14:2). Three peoples, historically the bitterest of Israel's foes—Edom, Moab, and the best of the children of Ammon—will escape his fury. We would identify these countries on a modern map as the country of Jordan. No explanation is given as to why these countries escape his wrath. It may be that Jordan will hasten to make its peace with this dreadful king. Or perhaps, as the territory of Israel's ancient foe, Jordan will be reserved for special humiliation at the time of the Lord's return. We find a hint of this in Isaiah 11:14, a Messianic passage.

The antichrist will take firmly in hand the countries he overthrows on his westward march, and finally he will reach Egypt itself. He will summarily deal with the king of the south; he will ransack the country of all its wealth; and he will accept the swift submission of Libya and Ethiopia, which had joined in the revolt. These two countries will now be added to the ranks of his obedient and subservient allies.

> But tidings out of the east and out of the north shall trouble him: therefore he shall go forth with great fury to destroy, and utterly to make away many (Daniel 11:44).

It is the beginning of the end. His mighty, monolithic, worldwide empire—held together by every form of wickedness, by Satanic energy, and by terror—is falling apart. The upheavals in the Near East have made possible even greater threats to his authority. The eastern half of his empire breaks away and, as we learn from the Apocalypse, mobilizes against him and marches back to confront him at Megiddo (Revelation 16:12-16). At this time the "kings of the east" invade Israel, gathering up allies in the distant north as they come. The fury of the beast will know no bounds. He will summon up all the remaining military might of his empire, including all the enormous industrial and military resources of the West, and will march to confront the rebels at Megiddo. Thus the stage is set for the battle of Armageddon.

> And he shall plant the tabernacles of his palace between the seas in the glorious holy mountain; yet he shall come to his end, and none shall help him (Daniel 11:45).

Somewhere between the Mediterranean and Jerusalem, the antichrist will pitch his resplendent military pavilion. With the armies of the West at his command, he will prepare for the final confrontation with the powers of the Far East. But his time has run out. The divine clock, set for seven years, has been ticking relentlessly away and now it chimes the hour. The Lord Jesus rises up from His throne on high, descends the sky with the armies of Heaven at his back, and bursts on the assembled millions, drawn from east and west, to put an end to man's ravishing of the planet Earth.

"None shall help him" is Daniel's final word on the fate of the beast. The book of Revelation adds the details to the destruction and ultimate doom of this wicked man of whom Antiochus Epiphanes, with all the atrocities and outrages he committed, was, after all, a mere shadow.

THE CLIMAX OF THE LAST DAYS (DANIEL 12)

The closing visions of Daniel focus on the endtimes themselves. Daniel's attention is drawn once more to the coming universal persecution of the Jewish people. And, for the second time in this book, we learn that Michael the archangel is "the great prince which standeth for the children of thy people" (Daniel 12:1).

According to the book of Daniel there are, in the unseen spirit world, angelic forces, both good and bad, which are directly involved in the government of this planet. It appears from Daniel 10 that an angel was sent with an answer to one of Daniel's prayers. Notwithstanding the exalted rank of the messenger and the importance of his commission (an errand commanded by God Himself), the angel was delayed for three weeks of our time by adversaries in the spirit world. He was resisted by one he calls "the prince of Persia," obviously no mere human prince (Daniel 10:13). One angel in one night could smite with death all of Sennacherib's mighty invading forces. After delivering his message to Daniel, the angel told the prophet that he was now returning to do battle with the "princes" of Persia and Greece, and he was counting on help from "Michael, your prince."

All of which opens up a fascinating area of truth. It would seem that Satan, as "the prince of this world," sets up his own fallen angelic princes over the various nations of the earth. Here on earth the nations are ruled by their various governments; in the spirit world those same nations are governed by angelic powers answerable to their master the devil. Paul refers to these spirit forces when he warns us that we do not battle flesh and blood but "against principalities, against powers, against the rulers of the darkness of this world, against spiritual wickedness in high [heavenly] places" (Ephesians 6:12). Satan's empire in the unseen spirit world is organized, rank above rank, in an orderly fashion, with himself at the head. To deny the existence of such beings is about as sensible as a medieval man's denying the existence of microbes.

When God said to Abraham, "I will make of thee a great nation" (Genesis 12:2), it marked a new beginning, not only on earth but also in the spirit world where Satan has his princes ruling over all the lands of earth, from pole to pole, from sea to sea. He has his own emissaries influencing the decisions made by the men in the Kremlin, by the leaders of Libya, Ethiopia, Iran. He has his high princes presiding over the affairs of China and the other nations of the Far East to ensure that these nations work out his diabolical will. He has them carrying out his designs in Rome, in Paris, in all the lands of the western world.

Prayer enters the scene at this point. Prayer hinders those Satanic plans; prayer engages the enemy in the unseen world; prayer frustrates and foils many of Satan's best-laid plans for this planet. That is why Satan does his best to keep us from our knees.

The nation of Israel differs in all of this. Despite its national sins, its faults, its failures, and its guilt in the matter of the Messiah, Israel is unique. It is a nation deliberately created by God. Over this nation, in the spirit world, God has placed one of *His* angels, the mighty warrior angel we know as Michael. He is called the archangel. He is the commander-in-chief of the armies of Heaven. He is mighty in power, and he is the angelic prince over Israel (Exodus 32:34; 33:1-3). There are hints of this elsewhere in the Bible. God wrote the truth of it right into the Mosaic law.

> Behold, I send an Angel before thee, to keep thee in the way, and to bring thee into the place which I have prepared. Beware of him, and obey his voice, provoke him not; for he will not pardon your transgressions: for my name is in him (Exodus 23:20-21).

This significant fact helps us to understand something of Israel's history in the world. Israel, it would seem, has one of God's highest angels to rule over it in the spirit world; and Satan, by the same token, has no prince of his ruling over Israel. It is a maverick among the principalities and powers as it is among the nations of men. This accounts for antisemitism, that strange, worldwide, age-long, universal hatred of the Jewish people which is always endemic in the world and which from time to time becomes epidemic.

Satan hates the nation of Israel with special venom because no prince of his presides over its affairs.

Some of this comes out in the Apocalypse, where it is Michael who fights with Satan and casts him out of Heaven with the result that Satan at once stirs up the nations against Israel (Revelation 12:7-17). Here, then, in his last chapter, Daniel referred to this final outburst of antisemitism; he spoke of it as "a time of trouble, such as never was since there was a nation" (Daniel 12:1).

Next he spoke about the resurrection (Daniel 12:2-3). A remnant of the Jewish people will survive the coming great tribulation period. These will be referred to by the Lord as enduring to the end and thus being saved (Matthew 24:13). Some will escape the wrath of the beast by flight, others by the kindness of a few brave and believing Gentiles who will offer them shelter at great personal risk. All this remnant will be ultimately delivered by the intervention of God in human affairs at Armageddon.

Besides these who manage to live through the persecutions of the period and thus are able to go right on into the millennial kingdom, there will be a general resurrection of the Jewish people. Daniel told us that for some this resurrection will mean "everlasting life," but for others it will mean "shame and everlasting contempt" (Daniel 12:2). There will be special rewards for the wise counselors ("they that be wise"), those who will guide many into the ways of righteousness during the great tribulation (Daniel 12:3).

Daniel wrote down these coming realities and was then told to "seal the book, even to the time of the end" (Daniel 12:4), not so much to conceal its contents as to secure them until a later day. Many of the prophecies of Daniel, in other words, would have special significance at "the time of the end."

Once again the prophet was told that the three and a half year period set aside for the suffering of Israel, would be the time during which Israel would be shattered and its self-reliance brought to an end. Daniel was told that the persecutions of the endtimes would accomplish two things. They would bring to light a number of pure-hearted people who would be refined and ennobled by their sufferings; at the same time they would expose those who would actually enjoy the wickedness of the age. The lawlessness, the permissiveness of the reign of sin, would find an answering echo in their unregenerate hearts.

Just before the prophet came to the end of his book, he was given a revelation of two mysterious time periods—time periods that are today still in the future.

> And from the time that the daily sacrifice shall be taken away, and the abomination that maketh desolate set up, there shall be a thousand two hundred and ninety days. Blessed is he that waiteth, and cometh to the thousand three hundred and five and thirty days (Daniel 12:11-12).

Throughout both Daniel and Revelation a period of 1,260 days is kept before us. This period refers to the second half of Daniel's seventieth "week" (Daniel 9:27). It is referred to elsewhere as "a thousand two hundred and threescore days" and also as "forty and two months" (Revelation 11:3; 12:6; 13:5).

Daniel, then, has three terminal points in time revealed to him: a terminal point after 1,260 days; another 30 days later (1,290 days); and yet another 45 days after that (1,335 days). Commentators have puzzled much over these periods of time and especially over the last two. Actually there is an interesting correspondence between these future dates and what actually happened when Antiochus Epiphanes (the great type of antichrist) shamed Jerusalem. From the time Antiochus profaned the temple in Jerusalem until the restoration of divine worship by Judas Maccabeus was 1,290 days, and from that date to the death of Antiochus and the end of his persecutions was another 45 days, making a total in all of 1,335 days.[6]

We can only conjecture how these numbers will relate to the endtimes. The starting point is marked for us as the time when the antichrist sets up his image in the temple in Jerusalem. That will be the signal for the commencement of the great tribulation which will end 1,260 days later at the return of Christ at Armageddon. A month is added, during which time, perhaps, mopping-up operations are completed and the great assize in the valley of Jehoshaphat is convened. A further period of a month and a half is added, perhaps to give time for the ceremonial cleansing of the land of Israel and to prepare the Jewish remnant for their coming roles as leaders of world affairs during the millennium. Then the glorious millennial reign of Christ will begin. "Blessed is he that waiteth, and cometh to the thousand three hundred and five and thirty days."

1. F. F. Bruce, *The Books and the Parchments* (Westwood, NJ: Revell, 1963), pp. 114-115.
2. Robert Dick Wilson, *Is the Higher Criticism Scholarly?* (Philadelphia: Sunday School Times, 1953), p. 22. Also his *A Scientific Investigation of the Old Testament* (Chicago: Moody Press, 1959), pp. 96, 99, 127, 146.
3. Sir Robert Anderson, *The Coming Prince* (Grand Rapids: Kregel, 1954), p. 72.
4. Those interested in pursuing the subject further are referred to Anderson, *The Coming Prince*, p. 72, and to his *Daniel in the Critic's Den* (London: James Nisbet, 1902), pp. 112-134.
5. See Alexander Hislop, *The Two Babylons* (Neptune, NJ: Loizeaux, 1959).
6. Frederick A. Tatford, *The Climax of the Ages* (London: Marshall, Morgan & Scott, 1953), p. 235.

4

The Prophecies of Revelation

The divine title of this book is "The Revelation of Jesus Christ" (Revelation 1:1). It is often called the *Apocalypse*, the transliteration of the Greek word for "revelation." The word carries the idea of an *unveiling*. In this book we have an unveiling of the person of Christ and of the purposes of God. In its chapters the Holy Spirit brings us repeated views of the Lord Jesus in His glory. Here, too, the Spirit sets before us clear pictures of God's impending purposes for both the human race and the planet on which we live.

There are more quotations from and allusions to the Old Testament in Revelation than in any other book of the New Testament. Matthew, which has a strong Jewish flavor, has 92 references to the Old Testament. Hebrews, which was written for Jews, has 102 references. But the book of Revelation has 285 such references, more than three times as many as Matthew and nearly three times as many as Hebrews. This preoccupation with the Old Testament is significant. It suggests that the book of Revelation anticipates a time when God will be dealing primarily with Jews and Gentiles, a time when the church will no longer be here. This truth is endorsed by the book itself because, after chapter 3, there is no further direct reference to the church until the closing remarks in the last chapter (Revelation 22:16).

Few books are so controversial, which is not surprising when one considers the unusual structure and the wealth of symbolism found in Revelation. Much could be said about its structure. One evident fact is that its scenes alternate between Heaven and earth: a scene on earth is followed by a scene in Heaven; a scene in Heaven is followed by a scene on earth. The following diagram reveals how the scenes change throughout the book.

Heaven and Earth in Revelation

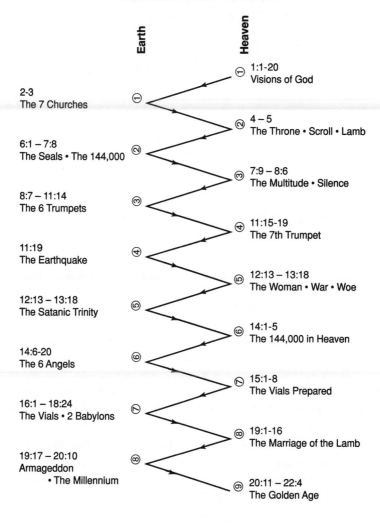

Earth / Heaven

① 1:1-20
Visions of God

2-3
The 7 Churches ①

② 4 – 5
The Throne • Scroll • Lamb

6:1 – 7:8
The Seals • The 144,000 ②

③ 7:9 – 8:6
The Multitude • Silence

8:7 – 11:14
The 6 Trumpets ③

④ 11:15-19
The 7th Trumpet

11:19
The Earthquake ④

⑤ 12:13 – 13:18
The Woman • War • Woe

12:13 – 13:18
The Satanic Trinity ⑤

⑥ 14:1-5
The 144,000 in Heaven

14:6-20
The 6 Angels ⑥

⑦ 15:1-8
The Vials Prepared

16:1 – 18:24
The Vials • 2 Babylons ⑦

⑧ 19:1-16
The Marriage of the Lamb

19:17 – 20:10
Armageddon
• The Millennium ⑧

⑨ 20:11 – 22:4
The Golden Age

This alternating pattern gives us the answer to the Lord's prayer: "Thy kingdom come. Thy will be done in earth, as it is in heaven" (Matthew 6:10).

The structure of the book is complicated by the fact that its basic chronological sequence of events is constantly interrupted by parenthetical passages. These passages comment on the action described in the chronological segments of the book.

Imagine, for instance, a newscaster broadcasting to a radio audience his account of a parade that is passing before him. He describes the floats, bands, and other scenes of interest. Presently he finds himself with a few moments to spare, so he takes his audience back in time. He says, "A few minutes ago, when the parade was at the last intersection, something interesting happened. I didn't have time to describe it then, but let me fill you in on the details now." After that account, he continues his description of the passing parade. Again he finds himself with moments to spare, so this time he anticipates. He says, "In a few minutes the parade will reach the square, where a ceremony is to take place. Let me prepare you for that event . . ." Then once more he comes back to continue his description of the parade.

Revelation is written in such a style. Action is interrupted by commentary. It is not always easy to decide where these parentheses begin, where they end, or where they fit in relation to the action segments of the book, although most seem to refer to the trumpet judgments—the time when the antichrist is in power. These comments tell us how he can so swiftly take over the planet, what happens once he is in control, and how God intends to bring his schemes to nought. The following diagram shows how the more important parenthetical chapters relate to Revelation 8 and 9 and the trumpet judgments.

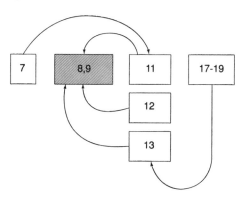

The symbolism of the Apocalypse also causes confusion because commentators often forget that God is His own interpreter (Genesis 40:8). In the book of Revelation about half the symbols are explained. Thus *lampstands* are said to represent local churches, *stars* symbolize angels, *torches* stand for spirits, *horns* and *eyes* are said to represent spirits, *incense* symbolizes the prayers of saints, the *dragon* symbolizes Satan, *frogs* represent evil spirits, the *wild beast* represents a king, the *heads* of the wild beast stand for kings and also for mountains, *horns* stand for kings, *waters* represent peoples, the *woman* symbolizes the city that sits on the seven hills (Rome), *fine linen* stands for the righteousness of saints, and the *city of God* symbolizes the bride of the Lamb.

Where the symbols are not explained in the immediate context, often they are explained elsewhere in the book of Revelation or, almost certainly, elsewhere in the Bible. Sometimes the same symbol stands for more than one thing in Scripture, and sometimes one thing can be symbolized in more than one way. The context is always the determining factor.

Before we proceed further we need to get the overall plan of the book in mind. It can be divided as follows:

I. Introduction (Revelation 1:1-3)
II. Visions of God (Revelation 1:4-20)
III. Visions of Grace (Revelation 2:1–3:22)
IV. Visions of Government (Revelation 4:1–20:15)
   A. Hallelujahs in Heaven (4:1–5:14)
   B. Horrors on earth (6:1–20:15)
      1. The seals: a world ruined by men
      2. The trumpets: a world ruled by Satan
      3. The vials: a world rescued by God
V. Visions of Glory (Revelation 21:1–22:7)
VI. Conclusion (Revelation 22:8-21)

The above outline is intended merely to sketch in the broad outlines of the book.[1]

The chart on the following page visualizes the major themes of the Apocalypse. This chart makes no attempt to separate the chronological sections of the book from the commentary sections and simply summarizes the major themes in the order in which they appear. Read through the book of Revelation with the aid of

The Seven Churches — Chapters 1, 2, 3

Introduction • Visions of God the Son	1 Ephesus	2 Smyrna	3 Pergamos	4 Thyatira	5 Sardis	6 Philadelphia — 7 Laodicea

The Seven Seals — Chapters 4, 5, 6, 7, 8

	1	2	3	4	5	6	7
The Throne • The Scroll • The Lamb	Anti-God Ideology / White Horse	World War / Red Horse	Famine / Black Horse	Plagues / Pale Horse	Persecution	The Sealing of the 144,000 / Panic	Silence in Heaven

The Seven Trumpets — Chapters 8, 9, 10, 11, 12

	1	2	3	4	5	6	7
The Beast • The False Prophet	The Brewing Storm	The Boiling Sea • The Beast Surfaces	The Banished Star • Satan Falls	The Blackened Sky	Woe / The Locusts • Demonic Delusion	Woe / The Four Angels • Russia Goes to War	Woe / War in Heaven • The Great Tribulation
The 144,000 in Heaven						The Little Book • The Two Witnesses	
Three Angels Call	Harvest Vintage	The Vials of Wrath Prepared					

The Seven Vials — Chapters 13, 14, 15, 16, 17, 18

1	2	3	4	5	6	7		
Sores	Sea Turned to Blood	Streams Turned to Blood	Sun Scorches Men	Throne of Beast Smitten	The Kings of the East	The Fall of Babylon	Mystical Babylon	Material Babylon

The Seven Last Things — Chapters 19, 20, 21, 22

Marriage Supper of the Lamb / Return of Christ	The Beast and False Prophet Slain • Satan Bound	The Millennium	Satan Loosed • The Last Rebellion / Satan Cast into the Lake of Fire	The Universe Destroyed • The Great White Throne / The New Universe — The Celestial City	Conclusion

this chart; then reread chapters 7–9, 11–13, and 17–19 in the light of the diagram on page 63, which shows how these chapters overlap.

Opening Visions (Revelation 1)

The visions of the Apocalypse were given to John when he was a prisoner on Patmos, a small island off the coast of Asia Minor (Turkey). Before him lay the mainland and thriving churches in a dozen cities of the empire; to the west lay Rome; to the east the Holy Land, the Euphrates, and Babylon.

The book was addressed to seven chosen churches in Asia Minor and begins with a blessing and a benediction (Revelation 1:4-6). How like God to begin with grace and peace, even though the book is to deal with the most appalling judgments.

This book describes judgment after judgment being poured out by a God whose patience has been exhausted. We see men getting just what they deserve. But God begins by telling them that even in the hour of His wrath He remembers His mercy, and they can have what they don't deserve—grace. The line of sovereign grace runs through much of the book: grace to defy the devil to the last; grace to win souls from beneath the very throne of the beast.

And peace. This book deals with the opposite of peace: bloodshed and war. It rings with the din and noise of strife. It tells of carnage and conflict; of earthquake, pestilence, and woe; of purges and persecutions that dwarf all those in previous history. It tells of the crash of empires, the downfall of the establishment, and the upsurging of the mob. It tells of anarchy, oppression, and terror; of a beast rising up from the sea; of Satan flung down from the sky. It tells of war in heaven and war on earth. Martyrs are countless, thunder rolls, stars fall from heaven, and demons pour up from the abyss. Armies are mobilized until East and West meet in furious confrontation on the plains of Armageddon. Yet God begins the book with the word *peace*.

Yes, and grace and peace win through at last. In the end the storm clouds roll away, the drums of war are stilled, the earth is purged with fire, and there emerges a new heaven and a new earth where all is grace and peace. John could not wait to tell us the glorious end of the story. "Behold, he cometh with clouds," he said, "and every eye shall see him, and they also which pierced him . . . Even so, Amen" (Revelation 1:7).

The book begins with *visions of God*, visions of the God the Son (Revelation 1:5). When He came the first time, it was as *the faithful witness*. He was a prophet; He was God's Word, clothed in flesh and dwelling among us, full of grace and truth. Today He is *the first begotten of the dead*, ascended to God's right hand in glory to be a priest, made like unto His brethren, touched with the feelings of their infirmities, upholding them on high. When He comes again it will be as *the prince of the kings of the earth*, the long-awaited Prince of Peace, earth's rightful King.

That's the first vision. The second is more detailed. The glories of the Lord Jesus are suddenly unveiled, and John, who once had leaned on Jesus' breast, was terrified and "fell at his feet as dead" (Revelation 1:17). He saw the blaze of Christ's glory, the glory He had with the Father before the worlds began. He saw Him walking between the seven lampstands (i.e., the seven churches), and each detail of the description is applied later to the seven churches (Revelation 2–3). Yet it was "this same Jesus" after all, the Jesus whom John had known on earth, and gracious as ever. Tenderly He laid His right hand on John and told him, "Fear not" (1:17).

Nor did John ever fear again. We see him as he moved through scenes of devastation and terror undaunted. He soared to worlds unknown and stood among angels, archangels, cherubim, and elders on their thrones—completely unafraid.

THE SEVEN CHURCHES (REVELATION 2–3)

There were more than seven churches in Asia Minor in John's day. Paul's remarkable ministry at Ephesus had resulted in the evangelization of the entire surrounding countryside. We know from the New Testament that there were churches at Colossae and Hierapolis besides the ones addressed in these two chapters of Revelation. The choosing of these seven and the order in which they are addressed is therefore significant.

There are three primary ways to view these seven letters. First, they contain *practical* truth; they were letters addressed to existing churches and dealing with real problems.

Picture the postman from Patmos arriving at each of the

churches in turn. In each of them he finds exactly the state of affairs described in the letter addressed to that church. He found the church at Ephesus fundamentalist to the core, busy with a tremendous program, and cold as clay. He found the church at Smyrna facing the hatred of the world and harboring in its fellowship a dangerous sect, a "synagogue of Satan." At Pergamos he found compromise with immorality and idolatry. At Thyatira he found believers under the spell of an attractive but dangerous woman who claimed to be a prophetess and who openly advocated idolatry and immorality. At Sardis he discovered a church with a tremendous reputation, which was not only dead but in danger of losing whatever shreds of spirituality remained. Philadelphia was a refreshing change; there he found a church living in ecclesiastical, eschatological, and evangelical revival. At Laodicea he found a wealthy and arrogant church, so inflated with its own importance that Christ was outside its doors altogether.

These seven letters give us a picture of what the church was like toward the end of the first century of the Christian era. They deal with practical truth and address themselves to relevant issues.

These seven letters also contain *perennial* truth. From Pentecost to the rapture the messages to these churches will always be pertinent; there have always been churches that have grown cool toward Christ, churches facing persecution, and churches falling in step with the world. The warnings, exhortations, and promises in these letters have met the needs of churches in all ages.

Then, too, the letters contain *prophetic* truth. This is not surprising since they are found in a book devoted to prophecy. They contain in embryonic form the history of the church on earth.[2]

In each of these letters a key phrase can be found that highlights its prophetic significance. With *Ephesus* it is "thou art fallen"; with *Smyrna*, "tribulation ten days"; with *Pergamos*, "the doctrine of Balaam"; with *Thyatira*, "that woman Jezebel"; with *Sardis*, "a name . . . but dead"; with *Philadelphia*, "an open door"; and with *Laodicea*, "thou art lukewarm."

Ephesus illustrates the rapid cooling of love for Christ in the early church. Already in apostolic times error and apostasy raised their heads and gnosticism took root, so that the existence of the church was threatened.

A terrible period followed when the church went through

The Seven Churches

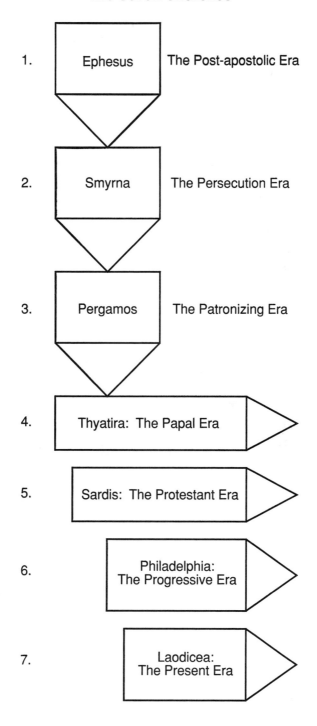

1. Ephesus — The Post-apostolic Era

2. Smyrna — The Persecution Era

3. Pergamos — The Patronizing Era

4. Thyatira: The Papal Era

5. Sardis: The Protestant Era

6. Philadelphia: The Progressive Era

7. Laodicea: The Present Era

persecution. Smyrna epitomized this period. For three hundred years the fires of intolerance burned, sometimes smoldering, sometimes raging. Historian Philip Schaff drew our attention to "the tenth wave" of persecution (under Diocletian), when for ten years all the might of imperial Rome was mobilized to uproot the church and stamp out Christianity.[3]

Diocletian was followed by Constantine, the first of the patronizing caesars. He embraced Christianity and made it the state religion of the empire. This was foreshadowed in the letter to Pergamos in the reference to Balaam. Balaam's philosophy was this: "You cannot conquer the people of God, my lord king, so corrupt them." Constantine's royal favor made the church popular, the world moved in, pagan rites and festivals were given new names and incorporated into Christianity, and the church lost its separation from the world.

In time, pagan Rome gave way to papal Rome. This is suggested by the reference to Jezebel in the letter to Thyatira. Jezebel was the wife of Ahab, the weak and wicked king of Israel. She imported idolatry into Israel. She became the power behind the throne, and she used that power to persecute the saints of God. In Jezebel we have the first instance in Old Testament history of the secular arm being used to attack God's saints. The religious system that Jezebel forced on Israel was pagan, idolatrous, and impure, and was served by an elaborate and false priesthood. All this has had its counterpart in church history, especially in the shameless lives of some of the popes and in the Inquisition. In these things we see the long dark shadow of "that woman Jezebel."

Not that Protestantism has been much better. As the letter to Sardis implies, Protestantism for all its initial life and vitality was soon a dead system. The reformers leaned too readily on the arms of princes, and state churches sprang up. Many glorious truths were rediscovered during the Reformation, but it was not long before Protestantism became weak, divided, contentious, and preoccupied with outward forms. Almost every major denomination was born in revival or in the rediscovery of some great truth, but it has never taken long for the new infusion of life to be replaced by deadness and formality, tradition and ritual.

The phase of church history foreseen in the letter to Philadelphia is that of the great revivals of the eighteenth and early nineteenth centuries. Men like David Livingstone, Hudson Taylor,

William Carey, and Adoniram Judson blazed new trails to evangelize Africa, China, India, and Burma, and spread the gospel to the ends of the earth. Men like John Wesley, Charles Finney, and D. L. Moody found new ways to bring the gospel to the masses. A "great door and effectual" was opened and millions poured through it into the kingdom of God (1 Corinthians 16:9).

The letter to Laodicea anticipated the final stage in church history, one of material wealth, complacency, and lukewarmness—the condition of being neither one thing nor the other. Such is the condition of the church today. We have evangelism without the offense of the cross; conversion without conviction; emotional, ecstatic experience without doctrinal understanding; preaching without power; salvation without separation; truth without love; religion without the Holy Spirit; organization without spiritual life.

The conditions envisioned in the letters to Ephesus, Smyrna, Pergamos, and Thyatira are *successive*; each stage follows and replaces the one before. But from Thyatira on, the stages are *contemporaneous*. As each new stage is introduced, it does not replace the one before it, but runs concurrently with it until the end. The diagram on page 69 shows this. Once the papal era is introduced, it goes on to the end; the Protestant era does not replace the papal era—it coexists with it until the end. Nor does the age of revival replace either Roman Catholicism or dead Protestantism; both continue as before, with the new elements of revival, evangelism, and missionary enterprise existing alongside. Similarly, the final phase of apathy and lukewarmness, although it characterizes much of the church and gives rise to many ills, does not replace Catholicism, Protestantism, and revivalism.

At the second coming of Christ, the true church, made up of all born-again believers, in no matter what communion they are found, will be caught away. What will be left will be dead Christendom which in effect will be "spewed out" of Christ's mouth as He said (Revelation 3:16).

VISIONS OF THE LAMB (REVELATION 4 –5)

The magnificent scenes in these two chapters are set in Heaven, and they form the prelude to judgments about to break on the world. Nowhere else in the Bible is there a greater emphasis on the throne of God. It is mentioned directly seventeen times in two short chapters—the throne, the throne, the throne—repeatedly.

These two chapters prepare us for a wild and stormy sea. Horrendous scenes are about to be enacted, as man's wickedness is wedded to demonic iniquity, and the world becomes a battleground between Heaven and Hell. At times it seems that God has lost control and that everything is going Satan's way. Not so. God is still on the throne. That is the message of these two chapters.

John was caught up to Heaven and came away first of all with the memory of an *unforgettable throne*. His description of that mysterious throne is awesome. God is described as "a jasper and a sardine stone." Who would think to describe God in inanimate terms? Then, too, the four mysterious living creatures are there and so are "the seven Spirits of God."

There is a majesty about that throne. John told of a sea of glass, of an emerald rainbow encircling the throne, of thunderings and lightnings. He described the endless chants of the holy ones and the adoring worship of the elders. It is all solemn, impressive, and eloquently indicative of judgment to come.

John came away with the additional memory of an *unforgettable throng*. The angels, the cherubim, the four and twenty elders—all are there. He described them that we too might catch a glimpse of the dignity of divine government, sense something of its solemnity, and feel for ourselves what it is like to be in the presence of such holiness and exhilarating happiness.

The cherubim are there, those ancient guardians of God's creative and redemptive rights in the universe. We meet them first at the gateway of Eden, standing with flaming sword to keep fallen man away from the tree of life lest, in his folly, he become immortal in his sins. We meet the cherubim again in the holy of holies, where they form part of the mercy seat. We see them facing inward and downward, forever occupied with the blood splashed there, the token of God's method of dealing with sin. We see them again in Ezekiel's vision. There they are associated with dreadful wheels that run and turn and revolve, spanning the vast reaches between Heaven above and earth beneath—all so eloquent of those "wheels within wheels" and God's righteous movements in connection with this world. We meet them again as they cry before the throne, "Holy, holy, holy" (Isaiah 6:3). Their praise fills the high halls of

Heaven as God sits enthroned on the worship of these sinless sons of light.

The four and twenty elders are there, each sitting on a throne adjacent to the throne of God. These elders are beings of exalted rank, occupying the thrones mentioned by Paul (Colossians 1:16). They form a kind of celestial jury to witness God's righteous acts of judgment on the earth. We meet them on a number of occasions in the Apocalypse, and on almost every occasion they do what they do here. They rise from their thrones, cast their crowns at the feet of God, fall down before Him, and praise Him for the wisdom and justice of His ways.

Finally, John came away with the memory of an *unforgettable thrill*. He saw the Lord Jesus, the beloved Lamb of Calvary, step into the spotlight of eternity and become the center of everything.

The scene is impressive. In the hand of God there reposed a scroll sealed with seven seals. That scroll is the title deed of planet Earth. A call was given for any man *worthy* to do so to come and take that scroll. Nobody came. Nobody could. No son of Adam's fallen race was worthy. History is littered with the wreckage wrought by men like Alexander, Caesar, Napoleon, Hitler, and Stalin. All *willing* enough, but none worthy.

John wept because of the disgrace of mankind. There, in those bright regions of joy, no man was found worthy to take that scroll or even to look on it—not even Abraham, Isaac, or Jacob, not David or Daniel, not Peter, James, or John. Of all the millions of people who have lived, not a single individual could be found who was fit to govern the globe. No wonder John wept. Then Jesus stood forth, "the lamb as it had been slain," still bearing the marks of Calvary. He came and took the scroll, and instantly all Heaven burst into song.

The Lord Jesus is called a lamb only twice in the Old Testament (Isaiah 53:7; Jeremiah 11:19), only twice in the Gospels (John 1:29,36), only once in the book of Acts (8:32), and only once in the Epistles (1 Peter 1:19). In the book of Revelation, however, He is called a lamb twenty-eight times. It is the apocalyptic title of Christ. Moreover, the word John used literally means "a little lamb." Satan has his great red dragon, his beast out of the sea, his armies numbered in the millions. God has His little lamb. But He is no ordinary lamb. He has seven eyes, suggesting omniscience, and seven horns, symbolizing omnipotence. This little lamb is the Lamb of God.

To see Him take the scroll, to see Him fill all Heaven with praise, was an unforgettable thrill for John. Everything else that happens in this book stems from that act, for God has committed all judgment to the Son (John 5:22). As the Lord Jesus begins to break the seals on that scroll, so the judgments begin here on earth. The seals are broken, the trumpets are sounded, and the vials are outpoured. Each series of judgments, in an ascending scale of severity, flows from the other; each has its ultimate cause in the taking of the scroll by Jesus into His capable and pierced hands.

Everything that happens now in the book of Revelation happens because *He* precipitates the action. From start to finish *He* is in complete control.

THE SEVEN SEALS (REVELATION 6 –8)

With the seven-sealed scroll securely in the hands of Jesus, the stage is now set for the judgments of the Apocalypse to begin. The first thing we notice is that there are three major series of judgments: the seals, the trumpets, and the vials. The seal judgments set before us *a world ruined by man.* The symbolism is fairly simple, because it deals with familiar things, everyday occurrences in the world. When the seals are broken the restraint will be removed, and the national and natural disasters that plague mankind will be allowed to develop their full potential of horror.

The rapture of the church is only hinted at (Revelation 4:1), probably because it has already been thoroughly covered elsewhere (1 Thessalonians 4:13–5:10). The removal of the church and the resumption by the Holy Spirit of His former relationship toward mankind (that which existed in Old Testament times and in the era of the Gospels, prior to the beginning of the church age) clears the way for the judgments of the Apocalypse (2 Thessalonians 2:1-12).

God is going to break off diplomatic relations with the earth, so to speak, and wage war on the forces of wickedness then to be given full reign. The horrors of this age to come are latent in society today, but they are being mercifully restrained by the Holy Spirit operating through the church. Once those restraints are removed, human and Satanic forces of wickedness will be given a brief period to come to full flower. God who for some two thousand years in His grace has been making *peace* through the blood of Christ's cross (Colossians 1:20) will go to *war* over that blood. But first He will call home the nationals of Heaven and end the day of grace; then He will inaugurate the period of judgment and wrath. The diagram on page 76 gives a pictorial overview of this impending change.

The events that take place under the seals can be summarized as follows:

    I. The Four Horsemen of the Apocalypse
      A. Seal 1: Successful propaganda
      B. Seal 2: Sanguinary policies
      C. Seal 3: Severe privations
      D. Seal 4: Spreading plagues
    II. The Further Horrors of the Apocalypse
      A. Seal 5: Immense persecution
      B. Seal 6: Impotent panic
      C. Seal 7: Imprecatory prayer

The *first seal* is opened. The first four seals are linked together by the appearance of a horse and a rider after each seal is broken. These riders are often called "the four horsemen of the Apocalypse." The first horse is white; its rider has a bow and a crown and is sent forth "conquering, and to conquer" (Revelation 6:2).

The immediate problem before us is to determine who or what this rider symbolizes. The key is found in Revelation 6:8, where the rider of the fourth horse is identified as Death. We realize that the riders are not persons, but personifications. They symbolize forces that will be abroad in the world immediately after the rapture of the church.

The color of the first horse, the bow, the crown, and the victorious career of the rider are all clues. In the Bible a horse is sometimes used as a symbol for war. Here we have war symbolized, but a different kind of war from that which appears under the second seal. The rider on the white horse symbolizes bloodless conquest, possibly what we call "cold war." He represents the all-victorious, anti-God, anti-Christ ideologies of the last days. We have seen such ideologies change the world more than once in the

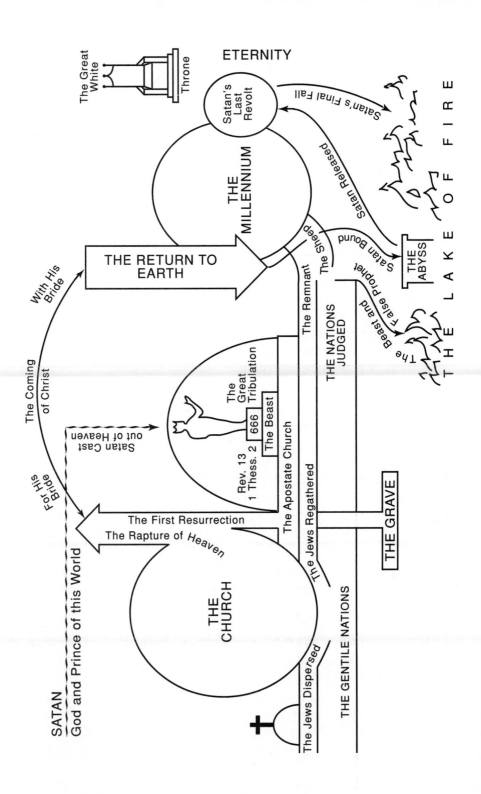

twentieth century. Nazi and communist ideologies are shadows of coming events.

The *second seal* is opened and a red horse appears. Its rider has a great sword given to him, and his commission is to "take peace from the earth" (Revelation 6:4). He symbolizes war on a global scale.

The *third seal* clears the way for a black horse whose rider carries a pair of scales. At his coming a voice calls out, "A measure of wheat for a penny, and three measures of barley for a penny; and see thou hurt not the oil and the wine" (Revelation 6:6). This symbolism depicts famine, privation, and shortage, but a kind that particularly affects the poor and does not impede the luxurious lifestyle of the rich. Ever since the Arab oil embargo in 1967 we have come to realize we are living in a world that is running out of many vital natural resources. Food shortages are endemic in many parts of the world today. Raw materials for industry are being depleted or are in the hands of a few key countries. What we are seeing is only the shadow of things to come.

The breaking of the *fourth seal* calls up a cadaverous horse whose rider is Death and whose companion is Hades. Authority is given to this rider to kill men "by sword, famine and plague, and by the wild beasts of the earth" (Revelation 6:8, NIV). The sword and famine referred to here are probably more local in scope than in the second and third seals. In any case, these disasters continue and two more terrors are added to them: beasts and pestilence (plague). It is uncertain whether the reference to "beasts" is to be taken literally or symbolically—whether "beasts" depict wild animals or bestial men. The word itself is used almost exclusively elsewhere in the Apocalypse for *the* beast, the devil's messiah. It is unlikely that wild animals could become a serious threat to mankind in an age of machine guns and napalm. The term *beasts* could refer possibly to vermin such as rats, since they are associated here with famine and pestilence. Rats are a menace both to human health and food supplies, and their fleas carry bacteria long associated with plague.

One way or another, this last horseman decimates the world of a quarter of its population. What the net effect will be of all these seal judgments is impossible to say, especially since once these riders are sent forth there is no word of their recall. Ideological struggles, warfare, famine, and plague will continue to the end until everything culminates in the battle of Armageddon.

The *fifth seal* removes divine restraint from yet another horror that curses mankind—persecution. John saw beneath the brazen altar those who had been martyred for their testimony to God and His Word. They appeal to God as "Sovereign Lord" (Revelation 6:10, NIV) to speed His vengeance upon their murderers. The name they use for God indicates they are not martyrs of the church age, but those who will be martyred in the age that lies ahead. They ask God how long He will hold back vengeance for their blood, another proof that these are not Christian martyrs. They are given white robes and told to be patient until the full complement of martyrs is made up. This seems to be a reference to those who will be martyred by the beast during the great tribulation. The coming age is to be one of persecution as well as judgment.

The *sixth seal* is broken, and great convulsions take place everywhere. The sun, moon, and stars are smitten; the heavens roll back like a scroll; the earth is shaken with violent earthquakes. All men, from kings on their thrones down to the meanest slaves, are seen running for shelter and calling on mountains and rocks to hide them from the face of the Lamb and from His wrath. These things could be literal. Many Scriptures tell of upheavals like this both in the heavens and on earth during the last days. But they could just as accurately be symbolic.

What we have is a description of the breakup of the old establishment on the earth, since sometimes in the Bible the sun, moon, and stars are used to symbolize ruling powers. Perhaps there is to be both a literal and a symbolic fulfillment of the events described here. Nevertheless, people will be in a state of panic, thinking that the end of the world has come. They will be mistaken. Both the trumpet and the vial judgments lie ahead; the terrors mentioned here are only "the beginning of sorrows" (Matthew 24:6-28). The sixth seal also looks on to the very end, because the forces set in motion under the seals are not recalled but go on operating until the day of wrath itself dawns.

Chapter 7 is a parenthesis in the Apocalypse. This parenthesis seems to be inspired by the martyrdoms mentioned under the fifth seal, but it really looks ahead to the time of the great tribulation. John saw four angels holding back further tumult on earth while

144,000 Jewish people are sealed, 12,000 from each of the various tribes of Israel. Dan and Ephraim are omitted from the list, and Levi and Joseph are inserted to take their places. This is fitting because the people who are now to be sealed by God are to be Jehovah's true witnesses during the coming age.[4] They will be not only saved, but also sealed, so that the beast will not be able to harm them.

The fruit of these true witnesses is described next. A countless multitude will be saved through their ministry. John saw this vast company standing before the throne of the Lamb in Heaven, arrayed in white robes and holding the palm leaves of triumph in their hands. He was told that this multitude, saved out of all nations, tribes, peoples, and tongues, have paid the price of martyrdom for their faith. "These are they which came out of great tribulation, and have washed their robes, and made them white in the blood of the Lamb" (Revelation 7:14). For them there is nothing now but eternal bliss and closeness to the Lamb Himself.

This first phase of apocalyptic judgment ends with a description of the *seventh seal*. The scene is once more cast in Heaven, where the opening of this seal brings about a solemn silence (Revelation 8:1). This is followed by the presentation to God of the prayers of His afflicted people on earth. Then seven angels are prepared, and now all is ready for the sounding of the trumpets and further scenes of judgment on earth.

THE TRUMPET JUDGMENTS (REVELATION 8–11)

With the blowing of the seven trumpets, a new dimension of horror is introduced into human affairs. Under the seals the world became a world ruined by man. Now, under the trumpets, it becomes *a world ruled by Satan*. The symbolism under the trumpets is much more complex than under the seals, because it deals with the world of the weird, the occult, the Satanic. Under the trumpets Satan's man takes over the world. He has been waiting while the seal judgments were tearing the world apart and reducing human affairs to chaos. Now men will be ready for anyone just so long as he is clever and strong enough to bring peace and sanity back to the world. Satan's man will be ready, but first, whatever is left of the establishment must be overthrown.

We can summarize the trumpet judgments as follows:

I. The War Trumpets (Revelation 8:1-13)
  A. The brewing storm
  B. The boiling sun
  C. The banished star
  D. The blackened sky
II. The Woe Trumpets (Revelation 9:1-21; 10:7; 11:15-19)
  A. Misery endured
  B. Mastery ensured
  C. Mystery ended

The action under the trumpet judgments is covered in two chapters, but much of the rest of the Apocalypse is commentary on this action. The following chart shows how the six connected trumpets unfold and how various later chapters relate to these judgments. The first four trumpets are *war* trumpets; the last three are *woe* trumpets, because an additional "woe" is sounded along with them.

The *first trumpet* brings a storm of fire, hail, and blood on the earth, as a result of which "the third part" of the trees and all green grass are burned up. This could, of course, depict a literal disaster, an ecological devastation of terrible proportions. Or it could symbolize some kind of political upheaval affecting those in authority as well as many others. *Trees* in Scripture are frequently used to symbolize kings and leaders, while *grass* is used to depict ordinary people. The disasters produced by the seals are continuing under the trumpets, only now a more specific goal is in view. The old establishment must be overthrown to make way for a new world order under the beast (as the antichrist is called in Revelation).

The expression "the third part" occurs frequently in connection with the trumpets. A clue to its significance is found in a reference to Satan's original fall (Revelation 12:4). The expression "the third part of the stars of heaven" refers to the angels who joined Satan's affairs in connection with this world. Satan has a second fall in this same chapter; he is now cast out of Heaven and confined to the earth. Consequently, a "woe" is pronounced against the earth's inhabitants (12:12). This is what makes the last three trumpets "woe" trumpets. The expression "the third part"

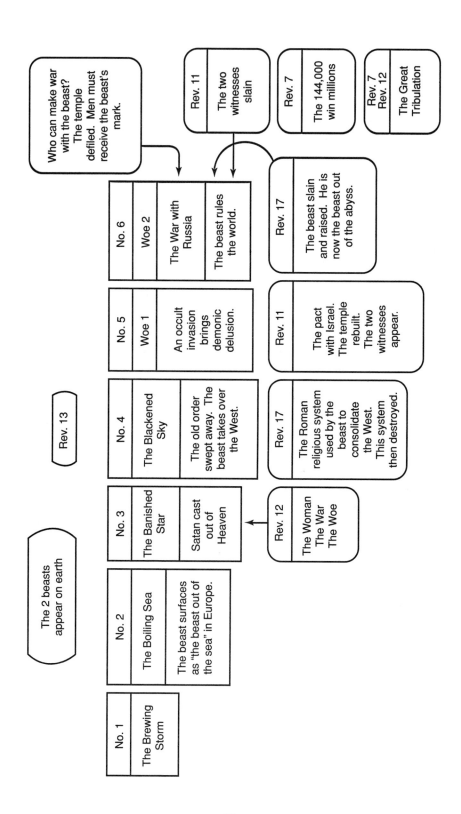

The 2 beasts appear on earth

No. 1	No. 2	No. 3	No. 4	No. 5	No. 6
The Brewing Storm	The Boiling Sea	The Banished Star	The Blackened Sky	Woe 1	Woe 2
	The beast surfaces as "the beast out of the sea" in Europe.	Satan cast out of Heaven	The old order swept away. The beast takes over the West.	An occult invasion brings demonic delusion.	The War with Russia / The beast rules the world.

Rev. 13

Who can make war with the beast? The temple defiled. Men must receive the beast's mark.

Rev. 11 — The two witnesses slain

Rev. 7 — The 144,000 win millions

Rev. 7 / Rev. 12 — The Great Tribulation

Rev. 12 — The Woman / The War / The Woe

Rev. 17 — The Roman religious system used by the beast to consolidate the West. This system then destroyed.

Rev. 11 — The pact with Israel. The temple rebuilt. The two witnesses appear.

Rev. 17 — The beast slain and raised. He is now the beast out of the abyss.

seems to be a reference to the sphere of Satanic influence which, under the trumpets, is to be confined to this world.

The *second trumpet* affects the sea. A great mountain burning with fire is cast into the sea so that "the third part" of the sea becomes blood, the third part of creatures in the sea die, and the third part of all shipping is destroyed. This could be a literal disaster. There is no reason why an omnipotent God could not uproot an erupting volcano and cast it into the sea. Or this trumpet could be describing a future ecological disaster affecting marine life and commerce. But probably we should interpret these things symbolically.

The sea is a well-known Bible symbol for the Gentile nations, and a mountain sometimes stands for a great world power. If we interpret this judgment symbolically, we have described a further upheaval among the nations, one that enables the beast to emerge and begin his remarkable career. He is described later in the book as "a beast . . . out of the sea" (Revelation 13:1).

He will become prominent on earth, it seems, during a time of unrest in Europe. He will swiftly bring that continent to heel and will eventually spread his influence throughout the western world. From the standpoint of Bible prophecy the future lies with Europe, not with the United States. Revelation 17 puts the focus on Italy— and particularly on Rome—as the chief scene of the antichrist's early activities. According to the book of Daniel, he will first come to power in a small insignificant European nation, for he is described as "a little horn." He will emerge at a time when a ten-nation European federation is forming. He will seize the initiative, overthrow three members of the federation, and install himself in absolute power over all ten.

The *third trumpet* adds a new and ominous dimension to world affairs. A great star burning like a lamp falls from heaven on "the third part of the rivers, and upon the fountains of waters" (Revelation 8:10). The star is given the symbolic name of "Wormwood," and its fall makes "the waters" bitter (8:11).

Angels are symbolized as stars in the Bible (see Job 38:7). This fallen star is Satan himself, who is now cast down from Heaven (Revelation 12:7-9). He is infuriated because he is no longer the "prince of the power of the air" (Ephesians 2:2), only "the prince of this world" (John 16:11). He vents his rage against the human race, with the result that "the waters became wormwood." "Waters" stand for "peoples, and multitudes, and nations, and tongues" (Revelation 17:15), so the people of the world now take their character from Satan himself. He is called "Wormwood"; they become wormwood and, as a result, life becomes bitter and many people die.

The *fourth trumpet* affects the sun, moon, and stars, so that "the third part" of them are darkened. An angel now proclaims a threefold woe on mankind: the remaining three trumpets are to be far worse than the preliminary four. The world has now become the sphere of Satanic activity (Revelation 12:12).

The sun, moon, and stars, of course, are all literal realities, so this trumpet could be describing some upheaval in the solar system. On the other hand, it could be a symbolic description of the complete overthrow of whatever ruling power still remains to bar the beast from his control of the western world. The underlying restlessness and rebellion of our age will continue until Satan is flung from the sky. He will use the anarchist forces already at work in society to overthrow existing governments and clear the way to power for his protégé the beast.

The *fifth trumpet* heralds a truly fearful coming event. The fallen star (Revelation 9:1) is now given permission to open the abyss and let loose on the world a host of evil spirits. They are described as "locusts," but no such locusts have ever ravaged this world. These demons have the general appearance of locusts, but they are also likened to horses, men, lions, and scorpions. They remind us of the cherubim whose faces resemble those of a lion, a calf, a man, and an eagle (4:7). These demons from the abyss seem to be some form of Satanic cherubim. They are supernatural, incapable of death, and led by "the angel of the bottomless pit" (9:11). The form of these demons probably indicates the kind of torment they inflict. They are obviously not literal locusts, because their hunger is not for vegetation but for humans.

They have faces like men, which suggests a special appeal to the intellect. They have hair like women to portray the attractiveness of their appeal. They have teeth like lions to denote their fierceness and the tenacity with which they fasten on their victims. They have breastplates of iron to emphasize how impervious they are to human suffering. Their wings sound like horses and chariots rushing to battle to depict the terror they cause. Their tails sting like scorpions to symbolize the excruciating torment they inflict on people's souls. They are crowned because they will be given complete ascendancy over the human race. Finally, in the mercy of God, their reign of terror is limited to five months (the normal length of time when natural locusts flourish, from May to September).

What are we to make of all this? Simply that a world which has rejected the ministry of God's Holy Spirit and the truth of the gospel is eventually to be handed over to evil spirits. Men will believe a lie, an attractive lie, a dreadful lie, a soul-tormenting lie, a lie that will make them long in vain for death. This coming lie is part of the working of Satan; it is he who opens the abyss to release these demons. This lie will pave the way for the world-rule of the beast and for the strong delusion that will center in him when once he is finally unveiled (2 Thessalonians 2).

It should be noted here that the "bottomless pit" (the abyss) is one of God's prison houses. Twice the beast is described as coming up from this place (Revelation 11:7; 17:8), and it is in this same prison that Satan will be incarcerated for the thousand years of the millennial reign of Christ (20:1-3).

The sounding of the *sixth trumpet* moves Satan's plans forward toward completion. This time four angels are released from the Euphrates. The Euphrates was the ancient dividing line between east and west. It is connected in Scripture with Babylon and the four world empires of prophecy. These four angels are called "the four"; it is likely they are the angelic beings who ruled the world empires of Babylon, Persia, Greece, and Rome as Satan's vice-regents in the spirit world. They are released to bring about an empire that will embrace the world.

They have accomplices and the description we are given of them is highly symbolic. We read about horses and riders with breastplates of fire, jacinth, and brimstone. We are told that the horses have heads like lions and that fire, smoke, and brimstone come from their mouths. Evidently this is a description of spirit beings. These evil spirits goad men on to a battle, one which involves some 200 million people.

The enormous number of persons involved in this war has led many to conclude that this battle involves China. This cannot be, however, for "the kings of the east" come to the fore and the way is paved for Armageddon when the *sixth vial* is outpoured, not before. China will be involved in that battle, but not in this battle. This war is some other battle of vast dimensions, one involving millions of people, and one that leaves the beast in control of the world. But it is not Armageddon. The number two hundred is used on various occasions in the Bible to depict human *insufficiency* (the key to its use is in John 6:7), so the number here could be a symbolic number. But regardless of whether the number is literal or symbolic, a tremendous war is now fought which changes the world completely, making possible the global dominion of the beast.

Only one war in Scripture fits this description. It is the war described in Ezekiel 38 and 39, in which Russia attacks Israel to its own undoing. The Russian invasion of Israel has no connection with Armageddon (as I will explain in the chapter dealing with Russia). The Russian invasion seems to fit into the Apocalypse right here.

When the beast first comes to power in the West, Russia dominates much of the Middle East and large segments of Africa. Russia's domestic empire (if we include the various republics) stretches from Europe to the Bering straits and from the Arctic to the Mediterranean sea and the Indian ocean. What Russia will be doing while the beast consolidates the West is unknown. Possibly Russia will be embroiled in a war with China, perhaps one of the wars mentioned under the seals or the early trumpets. By the time Russia is able to pursue her interests in the Middle East again, things will have changed. The West will be united under the beast, and all its enormous military, economic, and industrial power will be harnessed by him, its supreme dictator.

The beast will have signed a pact with Israel that unconditionally guarantees Israel's frontiers and acknowledges Israel's right to rebuild its temple. The fury of the Muslim world can well be imagined. Russia will see an open door to new and decisive influence in the Middle East and will mobilize all its resources in an all-out attack on Israel. *This* seems to be the war that is brought about by these four angelic powers released from the Euphrates. Russia will be overthrown, and the path to world dominion will be cleared for the beast.

At this point the Holy Spirit draws attention to the fact that none of these terrible happenings brings men to their knees in repentance before God. On the contrary, they are hardened in unbelief. The collapse of Russia will bring a wave of wonder over the world, however, and people will be forced to acknowledge that God is still sovereign. But that impression will soon fade. People once again will give themselves over to idolatry, crime, immorality, and pleasure. In his mention of "sorceries" (Revelation 9:21) as being part of the now-emerging world picture, John used a word that points to a drug-demon culture. The foreshadowings of such a culture are in the world today.

At this point in the Apocalypse a lengthy parenthesis is inserted. The blowing of the last trumpet is mentioned in passing in Revelation 10:7 but is not described until 11:15-19. The sounding of this last trumpet will bring about an end to the mystery phase of God's dealings with men, and it will usher in His direct and wrathful intervention in human affairs. In the Apocalypse God's wrath is connected with the *vial* judgments. All the rest is preparatory. Now we leave the trumpets, with the world firmly in Satan's grasp and his man securely enthroned, and turn our attention to the parenthesis.

Most of this long section is a commentary showing how God brings His purposes to fruition even though Satan seems to be having it all his own way on earth. We shall concentrate on several of the key features.

The beast will have three capital cities. When he first comes to power everything will be centered at *Rome* (Revelation 17), his *political* capital, the center from which he will unite and rule the West. *Jerusalem* will be his *religious* capital. His pact with the Jews will be a means to an end. He will want their temple rebuilt so that he can seize it and defile it in contempt for the living God. *Babylon* will be rebuilt and will become his *economic* capital (Revelation 18).

In Revelation 11 two witnesses appear, sovereignly raised up by God to bear witness to Him in the days when the beast is in control. The center of their activity will be Jerusalem. So then, God will have two men down here and Satan will have two men (Revelation 13). Both will be empowered to perform miracles (Revelation 11:6; 13:14-15). There will be a battle of miracles as God's witnesses call down fire, plague, and judgment and as the beast and the false prophet deceive men with "signs and lying wonders" (2 Thessalonians 2:10). In the end the beast will slay the two witnesses, much to the joy and delight of the whole earth, and will leave their bodies to rot in the streets of Jerusalem. His triumph will be televised to the world and universal celebrations will result. Those festivities will be short-lived, because the sudden resurrection of the two witnesses and their ascension into Heaven will be accompanied by a devastating earthquake that will wipe out a tenth of Jerusalem. The two witnesses will leave behind them 144,000 witnesses, so that instead of just two witnesses, the beast now has thousands with whom to contend. They in their turn will win multitudes of Gentiles to Christ. Many of these will doubtless be people who have been awakened by God's judgment on Russia (Ezekiel 39:21-22,27-29) and who will therefore be ripe for this witness. We do not know how long this worldwide revival will last, but probably not very long. Things now begin to move at a fast pace (Revelation 12:12).

Revelation 12 shows the place the believing Jewish remnant will have during the beast's rule. One of the things Satan will do after his expulsion from Heaven will be to stir up persecution against the Jewish people. Here we have a parenthetical description of the coming great tribulation period. It is to last three and a half years (12:14), and during this time the Jews will be the special targets of Satan's wrath. The beast, having used the Jews to provoke Russia into her fatal attack on Israel, will have no more use for them. He will throw off his mask, reveal himself for what he is— their most inveterate and vicious enemy—and launch a global campaign to exterminate them. The fleeing Jews will not be without friends, however, for when the serpent "cast out of his mouth water as a flood" to destroy the Hebrew people, "the earth helped the woman" (12:15-16). Many Jews will find refuge at Petra and other desolate mountain and wilderness places, and here and there God-fearing Gentiles will hide the persecuted Jews at great personal risk.

Revelation 13 describes the coming of the two beasts to power in the earth. The political beast is described first, the one who is Satan's heir and who has the full family likeness, as the following chart shows.

SATAN		THE BEAST	
REV. 12		REV. 13	REV. 17
7 HEADS		7 HEADS	7 HEADS
10 HORNS		10 HORNS	10 HORNS
7 CROWNS ON HEADS		10 CROWNS ON HEADS	
RED			SCARLET

The description of the beast in Revelation 13 shows him as combining in himself the characteristics of a leopard, bear, lion, and dragon. This symbolism shows that he is heir to the empire of the world.

He is described more than once as the beast "whose deadly wound was healed" (Revelation 13:3). Some think that what we have here is the revival of the Roman empire, and that view partially explains the symbolism. The second beast, however, is clearly a *person*, so the first beast must be a person too. He will be what all modern dictators have been—the embodiment of the state. He will be an absolute dictator with all the powers of the state concentrated in himself. That, however, also only partially explains the symbolism. It is clear from Revelation 17 that the beast (the antichrist) is to be killed and brought back to life again by the power of Satan. He has two comings in the Apocalypse. In his human form he is the beast "out of the sea," a brilliant and dynamic world leader with charisma and vision, demon-possessed as Hitler was. He will be killed, will have a "second coming," and from then on will be the beast "out of the bottomless pit." As such he will be superhuman, awesome, and in a position to command and receive the worship of mankind (13:4). All Satan's efforts in the world are directed to this end.

The world will be awed by the beast. The fall of Russia will have made him heir to all the vast domains formerly ruled by this nation. His authority, now coupled with his supernatural character, will convince the rest of the world that they must accept his rule. "Who is able to make war with him?" (Revelation 13:4) will be the universal attitude of the nations, particularly those of the Far East who will make peace with him on his terms. For a brief while his rule will be universal (13:7).

His true character as a blasphemer and persecutor is now revealed (Revelation 13:6-7), and with the exception of the redeemed, all men will worship him. Those who refuse to do so will be subjected to horrifying persecutions.

This beast is the "antichrist" of Scripture. He will be the world's last caesar, ruling empires far beyond those ever ruled before from Rome. He is the "man of sin" of 2 Thessalonians 2:3, the one in whom Satan will invest his power and through whom he will rule the world and be worshiped. The Jews will be among the first to acknowledge him and will hail him as messiah. Just as many unbelieving Jews were willing to accept Antiochus and his blasphemous claims, so unbelieving Jews in a future day will give this Satanic being the place they have refused to Christ. The Lord Himself foretold this (John 5:43).

John saw the second beast come up out of the earth, which suggests that he will be a Jew; for as the sea symbolizes the Gentile nations in Scripture, so the earth symbolizes Israel. Three times he is called "the false prophet" (Revelation 16:13; 19:20; 20:10) to distinguish him from the antichrist. The false prophet looks like a lamb but speaks like a dragon. That is, he seems harmless enough, but when he speaks, it is with the voice of Satan. It seems we have here a Satanic trinity. Satan is the anti-God; the beast is the anti-Christ; the false prophet is the anti-Spirit. The task of the false prophet will be to deceive the world by directing its attention and admiration to the beast, so that men will believe in him and give credence to his blasphemous claim to be God. One of the chief methods the false prophet will use will be "signs and lying wonders" (2 Thessalonians 2:9).[5]

The false prophet will make an image of the first beast, set this image up in the holy place of the temple (Matthew 24:15), and command the world to worship it. He will give life (breath) to the image and endow it with power to kill those who refuse to fall down and worship it. Some idea of the importance attached to this image can be seen in the fact that it is mentioned seven times (Revelation 13:15; 14:9,11; 15:2; 16:2; 19:20; 20:4). Worshiping the beast's image will be the final form of idolatry toward which all other forms of idolatry in the world today are pointing. The setting up of his image will be the sign that the great tribulation is about to begin (Matthew 24:15-21).

To enforce universal compliance, the false prophet will institute tight worldwide economic controls, which will reach down through all strata of society. Everybody will have to receive the beast's mark, either on the right hand or on the forehead; without this mark all commercial transactions will be forbidden. The Greek word for "mark" in Revelation 13:16-17, *charagma*, was often connected with the Roman emperor in John's day and is found on all sorts of documents. It denotes an official seal. The future slogan will be: "No seal, no sale." Trends in computerized marketing today foreshadow the time when all earth's peoples will be obliged to

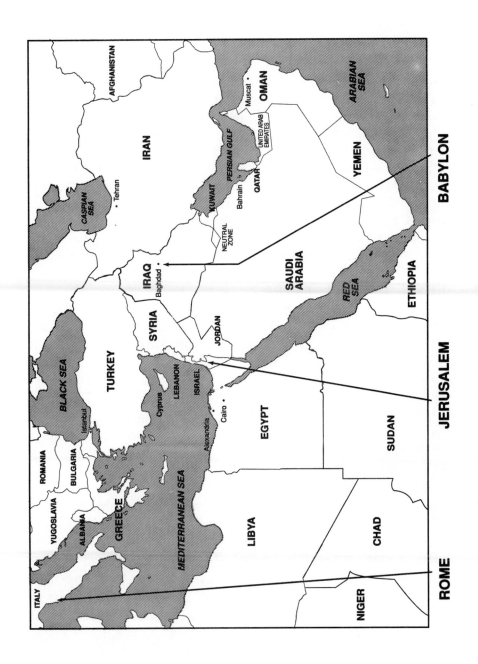

receive an identifying brand in their flesh in order to transact business.

Finally, the mysterious number 666 is given (Revelation 13:18), by which the people of that day will be able to identify the name of the beast. Astonishing guesses have been made by commentators in vain efforts to identify living or historical figures as the beast by means of this number. It is generally taken that the beast's name will be known by *gematria*. In the Greek and Hebrew languages, letters of the alphabet do double duty as figures in their numerical systems. It is evident, therefore, that any word written in Greek or Hebrew can be regarded either as a collection of letters or as a collection of figures. When the name of the beast is revealed it will be recognized in this way because the letters of his name, when viewed as Greek or Hebrew numbers, will yield the number 666 just as the name of Jesus in Greek yields the number 888.

The next two chapters, Revelation 14 and 15, are set back up in Heaven. The first sight is that of the 144,000 standing before God on mount Zion. Their work on earth is done. They have been preserved by God from the hatred and fury of the beast, and now they have been raptured to Heaven as a separate and distinct body of believers.

Next we see three angels sent to earth. One is commissioned to preach the "everlasting gospel," an evangel that reduces the gospel message to its simplest terms for the benefit of people living in such a fearful hour. A second angel is sent to announce the fall of Babylon and a third to warn mankind that God's abiding wrath will rest on any who succumb to the beast, receive his mark, and worship his image.

These visions are followed by two more, one to portray the Lord as the reaper of the harvest and one to show Him trampling out the vintage where the grapes of wrath are stored.

The way is now cleared for the vials of wrath to be poured out. Our minds are unable to comprehend the dreadful nature of this coming time of wrath, when God will deal with this godless world in accordance with His holiness. The way into the holy of holies in Heaven is now closed, and it is filled with smoke from the glory of God. No intercession can now be made; the time for praying is over.

THE VIALS OF GOD'S WRATH (REVELATION 16)

There is a striking similarity between the judgments under all the vials (except vial four) and the plagues poured out in Egypt in the days of Moses:

VIAL	PLAGUE	SIMILARITY
1	6	Boils
2,3	1	Blood
5	9	Darkness
6	2	Frogs
7	7	Hail

This suggests that for the most part the events described under the vials depict literal happenings. The purpose of the vial judgments is to break the grip the beast has on the planet. The world, which under the seals was ruined by man and under the trumpets was ruled by Satan, now under the vials becomes a world *rescued by God*. Men will now learn that the beast's power is limited, that he is impotent to stay or mitigate the terrible things now aimed against him and his subjects by the true God.

The *first plague* will be directed against those who have received the beast's mark imprinted on their flesh. God has warned that those who do so will suffer for it in this life and the life to come (Revelation 19:20), and the time now comes when they must pay the price for believing the lie of Satan rather than the Word of God.

The *second plague* will turn the sea to blood (Revelation 16:3), and every living creature in the sea will die. Whether this envisions some kind of global "red tide," such as occasionally visits various coastlines of the world and is caused by the proliferation of billions of tiny dinoflagellates, or whether this means that the sea will be turned to literal blood is unsure. The result is certain enough, however; all life in the sea will become extinct.

The *third plague* will carry the disaster of the second vial a step further as the rivers and fountains of earth are turned to blood. One of God's angelic administrators, called "the angel of the waters," acknowledges at once the justice of this plague: "They have shed the blood of saints and prophets, and thou hast given them blood to drink" (Revelation 16:6). One can scarcely imagine the panic on earth when the world's water supplies are contaminated beyond use.

The *fourth plague* will upset the delicate balance by which the sun, pouring forth its energy, maintains earth at just the right mean temperature to sustain life. The heat of the sun will be greatly increased and people will be scorched and burned. But instead of repenting, they will blaspheme God as the author of these plagues.

Then, as the *fifth plague* is outpoured, an uncanny supernatural darkness will grip the planet. Also the throne of the beast will come under direct divine attack. His impotence to defend either himself or his subjects against these divine visitations will be obvious. He will be as powerless to ward off God's judgment as pharaoh was in his day. This plague will also bring with it sufferings of such dimensions that men will gnaw their tongues for pain (Revelation 16:10) and pour out further blasphemies against God.

The glamour with which men viewed the beast will disappear fast; he will no longer be the charismatic leader he once was. People will be more prepared to dispute his right to rule the earth; and as the old Roman empire once split in two, so now the beast's world empire will be divided.

The eastern nations will break off allegiance to him and confederate against him; by the time the next plague is outpoured, the "kings of the east" will be in a position to challenge him and contemplate war against him. The eastern nations would seem to be latecomers to the empire of the beast, coerced into cooperation at a time when it was deemed impossible to make war on him. Those days will have gone forever, and henceforth the beast will be increasingly challenged (Daniel 11).

The *sixth plague* will pave the way for Armageddon. Reference is made to the drying up of the river Euphrates, so that "the way of the kings of the east might be prepared" (Revelation 16:12). Some take it that the drying up of the Euphrates will be literal. In ancient times a great river like the Euphrates was a formidable obstacle to an advancing army; but with today's technology, a river like the Euphrates is no more than a passing nuisance. So probably the drying up of the Euphrates has to be taken symbolically. Whatever it is that keeps the eastern hordes in the East is now to be removed.

For centuries the armies of the Far East have been kept in their place by the presence in the Middle East of a world power such as Britain, the United States, or Russia. In a coming day it will be the beast whose might will hold the eastern armies in their place; but with the faltering of his power, brought on by the fifth plague, his ability to control and contain them will be greatly eroded. The road will be cleared for them to attack the western world. Their millions will be united by a coalition of kings, and they will be fired by age-old resentments against the West.

Their mobilization will be inspired by Satan. Three froglike demons will be sent forth by the dragon, the beast, and the false prophet to bring about a world mobilization of all nations and the deployment of all earth's armies at Megiddo. Behind this demonic activity is God Himself, who is about to send back His Son to put an end to this world's tyrannies and insanities (Revelation 16:15). Armageddon itself is part of the plain of Esdraelon in Israel. Armies have fought there from the beginning of time, and here it is that the last battle before the coming of the Lord will be fought.

The *seventh plague* will bring a cry from on high, "It is done" (Revelation 16:17). Upon finishing the work of creation, God declared His work completed (Genesis 2:1). When the work of redemption was accomplished at Calvary, Jesus said, "It is finished" (John 19:30). With the coming of the seventh plague, the way will be paved for the personal return of Christ to end man's abuse of the planet, and once again the cry will go forth—"Done!"

When the seventh angel pours out his vial, there will be outbursts in the sky and accompanying convulsions on earth. The worst earthquake in all of history will take place, and the rebuilt, magnificent city of Babylon will be catastrophically overthrown.

THE TWO BABYLONS (REVELATION 17–18)

Revelation 17 and 18 are commentary. They take us back to give more details of the rise to power of the beast, and they take us forward to tell of the overthrow of Babylon. Revelation 17 deals with *mystery* Babylon, chapter 18 with *material* Babylon. One chapter has to do with a great Babylonian *system*, the other with a great Babylonian *city*.

Revelation 17 sets before us the world system that will be basic to the beast's rise to power in the West. In his vision John saw a scarlet woman sitting astride a scarlet beast, a beast we have met before (Revelation 13). It symbolizes the antichrist and the political system he will control in the West, the ten-nation European confederacy sometimes called "the revived Roman empire." The beast has seven heads and ten horns, and John was told what these symbolize. The seven heads are "seven mountains, on which the woman sitteth" (17:9). This clearly identifies the woman with Rome. She is also described as "the great whore that sitteth upon many waters" (17:1). The waters are said to represent "peoples, and multitudes, and nations, and tongues" (17:15); so clearly the scarlet woman has power and influence in many parts of the world. She is positively identified for us in the last verse of the chapter: "And the woman which thou sawest is that great city, which reigneth over the kings of the earth" (17:18). In John's day that city was Rome, so we need no further identification.

The woman does not represent the coming *political* system centered at Rome. The ten horns of the beast symbolize that, for John was told "the ten horns which thou sawest are ten kings, which have received no kingdom as yet; but receive power [*exousia*, "authority"] as kings one hour [at one and the same time] with the beast" (Revelation 17:12). He was further told that God will put into the heart of these European rulers to give their kingdom to the beast and to do his will (17:17). They will be motivated by hatred of Christ (17:14), which in the end will prove their downfall.

The scarlet woman represents a *religious* system centered at Rome. The description of the scarlet woman as a whore refers to her spiritual wickedness; she has prostituted the truth of God and perverted it to her own ends. She makes the people of the world "drunk with the wine of her fornication" (Revelation 17:2). That is, she seduces people into accepting her adulterated doctrines and her heady wine of power. Also the kings of the earth "have committed fornication" with her (17:2), which means that they live on terms of unholy intimacy with her. She offers them what they want, and they are willing to pay her price to get it. The picture symbolized by this scarlet woman is that of a religious system centered at Rome, one that craves secular power and is quite prepared to sacrifice its calling to any kind of debauchery to get what it wants.

The scarlet woman rides a "scarlet coloured beast, full of names of blasphemy" (Revelation 17:3). We have already identified this beast as the coming antichrist. It is not clear whether the beast supports the woman or whether the woman controls the beast. It is to the advantage of both to cooperate at first. The woman thinks she can use the beast to regain her waning influence in the world; the beast thinks he can use the woman to bring the nations under his control. He will already be supreme in western Europe (as represented by the ten horns), but he will want to rule the whole world and will see in the woman a system he can use to achieve his ends. If the religious system thinks it will be able to control the beast and his political system, it will be mistaken.[6]

The woman was arrayed in magnificent vestments, reveled in her wealth, and had in her hand "a golden cup . . . full of abominations and filthiness of her fornication" (Revelation 17:4). The religious system she represents already has a history of worldliness and wickedness, as anyone who has studied church history knows.

Although the vision identifies her with Rome, the system she represents is much older, for "upon her forehead was a name written, MYSTERY, BABYLON THE GREAT, THE MOTHER OF HARLOTS AND ABOMINATIONS OF THE EARTH" (Revelation 17:5). Ancient Babylon was the fountainhead of idolatry, Satan's invention for channeling worship to himself. After the overthrow of Nimrod's Babylon, idolatry spread to the ends of the earth but Babylon remained its home. God exiled the Jews to Babylon that there they might be forever cured of their penchant for idolatry. Babylon remained the seat of the pagan mysteries and of idolatry until eventually they were transferred by way of Pergamos to Rome. The caesar became the Pontifex Maximus of pagan religion and, in due course, as the church became more powerful and the caesars vanished, the title was passed on to the bishop of Rome. He is known to this day as the supreme pontiff.[7]

Many idolatrous systems in the world today, of course, have no connection with Rome. After the rapture of the true church, what is left of apostate Christendom will doubtless be absorbed quickly by the Roman religious system. The beast will manipulate this system on his way to supreme power. The other branches of idolatry in the world will doubtless make their own deal with the beast when finally he extends his power to the Far East.[8]

John saw this scarlet woman "drunken with the blood of the saints, and with the blood of the martyrs of Jesus." The sight astonished him beyond measure (Revelation 17:6). That pagan Rome should persecute the saints of God was not surprising; but that this system, which was supposedly Christian, should persecute God's people amazed the apostle. It was inconceivable to him that the church as he knew it could ever become the thing he now saw.

The fate of the woman was later described to John. "The ten horns which thou sawest upon the beast, these shall hate the whore, and shall make her desolate and naked, and shall eat her flesh, and burn her with fire" (Revelation 17:16). The political schemes of the scarlet woman will come to nothing; the beast will simply use them to bring the West under his control. Then, having no more use for it and seeing this meddlesome religious system as a hindrance to his own plans, he will turn it over to his confederates to be dismembered.

The chapter now concentrates on the lineage and history of the antichrist. "There are seven kings: five are fallen, and one is, and the other is not yet come; and when he cometh, he must continue a short space. And the beast that was, and is not, even he is the eighth, and is of the seven, and goeth into perdition" (Revelation 17:10-11).

Attempts have been made to identify these seven kings with various world empires or with phases of the Roman empire. The passage, however, refers to an individual. This is clear from the fact that he comes from perdition (Revelation 17:8) and goes back to perdition (17:11). Perdition is for individuals, not empires. The word translated "perdition," occurring twenty times in the New Testament, was used by the Lord Jesus to describe Judas. He called him "the son of perdition" (John 17:12), a phrase also used to describe the coming antichrist (2 Thessalonians 2:3). It is clear then that the description we have here is not that of an empire but of an individual, namely, the antichrist.

Five of the rulers had already come and gone and one (Domitian) existed at the time John wrote. One was still to come, one who would "continue a short space." If we wish to speculate about this seventh ruler, we can draw on history from John's day to our own. Mussolini is a likely candidate. He saw himself as a Roman caesar and deliberately set out to recreate the Roman empire. Napoleon is another. Most likely, however, the seventh king will be the antichrist himself in his mortal life, the "little horn" of Daniel's visions.

We are told further that "the beast that was, and is not, even he is the eighth" king. In other words, he will be one of the previous seven brought back to life to reign for a while in superhuman power (Revelation 17:11).

Thus, the antichrist has two comings, in imitation of the two comings of Christ. He will come first as an ordinary man, brilliant no doubt and demon-possessed, but an ordinary man. He will come again as a supernatural being and as such will be worshiped by mankind (Revelation 13:3-4). We can picture some impressive state occasion when the television cameras of the world are focused on the charismatic figure who has revolutionized the life of Europe. Suddenly he is cut down, as President Kennedy was, in his prime. The whole world watches with horror as he lies there in his own blood and is pronounced dead. There he lies—stiff, cold, and ready for a state funeral—when, before the eyes of a startled world, he rises and looks about him with flashing eyes. He is alive from the dead, arrayed in all the mystery and majesty of a being from another world. It does not take much imagination to see the world at his feet in worship.

Revelation 17 describes much that is passed over with barely a comment in those chapters that describe the coming of the beast (Revelation 8–9). It explains how the beast will be able to make those few remaining moves that will make him master of the world.

One of his moves (presumably after the collapse of Russia and the unification of the world under his control) will be to rebuild ancient Babylon on the Euphrates. The catastrophic overthrow of this new Babylon is the subject matter of Revelation 18.

Babylon must be rebuilt, because many of the ancient prophecies concerning the city have never yet been fulfilled. In his prophecy of the forthcoming seventy-year captivity of Judah in Babylon, for instance, Jeremiah said, "And it shall come to pass, when seventy years are accomplished, that I will punish the king of Babylon, and that nation, saith the Lord, for their iniquity, and the land of the Chaldeans, and will make it perpetual desolations" (Jeremiah 25:12). The context makes clear that although this visitation of judgment on Babylon was to have an immediate and partial fulfillment, the full scope of the prophecy would be in a time when God's hand would be against all the nations of the earth. Babylon will have to be rebuilt to fulfill this prophecy.

Later Jeremiah sent his prophecy about "all the evil that shall come upon Babylon" directly to Babylon with Seraiah. Seraiah was instructed to read its words of doom, and then tie that written message around a stone and cast it into the Euphrates while proclaiming, "Thus shall Babylon sink" (Jeremiah 51:63-64). Babylon will have to be rebuilt to fulfill this prophecy.

About a century earlier, the prophet Isaiah had declared, "And Babylon, the glory of kingdoms, the beauty of the Chaldees' excellency, shall be as when God overthrew Sodom and Gomorrah. It shall never be inhabited" (Isaiah 13:19-22). Babylon will have to be rebuilt to fulfill this prophecy, because Babylon saw no such violent overthrow when it fell to the Medo-Persians. They marched into the city with comparative ease, and the transfer of power was effected swiftly and efficiently.

Babylon continued for centuries afterward as a great city in world affairs. In the days of Christ there were a million Jews in Babylonia. After the fateful Bar Kochba uprising, large numbers of Jews fled to Babylon, where they were given a ready welcome by the Jews who had been established there in thriving communities since the exile. So great were the Jewish settlements in Babylon that their academies rivaled those of Palestine. The Babylonian Jews boasted that when the remnant returned to Israel from the exile, the best of them remained behind.[9]

Ancient Babylon was never overthrown like Sodom and Gomorrah. Its demise, when it came, occurred during the time of the Sassanids in the third century.

Since these Old Testament prophecies must be literally fulfilled, Babylon has to be rebuilt. Napoleon, the master strategist, believed that whoever held Babylon held the key to India and the world. He drew up plans for the building of a new Babylon with quays, river walls, and all the facilities of a large commercial city. These plans were deposited in the war office in Paris.[10] Britain also saw the strategic importance of the Euphrates valley and brought the whole area under her control in the interests of her world empire. Russia, following hard on Britain's heels, has been active in the area since the end of World War II.

The prophecy of Revelation 18 envisions a great city (actually called "Babylon the Great"), into which will flow all kinds of worldly wealth. Merchants, mariners, and monarchs will all bewail the fall of this "Vanity Fair." How and when it will be rebuilt we are not told, but why it will be rebuilt is clear. It is to be the commercial capital of the world. A glance at the map will show its strategic importance as the geopolitical center of the world's population, the natural meeting place of east and west. Babylon is Satan's world center as Jerusalem is God's world center. World history began at Babylon (Genesis 11), and world history will end at Babylon.

Already the whole area has assumed tremendous importance in world affairs. It lies at the heart of the Middle East, where the world's greatest oil reserves are located. In recent years the wealth of the world has flowed steadily in that direction. Oil sales have given the Arab nations of the area the greatest transfer of wealth in history. With some 115 billion Arab petro-dollars (1980) in circulation in various banks around the world, the Arabs are becoming the world bankers. The United States freeze on Iranian oil assets during the hostage crisis taught the Arabs a lesson. Their deposits in American and European banks could just as easily be frozen. Unsettled by their vulnerability, they have begun to move slowly but surely into the world of international banking. Once they have mastered the essentials they will undoubtedly start putting the enormous OPEC surplus into their own institutions.[11] No Arab banking system would be able to function without the cooperation of the present international banking system; but it might be equally true, one of these days, that no international banking system will be able to function without the cooperation of OPEC banks. It would never have been considered possible some years ago that the Arabs would become a world economic power, but it has happened. Their part of the world now controls a vast proportion of the world's wealth. We can see now how a rebuilt Babylon could become the financial center of the world.

The beast, at any rate, will see the value of rebuilding Babylon and making it the economic capital of the world. It also seems clear that the ancient Babylonian mysteries will be returned to their natural home in Babylon (Zechariah 5:5-11). No doubt, too, after he has satisfied his hatred of God and the Jews by defiling the rebuilt temple, the beast will allow Jerusalem to decline in importance, though all three cities—Rome, Jerusalem, and Babylon—will have their place in his plans. So then, Babylon will be rebuilt only to fall under the judgment of God exactly as foretold by the Old Testament prophets and as seen in this vision by John.

LAST THINGS (REVELATION 19–22)

The fall of Babylon on earth will be followed by rejoicing in Heaven (Revelation 19:1-6). Four hallelujahs reverberate around the throne of God as the hosts on high celebrate the removal from the earth of this cursed city, which has been "the habitation of devils, and the hold of every foul spirit, and a cage of every unclean and hateful bird" (18:2) since earliest times.

Next follows the marriage of the Lamb (Revelation 19:7-8). The church, of course, is frequently referred to in the New Testament as the bride of Christ, just as Israel is portrayed as the "wife" of Jehovah in the Old Testament.

Between the time of the rapture of the church to Heaven and the time of its formal union with the Lord, the dreadful events described in the Apocalypse have been taking place on earth. During this same period the saints of God will appear before the judgment seat of Christ (Romans 14:10-12; 2 Corinthians 5:10-11). Here believers will receive rewards for faithful service and also face the consequences of the way they have lived. The question of sin and salvation is not at issue at the judgment seat, but the believers' "work" will be brought into review (1 Corinthians 3:12-15). Position in the kingdom and capacity for eternity, being decided now in this life, will be confirmed at the judgment seat. That occasion, one of great heart-searching, is presented to us in the most solemn terms in Scripture. Paul used such words as *fire* and *terror* to describe it. At the same time the judgment seat of Christ will be a private, family affair and, once it is over, the people of God will be "arrayed in fine linen, clean and white." The fine linen is the "righteousness of saints" (Revelation 19:8). Believers will be forever sinless, and in that glorious condition as the bride of Christ, the church will be ready for the marriage supper of the Lamb.

John now began to use a very precise formula to describe the remaining sequence of events. He used the expression "and I saw" (Revelation 19:11,19; 20:1,4,11; 21:1) to describe things that follow in strict chronological sequence. The formula takes us in giant strides from the return of Christ through the millennial age and on into eternity.

The formula is first used to describe the return of Christ, as "KING OF KINGS, AND LORD OF LORDS" to meet His foes at the battle of Armageddon (Revelation 19:11-21). We speak of Armageddon as

101

though it were a protracted battle, but in reality it is over in an instant. The nations of the world will be drawn to the scene of conflict by demonic power (16:12-16), seemingly to settle once and for all whether the East or West shall rule the world.

The armies of earth will scarcely be deployed in the great arena before there will be an invasion from outer space. Jesus is coming again. The signs of His coming will blaze across the sky, and the gathered hosts will forget their differences to make common cause against Him (Psalm 2). Out of the mouth of the Lamb will go forth a sharp sword and with one word it will all be over. The battlefield will be strewn with the dead; vultures will come from afar to glut themselves upon the slain. The beast and the false prophet will be taken and flung headlong into the lake of fire, and Satan's empire will collapse in blood. The Lord will sweep on to Jerusalem; His feet will alight on Olivet, which will cleave instantly asunder (Acts 1:11; Zechariah 14:1-7). Other topographical changes throughout Israel will also take place. The Dead Sea will be cleansed and a river will flow out of the temple of God (Ezekiel 47:1-12).

During the kingdom age a new temple will be built, suitable for the golden age. The tribes of Israel will be restored, and each one will be given a wide strip of territory running west and east from the Mediterranean to the Euphrates. Dan will occupy the northern strip; south of Dan will be Asher, then Naphtali, Manasseh, Ephraim, Reuben, and Judah, in order. Next will come "the prince's portion," the largest of all the strips of territory. In the prince's portion will be located the holy city, territory for the Levites, territory for priests, and of course the new temple. Then finally will come the portion of Gad in the extreme south (Ezekiel 45:7-8; 48).[12]

With the return of the Lord, Satan is to be incarcerated in the abyss for a thousand years (Revelation 20:1-3), and thus the millennial age dawns. Little is said about this golden age in the Apocalypse, because its glories have been fully revealed already in scores of Old Testament prophecies. Satan will be bound, the curse will largely be removed from the earth, and all nature will conspire with the Lord to lavish on the planet the pristine glories of Eden (Romans 8:18-22). The lamb and the lion will be at peace (Isaiah 11:6-9). Swords will be beaten into plowshares (Isaiah 2:4). So bountiful will be the harvests that the plowman will overtake the reaper (Amos 9:13), and every person will have a fair share of this world's wealth (Zechariah 3:10). The twelve apostles will sit on thrones judging the twelve tribes of Israel (Matthew 19:28). Jerusalem will be the world's capital city (Isaiah 62:1-7), and all nations will come there to worship (Isaiah 66:19-20; Zechariah 14:16-17). A man will be but a boy at the age of a hundred (Isaiah 65:20), death will be virtually banished from the earth, and the world will be as filled with the knowledge of God as the waters now fill the sea (Isaiah 11:9).

After the judgment of the nations in the valley of Jehoshaphat (Joel 3:2,12; Matthew 25:31-46), the millennial age will begin with a believing nucleus of saved Jews and Gentiles. As the age rolls on, millions of children will be born who have never known the world as we know it: ravaged by famine, war, pestilence, and crime. Although born in the glory age, they will still be born of Adam's fallen race and like people in all other ages will need to be born again. Increasing numbers of them will remain unregenerate, and these will resent the iron discipline of the kingdom. Instant punishment will be meted out to those who offend against the laws of the kingdom; and people coming up to Jerusalem to worship will be given a tour of the dread valley where the carcasses of those who transgress will be burned (Isaiah 66:24).

With the passing of time the numbers of the unregenerate will multiply. Out of fear they will yield "feigned obedience" to the Lord (Psalm 18:44; 66:3; 81:15), and they will begin to congregate as far from the central glory as possible. They will long for emancipation from the strict enforcement of the righteous laws of the kingdom.

At the end of the millennial reign Satan will be released from his prison. The dissidents will hail him as an emancipator, one who can free them from the obligation to do right, who will give them freedom to sin, who will deliver them from the hated rule of Christ. They will flock to his standards and rally around him, rejoicing in the name of "Gog and Magog," in memory of a former age when God was dethroned from human thinking and the spirit of antichrist was abroad in the world. Blinded and deluded, they will march on Jerusalem, there to be consumed by fire from God on high (Revelation 20:7-9). At this point God will dissolve the entire universe in a holocaust of nuclear fire (2 Peter 3:9-13), Satan will be hurled into the lake of fire, and his dreadful career will be terminated forever (Revelation 20:10).

Time will have ended and eternity will have begun. The first act in eternity will be the setting up of God's great white throne, before which the wicked dead of all time will be summoned for judgment (Revelation 20:11-15). God's books will be opened. The dead will be judged according to their works (in the Bible salvation is always according to faith, and judgment is always according to works). The Lamb's book of life will be opened, and people will be pronounced lost because their names are missing from that book. The crowning sin of mankind is that of rejecting the salvation God has provided in Christ (John 3:16-19).

John used his formula "and I saw" for the last time to give us a glimpse of the eternal state (Revelation 21:1-8). He saw a new heaven, a new earth, and the holy city—the new Jerusalem. He saw the eternal ages free from sorrow and sin. He saw a place from which "the fearful, and unbelieving, and the abominable, and murderers, and whoremongers, and sorcerers, and idolaters, and all liars" are forever banned (21:8).

We could wish that the Holy Spirit had devoted whole books to describing the eternal state. When I was a little boy my father often went away on business. If he was to be away for several days he would say to us, "If you children are good, when I come back I'll bring something home for you." We would always want to know what it was going to be. "Is it going to be big?" "Is it going to be this?" "Is it going to be that?" To all of those questions my father had one standard reply, "You'll have to wait and see." That is what the Holy Spirit tells us about eternity. "You'll have to wait and see." But this we know: we have a God of omniscient genius, a God of omnipotent power, a God of overwhelming love, and we can be quite sure that He is making eternity an exciting place for a child of God to be.

Then follows the last great parenthesis of the Apocalypse (Revelation 21:9–22:5). John was taken back to have another look at the new Jerusalem. What he saw is a real place, the capital of the millennial kingdom as well as of the eternal state. He described its jasper walls and its pearly gates, its foundations ablaze with precious stones, its crystal stream and its streets of gold. He saw the wondrous tree of life growing there. He told us of things not needed there. That city will need no sea, no sun, and no temple. It is a city where night is unknown, where there will be no need for defense, and where no lost sinner can come.

Behind this symbolic description is a literal reality. This surely is the place Jesus has gone to prepare for us (John 14:1-3), a real place for real people. The city is even now being prepared somewhere in space, somewhere in eternity. During the millennial reign this celestial city will be brought out of eternity into time, brought from wherever it is right now in the mysterious depths of space to a position related to earth. It will be put into stationary orbit over the earthly Jerusalem so that people coming up to Jerusalem to worship during the millennium will be able to see it shining like a diamond in the sky. That glorious celestial city will be the home of the redeemed who, having their resurrection bodies, will be able to come and go between that city and earth at will.

For the people of God are going to have earthly responsibilities during the millennium. According to Isaiah 24:21, the Lord will depose two kinds of government at His return. He will "punish the host of the high ones that are on high, and the kings of the earth upon the earth." The Gentile rulers will have the government of the world taken away from them, and it will be handed back to the Jews (Romans 11:15,21-29). The fallen angelic powers, which rule in the spirit world, will be dethroned, and the church will rule in their place. This will involve rule on earth as well (Luke 19:11-19). But all authority during the millennial reign will come to rest in the Lord Jesus; the high courts where the final decisions are made will be in the new Jerusalem.

The millennial age will end in rebellion, as we have seen. Before God detonates the universe, the celestial city will become another "Noah's ark" for those of earth's people who love the Lord. They will be transported, one supposes, to the celestial city. The city will then be taken back out of time into eternity, from whence it came, far from the flaming fires that will embrace the earth, the solar system, and all of space. The new heaven and the new earth which will replace the old ones will be related forever to the holy city (Revelation 21:2).

Thus ends the Apocalypse. A closing paragraph or so gives warnings and admonitions and records the ringing promise of the Lord, "Surely I come quickly," and the answering cry of His own, "Amen. Even so, come, Lord Jesus" (Revelation 22:20).

1. For a detailed outline and a verse-by-verse exposition of the entire book, see John Phillips, *Exploring Revelation* (Neptune, NJ: Loizeaux, 1991).
2. Andrew Miller, *Miller's Church History* (Fincastle, VA: Scripture Truth, n.d.), pp. 1-6.
3. Philip Schaff, *History of the Christian Church*, vol. 2 (Grand Rapids: Eerdmans, 1910), p. 64.
4. Moses warned that the "man, or woman, or family, or *tribe*" [italics added] who introduced idolatry into Israel would fall heir to the curses of the law. He said, "And the Lord shall separate him unto evil out of all the tribes of Israel" (Deuteronomy 29:18-21). It was the tribe of Dan that first came under this curse (Leviticus 24:10-16). Later both Dan and Ephraim participated in idolatry (Judges 18:2,30-31). Later still it was Jeroboam an Ephraimite who made the golden calves and set them up in the tribe of Dan (1 Kings 12:28-30; Hosea 4:17). It would seem in the coming age that people from the tribes of Dan and Ephraim will take the lead in Israel in setting up the beast's image. Some have surmised that the false prophet will be a Danite. In any case, these two tribes will contribute none of their numbers to the glorious ranks of the 144,000.
5. Miracles in themselves are no evidence that God is at work. Even the miracles of Christ—gracious, multiplied, and amazing as they were—did not in themselves prove Him to be God (Matthew 11:1-6). What gave His miracles their authenticating power was that they were just the kinds of miracles the prophetic Word had declared He would perform. That is why they are so often called "signs." They were not mere wonders for the multitudes to marvel at; they were authenticated by the Word of God and bore witness to the truth of Scripture. This is what gave them their validity as signs of Christ's divine person and work. The false prophet will use "signs and lying wonders" to deceive mankind.
6. The Roman religious system today seems to think it can strike a deal with communism. The Kremlin and Rome have much in common. See Paul Blanshard, *Communism, Democracy and Catholic Power* (Boston: Beacon Press, 1952). Pope Paul VI tried to stack the college of cardinals to ensure the election, upon his death, of a Marxist-leaning pope, according to former Jesuit Malachi Martin. See his *The Final Conclave* (New York: Stein & Day, 1978).
7. Hislop, *The Two Babylons*, p. 206.
8. For a graphic illustration of Rome's addiction to image worship, see Miller, pp. 289-291. Miller described the failure of Emperor Leo III to purge the church of idolatry and recorded the steps taken by Pope Gregory III to establish image worship more firmly than ever in the church.
9. Alfred Edersheim, *History of the Jewish Nation* (Grand Rapids: Baker, 1954), pp. 46-48, 209-211.

10 . G. H. Pember, *The Great Prophecies* (London: Hodder & Stoughton, 1897), pp. 175-176.

11 . "Bankers in Burnooses," *Time* (July 14, 1980), pp. 45-46.

12 . A visualization of the new arrangement of the tribes, the holy city, the temple, and its surroundings can be seen in Clarence Larkin, *Dispensational Truth* (Philadelphia: Clarence Larkin, 1918), pp. 93-94; also *The Companion Bible* (London: Samuel Bagster, 1964), Appendix 88.

5

The Prophecies of Jacob
Genesis 49

Genesis 49 records the last words of Jacob, words freighted with prophetic insight. Jacob knew that he was about to speak under inspiration of the Holy Spirit and that his last words to his sons would be of prophetic significance.

He said to his sons, "Gather yourselves together, that I may tell you that which shall befall you *in the last days"* (Genesis 49:1, italics added). This is the first time this important phrase occurs in Scripture. It is used fourteen times in the Old Testament. In ten of them it is rendered "the latter days." The phrase is used, for instance, in the famous thirty-eighth chapter of Ezekiel, which prophesies the rise and fall of Russia. Its ultimate focus is on the Messianic era.

The scene in Genesis 49 is of great interest. Jacob had been in Egypt for seventeen years. He had seen his favorite son Joseph exalted to the right hand of the majesty of the pharaoh and given a name above every name, that at the name of Zaphnath-paaneah every knee should bow (Genesis 41:41-45). Everything that power and wealth could command was Jacob's for the asking, but he refused it all. Egypt was not for him. His heart was in Canaan.

The time had now come to die, so he summoned his sons to his side. They were the tribal heads of the embryonic nation of Israel. What he had to say to them was both personal and prophetical. The passing incidents of their lives became the basis for Jacob's prophetic edicts. The destiny of the nation from that day to this, and on until time shall be no more, was now described in cryptic statements, in flights of oratory, and in poetic mold.

It is astonishing how much is packed into this neglected prophecy. It begins with the sons where they were, down in Egypt; it takes them through the wilderness and into the promised land; it takes them through the days of the judges; and it marches majestically through the days of the monarchy. It focuses briefly on the desperate struggle of the Maccabean age, hurries on to embrace the first coming of Christ, takes in the dispersion and the end-time troubles, and ends on the triumphant note of the final return of Christ to establish His kingdom on earth.

Of course we can not expect a great deal of detail in a mere twenty-seven verses. We might expect some of the low-lying land to be obscure and that some of the peaks might rise like sentinels against the sky. We might expect too that, with much of the prophecy already fulfilled, its details would be clearer now than then. And all those things are so. Nevertheless, this prophecy stands as one of the monumental prophetic utterances of Scripture, and all the more so because it is the first such full-length prophecy to be found in the Scriptures.

Before we begin, let us look at the broad outline of Genesis 49.

   I. A Specially Purchased People (49:3-7)
     A. How disappointing they would be (Reuben, 49:3-4)
     B. How disunited they would be (Simeon and Levi, 49:5-7)
   II. A Supremely Privileged People (Judah, 49:8-12)
     A. The monarchial age (49:8-9)
       1. The wonderful years (49:8)
       2. The willful years (49:9)
       3. The woeful years (49:9)
     B. The messianic age (49:10-12)
   III. A Sorely Persecuted People (49:13-15)
     A. Widely dispersed (Zebulun, 49:13)
     B. Woefully distressed (Issachar, 49:14-15)
   IV. A Satanically Perverted People (Dan, 49:16-18)

V. A Sovereignly Protected People (49:19-21)
    A. Israel's tribulation warfare (Gad, 49:19)
    B. Israel's tribulation welfare (Asher, 49:20)
    C. Israel's tribulation witness (Naphtali, 49:21)
VI. A Suddenly Promoted People (49:22-27)
    A. The moral glories of Messiah (Joseph, 49:22-26)
        1. His sufficiency (49:22)
        2. His sufferings (49:23)
        3. His strength (49:24)
        4. His supremacy (49:25-26)
            a. The utmost blessings are to be His
            b. The utmost bounds are to be His
    B. The millennial glories of Messiah (Benjamin, 49:27)
        1. The commencement of the age
        2. The completion of the age

Such is the breadth of this prophecy. Let us take our staff in hand and prepare ourselves for a march down the centuries with old Jacob as our guide. Before commencing our journey we have a choice to make. Shall we make this a leisurely expedition, stopping to point out all the details of the way and the reasons for this or that signpost along the path? If so, we shall have to tarry in this chapter for a considerable time. Or shall we try to keep pace with Jacob, who is clearly in a hurry? He is on his way home, about to leave time for eternity, with the moments ebbing quickly away. He is a fast mover, this aged pilgrim, and we shall be out of breath if we try to match his pace down the centuries. But since the patriarchal prophet hurried past the ages, perhaps we should hurry past them too.

The sons gathered around the bed of their father. He looked away from the lotus pillars, the painted walls, the gilded couches that adorned his room. Seventeen years of Egyptian luxury had not touched him at all. He looked impatiently away from it all at each of the sons: at Reuben, Simeon, Levi, Judah, Zebulun, and Issachar, the six sons of Leah; at Dan, the son of Rachel's slave; at Gad and Asher, the sons of Leah's slave; at Naphtali, another son of Rachel's slave; and, at last, at Joseph and Benjamin, the two sons of his beloved Rachel. He addressed them in that order, not strictly the order of their birth. He set aside historical order for prophetic order; he was going to deal with them in the order of the unborn ages of time. Prophecy, not history, is paramount in this deathbed scene.

The prophecy begins with Jacob's three oldest sons—Reuben, Simeon, and Levi. What he had to say to them shows that the people then developing among his sons was to be *a specially purchased people* (Genesis 49:3-7), a people purchased by the shedding of blood who were constituted God's firstborn at the Passover in Egypt (Exodus 4:22; 12:11-12,23). Looking back at the way God led this emerging nation we can see that, in embryonic form, these verses anticipate the exodus, the way through the wilderness, and the settlement in Canaan.

Jacob began by fixing his eye on the firstborn. How Reuben must have quailed beneath that gaze. Years ago, hopefully long enough ago to have been forgotten, Reuben had committed adultery with one of Jacob's wives. The sin had never been confessed, never put right. The other two sons, Simeon and Levi, both had shameful pasts as well involving treachery and vengeance. Looking at these first three sons of his, knowing the flaws in their characters and pondering what kind of people could come from such unpromising stock, Jacob must have been dismayed. Failure is more than evident. Such would be the initial history of this specially purchased people.

In Reuben Jacob saw how *disappointing* they will be (Genesis 49:3-4) because of the disappointment Reuben had been to him. Reuben, who was his firstborn; Reuben, who should have been the beginning of his strength; Reuben, who should have worn the robes of excellency and dignity—he had expected so much from Reuben, and it had all been so bitterly disappointing. Reuben's instability was written large in a dreadful deed of shame, made more despicable because it was committed when Jacob's heart was sore over the death of Rachel and when he would naturally have turned to Bilhah, Rachel's maid. That was the moment Reuben had chosen to indulge his ungoverned passion, and Bilhah was the woman he chose to make the partner of his shame. Apparently Jacob had said nothing at the time (Genesis 35:22), but now, with the burden of prophecy on him, he seized on that incident as an ill omen of things to come.

That was how the nation's history would begin. Instead of being all that God looked for in His firstborn among the nations, instead of being the excellency of dignity and power, this nation would be a failure. It would fail miserably in Egypt. The fascination of Egypt's gods would soon take root in the minds of the people, and they would become a nation of slaves, bowing down to this world's prince. That was the first line of prophecy written in Reuben's personality.

In Levi and Simeon Jacob saw how *disunited* the tribes would be (Genesis 49:5-7). These two sons had once engaged in a particularly villainous piece of infamy. Under the pretense of salvaging their shamed sister's honor, they had entered into an agreement with the people of Shechem. Then, using religion as the cloak for their wickedness, they had fallen on the unsuspecting Shechemites and slaughtered them to the very last man. Jacob eyed them dispassionately. Partners in this crime, they would henceforth be scattered and divided in the nation. Jacob summed up their character in a single word, *self-will.*

It was thus that Israel's history after leaving Egypt began. It was the story of disunity brought on by self-will. Was there ever such an ungrateful, quarrelsome, complaining crowd? The children of Israel drove Moses almost to distraction. They brought down on themselves the repeated chastening hand of God. Nothing but the sovereign grace of God can account for their ever getting into Canaan at all. Instead of marching forward, heads held high, arms swinging, feet marching in step with the will of God, and the triumphant song of salvation in their souls, they quarreled with Moses at every step. The moment his back was turned they reverted to the gross idolatries learned in Egypt and then fell prey to civil war, Levi against them all.

Continuing in the grip of self-will, they came to Kadesh-barnea, where each tribe chose a man to go on into Canaan to spy out the land. Back they came with a disunited verdict, ten electing to return to Egypt, two demanding that they march right in and possess the land. In self-will, when once they did begin to conquer Canaan, two and a half tribes elected to stay on the wilderness side of Jordan. In self-will and division they lived out their chaotic history through the days of the judges—divided, scattered, disunited, a motley collection of tribes, hardly a nation at all.

Then, in further self-will, they demanded a king, not in order to fulfill God's purposes, but in order to be like the other nations around them. Saul became that king and proved to be a vacillating weakling who only furthered the discord and division in the land.

This disastrous period ends in prolonged civil war, with tribe fighting tribe over the shreds of Saul's bloodstained robe of sovereignty.

This, then, was the beginning of this specially purchased people, this people constituted to be God's firstborn among the nations. Jacob could write the dismal word *failure* across the early centuries, just as he could write the same word across the personal lives of his first three sons.

Then he turned his prophetic gaze on Judah; for a moment his eyes kindled, only to grow sad and dull again. In Judah he could see foreshadowed *a supremely privileged people* (Genesis 49:8-12). He caught fleeting glimpses of two ages, the first of which we call the *monarchial age.* Judah was to be the royal tribe.

Jacob began with the wonderful years of early promise when Judah would come into his own. "Judah, thou art he whom thy brethren shall praise: thy hand shall be in the neck of thine enemies; thy father's children shall bow down before thee" (Genesis 49:8). The monarchial age really began when David, a scion of Judah, came to the throne. It was David who formed a nation of the disunited tribes, who put his hand to the neck of their enemies, who founded the Messianic dynasty, who put the religious life of the nation in order, and who purposed to build a temple. Those were the wonderful years.

The wonderful years did not last long. They were followed by the willful years. Jacob went on: "Judah is a lion's whelp: from the prey, my son, thou art gone up" (Genesis 49:9). A lion's whelp may be a fitting symbol of royalty, but it is a symbol of royalty unrestrained. No one tells a lion what to do. Self-will became the mark of Israel's royalty throughout the greater part of the centuries when it stood intact.

The lion's whelp was Solomon. He was a splendid, lionlike figure of a man, every inch an oriental king. He paced across the page of Hebrew history in a magnificence unsurpassed, but he swiftly degenerated into pride and self-will. He was as destructive to the interests of his people as a rampaging lion. For all his pomp and majesty, Solomon did more to pull down the kingdom David had founded than any other single king. He laid the foundations for all its future wretchedness and sin. He, and those who followed him, pulled down the kingdom by their idolatries and apostasies faster than the prophets could rebuild.

Then came the woeful years: "He couched as a lion, and as an old lion; who shall rouse him up?" (Genesis 49:9). Poor Judah. What in nature is more pitiable than an old, enfeebled lion? Its mighty teeth decayed, its massive strength wasted away, mangy, famished, tired, and beyond any hope of recovering its former majesty—such is an old lion. And such was the fate of Judah's monarchy. We see Judah in declining years of the monarchial age, still managing to get out an occasional roar but broken, enfeebled, worn out by apostasy and sin—unresponding to the hunting calls of the prophets who tried to rouse up the old lion at last. At length all that could be seen in the future was a gilded Babylonian cage.

Jacob's prophetic eyes moved on down the unborn ages, still looking at Judah, but seeing now beyond the monarchial age to *the messianic age*. He said, "The sceptre shall not depart from Judah, nor a lawgiver from between his feet, until Shiloh come; and unto him shall the gathering of the people be" (Genesis 49:10).

We know now what happened after the Babylonian captivity came to an end. A small remnant of faithful Jews returned to the desolate land as pioneers to drive in their stakes and await the coming of Messiah. But the nation was no longer a monarchy, no longer even a theocracy; it was now a dependency. However, though the throne was gone, the royal line was still intact in the person of Zerubbabel. The scepter was still to be found in Judah, in that little inconspicuous province of the vast Persian world. And that scepter was handed on from generation to generation, despite all the attempts of Satan during the dreadful years of the Seleucids to root out and destroy the royal line. No power in earth or Hell could succeed in that. God stood ever watching in the shadows, guarding the fortunes of that scepter until Shiloh (Christ) should come.

When Antiochus Epiphanes appeared, the most dreadful persecutions were launched against the Palestinian Jews until it seemed that Satan must surely win. But God raised up the Maccabees, and the Syrians were flung back across their frontiers. The exhausted land enjoyed a breathing spell until the Romans came and, hard on their heels, the promised Messiah.

Jacob's eyes brightened again as he saw it at last—the coming Christ. One suspects that Jacob, lying there on his bed, must have hugged himself for joy. His face beamed on Judah but then, almost at once, the glow faded and the teardrops started from his eyes. What dark cloud is this that blackens that promising sky?

First he saw Messiah's career (Genesis 49:11). "Binding his foal unto the vine, and his ass's colt unto the choice vine," mused Jacob. He saw the Messiah coming in humility and lowliness, in disguise, as it were. He is a king, but a king riding an ass rather than a war-horse with arched neck and prancing feet and panoplied in the accoutrements of war.

Then he saw Messiah's cross (Genesis 49:11). He saw His garments dyed red in wine and His clothes crimsoned with the blood of grapes. He sees the Messiah (Oh! Can it be?) stained with blood. Is this the Messiah's own blood or the blood of His foes? Of course, we now know that the cross had to come before the crown, that the blood of the vine that Jacob saw poured out was nothing less than the precious blood of Christ.

Jacob's vision leapt the ages. He saw Messiah's conquest: "His eyes shall be red with wine, and his teeth white with milk" (Genesis 49:12). The wine and the milk suggest something to us, from our perspective, that they could hardly have suggested to Jacob from his. Prophecy is often vague in prospect and clear as crystal in retrospect (1 Peter 1:10-12).

We know now that after the finished work of the cross, the Lord Jesus ascended into Heaven to minister on behalf of His own. Even today He is carrying on a twofold work on our behalf. He is there to *safeguard* us, and when Satan comes as the accuser of the brethren, what does our Lord do? He presents the blood. The wine suggests that. The blood is God's answer to every charge brought against us. But Christ is also there to *sustain* us in our continuing needs. To do this He has sent His Holy Spirit, who draws our attention to a book. The milk suggests God's Word, for in it we find the "sincere milk of the word" (1 Peter 2:2) and all else we need to sustain us on our journey home.

Jacob associated the Lord's *eyes* with the blood-red wine; for when the Lord sees our sins, He sees them through the blood. The scarlet blood cancels out our scarlet sins, and He sees them no more. Jacob saw the Lord's *teeth* associated with the milk, because there's more to the book than milk; there's meat as well. Thus, in sketchy outline, Jacob saw the ministry of the Lord Jesus during this present age. It passed swiftly and dimly before his eyes, perhaps barely comprehended.

No wonder the dying patriarch looked so long at Judah. There was so much to see in that supremely privileged people to whom, through the line of Judah, the Messiah would come. As Paul put it: "What advantage then hath the Jew? . . . Much every way: chiefly, because that unto them were committed the oracles of God. . . . and of whom as concerning the flesh Christ came, who is over all, God blessed for ever" (Romans 3:1-2; 9:5).

The prophet's eyes moved on. He contemplated Zebulun and Issachar, and then he saw *a sorely persecuted people* (Genesis 49:13-14). "His blood be on us, and on our children," cried the mob when Pilate proposed to set Christ free (Matthew 27:25), thus pulling down on their heads the most fearful curse in history. When confronted with the conquest of Canaan they had cried, "Would God we had died in this wilderness!" (Numbers 14:2) and God answered their prayer. Now the full weight of the law's curse came home to roost on this people (Deuteronomy 27:14-26; 28:15-68). Jacob, looking at Zebulun and Issachar, the two remaining sons of Leah, saw the long ages after Calvary pass swiftly before his eyes.

He saw the nation widely dispersed as he looked at Zebulun: "Zebulun shall dwell at the haven of the sea; and he shall be for an haven of ships; and his border shall be unto Zidon" (Genesis 49:13). The Jews were never great sailors. The sea was foreign to them; they preferred the land. The Phoenician people of Tyre and Sidon on the Palestinian coast loved the sea, the gateway to the world. Jacob saw his sons engaging in seafaring interests like the maritime and mercantile Sidonians.

Little did Jacob know how far across those stormy seas events would carry his people. Little did he know they would become the world's merchants and bankers. Little did he know to what extent Jews would dominate the business of the world or how their commercial affairs would be entwined with the concerns of empires and nations then unborn. During the middle ages, for instance, the Jews filled a niche that was foreign to the serfs and despised by the barons. They alone had the worldwide facilities to carry on commerce on a global scale. Their trade reached all the way from China to the new world.[1] Their dispersal among the nations gave them international contacts unknown to any other people. In our own day, the Jews are dominant in the business affairs of at least twenty of the major nations of the world.

Jacob caught a glimpse of this in Zebulun. In Issachar he saw the other side of this coin, a nation woefully distressed (Genesis 49:14-15). He said, "Issachar is a strong ass couching down beneath two burdens: And he saw that rest was good, and the land that it was pleasant; and bowed his shoulder to bear, and became a servant unto tribute." Jacob saw his scattered people bearing two burdens, the burden of exile and the burden of exploitation. In the far-flung lands of his adoption, the Jew has always settled down, deciding that the land of his exile is good. He settled contentedly in Babylon, Persia, Greece, and Rome in ancient times. He settled in a business-like way in Spain, Poland, and Egypt in the middle ages. He has settled comfortably in Britain and America today. He has always settled down and done well in any part of the world, until his "rest" has been disturbed by the dislike, jealousy, and hate of his Gentile neighbors.

It has always been the same. In ancient times, in the middle ages, in the modern world, sooner or later the hands of his hosts turn against him; and the Jew is forced out of his comfortable niche and back to wandering. He is hailed one day, hated the next; cultivated, then cursed. And haunting him from land to land is the specter of incipient antisemitism. Always, just over the horizon, new storms are brewing. And always, not far from the surface, new holocausts are being prepared. This is the fate of the Jew in lands that are not his. Jacob caught a fleeting glimpse of this.

Jacob's restless eyes moved on to Dan. He saw *a satanically perverted people* (Genesis 49:16-18). He saw past the days in which we now live to the judgment age ahead. He saw the coming of the antichrist and Dan having a part in that dreadful episode of his people's future. Jacob said, "Dan shall judge his people, as one of the tribes of Israel. Dan shall be a serpent by the way."

The tribe of Dan, the first to embrace idolatry, will give none of its sons to the ranks of the 144,000 witnesses who will preach the gospel in those days (Revelation 7:4-8). On the contrary, it seems that Dan is to have some link with the serpent. Some people believe that the second beast, the false prophet of Revelation 13, will actually come from the tribe of Dan. Jacob said that Judah is a lion, Naphtali is a hind let loose, Issachar is a strong ass, Benjamin is a wolf, but Dan is a serpent in the path. And a ruling one at that. He will sit in judgment on the tribes of Israel.

The old prophet turned his eyes next to look at three remaining slave-born sons: Gad, Asher, and Naphtali. What he saw there is not altogether unencouraging. He saw in these three sons *a sovereignly protected people* (Genesis 49:19-21). The great tribulation, that time of Jacob's trouble, terrible as it will be, will not be entirely bad. God will have His remnant among the children of Israel even then.

Jacob looked at Gad, the first son of Leah's slave, and in Gad he saw Israel's tribulation-age warfare: "Gad, a troop shall overcome him: but he shall overcome at the last" (Genesis 49:19). In the days of the Maccabees all Jews did not bend before the persecutions of Antiochus Epiphanes. Many, goaded to desperation by their sufferings, took to the hills and fought battle after successful battle with their tormentors. It will be so again. Many Jews will perish during the great tribulation. But many more will flee, and some will resist and fight to the end. They will be overcome, but they will be victorious at the last. Just when it seems that all must be lost, the Christ of God will come and overthrow their foes.

Jacob looked then at Asher and saw Israel's tribulation-age welfare: "Out of Asher his bread shall be fat, and he shall yield royal dainties" (Genesis 49:20). When Israel marched out of Egypt and headed south along the rim of the Sinai peninsula, straight into some of the most fearful desert regions on the planet, the world must have shaken its head. In Egypt the news would have been greeted with incredulous delight. "The desert will avenge us on them"; that would be the general opinion. "That fellow Moses must be a lunatic. Imagine! Taking three million people into that wasted, howling wilderness. Where will he find food? Where will he find water? Men, women, children, herds of cattle, flocks of sheep, all trekking south into Sinai!" Yet God sustained them in that formidable desert for forty years. He rained manna from heaven, summoned quails from afar, split open the flinty rock for water, turned bitter water into sweet, fed them with angel's food, and spread a banquet in the wilderness. They grew fat on royal dainties.

During the great tribulation many Jews and other believers will flee into the hills and the deserts, some, it is believed, into Petra.

There God will repeat His former miracles and furnish a royal table for His believing remnant.

Then there was Naphtali. In him Jacob saw Israel's tribulation-age witness: "Naphtali is a hind let loose: he giveth goodly words" (Genesis 49:21). The more the beast will persecute this people, the more the Word will spread. The Jewish remnant, fleeing from land to land, penetrating the remotest corners of the earth where the name of the true and living God has scarcely been heard, will take the gospel of the kingdom with them. They will be the heralds of that gospel and will give "goodly words" to millions of people, sick and tired of the torments of that bestial age. Millions will believe. Indeed, John told us that there will be "a great multitude, which no man could number" (Revelation 7:9) who will turn at last to the living God in the great tribulation age.

Then Jacob's eyes came to rest on his favorites in the family, on dear dead Rachel's sons. He looked at beloved Joseph, so royal, so regal in his rich robes, a minister at the highest levels of government, with even the pharaoh paying deference to his wisdom and endorsing his will. He looked at Benjamin, his baby, the last of his sons. Jacob's voice strengthened. All he could see now is good.

Looking at these two sons he saw *a suddenly promoted people* (Genesis 49:22-27). He saw Jesus, only Jesus. From now on all is Christ. Christ in His moral glories in Joseph; Christ in His millennial glories in Benjamin. Jacob's words flow like lava; they come gushing from the fountains of his soul.

He looked at Joseph and saw the sufficiency of the Savior as reflected in His divine life: "Joseph is a fruitful bough . . . whose branches run over the wall" (Genesis 49:22). The Savior was like a generous vine (the figure of speech He used to describe Himself and those whose lives are forever linked with His). His was a life of prodigious, prodigal fruitfulness. He healed the sick. He raised the dead. He cast out demons. He fed the hungry and turned water into wine. He made the blind see, the deaf hear, the mute speak, and the lame walk. He distilled the wisdom of omniscience into inimitable parables, delightful discourses, unforgettable words. "Never man spake like this man" (John 7:46). Because Jesus lived, the world will never be the same. The branches ran over the wall.

Jacob saw too the sufferings of the Savior. He caught a glimpse of His death: "The archers have sorely grieved him, and shot at him, and hated him: But his bow abode in strength . . . the shepherd, the stone of Israel" (Genesis 49:23-24). Although all this applies to Joseph, it goes beyond Joseph to Him of whom Joseph was a type. Jacob saw the armed might of the world marshaled against the Christ of God. He saw them take aim and shoot. But even as the concentrated hatred of the world found its target, Jesus died not in weakness, but in strength, with a mighty shout on His lips that split creation's rocks and burst wide Canaan's tombs.

Jacob also saw the strength of the Savior as reflected in His dynamic resurrection. He went on to speak of blessing after blessing after blessing (Genesis 49:25). It seems as though old Jacob's heart was aflame as he thought of the boundless blessings that are centered in Jesus. His words would be mere hyperbole, a doting father's excess, if they were restricted to Joseph. But when applied to Jesus, even Jacob's eloquence fell far short of the mark. Every blessing on earth beneath, every blessing in Heaven above, is centered in Jesus. He lives in the power of an endless life to pour out those blessings upon men. No wonder Paul burst out, "Blessed be the God and Father of our Lord Jesus Christ, who hath blessed us with all spiritual blessings in heavenly places in Christ." No wonder he prayed that we might know "what is the exceeding greatness of his power to us-ward who believe, according to the working of his mighty power, Which he wrought in Christ, when he raised him from the dead, and set him at his own right hand in the heavenly places" (Ephesians 1:3,19-20).

Jacob saw the supremacy of the Savior in His dazzling enthronement on high. He saw the utmost bounds of the everlasting hills beneath His sway. All the blessings that Jacob's quickened heart and mind could conceive are to be heaped on the head of "him that was separate from his brethren" (Genesis 49:26). Again the immediate reference is to Joseph, but the fullness of the reference has to be to Jesus.

Last of all, the energized patriarch looked at Benjamin and saw in him the millennial glories of Christ. "Benjamin shall ravin as a wolf: in the morning he shall devour the prey, and at night he shall divide the spoil" (Genesis 49:27).

Jacob saw the commencement of Christ's coming reign. Jesus is coming back to subdue all of Israel's foes. He is coming back to engage His enemies in fierce combat at Megiddo. He is coming to seize the beast and the false prophet and to fling them into the lake of fire. He is coming to lock up Satan in the abyss and reserve him there in chains against a later visitation of undiluted wrath. He is coming to sweep the world clean of wicked men. That is how the millennial reign will begin.

Jacob saw, too, the completion of Christ's coming millennial reign. Satan will be loosed; the unregenerate of earth will flock by the millions to his standards of rebellion. They will march on Jerusalem like madmen. Then the Lord will divide the spoil. He will erase this planet and replace it with another—one free forever from sin, more glorious than Eden, more enduring than the stars. The fruits of His victories will be complete.

Exhausted, Jacob lay down on his bed. The room still rang with his tones. Awed and silent, the sons gathered closer to their wonderful father. He had one more word. "Bury me in Canaan," he charged (Genesis 49:29-30 paraphrased). Such exciting things are to happen in that narrow strip of land, and Jacob wanted his bones to be there for the moment of resurrection. Then, with his poor, tired, pilgrim feet safely back in bed, he took his final pilgrimage to the land of fadeless day.

---

1. See Phillips, *Exploring the World of the Jew* (Chicago: Moody Press, 1981).

6

The Prophecies of Balaam
Numbers 23–24

I n Old Testament times God normally said anything He had to say in Hebrew, through a Hebrew, to Hebrews. Balaam, a Gentile prophet, was an exception. He spoke four times, each time to a Gentile king.

Israel's tribes had left Hor and had journeyed by the way of the Red Sea to the outskirts of Edom. They were discouraged and complained bitterly because of the hardness of the way, despite the notable victory just won over Arad, the Canaanite king. Then it was that the fiery serpents attacked them. They were saved only when Moses made a serpent of brass and hung it up on a pole in the midst of the camp, so that anyone who looked on it might live (Numbers 21).

The lifting up of that serpent marked a great change in the people. After that there was no more murmuring, no more impatience. The march was resumed with a new sense of assurance. About that time, too, poets began to give song to the ways of God with His saints. Moses made mention of "the book of the wars of the Lord" (Numbers 21:14), evidently a collection of poems and hymns, some of which have found their way into the sacred text. Victories now came one after another as the people advanced toward Canaan.

Presently they reached the plains of Moab, and now just the Jordan stood between the people and the promised land. The Moabites, half-kin to the Israelites, were alarmed and, fearing that they were to be attacked next, sought desperately for aid. No mere coalition of kings would do. The Israelites had already swept aside some formidable Amorite foes; so Balak, king of Moab, took counsel with his allies the Midianites and decided to try prophecy. He would hire a prophet to curse this people. But who should be summoned for such an important task? Then someone thought of Balaam.

THE FIRST PROPHECY OF BALAAM (NUMBERS 23:7-10)

Balaam was a renowned soothsayer, cursed by the Mosaic law (Deuteronomy 18:10-11). But to Balak that was an endorsement rather than a hindrance; Balaam could not be expected to think kindly of a people who cursed his ancient profession. So Balak sent messengers with all haste to hire Balaam to curse the people of God.

Balaam was eager to come. But God opposed him and, in the end, allowed him to have his own way only when the prophet understood that God Himself would put words in his mouth. We are not concerned here with all the background, but rather with the four prophecies this pagan prophet gave. That God should use the tongue of this wicked man for His own glory is not remarkable; after all, God even seized the tongue of Balaam's own ass and made her speak (Numbers 22:22-34).

Balaam's prophecies give remarkable details about the future of the nation of Israel. Their significance is enhanced by the fact that they were given when the nation was in its infancy and marching forward to the conquest of Canaan, by the fact that they fell from pagan Gentile lips into pagan Gentile ears, and by the fact that their focus is particularly on the last days.

Here is an outline of Balaam's first prophecy.

I. A Great Imperative (Numbers 23:7)
  A. Balaam's mandate
  B. Balaam's mission

Balaam began with *a great imperative* (Numbers 23:7) and explained both his mission and his mandate. To understand his prophecies, we must appreciate his perspective. He was standing on "the high places of Baal, that thence he might see the utmost part of the people" (22:41). The "high places of Baal" were places where the fertility gods and goddesses of Moab were worshiped, places where immorality and obscenity were an integral part of worship. If ever there was a place where God could be expected to curse Moab rather than Israel, it was there. Those high places came under God's curse. One of the clauses in Israel's commission enjoined them to wipe out all such places. Their failure to do so led directly to their own national apostasy and judgment.

Balaam began his prophecy by stating *his mandate*: "And he took up his parable, and said, Balak the king of Moab hath brought me from Aram, out of the mountains of the east" (Numbers 23:7). Balaam's mandate was from Balak, not from God. He had come from Mesopotamia, the country from which Abraham had come. There was a notable difference, however: Abraham had come in the pursuit of God; Balaam in the pursuit of gold.

Balaam's name means "devourer," or "devourer of the people," a hint of the terrible power supposed to reside in his curses. He is described as "the son of Beor," a name meaning "consumer" or "destroyer," a name doubtless given to Balaam's father for much the same reason. Balaam apparently came from a family of seers or magicians, probably the great family of Chaldean magi whose duties included the pronouncing of curses.

Balaam came from Pethor, a name meaning "interpretation." Probably a college of the magi was located there, or the city may have been exclusively a magi city. Balaam's reputation as a magician was well established and had reached as far as Moab.

His mandate was impressive enough in human terms. He

carried a commission, signed by the king of Moab and sealed with the seal of Moab, which gave him wide scope and promised him generous rewards. But his mandate was a wretched one in the light of eternity. It carried no weight with God, the One with whom Balaam really had to do. God was not impressed by the signature of Balak nor by the seal of Moab.

Next, Balaam told *his mission*: "Balak . . . hath brought me . . . saying, Come, curse me Jacob, and come, defy Israel" (Numbers 23:7). That was his mission, and quite an undertaking it was. To curse Jacob and to defy Israel meant that Balaam had to curse and defy their God. "Jacob" was weak enough, "Israel" small enough, but behind that weakness was omnipotence, and behind that smallness was a God whom the Heaven of heavens could not contain. Others beside Balaam have undertaken a similar mission, only to be swept aside and dumped on the garbage heap of history. Where are now the pharaohs of Egypt, the proud Assyrian emperors, the haughty Babylonian kings, the imperial Persian warlords, the Greek oligarchs, the Roman caesars, the proud Crusaders, the papal inquisitors, the Hitlers and the Stalins of modern times? They have all passed away. One and all they undertook to curse this people and brought down the curse of God on themselves instead.

So Balaam had a great imperative, a commission from Balak urgent enough, enticing enough, to bring him from Chaldea to Canaan, from the mountains of Mesopotamia to the mountains of Moab. After all, his contract was confirmed by a king. Fame and fortune were to be his. Promotion and preferment under royal patronage were his. Who could resist that?

But then came what was obviously *a great impossibility*. Balaam had already been told he was not going to succeed. Perhaps the honorarium kept him pressing on, or perhaps the secret hope that somehow he would be able to outwit God. His was an impossible task. Balaam was skilled at his job, but the task he had undertaken was far beyond the skills of all the magi of Mesopotamia together.

First, we note *what was involved*: "How shall I curse, whom God hath not cursed? Or how shall I defy, whom the Lord hath not defied?" (Numbers 23:8) His task was to countermand the purpose of God. He might as well have told the sun to stand still, the moon to reverse its orbit, or the earth to stop spinning through space. He

125

might as well have commanded the tides to cease to flow or told Orion to disband its stars.

There was once a king of England known as King Canute. He was so wise a king that his subjects wished to worship him, but King Canute wanted no such adulation. To convince his courtiers of his mortality, he set up his throne on the sand below the level of the high tide mark and sat there watching the march of the oncoming waves. Presently the waters began to swirl about his feet. When they did, the king arose, swayed his scepter over the sea, and said, "Stand back, ye ocean tides." But the waves rolled on, and thus King Canute taught his people that he was no god.

Balaam had as little hope of countermanding the decrees of God concerning Israel as Canute had of countermanding the law of the tide. There was a tide in the affairs of Israel that had been on the ebb for four hundred years. Now the tide had turned. It was on the flood, it was leading on to Canaan, and it was soon to engulf that land. Balaam could not stop it, and he knew it. He knew he had a problem, and he was beginning to wish he had not come. If he hadn't been dazzled by the glitter of Moabite gold he would have resigned his commission and gone home.

"How shall I curse, whom God hath not cursed?" There are some other instances of trying to change God's mind. The patriarch Abraham had tried to change it. Abraham's heart longed that the blessings of the covenant might come true in his beloved Ishmael. "O that Ishmael might live before thee!" he said. But God had no intention of changing His mind: "In *Isaac* shall thy seed be called" (Genesis 17:18; 21:12, italics added).

Isaac, son and heir of Abraham, standing in direct line to the Messiah, child of promise—even Isaac could not reverse the made-up mind of God. "The elder shall serve the younger" (Genesis 25:23), God had said. But the elder was Esau and the younger was Jacob, and Isaac loved Esau because Esau supplied him with venison. Esau was a cunning hunter and Jacob was a sneak. But the blessing of God lay with Jacob, and though Isaac did his best to change God's mind, he ended up blessing Jacob after all. "Yea, and he shall be blessed," was his conscience-smitten affirmation when all was said and done (Genesis 27:33). In spite of himself, he had blessed the one whom God had blessed.

Yes, and Jacob as well. There seems little doubt that Jacob wished the full blessing of the covenant to go to Joseph. We have noted how long and lovingly Jacob lingered over the name of Joseph in his final blessing of his sons (Genesis 49). But the royal blessing was for Judah, and to Judah it went.

If Abraham, Isaac, and Jacob could not change God's mind, what chance did this pagan prophet have? This money-loving prophet, willing to sell his talent to the highest bidder? None at all.

Note next *who was involved.* On one side stood Balaam, a seer with a reputation among the heathen as a man versed in cursing people. On the other side stood God. Balaam used two names to describe Him.

He called Him *El,* "the mighty God," and he called Him "the Lord," *Jehovah.* He was opposing *El,* the God of power, and he was opposing *Jehovah,* the God of promise. He was up against two impossibilities, the impossibility of challenging God's power and the impossibility of changing God's promise. By those two immutable things, God's sovereign power and God's sovereign purpose, any hope he might have had of reversing the fortunes of Israel were dashed in pieces. The prophet recognized it right from the start.

Israel's future is as assured today as it was then by those same two immutable things. God's power has not changed; neither has His promise. If we want to understand the Word of God, the events of history, and what is happening in the Middle East today, we *must* take these facts into account. The Arabs can no more change God's mind about Israel than Balaam could. Israel's national future is guaranteed by *El,* by *Jehovah.*

Balaam concluded his first prophecy with *a great impression* (Numbers 23:9-10), one that seized the prophet and bore him along despite himself, an impression he could neither deny or defy. It was an impression of the greatness and grandeur of the Hebrew people camped below him there on the plains of Moab.

He had something to say about *the perspective.* "From the top of the rocks I see him, and from the hills I behold him" (Numbers 23:9). Step by step Balaam had climbed the heights. Down there on the plains he had been on the same level as the Israelites. Down there, perhaps, he might have been able to detect their imperfections. But the higher he went, the broader his perspective became, the more the petty everyday things receded, and the more the gathering as a whole came under his gaze.

Balaam saw a host organized like a military camp. In the center was the tabernacle with its precise contours draped with sealskins, its smoking altar, its brazen laver, and the glory-cloud brooding over all.

Around three sides of the tabernacle were the Levitical families and on the east, by the entrance to the court, were the tents of Moses, Aaron, and the priests. Around them, in a mighty protective fold, were the tribes in four divisions, each with its divisional standard and its distinctive ensign (Numbers 2:2-3).

We can only conjecture what the ensigns really were, but there is considerable support for the following suggestions. On the south side Gad was camped with the ensign of a tent, Simeon with the ensign of a gate, and Reuben with the ensign of a plant. On the west camped Ephraim and Manasseh (the two tribes descended from Joseph), whose ensign was a sheaf, and with them Benjamin (descended from Rachel's other son), whose ensign was a wolf. On the north camped Dan with the ensign of a set of scales. In the middle was Asher with the ensign of an olive tree and Naphtali, whose ensign was a hind. On the east was Judah with the ensign of a lion, Issachar with the ensign of the stars, and Zebulun with the ensign of a ship under sail.[1]

As Balaam gazed down at this, he could see order everywhere. There was an air of quiet and deliberate purpose in those ranks, which stretched away north and south, east and west, to the distant horizons. The precision of it awed the hireling prophet. The future of *that* people, he felt, was as sure and as solid as the rocks beneath his feet. He wished he had not climbed so high or seen so much. The vision gripped his soul and would not let him go.

He spoke next of *the people* (Numbers 23:9-10), with the Spirit of God inspiring his words. This was no incantation, no speaking in tongues, no ecstatic utterance, no demonic oracle. This was something he had never known before. This was the Spirit of the living God proclaiming truth, whether Balaam and Balak liked it or not. The same Spirit who had spoken through Moses to the Hebrew people now spoke through Balaam to a heathen people.

Balaam saw two facts about the Hebrew people which are as relevant today as they were when they were first uttered nearly thirty-five hundred years ago. He saw, first, that no nation would ever *absorb* them. "Lo, the people shall dwell alone, and shall not be reckoned among the nations," he said.

The principle of assimilation works for all other peoples. When they are scattered and take up their homes in other lands, they are eventually absorbed. But this does not work for the Jewish people. They are a gulf stream in the ocean of mankind. No matter where they go, no matter what their condition, no matter whether they are scattered in judgment to earth's remotest bounds to wander as fugitives from land to land or whether they settle down and prosper among the Gentiles, Jews remain Jewish. They might be French Jews, German Jews, American Jews, or Russian Jews, but they are always Jews. They are set apart from the nations wherever their lots are cast. Here and there some Jews might seek assimilation, but the Jews as a people will never be fully assimilated. To this day the Jews are the purest-blooded people on earth. No other people can trace its line and lineage back so far.

The Jews were already an ancient people with recorded family trees when barbarian Britons fought the legions of Rome. They were an ancient people when Rome was founded, when Alexander's armies marched eastward to fight the Persians, when Babylon fell, and when the Assyrians terrorized the world. Despite dungeon, fire, and sword, they can trace their roots back to Abraham and from him back to Noah and Adam.

The basic demands of the Mosaic law fostered their separation from the world. There was the law against idolatry, the rite of circumcision, the law of the sabbath, the law against marrying pagans, the complex sacrificial system, and the endless ritual of feasts and fasts. All such things set Israel apart.

Beyond those rules were the numerous traditions invented by the rabbis and imposed on the people, especially after the fall of Jerusalem in A.D. 70. Finding themselves adrift in a hostile world, without country or capital, without temple or sacrifice, cut off from their past and facing a stormy future, the Jews found identity in a book. That book was the *Talmud*, a vast book when finally finished, as large as the *Encyclopedia Britannica* and packed with laws and traditions, folklore and commentary, all designed to keep Jews apart from other people.[2] The *Talmud* locked them into a narrow, exclusive way of life, and eventually they found themselves in ghettos.

Thus Balaam's prophecy was true: "The people shall dwell alone, and shall not be reckoned among the nations." At first the Jews wanted it that way. In the promised land they developed an intolerance toward Gentiles that was bitter and fierce. Gentiles were considered unclean. Even the apostle Peter recoiled in horror when the Holy Spirit told him to go to a Gentile home and preach the gospel to a Roman family (Acts 11). The Gentiles, of course, retaliated in kind and excluded Jews from the mainstream of life. They pictured them as grasping moneylenders and Christ-killers, and made them scapegoats for the world's ills.

Balaam saw that no nation would ever absorb this people. He also saw that no nation would *abolish* them. "Who can count the dust of Jacob," he asked, "and the number of the fourth part of Israel?" (Numbers 23:10)

The Jews live in other people's countries. They are exclusive, and they differ in culture, custom, religion, history, ambition, and sometimes in morals. They hold key positions in the professions. They are often wealthy and successful. They know how to exert pressure on governments to further their interests. Human nature being what it is, jealousy and hatred take root; and sooner or later, public opinion turns against them. Laws are passed to curb their influence, to strip them of their wealth, to exclude them from the corridors of power. They are herded into designated areas and finally banished from the land or killed.

This has been the history of the Jewish people for nearly two thousand years. Numerous attempts have been made to exterminate them. Pogroms have been inflicted on them. Slanders have been circulated about them. Concentration camps have been built for them. Unrelenting, bitter, ruthless persecution has been unleashed against them. But no nation has been able to abolish them.

When Moses was sent to emancipate the Hebrew people, he met God at a burning bush, a bush that blazed but was not consumed. That bush was a symbol to Moses of a people always in the fires of persecution but never consumed, because God was in their midst. Down in Egypt, pharaoh launched history's first attempt to exterminate them. He tried. He failed. This people would prosper and multiply in spite of him.

Hitler killed an estimated six million Jews, but he failed to wipe out this people. It is estimated that there are some thirteen million Jews in the world today, of whom almost six million live in the United States, over one million in Russia, and almost four million in Israel. They exert an influence and pressure out of proportion to their numbers. There is scarcely a capital in the western world where Jews do not have considerable say in national and international affairs.

Balaam had another impression. He spoke of *the prospect:* "Let me die the death of the righteous, and let my last end be like his!" (Numbers 23:10) In his soul he knew that those tents down there were the tents of the righteous. The people may have had faults and failings, but they had been counted righteous by God. A way of life had taken root among those people that set them apart from all others. They had God-given laws—laws graven by the finger of God on tables of stone; laws enunciated midst earthquake, thunder, and fire; laws more righteous than any enacted by the peoples of the Gentile world.

That people down there, for all their limitations, knew God. Theirs was the secret of salvation from sin. They alone had hope beyond the grave. The smoke ascending from the brazen altar just inside the courtyard gate carried heavenward the message of salvation through the shed blood of the Lamb. Whatever Balaam might have known or apprehended of the eternal truths codified in the Mosaic law, he knew that truths such as Israel had were not to be found either in Moab or Mesopotamia. The Chaldean magus knew nothing of salvation as salvation was known and taught down there in that Hebrew camp.

A great longing seized Balaam's pagan soul—to die the death of the righteous. This man who "loved the wages of unrighteousness" (2 Peter 2:15) longed for the death of the righteous. It was not too late. Let him resign his Moabite commission and reimburse Balak for his expenses. Let him go down there and seek out Moses and ask if he could become a proselyte. Let him then live the life of the righteous, and the death of the righteous would be his. But the price tag seemed too high to Balaam. In the end he was to find that the price of dying the death of the unrighteous was far higher.

BALAAM'S SECOND PROPHECY (NUMBERS 23:11-24)

Balaam came down from the mount shaken but belligerent. His imperial employer was infuriated at what Balaam had been saying about the Jewish people. "What hast thou done unto me?" the king demanded, with some justification. "I took thee to curse mine enemies, and, behold, thou hast blessed them altogether." Balaam defended himself. "Must I not take heed to speak that which the Lord hath put in my mouth?" (Numbers 23:11-12)

Balak curbed his temper and his tongue. He could not afford to offend Balaam. "Come, I pray thee, with me unto another place, from whence thou mayest see them: thou shalt see but the utmost part of them, and shalt not see them all: and curse me them from thence" (Numbers 23:13). Balak decided that a different view of the Hebrews might help. Perhaps if Balaam saw only the rear guard . . .

The Moabites had seen Israel marching with mighty Judah in the vanguard, followed by Issachar and Zebulun. The Gershonites followed with the tabernacle and after them Reuben, Simeon, and Gad. After them came the Kohathites, with the sacred items of the sanctuary, followed by Ephraim, Manasseh, and Benjamin. Bringing up the rear were Dan, Asher, and Naphtali, the least significant tribes. Perhaps Balak had an inkling of this. Perhaps his spies had kept him informed. In any case, he thought that if Balaam could see just the unimportant tribes that trailed along in the rear, maybe that would help him pronounce his curse.

As though God would care less for the least of His own than He would for the greatest! On the contrary, God delights to make our weakness His strength:

> God hath chosen the foolish things of the world to confound the wise; and God hath chosen the weak things of the world to confound the things which are mighty; And base things of the world, and things which are despised, hath God chosen, yea, and things which are not, to bring to nought things that are (1 Corinthians 1:27-28).

So Balak took his paid preacher to Zophim, to the top of Pisgah. There, he hoped, Balaam would do better. Pisgah commands a tremendous view. It was from Pisgah that Moses was given his first and last views of the promised land. The whole land lies open to view, from En-gedi in the south, up the long winding valley of the Jordan, to the distant peak of Hermon in the north. There, on Pisgah, Balak built seven altars and, as before, offered a bullock and a ram on each. Religious ceremony (in imitation of Israel's ordinances) having been given its due, Balak turned expectantly to his prophet. But Balak was in for another shock. This time the prophetic urge that came upon Balaam from God spelled out the unique place that Israel as a nation occupies in the counsels of God.

I. Israel's Standing (Numbers 23:19-20)
   A. Due to God and His character (23:19)
   B. Due to God and His covenant (23:19)
   C. Due to God and His command (23:20)
II. Israel's Salvation (Numbers 23:21-22)
   A. Israel's perfection (23:21)
   B. Israel's promotion (23:21)
   C. Israel's protection (23:22)
III. Israel's Sovereignty (Numbers 23:23-24)
   A. Her spiritual sovereignty—because
      truth belongs to Israel (23:23)
   B. Her secular sovereignty—because
      triumph belongs to Israel (23:24)

The prophet began his second message with *Israel's standing* (Numbers 23:19-20). Israel's standing among the nations does not rest on any special merit in the Hebrew people. Rather, Israel's unique place among the nations has its roots in the person and the purposes of God. Thus Balaam, in taking up his second parable, began by relating everything to God: Israel's unique relationship to God makes her different from all other nations.

Balaam related Israel's standing to *God and His character.* "And he took up his parable, and said, Rise up, Balak, and hear; hearken unto me, thou son of Zippor: God is not a man, that he should lie" (Numbers 23:18-19). What Balak wanted more than anything else was some twisting of the truth regarding Israel, some assurance that somehow God could be persuaded to let Israel down, some prophetic word that there was really no future for Israel.

There are people today who preach that message: that Israel as a nation has no future; that all God's promises to Abraham, Isaac, and Jacob, to Moses, David, and Solomon can be explained away; that those promises are not to be understood as literal, concrete, substantial facts but as spiritual allegories. One school of interpretation says that God's Old Testament promises to the nation of Israel are being fulfilled spiritually in the church and are not to be taken literally. Therefore we must seek out their underlying meanings, dissociate them from their national context, and relate them to a spiritual context. The church, we are told, is spiritual Israel, and God's covenant promises are being fulfilled in the church. Consequently, there is no national future for the Jews.

Well, the rebirth of the state of Israel in 1948 should have put an effective end to such views. God is "not a man, that he should lie." The promises He made to Israel were literal, and they concern the destiny of a nation, not a church. Israel's national destiny is to be at the head of all nations in an actual worldwide kingdom. The promises of God along this line in the Old Testament are numerous and repeated, and their fulfillment is bound up in God's character and dependability. Nor can any national failure on Israel's part annul those promises; the Abrahamic and Davidic covenants were unconditional, and in no way related to the failings of the Hebrew people. Those failures were all foreseen and waived by God.

Some of these promises were partially fulfilled in Israel's Old Testament history. They will be completely fulfilled in a coming day. The character of God is all the guarantee Israel needs. That was lesson number one for Balak. He should have taken the lesson to heart and made his peace with Israel. The lesson Balaam sought to impart was that Israel's God was no deceiver. God's Word is His bond. He says what He means and He means what He says. The universe would come apart if God ever broke His Word.

Balaam moved on to speak of *God and His covenant.* "God is not a man, that he should lie; neither the son of man, that he should repent: hath he said, and shall he not do it? or hath he spoken, and shall he not make it good?" (Numbers 23:19) God does not change His mind.

Perhaps way back there in Mesopotamia Balaam had heard echoes of God's initial promise to Abraham:

> Get thee out of thy country, and from thy kindred, and from thy father's house, unto a land that I will shew thee: And I will make of thee a great nation, and I will bless thee, and make thy name great; and thou shalt be a blessing: And I will bless them that bless thee, curse him that curseth thee: and in thee shall all families of the earth be blessed (Genesis 12:1-3).

God had gone on adding to that initial promise. After Lot had made his fatal choice, pulled up stakes, and headed eastward toward the Jordan valley and the cities of the plain, God had confirmed His original promise to Abraham concerning the land.

> Lift up now thine eyes, and look from the place where thou art northward, and southward, and *eastward* [italics added; that was the direction in which Lot had gone, hoping to make that part of the land secure for himself—but God does not "repent" or change His mind], and westward: For all the land which thou seest, to thee will I give it, and to thy seed for ever [nothing can revoke this promise to Abraham of the land]. And I will make thy seed as the dust of the earth: so that if a man can number the dust of the earth, then shall thy seed also be numbered. Arise, walk through the land in the length of it and in the breadth of it; for I will give it unto thee (Genesis 13:14-17).

That was before Lot's final fall, his unutterable shame, and the incestuous birth of Moab, the father of the Moabite people.

Again, after the successful victory of Abraham over the invading kings of the East (the first invasion of the promised land after it had been deeded by God to Abraham), God had been even more specific:

> And he said unto Abram, Know of a surety that thy seed shall be a stranger in a land that is not theirs [Egypt], and shall serve them; and they shall afflict them four hundred years; And also that nation, whom they shall serve, will I judge: and afterward shall they come out with great substance. And thou shalt go to thy fathers in peace; thou shalt be buried in a good old age. But in the fourth generation they shall come hither again: for the iniquity of the Amorites is not yet full. . . . In the same day the Lord made a covenant with Abram, saying, Unto thy seed have I given this land, from the river of Egypt unto the great river, the river Euphrates (Genesis 15:13-16,18).

This particular covenant was ratified in the usual way for that day and age. It was the custom to slay and dismember an animal; then the contracting parties would walk up and down together between the pieces to solemnize the contract. On this occasion God put Abraham into a deep sleep, and He alone walked up and down between the pieces of the sacrifice. This was God's affirmation that He was assuming sole responsibility to make good the promise. Moreover, God now used the past tense. Up until this point He had said, "I will give." Now He said, "I have given." God, who sees the end from the beginning, thus guaranteed the literal fulfillment of this promise.

When Balaam stood on the heights overlooking Israel's encampment, the initial fulfillment of the promise was already underway. The fourth generation had come (Levi, Kohath, Amram, and Moses). Levi had gone down with Jacob to Egypt; and now his great-grandson Moses had brought the Hebrews to the borders of Canaan. The shackles of slavery had been shattered, and Israel was victoriously on the march.

Balaam spoke next of *God and His command*: "Behold, I have received commandment to bless: and he hath blessed; and I cannot reverse it" (Numbers 23:20). So that was that. No amount of wishful thinking was going to change God's blessing then any more than exegetical juggling is going to change it now. Israel stands in the blessing of God, both in Balaam's day and in ours. The Hebrew people might be unworthy of the future God has in store for them. They may falter and fail (and be punished for it), but their destiny stands sure because it is not based on their national performance, but on God's promise.

When Abraham was in his hundredth year, God once more endorsed this unconditional promise. The moment He appeared to him, Abraham fell flat on his face and remained prostrate while the glorious edicts rolled.

> And *I will* make nations of thee, and kings shall come out of thee. And *I will* establish my covenant between me and thee and thy seed after thee in their generations for *an everlasting covenant*, to be a God unto thee, and to thy seed after thee. And *I will* give unto thee, and to thy seed after thee, the land wherein thou art a stranger, all the land of Canaan, for *an everlasting possession*; and *I will* be their God (Genesis 17:6-8, italics added).

So that there might be no mistake, God also affirmed that the covenant was to be ratified in Isaac, not Ishmael (from whom the

Arabs have descended). Later He ratified it to Isaac personally and still later to Jacob personally.

In view of His repeated pledge to bless Abraham and his seed, God simply commanded Balaam to bless this people and be done with it. Balaam had enough sense to know that he could not reverse plans that were rooted in God's immutable character.

The prophet moved on next to Israel's *salvation* (Numbers 23:21-22). Again he saw three things. First, as he looked at Israel on the plains of Moab below, he saw their *perfection*. "He hath not beheld iniquity in Jacob, neither hath he seen perverseness in Israel" (23:21). That surely ought to end the argument that Israel has forfeited its covenant position by its sin. Israel's national sins were foreknown to God before He made His eternal promises to Abraham. In actual fact there *was* iniquity and perverseness in the Hebrew people. One of the first things they had done after leaving Egypt was to complain and to criticize Moses and Aaron. Then, they had crowned their unbelief first by making the golden calf at Sinai and later by turning back from the conquest of Canaan at Kadesh-barnea. But those sins had been dealt with and put away by God, who has His own way of seeing our sins through the blood of Christ, which means, of course, that they cannot be seen at all. God had given Israel an unassailable position. In His eternal counsels they were positionally perfect—as perfect as Calvary could make them. One day as a nation they will come into the good of Calvary, and they will inherit to the full all of God's national promises. Balaam, we must remember, was still looking down on the people from above and was seeing them from God's sublime point of view.

Balaam spoke next of their *promotion*. "The Lord his God is with him, and the shout of a king is among them" (Numbers 23:21). At the time Balaam spoke, Israel was a theocracy, a nation governed by God. God was their king. In due time God gave them a human king, David, a man after His own heart, a man who would found a dynasty that would climax in the coming of the King of kings Himself.

At the time of this prophecy, Israel had already overthrown Arad the Canaanite in the Negeb and conquered Sihon, king of the Amorites. Then, too, these warrior tribes had conquered Og, king of Bashan, a giant of a man, one of the nephilim monsters who haunted Canaan. Truly, the shout of a king was ringing through the Hebrew camp even as Balaam prophesied there on the mount.

Nor could any nation in that ancient world, much less Moab, hope to halt the coming of a kingdom long ago foreordained by God. Nor can any nation hope to stop the coming of that kingdom today. The Arabs have no hope at all of halting Israel's future. Nor will the Russians, when they cast caution to the wind and unite heart and soul with the Arab cause. The future in the Middle East and, indeed, of the world, lies with Israel. The shout of a king is among this people, a king who is absent today but who is coming back to claim the empire that belongs to Him.

Balaam also saw their *protection*. "God brought them out of Egypt; he hath as it were the strength of an unicorn" (Numbers 23:22). The word *unicorn* is often translated "buffalo." The proof that divine protection hovered over the Hebrew people was right in front of Balaam's eyes. This people had just despoiled mighty Egypt. Who but the true God could have preserved this people for four hundred years in "the house of bondage" where they had lived as a despised minority and, as their numbers increased, as a dreaded minority? Who but God could have countermanded the edict of the Egyptian throne to exterminate this people? Egypt was one of the world's great imperial powers.

Pharaoh had taken on the buffalo, and Israel's protector answered first with plagues and pestilence and finally in judgment at the Red Sea. This has been Israel's history—brought back from Egypt, brought back from Babylon, brought back now from the ends of the earth. Three times this people have returned to the promised land. At the time of their first return, they gave the world the Bible. At the time of their second return, they gave the world Christ and His church. Now at the time of their third return, they are destined to give the world the golden age of the millennium.

Their white and blue flag with its two equilateral triangles—the apex of one triangle pointing heavenward, the apex of the other pointing earthward—flies in the face of the world. It reminds us that God has a future for this people and that their protector is great. Balaam and Balak were being warned to leave this people alone. Balaam's parable is a warning also to all of this world's Balaams and Balaks to leave the Jewish people alone.

In the latter days there will arise another paid prophet and another Gentile prince (Revelation 13). Like their counterparts of old, these godless men will unite their forces to curse the Hebrew race. They too will find that they have taken a buffalo by the horns and that Israel's defender is just as able to save His people from them as He was from Balak in ancient times.

Finally, the prophet spoke of Israel's *sovereignty* (Numbers 23:23-24). He saw, first, that this sovereignty was a *spiritual sovereignty*, because *truth* was the inheritance of this people. "Surely there is no enchantment against Jacob, neither is there any divination against Israel: according to this time it shall be said of Jacob and of Israel, What hath God wrought!" (23:23)

Israel had recourse to God Himself. So great and glorious was God's guidance of this people that no enchanter or wizard or consulter with spirits could produce an effective curse. For forty years the Israelites had crossed and recrossed the desert, marching behind the moving shekinah cloud, fed with manna from heaven, and sustained by water from the riven rock.

Balaam, with a mere forty years of recent Hebrew history to draw on, could thus exclaim, "What God hath wrought!" How much more should we today echo his words! We can trace the path of this people through the wilderness of the whole world for fifty times as long. We see them emerging from persecutions spread over nearly twenty centuries. We see them leaving an indelible mark on the arts, sciences, economies, and politics of many nations. We see them in advancement and in adversity. We see them in royal palaces as the counselors of kings; we see them burned at the stake. And we see them now established again in their land, defying the Arabs, Russians, and United Nations alike. This is not little Israel's doing alone. This is the hand of God.

Israel is back in the land because God *said* they would be back in the land. For the past 150 years those who have rightly understood the Word of God have been positively affirming that Israel would be reborn as a nation. Israel is back in the land because she has a spiritual sovereignty yet to be worked out in history. She is there because God's truth is on her side.

Finally, Balaam saw that this sovereignty was also a *secular sovereignty*, because *triumph* was to be the inheritance of this people. "Behold, the people shall rise up as a great lion, and lift himself as a young lion: he shall not lie down until he eat of the prey, and drink the blood of the slain" (Numbers 23:24).

The immediate reference was to the impending conquest of

Canaan, but its implications go far beyond that. The prophecy looks on to the endtimes, when the Lion of the tribe of Judah will return to espouse Israel's national cause in the face of the opposition and hatred of the world. The day is yet to dawn when Israel will be a lion among the nations. World empire is yet to be centered in Israel. Jerusalem is yet to be the world's capital, and the nations of mankind are yet to make their annual pilgrimages to Jerusalem to worship at the throne of the Lion.

"There, my lord Balak!" Balaam might have said, "What do you think of that?"

BALAAM'S THIRD PROPHECY (NUMBERS 24:3 -9)

Twice now Balaam had tried to curse the Hebrew people and twice he had failed. In disgust Balak snapped at his paid preacher, "Neither curse them at all, nor bless them at all" (Numbers 23:25). It would be better to say nothing at all, he thought, than to say the kind of things Balaam had been saying. But then he must have read something in Balaam's crafty face, for he changed his mind. It was obvious, despite the words which had been coming out of Balaam's mouth, that Balaam was really on Balak's side. It was suddenly obvious to Balak that Balaam didn't like what he had been saying any more than the king did.

Balak decided to try again. "Come, I pray thee," he said, "I will bring thee unto another place; peradventure it will please God that thou mayest curse me them from thence" (Numbers 23:27). That's how much he knew or cared about God. After all the blaze of divine revelation through Balaam's first two prophecies, Balak still thought that God could be outwitted.

He took Balaam to the top of Peor looking toward Jeshimon. Mount Peor was one of the peaks on the northern part of the mountains of Abiram near the town of Beth-peor, a place celebrated as a center of idolatrous practice. It was here that Baal was worshiped. It was a Moabite "holy" place and not far from where Moses was to be buried by the angels of God. Balak wanted his preacher to look down on the people, but with his face toward Jeshimon on the north side of the Dead Sea. The word *Jeshimon* means "wilderness." It was a name for the wilderness of Judea, twelve hundred square miles of brown and yellow sand, of crumbling limestone, of scattered shingle dotted here and there with an occasional shrub or thornbush. The place carries the violence and desolation of the Dead Sea valley right up into the heart of the promised land and to the foot of the mount of Olives. If ever a site bespoke the curse and judgment of God, that was it. The fire and brimstone of God's wrath had already fallen on that area once. "There!" Balak said in effect to his prophet, "Take a look at them from that point of view. That should inspire you to curse if anything will!"

So once again prince and prophet went through their performance, building seven altars and sacrificing seven more bullocks and rams, in the hope that this might impress Israel's God. It was all in vain. God was not impressed; the sacrifice of the wicked is an abomination to Him (Proverbs 15:8). Balaam seemed to sense that it was hopeless; he did not even go through his magic formulas. He simply stared at the arid scene below him—at the frightful desert, at the ominous stillness of the Dead Sea swallowing up endlessly the generous flow of the Jordan, giving nothing but death and desolation in return. He also saw the orderly camp of Israel waiting patiently for God's word to march. And once again the Spirit of God seized the reluctant prophet's tongue.

Once more it will help to have the outline of his prophecy before us.

> I. The Brightness of the Light (Numbers 24:3-4)
> A. Balaam autographs his prophecy (24:3)
> B. Balaam authenticates his prophecy (24:4)
> II. The Beauty of the Land (Numbers 24:5-6)
> A. The camp (24:5)
> B. The country (24:6)
> III. The Bravery of the Lion (Numbers 24:7-9)
> A. The nations trembling before Israel (24:7)
> 1. Israel responding to the nations
> 2. Israel residing among the nations
> 3. Israel ruling over the nations
> B. The nations tumbling before Israel (24:8)
> 1. The past: triumph over Egypt
> 2. The prospect: triumph over everyone
> C. The nations tranquil before Israel (24:9)
> IV. The Blessing of the Lord (Numbers 24:9)

The prophet began with a word about *the brightness of the light* (Numbers 24:3-4). He knew well by now that the words pouring from his lips were coming from God, that light from Heaven was filling his soul. His usual enchantments had no part at all in what he now had to say. He hadn't even tried to conjure up a message. He wanted to make that clear and plain.

So first he *autographed his message.* "And he took up his parable, and said, Balaam the son of Beor hath said, and the man whose eyes are open hath said" (Numbers 24:3). Or, as Joseph Bryant Rotherham translated this verse: "Balaam . . . the man of the opened eye." Like the blind man in John's Gospel Balaam could testify, "Whereas I was blind, now I see" (John 9:25).

Balaam knew he was speaking under the influence of the Spirit of God. Although it was Balaam the son of Beor who was speaking, the message was the message of God. That is what invested these prophecies with a significance out of all proportion to the stature of the soothsayer from Chaldea. He was only a covetous crystal-gazer from a demon-haunted land, but the words he spoke were the words of the living God. The same God who put Saul among the prophets and who put a prophetic utterance on the lips of Caiaphas put the words of truth into the mouth of this mountebank from Mesopotamia. Balaam's sole claim to fame is that God deigned to cancel out his curses and replace them with the word of God. Had it not been for these four prophecies concerning the nation of Israel, nobody would ever have heard of him.

Balaam next *authenticated his message*: "The man whose eyes are open hath said . . . which heard the words of God, which saw the vision of the Almighty, falling into a trance, but having his eyes open" (Numbers 24:3-4).

Balaam affirmed in the most solemn way that his words were from God, not from himself. He used the name *El* ("the mighty God") and also the name *Shaddai* ("God the all-bountiful, God the all-sufficient, God the giver")—the name first used by God when revealing Himself to Abraham at the time of the most far-reaching confirmation of the covenant (Genesis 17:1). The name formerly intended to assure Abraham that God had all the resources necessary to fulfill that covenant was used now to affirm the fact that this almighty, all-sufficient God was Israel's God still.

Someone once asked Baron von Rothschild why, with all his vast resources, he did not simply *buy* the land of Palestine and *give* it to the Jewish people. He replied, "Why should I do that when we already have the title deeds?" Well said.

By using the name *Shaddai* for God, Balaam affirmed the same thing. Israel had no need to wonder whether or not the land lying before them would be theirs. God had deeded it to Abraham hundreds of years before. He was with that people down on the plain. He was the giving God, able to make good on His promises. He was able to put the Hebrews in possession of the promised land.

We should remember that. The land has had many alien tenants in the course of history, but the title deed has not been changed. The land does not belong to the Palestinian Arabs.

The last time a state existed in the country that came to be called Palestine, it was a *Jewish* state, which the Romans vengefully destroyed in A.D. 70. They burned its temple, deported its people, and minted a coin to celebrate their achievement. The coin bore the inscription *Judea Capta*. A special and magnificent triumphal arch was erected in Rome to celebrate the "victory" of Titus.

It had been a costly victory; the Jews did not surrender their land to the invader without a fierce fight. Julius Caesar had needed only twenty-five thousand troops to conquer Gaul and invade Britain, but Titus needed eighty thousand just to conquer the beleaguered Jews of Jerusalem. In the end he won by starving them out and by butchering any who tried to escape. Historians say that it was common for as many as five hundred Jews to be crucified in a single day. It took the Romans four years of costly fighting to subjugate Jerusalem, and they retaliated by sacking the city with unprecedented ferocity. Tacitus said that as many as six hundred thousand Jews were massacred in the wake of the siege.

But the Jews were not wiped out. In A.D. 113, when the Romans were preoccupied trying to subdue their ancient Parthian enemies, a new Jewish revolt forced the Romans to divert troops they could ill spare from the Parthian war. The emperor Hadrian was so thankful to see this second Jewish revolt put down that he promised moderation. The Jews, he said, could rebuild their temple. Instead, lulled by the false calm that settled over the country of Judea, he built a temple to Jupiter, changed the name of Jerusalem to Aelia Capitolina, and converted it into a Roman city.

The infuriated Jews retaliated a third time, this time led by the pseudomessiah, Bar Kochba. This eruption in A.D. 132 took the Romans by surprise. Again the Jews fought fiercely for their land.

They cut to ribbons the armies Caesar sent against them. At last the emperor was forced to summon his ablest general Julius Severus from Britain, where he was quelling another revolt, and send him off to Judea to subdue the Jews once and for all. Bar Kochba promptly defeated the forces Severus sent against him. After this, the general decided that the only way to deal with this people was to burn all before him as he marched; so he systematically slaughtered everything in his path. Men, women, children, and cattle alike were slaughtered in ruthless butchery, the aim being to reduce the population to zero.

The Jews held out until A.D. 135, when this last revolt was finally crushed. Hadrian at once proclaimed Jerusalem and all of greater Judea out of bounds to all Jews, and as a final act of spite, he renamed the country *Palestine* after the Jews' hereditary foe, the Philistines. This is the way that the name "Palestine" entered into Latin and church history and literature.

Neither a Palestinian state nor a Palestinian people has ever existed in fact. The country has been held from time immemorial by invaders. During the middle ages it was conquered by the Arabs in Islam's holy wars. Muslims and Crusaders fought over the country for centuries until the Crusaders were driven out by the Mamelukes of Egypt. In the sixteenth century the country was conquered by the Ottoman Turks. The Turks ruled it with such corruption and neglect that it was denuded of trees and vegetation, converted into a wasteland of stones, and left to bake and blister under the eastern sun.

In the nineteenth century Jews began to return to the country again in appreciable numbers, fleeing persecution in eastern Europe and Russia. Then the Zionist movement was born, and an ever-increasing flow of Jews began to trek back to their ancestral home.

During World War I the country, under Turkish rule, was aligned with Germany, which made it a target for the western powers. It was taken from the Turks by the British general, Lord Allenby, and it was mandated to Britain by the charter of the League of Nations. Under international law, Britain was commissioned to establish a national home for the Jewish people in that country. One of Britain's first acts was to carve out a sizeable strip of the land and create the country of Jordan.

That there ever was a Palestinian nation is a fiction of Arab propaganda. After World War II, Britain surrendered the mandate because of the incessant strife in the country between Jews and Arabs. The United Nations was given the "Palestine problem" to solve. Its solution was partition: divide the land between Jew and Arab.

No sooner was the partition plan put into effect and the Jewish state officially born than the Arabs tried to push the Jews into the sea. The war that erupted in 1948 swiftly went against the Arabs, and thousands of former Arab residents fled the country. They found new homes in Libya, Jordan, Saudi Arabia, and the gulf states. Lebanon hospitably took in many of them, and the Palestine Liberation Organization rewarded Lebanon by setting up a state within the state and using the unfortunate host country as a base from which to wage terrorist war against Israel.

Three times as many Jews were forced out of Arab countries in the Middle East as there were Arabs who fled partitioned Palestine in 1948. These Arabs left the country, not because the Jews threw them out, but because they fully expected to return with victorious Arab armies. To leave was their decision. The oil-rich sheikdoms of the Middle East, with their vast wealth and great land holdings, could easily have absorbed these voluntary refugees just as the little state of Israel absorbed displaced Jews from Libya, Egypt, Iraq, Syria, and elsewhere. The Arab states have preferred to let these displaced Arabs sit in squalor in refugee camps so as to make political capital out of them, keep alive hatred of the Jew in the Middle East, and promote anti-Jewish sentiments around the world.

The land, styled "Palestine" by the Romans, was never deeded to the Arabs but to the Jews. The vicissitudes of history have not changed God's mind. He is still *Shaddai*, "the giver." He is still the One Balaam saw down there in the Hebrew camp on the plains of Moab, wrapped around with the mysterious shekinah cloud. The God who promised the Hebrew people the land *then* has not changed His mind *now*.

When Balaam saw that God was down there with the Hebrew people, he knew that nothing could keep Israel out of the land. Moreover, the Abrahamic covenant was an *everlasting* covenant, without conditional clauses. The conditional clauses found in the later Palestinian covenant were of a temporary nature and have had their fulfillment in the Jewish age-long exile during the Christian era. Those appended clauses did not abrogate or annul the original unconditional promise of God concerning the future of this people and this land.

The prophet's vision next took in *the beauty of the land* (Numbers 24:5-6). Balak had tried to influence Balaam by showing him a land under a curse, the arid areas around the Dead Sea where Israel was making its temporary camp. The Spirit of God simply swept aside that view and gave the prophet a different picture altogether. He saw, first, *the camp.* "How goodly are thy tents, O Jacob, and thy tabernacles, O Israel!" (24:5) Over three million people camped down there, a new generation of Hebrews. The generation that had left Egypt under Moses and been so bitterly critical of everything had been replaced by a new generation. It was no disorderly mob of refugees but an orderly encampment with strict laws, high moral principles, superb organization and discipline, with martial fervor, a taste of victory, clear goals, and God in its midst. It was "terrible as an army with banners" (Song of Solomon 6:4). It had survived forty years in the wilderness, it was marching by divine command, and it was a sight to make the boldest foes tremble. Balaam could see that camp spread out before him in perfect order and symmetry, and he could not help but comment on it.

Then God showed him *the country*, just as He was soon going to show it to Moses. "As the valleys are they spread forth, as gardens by the river's side, as the trees of lign aloes which the Lord hath planted, and as cedar trees beside the waters" (Numbers 24:6). The arid plains of the Dead Sea vanished from the prophet's sight, and he saw this people in a different environment. He saw them at home in this land. He saw the curse removed and blessings flowing like a river. His vision carried him on—not just to the promised land, as it was to be after the conquest under Joshua, but to the promised land as it will be in the golden age when paradise will be regained, the curse will be removed, and the deserts will blossom as the rose.

Then the prophet spoke of *the bravery of the lion* (Numbers 24:7-9). He further contemplated the distant but glorious millennial age, when the people of Israel will become the blessing to the nations that God has always intended them to be.

Balaam saw *the nations trembling before Israel* (Numbers 24:7). The scene that filled his vision was that of an earthly paradise, a world transformed into a garden because Israel had come at last into its own. He saw Israel as the head of the nations.

Balaam saw *Israel responding to the nations.* "He shall pour the water out of his buckets" (Numbers 24:7). Israel's coming blessings will not be kept selfishly to herself, but will be shared with others.

During the week of the feast of tabernacles, the gladdest of all of Israel's annual feasts, the one feast that was intended to prefigure the coming millennial age, water was poured forth as part of the ritual. The feast itself always lasted a full week, but an eighth day was added for a new beginning. That added day, by law, was always observed as a special sabbath.

The symbolism that grew up around the feast was interesting, and Jesus used it to draw national attention to Himself and to His claims. For the first seven days of the feast, a procession of priests went to the pool of Siloam or to the Kidron with golden vessels that they filled with water. When they arrived back at the temple, the priests poured that water out within the temple courts.

The ritual was intended to convey two truths: one related to the past, the other to the future. The symbolism pointed to the past as it reminded the people how God had miraculously supplied Israel with water in the wilderness. It pointed to the future as it reminded Israel of the prophecies in Ezekiel, Joel, and Zechariah of a coming day when God will send rivers of water to revive the deserts and when Israel will come into full spiritual blessing. This ritual continued for seven days.

According to Dr. G. Campbell Morgan there was a deliberate change on the last day, the eighth day. There was no procession of priests, no drawing of water, no water outpoured in the temple court. The omission symbolized the fact that Israel was now in the land; there was no need for a supernatural supply of water. It was also intended to remind the people that the promises of spiritual refreshment and the reviving of the desert lands had not yet been fulfilled.

Jesus stood on the temple steps on the last day of this feast, shortly before going to Calvary, to announce that He had come to fulfill the spiritual side of the promise. "If any man thirst," He cried, "let him come unto me, and drink. He that believeth on me, as the scripture hath said, out of his belly shall flow rivers of living water" (John 7:37-38). He was there, too, to guarantee that the other part of the promise would be fulfilled at His second coming—the promise that the desert would blossom as the rose and that Israel would become a source of blessing to mankind. Israel, as Balaam put it, will "pour the water out of his buckets," not in the symbolic way commemorated at the feast of tabernacles, but in a literal way, both physically and spiritually.

Balaam then saw *Israel residing among the nations*. "His seed shall be in many waters" (Numbers 24:7). This has been Israel's lot in judgment for many a century, but that was not what the prophet meant. The context is clearly millennial. During the millennial age, Israel's sons will take up their place among the nations as ambassadors of the King and as the administrators of the affairs of His empire. They will be there to bring to all mankind the blessings of the kingdom and to see that the laws of the kingdom are obeyed.

In keeping with this, the prophet saw *Israel ruling over the nations*. "And his king shall be higher than Agag, and his kingdom shall be exalted" (Numbers 24:7). This sentence alone warrants our seeing millennial blessing in these verses.

The name *Agag* here has caused some problems, because the only Agag mentioned in Scripture is the Amalekite king slain by Samuel in the days of Saul (1 Samuel 15:33). It may be, however, that the name *Agag* was a title for the Amalekite kings, just as the names *pharaoh* and *caesar* were titles of Egyptian and Roman rulers. The word *Agag* means "the fiery one." That gives the word significance in this context. The first thing the returning Christ will do will be to smash the power of the fiery one—that is, the power of Satan himself. Then He who is, indeed, "higher than Agag" will set up His kingdom on earth, basing everything on the covenant signed with Abraham long centuries ago.

Having caught this glimpse of the nations trembling before Israel, the prophet then saw *the nations tumbling before Israel*. His ecstatic vision embraced first *the past* as it took in this nation's triumph over Egypt. "God brought him forth out of Egypt; he hath as it were the strength of a unicorn [buffalo]" (Numbers 24:8). Israel's triumph over all the might of Egypt was well-known in Balaam's day. It was spoken of with bated breath in Canaan, as the two spies were soon to discover (Joshua 2:9-10). Mention of the overthrow of Egypt was probably the last thing Balak wanted to hear.

The prophet's vision also embraced *the prospect* as it took in this nation's triumph over everyone. "He shall eat up the nations his enemies, and shall break their bones, and pierce them through with his arrows" (Numbers 24:8). The immediate vision, of course, had to do with the impending conquest of Canaan; but the ultimate vision ran on to the endtimes, to the battle of Armageddon and Israel's final triumph over the Gentiles at the coming of the King.

No nation that has tangled with the Jewish people has prospered. Antisemitic practices might seem to triumph, but in the end the nation that espouses them is pulled down by divine decree. The Arab nations that surround Israel have already been taught the high cost of meddling with Israel, but meddle they do and will. Russia will meddle with Israel too, as will all the nations of earth before the end. The fate of Egypt awaits them one and all.

The prophet then saw *the nations tranquil before Israel.* "He couched, he lay down as a lion, and as a great lion: who shall stir him up?" (Numbers 24:9) What a picture of the millennium! The Lion of the tribe of Judah has thrashed all Israel's foes at Armageddon, and the surviving wicked have been weeded out and banished from the earth. The remnant of both Jews and Gentiles, all believers, have begun to rebuild a shattered world. War has been abolished, the world's military academies dissolved, and weapons of war converted into implements of peace. The great Lion lies down in the midst of the land. The nations do not dare to arouse Him. Peace comes at last to this poor old planet—peace through strength.

Finally the prophet mentioned *the blessing of the Lord.* "Blessed is he that blesseth thee, and cursed is he that curseth thee" (Numbers 24:9). All Balaam could do was reiterate the original promise of God to Abraham and his seed. It is a promise God has never withdrawn or forgotten, even during the long centuries of Israel's dispersal and chastisement. History affirms that nations that have harbored and protected the Jews have prospered, and the nations that have hated and persecuted the Jews have perished.

This was the note on which Balaam finished his third prophecy, a note of wonder and warning, a note that left Balak almost speechless with rage.

BALAAM'S FOURTH PROPHECY (NUMBERS 24:16 - 24)

Three times the prophet had tried to curse the people of God, three times he had failed, and three times his attempted curse had been changed into a blessing. Sobered, the prophet decided to leave the scene of his debacle, anxious to get away before the wrath of the Moabite king was poured out on his head.

Before the alarmed prophet could leave, however, God forced him to say more. This time there was none of the usual ritual preparations. Feeling the Spirit upon him, the prophet abruptly turned to his angry sponsor and announced, "And now, behold, I go unto my people: come therefore, and I will advertise thee what this people shall do to thy people in the latter days" (Numbers 24:14). The prophecy that followed had its focus on the endtimes. The expression *the last days* was first used by the dying Jacob when forecasting the future of the Hebrew people (Genesis 49:1).

The whole episode is full of interest for us. The seer himself came from the region of Babylon. The city of Babylon was to be the first of the world empires of Scripture, and it is to rise again in the last days under the sponsorship of the antichrist. The prophecy was made by one pagan to another. It made clear what would happen to any nation that tangled in enmity with the Israelites.

Here is the outline of this prophecy that brings to a climax all that Balaam had to say.

    I. The Source of the Prophecy (Numbers 24:15-16)
        A. Balaam's signature (24:15)
        B. Balaam's sincerity (24:16)
    II. The Substance of the Prophecy (Numbers 24:17-19)
        A. Its time factor (24:17)
        B. Its true focus (24:17-19)
           1. The coming Messiah (24:17)
             a. The person of Christ: the star
             b. The power of Christ: the scepter
           2. The coming millennium (24:17-19)
             a. Israel's foes assailed (24:17-18)
             b. Israel's future assured (24:19)
    III. The Sequel of the Prophecy (Numbers 24:20-24)
        A. A coming military power (24:20-22)
           1. Nations hostile to Israel (24:20)

2. Nations helpful to Israel (24:21-22)
B. A corresponding maritime power (24:23-24)
    1. Initially useful, so employed by God (24:23-24)
    2. Intrinsically useless, so destroyed by God (24:24)

The theme of this final prophecy is the second coming of Christ to smite Israel's foes. We note first *the source of the prophecy* (Numbers 24:15-16). The prophet began this utterance in much the same way as the previous one—with *his signature*. "And he took up his parable, and said, Balaam the son of Beor hath said . . ." (24:15). He himself was the human instrument, he the soothsayer who once thought that God could be manipulated and that he could make money by cursing the people of God. Balaam was a kind of Old Testament Simon Magus, a man who thought that sacred things could be bought and sold, who had the reputation of being "the great power of God" (Acts 8:10), who really had no part in spiritual things at all and was full of "the gall of bitterness, and in the bond of iniquity" (8:23). He, Balaam, signed the prophecy.

That signature carries weight, if for no other reason than because it was the pledged word of a man who was a sworn enemy of the Jewish people. The words he recorded were not written out of any love for them. Balaam hated them, would have cursed them if he could, and in the end collected his wages by teaching Balak how to corrupt them. No friend of theirs, he died under the avenging sword of Joshua.

So what Balaam had to say is of interest, not only because it is the inspired word of God, but also because it is the testimony of a hostile witness. The truth was dragged out of him, so to speak. He was forced to bear witness, even against his will, on behalf of a people he personally disliked and for whom in his inner soul he wished ill. Then, his sworn statement having been taken, his signature is added to bind him to it.

Next we have *his sincerity*. "And the man whose eyes are open hath said: He hath said, which heard the words of God, and knew the knowledge of the most High, which saw the vision of the Almighty, falling into a trance, but having his eyes open" (Numbers 24:15-16).

Balaam used three names for God in this statement. He referred to Him as "God," as *El*, the mighty God. He referred to Him as "the Almighty," as *Shaddai*, God the bountiful giver, the all-

151

sufficient One. He referred to Him as "the most High," as *Elyon*, the high One over all the earth, and the One who has dominion.

There is a hint here of the triune nature of God. We have here God the Father, the mighty God, the ultimate power behind the universe, the original source of all that exists. We have God the Son, "the most High," the Lord of the earth. And we have God the Holy Spirit, God the bountiful giver, the all-sufficient One. There was no way, of course that Balaam could have known God in three persons except by direct illumination. It was this triune God, so different from the idols and demons worshiped by pagans, who now came upon Balaam, threw him into a trance, forced his eyes open, and filled his soul with a vision of end-time events.

The prophet wanted the king of Moab to know that the words which were now to spill from his mouth did not have their source in his own intuition, knowledge, or occult powers. They had their source in God. He affirmed this as solemnly as he knew how.

We now come to *the substance of the prophecy* (Numbers 24:17-19), and we notice that it deals with two major themes. Balaam made reference first to *the time factor*: "I shall see him, but not now: I shall behold him, but not nigh" (24:17). That was the prophet's way of saying that the coming of this mighty One was in the distant future and that the message had nothing to do with the immediate present. It related to One who had not yet appeared, nor would appear in the near future. We now know that this One's first coming was delayed by nearly fifteen hundred years, and His second coming has been delayed by an additional two thousand years. These vast periods of time were dissolved in the vision, but the time factor was there just the same, and had to be noted.

Then the prophet mentioned *the true focus* of his prophecy, its chief burden. Immediately everything becomes clear. He saw the coming of *the Messiah*: "There shall come a Star out of Jacob, and a Sceptre shall rise out of Israel" (Numbers 24:17). The star and the scepter. What can these symbolize but the two comings of Christ!

He saw the star, the person of Christ. He saw the first coming of Christ. He saw One who came from Heaven to shed light on the earth. This prophecy of Balaam eventually found its way into the camp of Israel and also, it seems, to the banks of the Euphrates. There the story lingered on in the traditions of the magi until some fifteen hundred years later a star did suddenly appear in the sky. Those of their ranks who had the knowledge to read the riddle of that star and the faith to follow it came at last to Bethlehem, where they saw the star Himself. And seeing, they worshiped.

Balaam saw also the scepter, the power of Christ; he saw the second coming; he saw One who was to rule the nations, One who was to be "King of the Jews." He saw this King coming in the endtimes to rule.

Moreover, Balaam proclaimed the fact that this star would come "out of Jacob" and that it would "rise out of Israel," firmly identifying the coming King with the Hebrew people.

The use of the names *Jacob* and *Israel* for the Hebrew people is also significant. *Jacob* is the name for the Hebrew nation in its faults and failures, in its worldliness, carnality, shortcomings, and sin. It was to just such a nation that the star came, only to be rejected and crucified. The name *Israel* signifies the nation in its spiritual state, cleansed, converted, consecrated, and crowned. The name *Israel* means "prince with God" and was the name given to Jacob, the father of the tribes, when God broke and blessed him at the ford Jabbok. As used here, the name anticipates the day when the nation of Israel, having been broken by the great tribulation, will be blessed at the return of Christ, converted and brought into the good of all the promises of God.

But Balaam saw further. He saw the coming of *the millennium* (Numbers 24:17-19). He had already announced that the focal point of this vision is the "latter days," that this is essentially an end-time vision.

He saw *Israel's foes assailed.* "And [he] shall smite the corners of Moab, and destroy all the children of Sheth. And Edom shall be a possession, Seir also shall be a possession for his enemies; and Israel shall do valiantly" (Numbers 24:17-18).

Moab was descended from Lot, and Edom from Esau. Both these nations were blood-kin to Israel and were offered peace by Israel, but both became her enemies. Balaam's reference to "the children of Sheth" seems to be a reference to mankind in general. Sheth, usually spelled Seth, was the son of Adam from whom Noah descended and from whom therefore all men living on the earth are descended.

Balaam's vision focused, at this point, on a worldwide coalition of nations against the Hebrew people in the endtimes, prior to the millennium, a coalition in which Israel's bitterest enemies will be its immediate neighbors in the Middle East. A similar vision was seen later by Isaiah (Isaiah 15). The ancient lands of Moab and Edom are today included in the country of Jordan. As ancient Moab was bitter toward Israel because Israel, by conquering Sihon the Amorite, seized land that had formerly belonged to Moab, so Jordan today is bitter toward Israel because it occupies land that Jordan once ruled. Indeed, all the ferment and turmoil in the Middle East stem from the fact that Israel occupies territory the Arabs believe belongs to them.

It would be foolish for us to draw too close a parallel between Moab and ancient Israel and Jordan and modern Israel. However, we do know that the hostilities in the Middle East generated by the rebirth of the state of Israel will continue. Dangerous alliances will be made by the Arabs, first with Russia and then with the beast. Those alliances will be aimed at getting rid of Israel and will rebound on the nations that enter into them.

Balaam, in this prophecy, was warning Balak against continued intransigence toward Israel, but Balak was not to be warned. Indeed, when he found that open hostilities against Israel were futile, he resorted to guile. He and his people were divinely punished by being excluded from any share in the spiritual riches of Israel (Deuteronomy 23:3). Moab, however, was not willing to accept the warning, and neither are the Arab states today.

The prophet also saw Israel being assailed in the last days by Edom. The Edomites occupied territory to the south of the Dead Sea which is also included in Jordan today. The Edomites were bitterly hostile toward Israel. Balaam made it clear that these ancient enmities will be revived in the last days, and that they will culminate in the Arabs' siding with the antichrist against Israel. Psalm 83 endorses all that Balaam had to say about this.

Balaam saw something else. He saw *Israel's future assured.* "Out of Jacob shall come he that shall have dominion, and shall destroy him that remaineth of the city" (Numbers 24:19). Or, as the American Standard Version renders that last clause, "And shall destroy the remnant from the city" (that is, the cities of Edom).

We know from other prophetic Scriptures that this whole area will be a battleground and that Israel will be kept in constant turmoil, always at the vortex of trouble. Russia will continue to press into the area, inflaming Arab passions until God Himself puts an end to the meddling. The antichrist will keep the pot boiling in his own interests, now siding with the Jews, now with the Arabs.

But it will all come to nothing; neither Arab enmity nor the combined hatred of all the nations (symbolized here by Seth) will change the ultimate outcome. The future belongs to Israel. So does most of the territory in what we call the Middle East. Out of Jacob is to come the One who will have dominion.

At this point in the prophecy there was a pause while Balaam took a breath, looked one last time at the people he had come so far to curse, and began *the sequel to the prophecy* (Numbers 24:20-24). He now saw two world powers come on stage. One was essentially a military power, the other essentially a maritime power. The details are hazy, both because of the distance in time and because the prophet was an alien to "the commonwealth of Israel" and a stranger to "the covenants of promise" (Ephesians 2:12). We can be sure, however, that when the time comes for the final fulfillment of this prediction, everything will be clear. We can sketch in some of the details even today.

Balaam saw the coming of *a future military power* (Numbers 24:20-22). The source of the coming scourge was to be "Asshur," the ancient name for the Assyrians. The Assyrians, when they came to power in the Middle East, were a terrible reality to all the smaller nations. They swept down from the north massacring, torturing, uprooting, and deporting at will, with a ferocity unsurpassed in ancient times; and they became an archetype. They symbolized destruction descending from the north.

The focus of Balaam's prophecy is on "the last days"; so "Asshur" must symbolize an end-time great northern power, one characterized by military thoroughness and cold-blooded cruelty, which has imperial designs on the Middle East. We do not have to look far for such a power. Russia, especially as that nation's future is chronicled by Ezekiel, is surely the "Asshur" of the last days seen by Balaam. With callous indifference Russia will scourge nations friendly to Israel as well as nations that are foes of Israel. This, too, the prophet foresaw.

Balaam envisioned this nation "Asshur" scourging a people *hostile to Israel.* "And when he looked on Amalek, he took up his parable, and said, Amalek was the first of the nations, but his latter end shall be that he perish for ever" (Numbers 24:20).

The Amalekites were descended from Esau and were kin to the Edomites. They hated the Hebrews because they feared that the blessing that Jacob had stolen from Esau was about to be made good to the Israelites. Amalek is called "the first of the nations" because Amalek was the first nation to attack the Hebrews on their march toward Canaan. They treacherously fell on Israel at Rephidim, attacked the rear of the marching Hebrews, and smote all who were feeble when they were faint and weary because, as the Holy Spirit says, Amalek "feared not God" (Deuteronomy 25:18). The Lord declared war on Amalek "from generation to generation" (Exodus 17:16).

One of history's attempts to exterminate the Hebrew people was inspired by an Agagite (Amalakite) by the name of Haman (Esther 3). This same spirit of bitter antisemitism prevails in the Middle East today among the Arabs and, indeed, it is the one common bond they have. It is Arab hatred of Israel that gives Russia her foothold in the area. God might yet use Russia to thrash some of these Arab countries before overthrowing her in turn. Russia has no real love for the Arabs nor for their Islamic faith and sees them only as pawns in a larger game. In any case, Balaam sees a northern power he calls "Asshur" defeating certain nations hostile to Israel.

The prophet also envisioned this northern power scourging nations *helpful to Israel*. "And he looked on the Kenites, and he took up his parable, and said, Strong is thy dwellingplace, and thou puttest thy nest in a rock. Nevertheless the Kenite shall be wasted, until Asshur shall carry thee away captive" (Numbers 24:21-22).

The Kenites were always as friendly to Israel as the Moabites were hostile. Their origin is shrouded in obscurity. Jethro, the father-in-law of Moses, was a Kenite (Judges 1:16; 4:11) and is also described as a "priest of Midian" (Exodus 2:15-16), so the Kenites might have been a tribe of Midian. In this case they would be related to Israel as descendants of Abraham and Keturah (Genesis 25:2). The Kenites accompanied the Israelites in their wanderings. Hobab, the son of Reuel, was a Kenite; and he acted as a guide for Israel in the wilderness for a while. The Kenites were still associated with Israel at the time of Jericho's fall (Judges 1:16; 2 Chronicles 28:15). After Israel was settled in the land, the Kenites seem to have moved to the wilderness of Judea south of Arad near where the Amalekites dwelt.

Balaam, in viewing the Kenites, mentioned the strong security they enjoyed in their rocky fastness. Their capital appears to have been the cliff which rises perpendicularly from the western shore of the Dead Sea, about ten miles south of En-gedi, the spot where later the famous city of Massada was built.

The Kenites, then, stand for a people helpful to Israel, which in itself would be enough to ensure their suffering at the hand of a latter-day Assyrian. In a coming day, to lend a helping hand to a Jew will be a mark of infamy in the sight of the godless Jew-haters who are yet to rule most of mankind.

Balaam, then, foresaw the coming of a military power to dominate the Middle East in the last days, one that would brood ominously over the area from the north. This power would have as little concern for the welfare of the nations it uses as pawns as for those it is determined to sweep completely off the board. We have small trouble today seeing such a power in Russia.

In concluding his vision, Balaam saw also the coming of *a future maritime power* (Numbers 24:23-24). Again he paused to take another breath and look around him before bringing to an end this series of remarkable pronouncements concerning Israel.

He foresaw the coming of a maritime power that would be *initially useful* so that God will *employ* it. "And he took up his parable, and said, Alas, who shall live when God [*El*] doeth this! And ships shall come from the coast of Chittim, and shall afflict Asshur, and shall afflict Eber" (Numbers 24:23-24). Asshur, we have suggested, is a symbolic name for a great northern power; Eber is another name for the Hebrew people.

What Balaam sketchily foresaw was a coming clash between the western maritime powers (here called *Chittim*, originally a name for the island of Cyprus, but a name that came to include other lands bordering on the Mediterranean sea) and the great military power to the north. We know from Ezekiel 38 and 39 that the western powers under the antichrist will challenge Russia's coming invasion of Israel and that they will mobilize against Russia. This may be the confrontation Balaam dimly foresaw. If so, then Balaam's prophecy adds another detail to the picture we have in Scripture of the coming confrontation between Russia and the West. The Russian invasion of Israel will be swiftly countered by the naval forces of the West, which will inflict a notable defeat on the Russian naval forces.

But in the end this maritime power will be of little use to God; it will be just as treacherous and evil as the great northern power it will have replaced as the world's leading power. Balaam foresaw that this maritime power would be *intrinsically useless* so that God will *destroy* it: "And shall afflict Eber, and he also shall perish for ever" (Numbers 24:24).

Once Russia is overthrown, the antichrist will see his way clear to world power. He will tear up his seven-year pact with Israel, pull off his mask of friendliness, and inaugurate a worldwide bloodbath of persecution against the Hebrew people. This in turn will bring down on him the outpoured wrath of Israel's God so "he shall perish for ever." The return of Christ will bring to a swift end the treacherous career of the beast, and he and his false prophet will be flung headlong into the lake of fire.

Thus ends Balaam's remarkable prophecy of the latter days.

---

1. Shortly after it became a nation, Israel issued a set of commemorative stamps. Each stamp represented a tribe of Israel, and each tribe was depicted by a different ensign as suggested above. Some authorities, however, have thought that the various tribes had the signs of the zodiac as their ensigns, in keeping with Genesis 37:9-10.
2. See Phillips, *Exploring the World of the Jew.*

7

The Prophecies of Zechariah

T he prophet Zechariah was born in exile in Babylon. He was born of priestly stock, and like Jeremiah and Ezekiel, he was both a prophet and a priest. His father seems to have died in Babylon, so he is known as "the son of Iddo." Iddo was his grandfather.

Zechariah was one of the little band of repatriated Jews, some fifty thousand in all, who responded to the decree of Cyrus giving the exiled Jews the right to return to their native land and rebuild their ancestral home.

Zechariah was only a young man when he began to preach. He began his ministry in the second year of the Persian king Darius Hystapses (521-520 B.C.), two months after Haggai began to protest the carelessness of the Jews in letting the unfinished temple lie neglected while they themselves were busy building their own houses and fortunes. Like his companion prophet Haggai, Zechariah was concerned about the neglect of the temple. His visions, however, were of greater scope. He soared far beyond his own day, taking in the unfolding drama of the ages, to focus at length on the last days at the time of Christ's return.

His apocalyptic visions are complex and not easy to unravel. They are couched in highly symbolic language. His visions were all given to him in a single night. Although no attempt is made here to exhaust their meaning, it is important to our overview of unfulfilled Bible prophecy to have at least the gist of their meaning before us.

Here is a summary of Zechariah's visions in outline form.

I. God Sees (Zechariah 1:7-21)
  A. The four horses (1:7-17)
    1. The imperialist powers (1:7-11)
    2. The impassioned plea (1:12-17)
      a. The plight of Jerusalem (1:12)
      b. The pledge of Jehovah (1:13-17)
  B. The four horns (1:18-21)
    1. Gentile power displayed (1:18-19)
    2. Gentile power destroyed (1:20-21)
II. God Speaks (Zechariah 2:1–4:14)
  A. The matter of Israel's restoration (2:1-13)
    1. A question of perspective (2:1-5)
      a. Jerusalem about to be measured (2:1-2)
      b. Jerusalem about to be magnified (2:3-5)
    2. A question of priorities (2:6-7)
    3. A question of punishment (2:8-9)
    4. A question of privilege (2:10-13)
  B. The matter of Israel's righteousness (3:1-10)
    1. The converted priest (3:1-7)
    2. The coming prince (3:8-10)
  C. The matter of Israel's revival (4:1-14)
    1. The testimony restored to Israel (4:1-7)
    2. The temple rebuilt in Israel (4:8-10)
    3. The tribulation resolved for Israel (4:11-14)
III. God Stirs (Zechariah 5:1–6:15)
  A. Implicitly to convict (5:1-4)
    1. The mystery of the flying roll (5:1-2)
    2. The ministry of the flying roll (5:3-4)
  B. Impartially to condemn (5:5-11)
    1. The container (5:5-6)
    2. The cover (5:7)

3. The contents (5:7-8)
4. The carriers (5:9)
5. The comment (5:10-11)
C. Imperially to conquer (6:1-15)
1. The timely coming of the chariots (6:1-8)
2. The typical crowning of the Christ (6:9-15)

From this expository outline we can extract the ten visions of the prophet. They were the visions of:

1. The Four Horses (Zechariah 1:7-17)
2. The Four Horns (1:18-19)
3. The Four Carpenters (1:20-21)
4. The Man with the Measuring Line (2:1-13)
5. The High Priest, Joshua (3:1-7)
6. The Branch (3:8-10)
7. The Candlesticks and the Olive Trees (4:1-14)
8. The Flying Roll (5:1-4)
9. The Ephah (5:5-11)
10. The Four Chariots (6:1-8)

The prophet Zechariah had other prophecies to impart to Israel. We are focusing on these, however, because of their apocalyptic nature.

1. The Vision of the Four Horses (Zechariah 1:7-17)

Zechariah saw four horses standing among the myrtle trees on low-lying ground. The first horse was red; those behind it were red, speckled, and white. Attention is drawn especially to the rider on the first horse. When the prophet asked who these riders were, he was told that their mission was to ride through the world, survey the nations, and report back to the angel of Jehovah, who was seated on the first horse. Their report was simple. The nations were at rest.

The myrtle trees symbolized the nation of Israel. The myrtle is a beautiful ornamental plant native to the lands of Persia and Assyria, where the tribes of Israel were to be found dispersed. The vision sees Jerusalem downtrodden and Judah scattered. The nations are at rest, unconcerned about the plight of the Jewish people. The vision brings to the fore the Lord's anger at the nations that dispersed His people and His even greater anger at the Gentile powers because of their indifference toward the needs of the Jewish people. The prophet was consoled by the Lord's promise that He will "yet comfort Zion, and shall yet choose Jerusalem" (Zechariah 1:17).

2. *The Vision of the Four Horns (Zechariah 1:18-19)*

The prophet then saw four horns. That was all—just four horns. Intrigued, he asked the interpreting angel what they stood for. He was told they represented the four world empires that have scattered Israel. A horn in Scripture is frequently used as a symbol of power, particularly Gentile power. It derives its significance from the horns of bulls and wild beasts which have their strength in their horns. Exactly which four nations are thus symbolized is not altogether clear. Assyria, Egypt, Babylon, Persia, Greece, and Rome all rode roughshod over Israel. Assyria, Babylon, and Rome, particularly, scattered the Hebrew people.

3. *The Vision of the Four Carpenters (Zechariah 1:20-21)*

The vision of the four horns is closely associated with the vision of four carpenters (smiths or engravers) who are commissioned to "fray" the four horns and to cast them out. The carpenters (or craftsmen) symbolize the nations God used to overthrow the empires which had overthrown Israel. Commentator David Baron thinks that these four craftsmen represent Medo-Persia, which broke the horn of Babylon; Greece under Alexander the Great, which broke the power of Persia; Rome, which in turn put an end to Greek power in the world; and since he sees the fourth horn as Rome, reasserting itself in the endtimes under the leadership of Satan, the fourth craftsman is none other than the Lord Himself, who will suddenly appear at the end of the age to cut down this final manifestation of antisemitic Gentile world power.[1] Not for nothing was the Lord Jesus known as the carpenter.

162

4. *The Vision of the Man with the Measuring Line (Zechariah 2:1-13)*

In his fourth vision the prophet saw a man with a measuring line in his hand preparing to measure Jerusalem. Before he can get started, a messenger is sent to tell him that while the Jerusalem of that day might be small enough to be thus measured, the Jerusalem of the future would be spread out far beyond its present parochial bounds.

The vision signifies the certain restoration and blessing of Israel and Jerusalem. The enlargement of the Jerusalem of today is nothing compared with the glory that awaits this city during the millennial reign. In clearing up some of the points of the vision for the prophet, the Lord adds a warning for the nations: "He that toucheth you toucheth the apple [pupil] of his eye" (Zechariah 2:8). Woe betide those nations that launch offensives against Jerusalem.

5. *The Vision of the High Priest (Zechariah 3:1-7)*

In this vision the prophet saw Israel's high priest, Joshua, standing before the Lord in filthy garments, with Satan standing at his right hand to accuse him. Joshua's sad case was championed by the Lord, who called him "a brand plucked out of the fire" (Zechariah 3:2). He rebuked Satan, absolved Joshua, gave him a new robe and miter, and invested him with a new ministry.

Joshua symbolizes the nation of Israel in its moral and spiritual guilt, the persistent object of Satanic hatred and opposition, yet with a powerful champion on high. Israel is seen rescued from the fires of the Gentile world as "a brand plucked out of the fire." The vision anticipates the time when the nation's guilt will be cleansed and Israel will have restored to her her spiritual ministry to the nations of earth.

6. *The Vision of the Branch (Zechariah 3:8-10)*

The title *Branch* is used for Christ in the Old Testament in a fourfold way. He is called a Branch of David (Isaiah 11:1; Jeremiah

23:5) or the Branch (Jeremiah 33:15), which is just how we meet the Messiah in the Gospel of Matthew. There He is set forth as the rightful heir to David's throne. Matthew is essentially the Gospel of the King. The Lord calls Him "my servant the BRANCH" (Zechariah 3:8). This is how Christ is portrayed in Mark's Gospel, as God's perfect Servant, ever busy, ever bearing other people's burdens, giving His life first in service and then in sacrifice. He is called "the man whose name is The BRANCH" (Zechariah 6:12), which is how Christ is described in Luke's Gospel. Luke's emphasis was on the true and essential humanity of the Lord Jesus. He is called "the branch of the Lord" in Isaiah 4:2, and depicted that way in John's Gospel. In that Gospel His deity is emphasized, and He is seen as the One who is coequal and coeternal with the Father.

The refusal of the Jews to accept Jesus, presented to them in this fourfold way, as their rightful Messiah, blinded them to the fact that the promised Branch had come. But He is coming back, and when He does, the broken nation of Israel will at last recognize Jesus as Messiah. The nation will then be cleansed and will enter into millennial peace and prosperity. This is evident from the closing statement of the vision: "In that day, saith the Lord of hosts, shall ye call every man his neighbor under the vine and under the fig tree" (Zechariah 3:10). Israel will enjoy a time such as it has never known before, but that time of bliss and blessing is linked with its acceptance of Christ.

7. The Vision of the Candlesticks and the Olive Trees (Zechariah 4:1-14)

The prophet next saw a candelabra of gold fed by two adjacent olive trees, which assured it an endless supply of oil. We know from Revelation 11:3-12 that fulfillment of this vision lies in the future. It anticipates the day when God will send two witnesses to the nation, in the days of the beast, to minister in power to the people through the Holy Spirit. The vision had a partial fulfillment in the ministry of Joshua the priest and Zerubbabel the prince, the two leaders of the restored nation in the days of the prophet Zechariah.

Fulfillment of the vision is by no means exhausted by its initial and partial application to the day and age of the prophet, nor by its more complete fulfillment in the days of the coming two witnesses.

Ultimately, the vision anticipates the day when the nation of Israel will have its spiritual ministry restored to it and it will be a source of truth and light to all nations. That, of course, will not happen until the nation turns to Christ, its true priest-king.

8. *The Vision of the Flying Roll (Zechariah 5:1-4)*

The last three visions of Zechariah are of a different character from the first ones. The earlier visions were consolatory in character. But before the things promised for Israel can be fulfilled (victory over her foes, cleansing, restoration of priestly ministry, illumination for the nations), there must be a time when God will judge the nation for its sins.

This time the prophet saw "a flying roll." It was very large, as large as the holy place of the tabernacle, twenty cubits by ten (about thirty by fifteen feet), and it was unrolled. The flying roll contained a curse against thieves and perjurers. The middle commandment from each table of the Decalogue was selected, probably as a sample and summary of the whole. Israel had broken both sets of commandments, those enjoining duty toward God and those emphasizing duty toward man. A roll in Scripture is a symbol for the written Word. The vision sees the nation under the curse of the Law. In its ultimate fulfillment, the vision no doubt anticipates the coming day when God will judge the Jewish people during the time of the great tribulation.

9. *The Vision of the Ephah (Zechariah 5:5-11)*

The prophet next saw an ephah (the largest Hebrew dry measure), a container larger than a bushel. In this container sat a woman, sealed in by a weight on the mouth of the container. The prophet was expressly told that the woman symbolized wickedness. Two stork-winged women, with the wind in their wings, lifted up the ephah with its contents and carried it away to the land of Shinar (Babylon). There it was to be set down on its own pedestal.

The ephah, seen as a measure, symbolized wickedness come to the full and ready for judgment. In Scripture an unethical woman always symbolizes that which is religiously out of place. The church at Thyatira was corrupted by a woman (Revelation 2:20). The Babylonian phase of the apostate church is symbolized by a scarlet woman (Revelation 17:1-6).

The local application of Zechariah's vision is evident. The Jews in the land had been captives in Babylon. They had cleaned up some of their more obvious sins, such as idolatry. But in Babylon they had imbibed a commercial spirit and a love for financial gain, something previously foreign to them as a pastoral people. For the Jews of Zechariah's day, the vision symbolized God's judgment on their new Babylonianism.

Prophetically, the vision sees sin being returned to the place from which it originally spread to contaminate the earth. We learn from Revelation 18 and elsewhere that Babylon as a city is to be rebuilt. It is to become the vanity fair of the antichrist's world empire and the economic and financial capital of the world. Symbolically sin is sent back there to be judged. When the beast has destroyed the apostate religious system centered in Rome, he will turn his thoughts eastward and eventually will center all his efforts at Babylon. The religious sins of Rome will be carried back to Babylon. Babylon will again become the sin capital of the world. Its judgment is the theme of Revelation 18.

10. The Vision of the Four Chariots (Zechariah 6:1-8)

Finally, the prophet saw four chariots come into sight from between two mountains of brass. He was told they represented the four spirits of Heaven. The chariots were drawn by four horses. As in the first vision in the series, they were horses of varying color— red, black, white, grizzled, and bay. While different points of the compass were the destinations of these chariots, special mention is made of the North. Special judgment was reserved for the North, and God's Spirit is said to have been quieted once that particular judgment was accomplished.

The vision turns our attention to God's judgment on the nations. The prophet was to be assured that the reestablishment of order and peace in Israel, guaranteed by the earlier visions, would not again be disturbed by the nations of earth which had so long molested and oppressed the Jewish people.

The chariots symbolize power and authority, and the four

166

points of the compass tell us that God's judgment is to be universal. The two mountains from which they come probably symbolize mount Zion and the mount of Olives, between which lies the valley of Jehoshaphat, where the final judgment of the nations prior to the millennium is to take place. The mountains are said to be of brass, because brass is a Bible symbol for judgment. The four spirits with whom the chariots are identified remind us of the cherubim and their "wheels" seen by the prophet Ezekiel (Ezekiel 1:4-28). The cherubim certainly have something to do with upholding God's claims, especially as those claims have to do with the earth.

The chariot drawn by the black horses was sent to the North, and the chariot drawn by the white horses followed. The chariot drawn by the grizzled horses went to the South. In Zechariah's day, the north stood for Babylon and the south for Egypt. Two teams were sent to the North. Something about the wickedness and oppression located in the North especially stirred the Spirit of God. Perhaps the twofold mention of the North refers, first, to the nation of Russia as the world center of atheism, God-hate, antisemitism, and opposition to Israel. Second, it may refer to the city of Babylon itself, as rebuilt by antichrist and made the center of global hatred of God. In any case, the twofold judgment on the North brings quietness to the Spirit of God.

Thus end the visions seen by Zechariah. He added a footnote. Joshua the high priest was symbolically crowned and enthroned. Since the Old Testament forbad the merging of the offices of king and priest, the crowning had to be symbolic. As Zechariah soon learned, the action pointed to the coming of Christ as the true priest-king and as the One who would rebuild the temple for the millennial reign. "And this shall come to pass" is the concluding word of assurance given to the prophet (Zechariah 6:15).

---

1. David Baron, *Visions and Prophecies of Zechariah* (London: Hebrew Christian Testimony to Israel, 1918), p. 46.

8

The Olivet Discourse
Matthew 24–25

The prophecies given by the Lord Jesus on the mount of Olives just before He went to Calvary must be regarded as among the most important utterances He ever made. Jerusalem and the temple complex lay before Him, the whole city already under divine sentence. The Lord had just told His disciples that Herod's magnificent temple, then still under construction, was to be so reduced to rubble that not one stone would be left standing on another. This statement prompted their questions as to when that would happen, when the end of the age would come, and what signs could be anticipated as heralds of the last days.

In recording the Lord's answer Matthew leapt over the details of the impending destruction of Jerusalem by the Romans and concentrated on what the Lord had to say about the endtimes. Here is a summary outline of this important prophecy.

I. A Prophetic View of the Last Days (Matthew 24)
A. Great troubles foretold (24:1-14)
1. Difficult problems foreseen (24:4-8)

      a. National disasters (24:4-7)
         (1) Messianic creeds (24:4-5)
         (2) Military conflicts (24:6-7)
      b. Natural disasters (24:7-8)
         (1) Drought
         (2) Disease
         (3) Destruction
   2. Dreadful persecutions foreseen (24:9-10)
      a. The emphasis on brutality (24:9)
      b. The emphasis on betrayal (24:10)
   3. Deceiving prophets foreseen (24:11-12)
      a. Numerous (24:11)
      b. Iniquitous (24:12)
   4. Dynamic preaching foreseen (24:13-14)
      a. The call to endure (24:13)
      b. The call to evangelize (24:14)
B. Great tribulation foretold (24:15-36)
   1. The wanton sin of the last days (24:15-26)
      a. The flight of the saints (24:15-20)
      b. The fury of the superman (24:21-22)
      c. The folly of the sinner (24:23-26)
   2. The welcome sight of the last days (24:27-31)
      a. The tribulation will end (24:27-29)
         (1) Swiftly (24:27)
         (2) Surely (24:28)
         (3) Solemnly (24:29)
      b. The truth will dawn (24:30)
      c. The trumpet will sound (24:31)
   3. The warning sign of the last days (24:32-36)
      a. A word of comparison (24:32-33)
      b. A word of confirmation (24:34-35)
      c. A word of caution (24:36)
C. Great testings foretold (24:37-51)
   1. The character of the endtimes (24:27-41)
      a. An appeal to the days of Noah (24:37)
      b. An appraisal of the days of Noah (24:38-39)
      c. An application of the days of Noah (24:39-41)
   2. The challenge of the endtimes (24:42-51)
      a. Be watchful (24:45-47)
      b. Be wise (24:48-51)

c. Be warned (24:48-51)
    (1) The evil servant's deeds (24:48-49)
    (2) The evil servant's doom (24:50-51)
II. A Parabolic View of the Last Days (Matthew 25)
  A. A marriage and its guests (25:1-13)
  The Wise and Foolish Virgins
    1. The marriage call (25:1-5)
      a. The heavenly groom (25:1)
      b. The Holy Ghost (25:2-5)
        (1) A serious neglect concerning the oil
        (2) A sad neglect concerning the bridegroom
    2. The midnight cry (25:6-10)
      a. The arousal of the guests (25:6-9)
      b. The arrival of the groom (25:10)
    3. The mistaken claim (25:11-12)
  B. A merchant and his gains (25:14-30)
  The Talents
    1. A time of responsibility (25:14-30)
    The Master's trust
      a. Solemnly bestowed (25:14-15)
      b. Surely believed (25:16-17)
      c. Sadly betrayed (25:18)
    2. A time of reckoning (25:19-30)
      a. The faithful servants (25:19-23)
        (1) Their work reviewed (25:19,20,22)
        (2) Their work rewarded (25:21,23)
      b. The faithless servant (25:24-30)
        (1) His confession (25:24-25)
        (2) His condemnation (25:26-30)
  C. A Monarch and His grace (25:31-46)
  The Sheep and the Goats
    1. The throne (25:31)
    2. The throngs (25:32-33)
      a. The Hebrew people
      b. The heathen peoples
    3. The thrill (25:34-46)
      a. Of happiness: grace received (25:34-40)
        (1) Their standing (25:34-36)
        (2) Their surprise (25:37-39)
        (3) Their salvation (25:40)

    b. Of horror: grace refused (25:41-43)
      (1) Their curse (25:41-43)
      (2) Their complaint (25:44)
      (3) Their condemnation (25:45-46)

This structural analysis shows how comprehensive and detailed the Olivet discourse is. The Lord Jesus gathered together the various threads of Old Testament end-time prophecies, added to them strands from His omniscient insights, and wove an overall pattern of truth. All later New Testament prophetic teaching rests on this discourse. For instance, the happenings under the seal judgments (Revelation 6) follow closely the pattern of Matthew 24:1-14.

THE PROPHECIES (MATTHEW 24)

The Jewish temple was one of the unsung wonders of the world. Herod had spent a fortune embellishing and beautifying it. The sinking sun, dipping behind the ramparts of Zion, would flood the marble walls and golden pinnacles with its afterglow until the whole gleaming edifice burned and blazed upon Moriah's brow like a glittering diadem.

But to Jesus, who could see A.D. 70 as well as A.D. 33, the setting sun would seem to bathe that temple in blood and fire. His knowledge of the temple's coming destruction at the hands of the Romans prompted His remark to the disciples that not one of its stones should be left on another. The disciples then asked the Lord three questions: "When shall these things be? and what shall be the sign of thy coming, and of the end of the world?" (Matthew 24:3) In response to those questions Christ foretold not only the immediate destruction of Jerusalem, but also passed on to a full-length discussion of end-time events.

Great Troubles Foretold (Matthew 24:1-14)

The Lord Jesus began His sermon by underlining some of the *difficult problems* of the last days (Matthew 24:4-8). He warned, first, that false messiahs would appear upon the scene leading many astray. It is an interesting fact that no false prophets surfaced among the Jews until after the Jewish national rejection of Jesus as Messiah. Thereafter a remarkable flock of them appeared, some of them odd characters indeed, and none of them at all resembling the Messiah foretold in the Old Testament Scriptures.[1]

Here, however, the focus is on the last days and on the end-time messianic movements. We are living in such a day. Hitler, for example, was a false messiah, as we will show in chapter 10 of this study. His hypnotic voice swept a nation into mass hysteria, antisemitism, and war. His speeches were spellbinding. Strong men would moan aloud, and women would burst into tears. He was able to brainwash and browbeat a whole nation. He inspired in many a fanatical loyalty that survived even his death.

Karl Marx was a false messiah—a bearded, angry, Jewish prophet, fired by an immense hatred of God, of Christianity, and of Judaism. Even devout Marxists admit that his work *Das Kapital* is difficult to understand and that Marx was often obscure and at times incomprehensible. Yet much of the human race has been influenced by Marxism's vitriolic atheism and virile materialism.

The abandonment by the West of its traditional Bible-based values in favor of secularism and permissiveness, has left an enormous spiritual vacuum in the world. The West has no message for the masses of mankind, and the void is being filled by all kinds of false religions, cults, and messianic appeals. What we are seeing today is only the beginning. After the rapture of the church, diabolical philosophies will take swift root, the devil's own messiah will appear, and people will rush to embrace what the Holy Spirit calls "a lie" (2 Thessalonians 2:11).

The last days, Jesus proclaimed, would be marked not only by the proliferation of messianic creeds but also by the dramatic increase in military conflicts. "Ye shall hear of wars and rumours of wars . . . but the end is not yet" (Matthew 24:6). That brief statement embraced the countless conflicts of history from Christ's day down to modern times.

The last days, however, will be heralded by a significant change in the character of war. It will assume a global aspect. "For nation shall rise against nation, and kingdom against kingdom" (Matthew 24:7). Up until the turn of this century, wars were fought army against army; even the Napoleonic wars were relatively limited in size and scope. Now we mobilize whole nations and empires, fight war on a worldwide scale, and call it "total war." Two such wars have already been fought in this century and these, terrible as they were in themselves, are nothing compared with what lies ahead. The book of Revelation mentions at least five future wars, two of them of almost unbelievable dimensions.

Along with these national disasters, the Lord Jesus foretold natural disasters. "And there shall be famines, and pestilences, and earthquakes, in divers places. All these are the beginning of sorrows" (Matthew 24:7-8).

The shadow of famine already lies heavy across the world. Half the world goes to bed hungry. Almost all the 3.6 billion acres of economically cultivable land is under the plow. Each year it takes about 1.2 billion metric tons of grain to supply the world's minimum demands. The problem of the world's starving millions is aggravated by the fact that most of the world's peoples live in its poorest countries.

Other factors compound the problem. Climatologists are hinting darkly at changing weather conditions that could bring disastrous droughts to the world's most heavily populated areas. Increasing water shortage, expanding deserts, and the skyrocketing price of energy and petroleum-based fertilizers all point to the inevitability of famines gripping much of the world by the end of the century.[2]

Along with spreading famine conditions, the Lord Jesus pointed to the outbreak of pestilence as another end-time factor (Matthew 24:7). We have made tremendous strides in eliminating such diseases as plague and polio. However, overuse of antibiotics and sulfa drugs has resulted in new drug-resistant bacteria, some of which can withstand several antibiotics at once. Some diseases such as AIDS have defied attempts by modern medical scientists to find a cure.

Worse still, scientists today are experimenting with DNA, the molecular compound that embodies the genetic codes that cells use to sustain and reproduce themselves. In one experiment scientists are combining segments of DNA of the bacterium *E. coli (Escherichia coli)* with segments of DNA from plants, animals, and other bacteria just to see what happens. They hope such experiments will lead to cures for cancer, diabetes, and similar diseases. But what if they produce something harmful to the human race, and what if it escapes from the laboratory, and what if it runs like a plague through the world?

Not content with these things, the superpowers are stockpiling chemical and bacterial weapons against the day of war. Such weapons certainly exist and, according to the U. S. State Department, have already been used by Russia in Indochina and Afghanistan. Formal charges have been laid against the Soviets for at least 432 attacks with these horrible weapons.

Along with famine and pestilence, Jesus included earthquakes as another indication of the approach of the end. Earthquakes have always rumbled their way through the earth. But they seem to be increasing. Certainly we are more aware of them than ever before and certainly, too, giant modern cities make us far more vulnerable than ever before.

Seismologists have mapped out the major areas of the planet most prone to earthquakes. They occur most regularly along nearly all of the western coastline of the Americas, in parts of Europe, throughout the Middle East and central and eastern Asia, throughout all of New Zealand, and in extensive areas of the Atlantic and Pacific. Maps show that earthquake zones coincide for the most part with the rift systems of the ocean floor, with the island archipelagoes, and with the major mountain systems of the planet. Eighty percent of the really big quakes occur within the so-called "ring of fire" that encircles the Pacific ocean.

Most Americans live in areas where earthquakes could erupt, the areas of greatest danger being Los Angeles, San Francisco, and Salt Lake City. The United States Geological Survey actually labeled the year 1976 as the year when earthquake activity in the world took on new significance.

The disastrous 1989 earthquake in San Francisco again brought to the forefront of the news the vulnerability of cities built on fault lines. Seismologists warn that Los Angeles is actually far more vulnerable than San Francisco. Moreover, Los Angeles has not suffered a major earthquake in this century and is due for one. The Federal Emergency Management Agency has warned that an earthquake registering 8.3 on the scale (sixteen times as powerful as the one that hit San Francisco) occurring on the southern San Andreas fault near Los Angeles, could cause anywhere from 3,000 to 14,000 deaths. Los Angeles sits on three fault lines, any of which could produce a devastating earthquake.

Having underlined some of the difficult problems that would mark the endtimes, the Lord Jesus then spoke of the *dreadful persecutions* of the last days (Matthew 24:9-10). We seem to have already entered the age of persecution, an age heralded by terrible atrocities committed against the Jews, Slavs, and other peoples by the Nazis. Their cruelties, however, are only the beginning. According to one estimate the communists, in their drive to dominate the world, have already killed more than eighty-three million people. Spread out a map of Central and South America. Shade in all the Spanish-speaking countries from Guatemala to the southernmost tip of the continent. Then envision every person in those countries being systematically murdered, and that will give some idea of the blood-guilt of the communist powers.

According to the Lord, two kinds of persecution will mark the endtimes. There will be, first, persecutions marked by *brutality*. "Then shall they deliver you up to be afflicted, and shall kill you: and ye shall be hated of all nations for my name's sake" (Matthew 24:9). In this summary the Lord did not, apparently, take in the persecutions that arise against political and intellectual dissidents such as those described by Alexander Solzhenitsyn. Jesus emphasized, rather, persecutions directed against His own people, those who will suffer for His "name's sake."

For the first three hundred years of its history, the church faced bitter persecution. The persecutions instigated by Nero were so terrible that almost immediately after his death rumors began to circulate that he was to return to earth in the last days as the antichrist. Christians were crucified, sewn up in the skins of animals, and tossed to mad dogs in the arena. They were covered with pitch, nailed to posts of pine, and then ignited to serve as torches for the amusement of the mob.

The prophecy of Jesus, however, focuses on the last days. The real age of martyrs is still ahead. The fierce purpose of the antichrist will be to exterminate from the earth all who have any vestige of a testimony for God. Gentiles will suffer along with Jews, but the real hatred of the beast will be directed toward the Jewish people.

Satan has had a number of dress rehearsals for this coming age of savage persecution, one of them in our own days. The horrors of Dachau, Treblinka, Belsen, Auschwitz, Ravensbrueck, and a score of similar extermination camps show us what the coming age will be like.

Second, the Lord indicated there would be persecutions marked by *betrayal.* "Then shall many...betray one another, and shall hate one another" (Matthew 24:10). Nowhere has this coming nightmare been more terribly illustrated than in the attempt made by the communists in China to eliminate the church.

After communism came to power in China, the leaders of the church were assembled and told that communism was not opposed to Christianity, just to foreign missionaries who were really imperialist agents. The missionaries were told to leave, and their departure was made as difficult and as embarrassing as possible. Thus a century of Protestant missionary work in China came to an end. Church leaders were forced to sever all ties with what the communists called "foreign imperialists" so that the church in China might be independent: self-governing, self-supporting, and self-propagating. Also, all "imperialist poison" was to be purged from church doctrine.

Then came the campaigns of intimidation. Vast meetings were convened at which Christian leaders were accused, terrorized, brainwashed, and forced to comply with the party's will. Converts accused their teachers; children accused their parents. Only when a denomination had successfully passed through this purging process could it be licensed as a "reform church." Then all home meetings and private gatherings were banned. The church, by then thoroughly cowed and cooperative, was enlisted to promote the "Great Leap Forward." There could be no more Sunday services. Everyone had to help China achieve her goals, and that meant ceaseless work supplemented by massive doses of communist propaganda. The visible church in China ceased to exist. It was wiped out by betrayals.

The Lord next turned His attention to the *deceiving prophets* of the last days (Matthew 24:11-12). First, He indicated that they would be numerous. "And many false prophets shall rise, and shall deceive many" (24:11). He had already warned of the coming of false messiahs; now He warns of the coming of false prophets too. Deception after deception will come until, at length, the false messiah himself will arrive together with the false prophet (Revelation 13). All lesser deceptions will then be swallowed up in this final global deception (2 Thessalonians 2).

These false prophets will be iniquitous as well as numerous. "And because iniquity shall abound, the love of many shall wax cold" (Matthew 24:12). Just how iniquitous latter-day cults can be is obvious everywhere in contemporary society, but the case of Jim Jones and his "cult of death" is surely one of the most blatant examples. We can still see the pictures which made the front pages of magazines and filled our television screens: the great tub containing the cyanide, the empty cartons and bottles of poison, and, above all, the corpses lying everywhere, fully clothed, strewn in all positions. It was just a sample of what a false prophet can do to people disillusioned by the materialism, secularism, and futility of modern times.

Along with those great troubles, however, Jesus gives us a glimpse of the *dynamic preaching* of the last days (Matthew 24:13-14). Jesus said that the "gospel of the kingdom" must be preached to "all nations." Then "the end" will come. He added, "He that shall endure unto the end, the same shall be saved." The context is important in understanding this. The preaching referred to here is end-time preaching. It is not the gospel of grace that is to be preached, but the gospel of the kingdom—the good news that the millennial kingdom is at hand. The key words in this statement are the words *saved* and *the end*.

The word for "saved" is *sozo*, the most common word for salvation in the New Testament. In its usual sense it means to be saved from death and judgment, from the consequences of sin; but it also means to be saved from danger, loss, or destruction. The context must determine the meaning. Here the context is evidently the coming great tribulation; so the word can legitimately be rendered "delivered" in the sense of being saved out of the horrors of that coming age. Those who endure to the end of it will be saved out of it by the return of Christ.

The word for "end" is *telos*, which denotes the actual end. This takes us back to the beginning of this discourse and one of the questions the disciples asked the Lord. "What shall be the sign of . . . the end of the world?" (Matthew 24:3) The Lord at once described some of the preliminary happenings of the last days but indicated that these things were but "the beginning of sorrows" (24:8), adding, "but the end [*telos*, the very end] is not yet" (24:6). Many more things must happen. The image of the beast must be set up in the rebuilt temple. The great tribulation must come. The gospel of the kingdom must be preached in all the world. This is the gospel that will be preached after the rapture of the church. Millions will be saved after that event, but while they will not be in the church, they will be in the kingdom. This gospel will be preached by the 144,000 sealed witnesses (Revelation 7). These zealous Jewish evangelists will reap a worldwide harvest; many hungry, frightened hearts will be longing for some message of hope, peace, salvation, and deliverance from the wrath to come. These converts will pay a fearful price for their faith, because the antichrist will wreak his vengeance on them as well as on the Jewish people.

Great Tribulation Foretold (Matthew 24:15-36)

In much that He had to say in this section of His prophecy, the Lord assumed that those who pay attention to Him have a working knowledge of the Old Testament prophetic Scriptures, especially the prophecies of Daniel. Let us take a moment to sketch in the main events between the rapture and the return. First, there will come a rapid deterioration in world affairs, climaxing in a universal longing for some kind of superman to come and bring order out of chaos. Satan will produce the antichrist who, having united the West and overseen the demise of Russia, will bring the world under his sway. At this point he will seize the rebuilt Jewish temple in Jerusalem and convert it into a pagan shrine dedicated to himself and the worship of Satan. He will install in the temple an image of himself and demand that all mankind worship it and him. The refusal of many Jews and their Gentile converts to comply will result in a blood bath of persecution known as the great tribulation. This is what the Lord next underlined in His discourse.

He mentioned *the wanton sin* of the endtimes. "When ye therefore shall see the ABOMINATION OF DESOLATION [i.e., the image of the beast], spoken of by Daniel the prophet, stand in the holy place . . . flee" (Matthew 24:15-16). As the first Gentile world ruler, Nebuchadnezzar, made his great image and summoned his subjects to fall down before it, so this last Gentile world ruler will do the same. History will have come full circle. As Antiochus Epiphanes desecrated the temple and set up a God-defying idol there, so the antichrist will do the same. History will have come yet another complete circle.

The installation of the beast's image in the temple will be the signal for the great tribulation to begin. The Lord urged instant flight. "Let them which be in Judaea flee into the mountains: Let him which is on the housetop not come down to take any thing out of his house: Neither let him which is in the field return back to take his clothes" (Matthew 24:16-18). The hour will be one of desperate urgency. All avenues of escape will swiftly close; to rush back into the house just to pick up a few things will make all the difference between safety or doom. "Woe unto them that are with child . . . pray ye that your flight be not . . . on the sabbath day" (24:19-20). Thus the Lord underscored the need for immediate flight from the cities and into the wilds. Just to escape will be hard enough, but to be cumbered by pregnancy or religious scruples will be fatal.

> For then shall be great tribulation, such as was not since the beginning of the world to this time, no, nor ever shall be. And except those days should be shortened, there should no flesh be saved: but for the elect's sake those days shall be short-ened (Matthew 24:21-22).

We know from other Scriptures that the great tribulation will last exactly 1,260 days. We must not confuse ordinary persecution with the great tribulation. Tribulation has been the lot of God's people on this planet ever since Cain murdered Abel. The great tribulation is a special period, marked off in the counsels of God, when Satan will be allowed to rule the planet and when God will pour out His vials of wrath on mankind. It is preeminently Jewish in character and is called elsewhere "the time of Jacob's trouble" (Jeremiah 30:7). During this period God will be dealing in judgment with all the nations, but especially with the nation of Israel because of its persistent, age-long rejection of Jesus.

The choices facing men will be terrible: refuse to worship the beast and his image and to wear his mark, and be slain; worship the beast's image and receive his mark, and be eternally damned. The alternative will be to flee and hide until the return of Christ at the end of the 1,260 days.

To lure people out into the open, Satan will dazzle the world with spectacular false signs. There will be persistent rumors that Christ has returned. The Lord therefore warned:

> Then if any man shall say unto you, Lo, here is Christ, or there; believe it not. For there shall arise false Christs, and false

prophets, and shall shew great signs and wonders; insomuch that, if it were possible, they shall deceive the very elect (Matthew 24:23-24).

The Lord then told how this terrible period of persecution will end. He mentioned *the welcome sight* of the endtimes, the sight of the Lord's returning with signs and in splendor from the sky. Swiftly, surely, and solemnly the end will come (Matthew 24:27-29). There will be no mistaking *this* sign. It will be in a blaze of splendor like lightning flashing from east to west across the face of heaven. In anticipation, vultures will gather to feed on the carcasses of those to be slain at Armageddon. All nature will be convulsed as the sun is darkened, the moon is veiled in blackness, and stars fall from heaven. Awesome signs like these will be in a category apart from the magic tricks of Satan and the beast. No false messiah this, with lying signs, but Christ Himself, with signs enough to convince His trembling people waiting in their hideouts.

As the tribulation ends, the truth dawns. "And then shall appear the sign of the Son of man in heaven: and then shall all the tribes of the earth mourn, and they shall see the Son of man coming in the clouds of heaven with power and great glory" (Matthew 24:30). Our Lord comes not now as "the carpenter's son," as they had referred to Him before, but in a robe of shimmering light, ablaze with that glory He had with His Father before the worlds began. The truth will dawn at last. The Bible was right all along. The gospel is true. Jesus is the Son of God. But for many the truth will dawn too late. Their bodies are already branded for Hell with the mark of the beast.

Then the trumpet sounds. "And he shall send his angels with a great sound of a trumpet, and they shall gather together his elect from the four winds, from one end of heaven to the other" (Matthew 24:31). The trumpet blast will herald the commemoration of the true feast of trumpets anticipated so long in Israel's annual feasts (Leviticus 23:23-25).

At this point the Lord paused to give *the warning sign* of the endtimes (Matthew 24:32-36). The sign that all these things are about to happen is the sign of the fig tree. Shortly before, the Lord had cursed a literal fig tree in the only judgment miracle He ever performed. From all outward appearance the fig tree He had passed that day on His way from Bethany to Jerusalem was fair and flourishing. Properly tended, we are told, the fig tree is the most prolific of trees. Its fruit appears before its leaves, and a healthy tree often has plenty of fruit from the previous season on its boughs. From a distance this tree gave every promise of fruit, but it was a lie, a fraud. All it had was leaves. Like Adam in the garden, it covered its nakedness with leaves and, like Adam, it was ripe for judgment. So the Lord cursed it.

That evening on the way back from the city He passed that tree again. It had already withered away. Its Creator had looked on it with disfavor, and it had shriveled and died. "Now learn a parable of the fig tree," Jesus said. "When his branch is yet tender, and putteth forth leaves, ye know that summer is nigh: So likewise ye, when ye shall see all these things, know that it is near, even at the doors" (Matthew 24:32-33).

That fig tree symbolized the nation of Israel. The Lord had come to the nation looking for fruit, but all He found was outward show, a worldly claim to be "Abraham's seed." The nation's religious life had degenerated so far that the annual feasts of the Lord were styled "feasts of the Jews." The temple was called "the Jews' temple." The faith imparted by divine decree to this favored people had become "the Jews' religion." Even worse, its leaders were actively planning His murder. So He withdrew His blessing from the nation and endorsed the curse they were about to call down on their own heads (Matthew 27:25).

Within a generation the Roman war burst on the nation, Roman legions marched across the land, Jerusalem was taken, and the temple was engulfed in flames. It was the beginning of the end. A further revolt and then the Bar Kochba rebellion saw the final dissolution of the nation. From then until recent times the Jews were a stateless people.

But now the nation of Israel has been reborn, and its people have begun to return. Moreover, as the parable of the fig tree implies, they are going back in unbelief. The nation is putting forth the leaves of national, economic, political, social, and religious life, but it is still Christ-rejecting and still unbelieving. It is one of the most significant signs of our times.

The Lord drove home the lesson. "So . . . when ye shall see all these things, know that it is near, even at the doors" (Matthew 24:33). There is hardly a nation on the face of the earth where the receding tide of Hebrew national life has not left its flotsam and jetsam of Jewish people. Again and again the surging waves of the great Gentile sea have washed this people from land to land. They have been cast here, picked up and dropped down there, strangers in foreign lands, at times desperately trying to preserve their Jewishness and at other times longing to be assimilated by the lands of their adoption. Now the tide has turned; and although the flood has not yet set in, and probably will not until after the return of Christ, the sea is returning the Jews to the shore from which they came and where they rightfully belong.

The Lord followed up His sign of the fig tree with a challenging word: "Verily I say unto you, This generation shall not pass, till all these things be fulfilled. Heaven and earth shall pass away, but my words shall not pass away" (Matthew 24:34-35).

We must now note the closing verses of Matthew 23, which led us directly into the prophetic discourse in Matthew 24. The Lord had been pouring out His woes on the leaders of Israel for their rejection of Him as their Messiah. Hear His words:

> Ye serpents, ye *generation* of vipers, how can ye escape the damnation of hell? Wherefore, behold, I send unto you prophets, and wise men, and scribes: and some of them ye shall kill and crucify; and some of them shall ye scourge in your synagogues and persecute them from city to city: That *upon you* may come all the righteous blood shed upon the earth, from the blood of righteous Abel unto the blood of Zacharias son of Barachias [the first and last martyrs in the Jewish Bible], whom ye slew between the temple and the altar. Verily I say unto you, *All these things* shall come upon *this generation* (Matthew 23:33-36, italics added).

The Lord then mourned over Jerusalem and said: "Behold, your house is left unto you desolate. For I say unto you, Ye shall not see me henceforth, till ye shall say, BLESSED IS HE THAT COMETH IN THE NAME OF THE LORD" (Matthew 23:38-39). Thus ends Matthew 23, and the Olivet discourse follows immediately in chapter 24.

Reading Matthew 24, we come to a repetition of the words "all these things" and "this generation." Obviously we must interpret the expressions in one place the same as in the other place. This contextual parallel shows first that Jesus, having no more to say to the Jews of His day, handed the nation over to judgment. In

Matthew 23 the expressions referred to the specific generation on whose head would come the blood of all the martyrs. And, sure enough, that generation witnessed the Roman war, the destruction of the temple, and an end to Jewish religious and most of Jewish national life in Palestine. Literally and historically, the generation *to which* He was speaking lived to see "all these things" begin.

In Matthew 24 the parallel expressions must be handled the same way; only in Matthew 24 the focus is not on the generation to which He was speaking, a generation which has long since passed away, but on the generation *of which* He was speaking, namely the generation that would witness the budding of the fig tree and the rebirth of Jewish national life in Palestine.

There can be little doubt that our generation is the generation that has witnessed the budding of the fig tree, the rebirth of the state of Israel, and the beginning of "all these things" which form the body of the prophecy. The shadows of the coming apocalyptical age lie thick and heavy on our generation, and we can read in them the heralding of the return of Christ and the consequent consummation of the age.

But we must be careful. Jesus warned, "But of that day and hour knoweth no man, no, not the angels of heaven, but my Father only" (Matthew 24:36). This puts an end to all speculation about the date of His return. The Lord told us just what to look for but firmly forbade guessing as to the actual date. To estimate how many years comprise a "generation" and to fix a starting point for a calculation based on the date of Israel's actual rebirth as a nation and hence to speculate approximately how long we have left is forbidden. The things spoken of by the Lord in this chapter have begun to be; so our generation can now pass off the scene. That is as far as we can go. The signs are for us to see; the seasons are hidden from us.

Great Testings Foretold (Matthew 24:37-51)

The Lord now spoke of *the character* of the endtimes (Matthew 24:37-41) and used the days of Noah as an illustration of what these times will be like. They will duplicate exactly conditions as they were in Noah's day. Later in this study we will take a careful look at the days of Enoch which, of course, were essentially those of

Noah, so we shall not describe those days here. Suffice it to say that in seven particulars the "days of Noah" as described in Genesis 4–6 are identical to our own days.

It was a time of spiritual decline, so much so that the true faith had almost vanished from the earth. There can be no doubt that people today in general have little regard for God. One Gallup poll, for instance, examined the impact of religion in various parts of the modern world. Less than ten percent of the people of Japan, Germany, France, or Great Britain thought that religion was an important factor in life; less than two people out of every five in France, Germany, and Scandinavia said they believed in God.

The "days of Noah" were days of social dilemma marked by a rapid rise in the world's population and a corresponding increase in crime. The outstanding feature of the age was social permissiveness, personal corruption of life, and widespread violence.

They were days of shameless depravity, characterized especially by polygamy and pornography. "Every imagination of the thoughts of . . . [men's hearts] was only evil continually" (Genesis 6:5).

They were days of scientific development with great strides being made in art, technology, and engineering. The descendants of Cain had discovered the art of smelting, for instance, and were changing the whole structure of life on this planet. The scientific advancement of our age is evident everywhere. The trip of *Voyager 2* to the planet Saturn is a case in point. The craft traveled for four years across 1.24 billion miles of space and arrived for its meeting with the planet only three seconds late and only 41 miles off course. It raced toward its rendezvous at 54,000 miles an hour, came within a hair of Saturn's clouds and then, like a stone from a slingshot, was sent off on a new course toward Uranus, propelled by the power of Saturn's gravity.

They were days of strong delusion. Jesus said of the people of Noah's day that they "knew not" until the flood came and took them all away (Matthew 24:38-39). The one feature of Noah's day the Lord chose to emphasize in this connection was the preoccupation of the antediluvians with material things. Theirs was a materialistic society and also a society probing deeper and deeper into occult mysteries—all of which are marked features of our age.

They were days of some devotion, however, since God never leaves Himself without a witness. Indeed, the more degenerate the times, the more definite the testimony. In an apostate age, God's witness to Himself invariably takes the form of faithful preaching on one hand and fulfilled prophecy on the other. The days of Noah were no exception; Noah was "a preacher of righteousness" (2 Peter 2:5) and so was Enoch. Noah's preaching was backed by "signs," notably by the gathering of the animals into the ark and the death of Methuselah. Methuselah's father was the prophet Enoch. The name he gave to Methuselah was a vivid prophecy: "When he dies, it shall come." When Methuselah died, it (the flood) did indeed come.

Finally, the days of Noah were days of sudden destruction. It would seem that God set a limit of 120 years on His patience in Noah's day. When the time ran out, His Spirit ceased to strive with man, and the restrainer having stepped aside, the judgment fell. Just so today, the day of grace is ebbing fast away and the day of judgment is about to burst on the world.

Having given us His appraisal of the days of Noah, the Lord made His application:

> For as in the days that were before the flood they . . . knew not until the flood came, and took them all away; so shall also the coming of the Son of man be. Then shall two be in the field; the one shall be taken, and the other left. Two women shall be grinding at the mill; the one shall be taken, and the other left (Matthew 24:38-41).

Controversy rages over His statement. Some believe it refers to the rapture, when saved ones will be snatched away and the rest of mankind left behind for judgment. Others are convinced that the end-time judgment is in view, when the Lord will return to earth and take all unbelievers out of it. The strength of this latter view is entirely contextual, the "taking away" being directly linked with that of the previous verse, where in Noah's day the lost were taken away in judgment. The contextual argument is convincing and has its powerful champions. But, on the other hand, so is the etymological argument of those who see in this "taking away" a reference to the rapture of the church.

In Matthew 24:39 the word translated as "took" is *airo*—"the flood came, and *took* them all away." It is a word that suggests taking away in violence, which is just what happened at the flood.

185

Having used this word, the Lord dropped it and changed to a different one, *paralambanomai* (Matthew 24:40-41). This word is also sometimes used in an adverse way, but it is frequently used in a tender way in the New Testament. The margin of the *Companion Bible* gives the primary meaning of this word to be "to take to one's side in peace and for blessing." Strong's *Concordance* defines it: "to associate with one's self in any familiar or intimate act or relation."

Why should the Lord have changed from *airo* to *paralambanomai* if He did not wish to convey a different sense? Instead of the thought of judgment, He deliberately used a word that often has exactly the opposite thought. It is the word used for the taking of a bride. The first time it is used in the New Testament, it is addressed to Joseph: "Fear not to *take* unto thee Mary thy wife" (Matthew 1:20, italics added).

Paralambanomai is used in connection with the transfiguration: "Jesus *taketh* Peter, James, and John . . . And was transfigured before them" (Matthew 17:1-2, italics added). It is used to describe the Lord's action after the return of the apostles from their evangelistic mission: "And he *took* them and went aside privately into a desert place" (Luke 9:10, italics added). It is used to describe the Lord's taking of the disciples into His confidence. Above all, it is used to describe the Lord's return: "I will come again, and receive [*take*] you unto myself; that where I am, there ye may be also" (John 14:3). It is the most appropriate word the Lord could have used to describe the rapture, and this is the word He chose to use here.

The chief objection to this view is that it seems to put the church through the great tribulation. This would be so if the Olivet discourse is to be taken in strict chronological sequence. The objection is annulled if we view the discourse as a three-point sermon. First, the Lord described the endtimes as they will affect the nations (Matthew 24:4-14). Then He picked up another topic and described the endtimes as they will affect the Jews (24:15-36). Finally, in His third topic He described the last days as they will affect His church (24:37-42). And, in so doing, He kept "the best wine till last."

Those who object to seeing the rapture of the church in Matthew 24 make much of the Jewish character of Matthew's Gospel. They forget that this Gospel mentions the church twice, once in its universal aspect (16:17-18) and once in its local aspect

(18:15-20). Also the parable of the pearl (Matthew 13) clearly seems to relate to the church; so the objection is unfounded. It is hard to see how the Lord could have given one overall definitive statement on prophecy and ignore what was closest to His heart, His church.

The prophetic section of the discourse ends with a threefold challenge to believers to be watchful (Matthew 24:42-44), to be wise (24:45-47), and to be warned (24:48-51). There are crowns to be won; there is a kingdom to be gained. We are not spectators. We are combatants, and we must behave as such.

THE PARABLES (MATTHEW 25)

Three parables supplement the Lord's prophetic discourse. They are parables of a marriage and its guests, of a merchant and his gains, and of a monarch and his grace.

A Marriage and Its Guests (Matthew 25:1-13)

We begin with the well-known parable of the five wise and the five foolish virgins, but first we need to get our bearings. The parable begins with the coming of the groom for the bride. From that point on in the story the church is no more, and the focus is on the nation of Israel. This parable belongs to the post-Christian era.

First comes *the marriage call* (Matthew 25:1-5). Three actors appear on the stage of the parable: the Lord, the virgins, and the Lord's "brethren." There are ten virgins, a number that denotes completeness in Scripture, as in the ten commandments, which sum up the entire Mosaic code. In the church the controlling number is not ten, but "two or three" (Matthew 18:20). The ten virgins go forth to meet the bridegroom. Those who are left behind at the rapture of the church will have missed all opportunity to attain bridal glory. They will have missed forever a chance to be in the church. Those to whom the gospel call will be sent after the rapture will have a different honor made available to them, the honor of being present at *the reception* of the bride and the groom.

Our attention is drawn first to *the heavenly groom*. "Then shall the kingdom of heaven be likened unto ten virgins, which took their lamps, and went forth to meet the bridegroom" (Matthew 25:1). In Biblical times the bridegroom went first to the house of the bride to conduct her to his home. They both returned together and at various points along the way were joined by their friends, until at length the whole procession went in to the marriage feast. As the parable begins, the heavenly groom has already come for His bride and has taken her to His home on high. The marriage call has been issued to Israel, and a company is being formed of those willing and ready to go forth and meet the Bridegroom and the bride at their return.

There is no mistaking who the groom is. He is referred to as "Lord" by the foolish virgins and as the "Son of man" by Christ. For in all ages the hope of Heaven is found in Him alone. Many people will be saved after the rapture of the church. These will be gathered from the mass of mankind to await the return of the Lord and the subsequent setting up of His kingdom. In all ages the coming of the Lord is the great purifying hope of His own. Old Testament saints looked for His coming to redeem, we today look for His coming in rapture, and in the tribulation age they will look for His coming to reign; always that anticipation helps keep His people pure.

Attention is next focused on *the Holy Ghost*, who is symbolized in the parable by the oil. "Five of them were wise, and five were foolish. They that were foolish took their lamps, and took no oil with them: But the wise took oil in their vessels with their lamps. While the bridegroom tarried, they all slumbered and slept" (Matthew 25:2-5).

We notice a serious neglect concerning the oil. In many ways the wise and foolish virgins were alike. They were alike in outward ways: they were all virgins, they all had lamps, they all went out to meet the bridegroom, and they all slumbered and slept. Outwardly there was nothing to distinguish between them. The one difference centered in the oil. The foolish virgins took no oil in their vessels. They had oil in their lamps, but no oil in their vessels.

Here is the crux of this parable. Oil in the lamp is one thing; oil in the vessel is something else. The lamp represents the Word of God. The psalmist said, "Thy word is a lamp unto my feet, and a light unto my path" (Psalm 119:105). We are living in a dark world. The murky twilight of the day is fast deepening into that "horror of great darkness" (Genesis 15:12) destined to descend after the rapture. The only hope for a person in this world of sin will be to have light from God's Word to show the way.

Each virgin had a lamp and knew it was necessary to use that lamp as a guide through the darkness. But in order to give light a lamp must have oil. The Word of God must be illuminated by the Spirit of God. Only by the operation of the Holy Spirit does God's Word become meaningful to people. Human intellect and natural genius are of no avail here. The Bible is not like a book on chemistry or physics which can be understood by human intellect. The Bible is a supernatural book, and its truths can be imparted only by the Holy Spirit. Paul wrote, "The natural man receiveth not the things of the Spirit of God: for they are foolishness unto him: neither can he know them, because they are spiritually discerned" (1 Corinthians 2:14).

All the virgins, then, had oil in their lamps. That is, each had come under the initial enlightening work of the Holy Spirit. They all had light from the lamps at the beginning, but through neglect the lamps burned out. That was the common experience of all. But here the likeness ends, because right from the start, some had oil in the vessels as well as in their lamps. What does the vessel represent?

The lamp represents the Word of God. The vessel represents the individual's life. David cried, "I am like a broken vessel" (Psalm 31:12). God told Ananias that Saul was "a chosen vessel unto me, to bear my name before the Gentiles" (Acts 9:15). Husbands are commanded to dwell with their wives "giving honour unto the wife, as unto the weaker vessel" (1 Peter 3:7). Concerning God's work in our lives we are told that "we have this treasure in earthen vessels, that the excellency of the power may be of God, and not of us" (2 Corinthians 4:7). So then, while all had light from the Word of God to begin with, some went further than others. The same oil that made their lamps shine was introduced into their vessels as well. In other words, some had the Holy Spirit in their lives and some did not.

All allowed the light in their lamps to go out, with the result that the darkness crept closer; neglect of God's Word always results in a deepening of the darkness. In the day that this parable describes it will be even more difficult than it is now to keep fresh in the Word of God. We can not begin to imagine the social, economic, and political pressures that will be brought to bear on those who make a decision for Christ in the post-Christian world. But although all neglected their lamps, some had the means to relight them, and some did not. Some were truly saved because they had the Holy Spirit in their lives. The rest did not have the vital, personal, indwelling Holy Spirit in their lives. They were therefore quite unable to rekindle the light they once had.

There was also a sad neglect concerning the groom. They had all been alerted to His coming, but as time went on all were overcome by the weariness of waiting and they all fell asleep. They yielded to natural desires, they felt the groom was never coming, and so they slept. That was natural enough, but the natural is always the enemy of the spiritual. Doing the natural always dims one's spiritual vision so that we fall asleep concerning the things of God.

The next theme of this parable is *the midnight cry* (Matthew 25:6-10). After a delay of unspecified length, a sudden burst of activity carried everything right on to the end.

We have, first, *the arousing of the guests* (Matthew 25:6-9). The parable does not say how they were aroused. The book of Revelation indicates that just before the final climactic judgments, an angel will be sent to span the world in a moment of time and to preach "the everlasting gospel" (Revelation 14:6). Perhaps this is what awakens these people to the imminent return of Christ. Or perhaps it is the setting up of the beast's image and the onslaught of the great tribulation. Some sudden quickening in the tempo of the times or some call from on high will awaken believers. What we do know is that "at midnight there was a cry made, Behold, the bridegroom cometh; go ye out to meet him" (Matthew 25:6).

It was then the foolish virgins made their tragic discovery. They were not ready. They had missed the most vital thing of all; they had no oil in their vessels. They begged those who did have oil to share it, but the wise virgins were unable to do that. "Go ye rather to them that sell, and buy for yourselves," they said (Matthew 25:9). A believer can share his testimony with a lost person, but he cannot share the Holy Spirit with him. Nobody can be saved on the strength of someone else's faith and readiness. There is no such thing as accumulated merit, so that one saint can share with others the merits they lack. Salvation is a personal matter and, in any age, can be obtained only where it is "sold." Salvation comes from God alone; He only can impart the Holy Spirit to men.

The wise virgins, thoroughly awake, trim their lamps and prepare for the immediate coming of the groom. They have fresh light now from their lamps, so they can see to walk in the darkness. The foolish virgins stumble off on a vain quest for the oil they neglected to bring.

The arousing of the guests is followed by *the arrival of the groom.* "And while they went to buy, the bridegroom came; and they that were ready went in with him to the marriage: and the door was shut" (Matthew 25:10). There is something very final about that. The groom has come for the guests, and the marriage supper of the Lamb begins. The foolish virgins had missed not only the rapture; they had now missed the reception as well. They are left behind, shut out in the dark with terror and horror mounting on every hand.

Last, the parable underlines *the mistaken claim.* "Afterward came also the other virgins, saying, Lord, Lord, open to us. But he answered and said, Verily I say unto you, I know you not" (Matthew 25:11-12). They claimed He was their Lord; He denied any such claim. They had the language of a believer, but not the life of a believer. It was not that they had made no preparation, but they had made the wrong preparation. The parable does not say what happened to them. All it says is that the door was shut, and they were on the wrong side.

The Lord adds a footnote to the parable: "Watch therefore, for ye know neither the day nor the hour wherein the Son of man cometh" (Matthew 25:13). The interpretation of the parable belongs to the post-rapture age. The application of the parable can be made to us today. The important question to ask is this: Do I have oil in the vessel? Am I truly saved? Does the Holy Spirit reside in my life? "If any man have not the Spirit of Christ, he is none of his" (Romans 8:9).

A Merchant and His Gains (Matthew 25:14-30)

The basic thought behind this parable of the talents is that of responsibility and accountability to the Lord. It covers the period between the noble's departure and his return, the period between the Lord's ascension and His second advent. It should not be confused with the parable of the pounds (Luke 19:12-36), although

191

both parables have certain elements in common. In both cases a rich man departs to a distant country, leaves a sum of money with his servants to be invested for him, and promises that when he returns he will deal with them according to the use they made of what was entrusted to them. In both parables faithfulness is rewarded and neglect is punished. But there the similarities end.

The parable of the talents was addressed to disciples of the Lord in a private, confidential session. The parable of the pounds was addressed to the multitudes when the Lord was speaking publicly at Jericho. In the parable of the pounds, the unsaved contrast sharply with the saved. The unsaved are called "citizens," and the saved are called "servants." It was to the servants that the Lord entrusted His all. It was the citizens who sent the insulting message after Him saying, "We will not have this man to reign over us" (Luke 19:14), a sentiment that the Jewish people expressed at Calvary and which they will finally express in the coronation of the beast. In the parable of the pounds all three servants were His servants, whereas the citizens were open rebels and were eventually sentenced to death. This punishment was quite different from the severe, though deserved, reproof handed out to the unfaithful servant.

In the parable of the talents the emphasis is on the three servants of the departed merchant. The basic teaching of the parable is about personal accountability. It deals with what we call kingdom truth, but it is kingdom truth for those living in the present age of grace when the kingdom is in mystery. The interpretation of the parable relates to us, since this is the age of the absent Lord. We are living in the day of responsibility. The day of reckoning will come when after the rapture we appear before the judgment seat of Christ. What is being determined by us in this church age is our future position in the kingdom. This parable doubtless has its application to the Lord's servants during the great tribulation, but its primary message seems to be for us.

The parable begins with *the day of responsibility*.

For the kingdom of heaven is as a man traveling into a far country, who called his own servants, and delivered unto them his goods. And unto one he gave five talents, to another two, and to another one; to every man according to his several ability; and straightway took his journey (Matthew 25:14-15).

192

We are living in the age during which the Lord is on that long journey of His to that far country where He makes His home. When the kingdom age dawns, the Lord will require many administrators; so He has deliberately interposed, between the time of His departure and the time of His return, a prolonged period for testing those He has left to administer His affairs. Our lives as believers are being watched and weighed to see what use we are making of the talents entrusted to us. The results will be revealed at the judgment seat.

The talents are the spiritual gifts that have been bestowed on us by the Lord through His Holy Spirit. Each of the talents in the parable itself belonged to the Lord, and all were given to His servants to be used for Him. They represent considerable trust; a talent, whether of silver or gold, was the heaviest weight among the Hebrews. We can not put an actual value on these talents, but even the servant who received just the one talent received something of great worth. The greatness of the trust made the occasion of its bestowal a solemn one. It was not every master who would hand over to his servants such responsibility.

These talents, then, represent the spiritual gifts the Lord has bestowed on each one of His own. He has given us the spiritual wealth that was His. He has gone away and left it all in our hands. The Lord knows the measure of our capacity and trusts us with what He knows we can handle. The Lord does not try to put an ocean in a saucer. We differ in our abilities, so the gifts of the Holy Spirit are sovereignly bestowed as He pleases (1 Corinthians 12:11). But although we differ in capacity, we all share a common trust and accountability.

Our first imperative is to identify what gifts the Lord has entrusted to us. Then, with the help of the Holy Spirit, we must get busy and invest those gifts in view of the coming kingdom and in the light of the judgment seat of Christ.

So then, the master's trust was solemnly bestowed. It was also surely believed. "Then he that had received the five talents went and traded with the same, and made them other five talents. And likewise he that had received two, he also gained other two" (Matthew 25:16-17). These two men took their master at his word and at once went into business for him. We are told nothing about where they went, what they did, or how they employed the talents. We only know that each according to his ability was faithful in the trust invested in him by the absent lord. Their lord did not commend them because they were clever but because they were conscientious; they were faithful.

The American Standard version adds an extra word. It does not simply say that they "went and traded"; it adds the word *straightway*. That is, they went to work at once. They did not know how much time they had, so they made the most of it. We are not going to be rewarded for our good intentions or for our promises to serve the Lord, but for our actual performance.

The master's trust was also sadly betrayed. "But he that had received one went and digged in the earth, and hid his lord's money" (Matthew 25:18). The lord, a shrewd judge of men, knew well that this servant had ability. He, however, refused to accept the lord's evaluation of himself. Off he went to dig a hole and bury the talent "in the earth." He had his eye on the wrong world. He should have been looking away to that land to which the merchant had gone and kept his mind on his master and his master's trust in him. Instead he grubbed away in the dirt of this world and buried his talent out of sight. He was not a thief. He was simply unwilling to do something worthwhile with what had been entrusted to him. Most believers do not set out deliberately to defraud their Master. Rather, they allow this world to loom too large in their thinking so that they amount to nothing and become, by neglect, unprofitable servants.

The parable proceeds to *the day of reckoning* (Matthew 25:19-30). There is to be a day of reckoning, even for those who are saved by sovereign grace and are as sure of Heaven as the blood of Christ can make them. "After a long time the lord of those servants cometh, and reckoneth with them" (25:19). It has been a long time since the Lord Jesus went away. This one statement fixes the interpretation of the parable to our own age. Although it can be applied to those saved during the tribulation age and although the Lord will be absent during that period too, that absence is going to be short; He said that those days would be shortened (24:22). This age in which we live is the one marked by the prolonged absence of the Master.

The reckoning begins with the faithful servants (Matthew 25:19-23). Each was brought before the master, each had his work reviewed, each was rewarded, and each heard the lord say, "Well done, thou good and faithful servant: thou hast been faithful over a few things, I will make thee ruler over many things: enter thou into the joy of thy lord" (25:21). Each had brought joy to the master. Each had spent his time and talents in faithful service, grateful for the trust received and with an eye fixed on the day of the master's return. At the judgment seat of Christ, reward for faithful service is to be in the form of a crown (2 Timothy 4:8), a throne (Revelation 3:21), and a kingdom (Matthew 25:34). What we gain in the church age we shall reap in the kingdom age.

Each of these servants was told to enter into "the joy of thy lord." This planet, the scene of His sorrow and suffering, is to be the scene of His glory and joy. Those who come into commendation in the day of reckoning will be promoted to royal rank and responsibility in the millennial kingdom.

The parable next focuses on the faithless servant (Matthew 25:24-30), and more is said about him than the others. Only three verses each are given to the faithful servants; seven verses are given to the unfaithful one. This is where the emphasis lies.

We must pause here and evaluate this servant's standing. In common with the others he was trusted by the lord with the conduct of his affairs during his absence. That is important. Since the Lord never entrusts His work to the unsaved, we conclude that this unprofitable servant was a truly saved man. Moreover, all three men are called "his own servants"; so the master clearly identifies himself with them. The word *servants* is the common word for "slaves." They are those he has purchased; they belong to him.

Then, too, although all three differed in capacity, all were the same in that the master bestowed his trust on each of them and gave them something that was theirs to invest for him. All three servants were judged at the same time. That is important because we know from the Scriptures that the wicked are not to be judged at the same time or at the same place as the people of God. Finally, all three men are judged as *servants*, not as sons. It is not salvation or sonship that is at issue in this parable, but service. These men are to be judged, not as to their persons, but as to their works—the essential difference between the great white throne and the judgment seat of Christ. Their standing is not brought into question at all.

The Lord emphasized two things about this servant. First, there is his confession. "Then he which had received the one talent came and said, Lord, I knew thee that thou art an hard man, reaping where thou hast not sown, and gathering where thou hast not strawed: And I was afraid, and went and hid thy talent in the earth: lo, there thou hast that is thine" (Matthew 25:24-25).

This man was not guilty of gross sin; he was no murderer, embezzler, adulterer, or apostate. He was simply charged with neglect. Moreover, he added insult to idleness by accusing his master of being "a hard man." If there is one thing our Lord is not, He is not hard. He who wept with Martha and Mary at the grave of Lazarus, He who forgave the woman taken in adultery, He who picked up fallen Peter, a hard man? No. A holy man, yes.

Next came the servant's condemnation (Matthew 25:26-30), and this was divided in two parts. First we have the Lord's summary. "His lord answered and said unto him, Thou wicked and slothful servant, thou knewest . . . Thou oughtest therefore to have put my money to the exchangers" (25:26-27). To have at our judgment only what we had at our conversion will be evidence of our neglect. This servant was "wicked"; that is, he was wicked in the sense of being both slothful in his service for the master and harsh in his thinking about the master. He represents those who take the attitude that since they can not be as holy as God expects, they will give up all thoughts of holiness. Since they can not produce as God expects, they will not even try. The slothful servant represents the person who has a saved soul and a lost life.

This brings us to the master's sentence: "Take therefore the talent from him, and give it unto him which hath ten talents. . . . And cast ye the unprofitable servant into outer darkness: there shall be weeping and gnashing of teeth" (Matthew 25:28,30). This is unquestionably the most difficult part of the parable.

Some say the servant was not saved at all—he was a mere professor of Christianity who was literally cast into Hell. But then how do we explain the fact that he was entrusted with the Lord's gifts in order to carry on His work in the world? And why was he judged at the same time as the profitable servants?

Some say that he was once saved but that he had lost his salvation; such an interpretation raises a different set of problems. It makes salvation rest on works, which is contrary to the teaching of Scripture (Ephesians 2:8-9). Also it equates salvation with reward, which is contrary to sound principles of Biblical interpretation.

Some say he was saved but was incarcerated during the kingdom age because of neglect of his responsibilities. This would imply some kind of Protestant purgatory, but that interpretation lands us in very hot water indeed. This view overlooks the fact that when the kingdom age dawns the church will be seated with Christ on high, having been presented to Him "not having spot, or wrinkle, or any such thing" and arrayed in the "fine linen" of personal righteousness (Ephesians 5:26-27; Revelation 19:7-8). To envision some members of Christ's body as being shut out of the kingdom is not consistent with such Scriptures as these.

Some say that the place of "outer darkness" is a place in the kingdom, but far removed from the central glory. This view leaves questions unanswered too. Where, for instance, is "the weeping and gnashing of teeth" going on?

There has to be an explanation that fits the facts and avoids the pitfalls. Between the rapture of the church and the final return of Christ, all believers will stand before the judgment seat of Christ. We will have been raised and will have our new bodies, but we shall still have to give account of our lives as believers (1 Corinthians 3:11-15; Romans 14:10; 2 Corinthians 5:10). The thorough sifting to take place at the judgment seat is always presented to us with great solemnity in the New Testament.

We know very little about the actual process of this judgment. The question of our personal salvation will never be raised, of course, since that was settled at Calvary. But might it not be that such servants as this one will be taken to that place of "outer darkness" where there is that "weeping and gnashing of teeth," taken there not to suffer but to see, not to be punished or purged but to perceive for themselves the end result of their wasted lives and sinful neglect? What could be more solemn than that? Could anything be more just than to be made to see what their criminal neglect has wrought? Then, in His grace, the Lord will wipe away all tears, the judgment seat will be over, and a church forever free from blemish will enter the kingdom age.

There is a Scriptural precedent. Jonah, the unprofitable servant of the Old Testament, refused to go to Nineveh and announce the coming of the judgment of God. So God put Jonah into the belly of the great fish (what Jonah called "the belly of hell" [Jonah 2:2]) and gave him a taste of what it is like for a soul to be lost. Jonah came out of that experience a chastened man, prepared to go at once to Nineveh and to warn the people of their impending doom.

So, here we have the unprofitable servant's sentence. He was given a sharp rebuke and sent to see what that dread place of outer darkness was like.

We must distinguish between the kingdom age and the eternal state. Our position in eternity depends entirely on the finished work of Christ, not on any works of ours. Our position in the kingdom does depend on *us* and will be determined by what comes through the fire as "gold, silver, and precious stones." The parable of the talents makes it clear that there will be relative positions in the millennial kingdom, positions that have to be earned. When the mother of James and John came with her two sons to Jesus to request that, in the kingdom, one might be allowed to sit on His right hand and the other on His left, the request was denied. The Lord Jesus said, "To sit on my right hand, and on my left, is not mine to give, but it shall be given to them for whom it is prepared of my Father" (Matthew 20:23). That place of honor must be earned. God gives unmerited salvation, but He never gives unmerited reward.

A Monarch and His Grace (Matthew 25:31-46)

In the last parable in the series the Lord Jesus called Himself a King for the first and last time. Twice in the parable He claimed the title. Then, as the Gospels reveal, He prepared Himself for the crown of thorns, the mocking purple robe, and Pilate's sneering title: "This is Jesus of Nazareth, the King of the Jews." The cross was only three days ahead.

This parable portrays the end of the great tribulation. The Lord Jesus has returned. He has quelled His foes at Megiddo, and He has summoned what's left of the human race to the valley of Jehoshaphat near Jerusalem to be judged. For three and a half years the beast and the false prophet will have tried to exterminate all Jews and all professing believers in Christ. Here and there some bold and believing Gentile will have offered refuge to a fleeing Jew and by God's grace will have survived the holocaust. Now the time has come for the remnant of mankind to appear before the great assize. All this is preliminary to the setting up of the millennial kingdom.

This judgment recognizes two basic principles. First, there is the principle of *natural blindness*. Both those called sheep and those called goats will say, "When saw we thee?" (Matthew 25:37).

They will claim, and rightly, that they had no *direct* knowledge of Christ at all. For those living in the lands of Christendom there will be little room for such excuse. But the countless millions of Muslims, Buddhists, Hindus, and communists in the world, who have been almost totally sealed off from knowledge of the gospel of Christ, might well plead, "When saw we thee?" The "strong delusion" will overtake millions in the lands of Christendom who once had access to the truth (2 Thessalonians 2:11-12). The majority of the people named "sheep" in this parable will likely be those who live outside the pale of Christendom, those to whom "the everlasting gospel" will be perhaps primarily addressed (Revelation 14:6). That gospel will reduce belief to its barest essentials: (1)conviction: "Fear God"; (2)confession: "Give glory to him, for the hour of his judgment is come"; (3)consecration: "Worship him that made heaven, and earth" (Revelation 14:7).

The principle of natural blindness, of ignorance, will be a factor in this coming judgment of the nations. Those counted righteous did not know that in siding with the Jews they were siding with Jesus.

This judgment also recognizes the principle of *natural behavior*. The criterion is not "What did you do with Jesus?" since they had never known Him. The criterion is "What did you do with the Jews?" In that day natural behavior will dictate caution, to say the least. Self-interest and self-preservation will suggest turning a blind eye to what is going on. Many in Germany and the Nazi-occupied countries of Europe did just that when faced with the Gestapo and widespread national persecution of Jews.

Since the criterion of this judgment will be "What did you do with the Jews?" it is obvious that two dependent factors will also be essential. First, the opportunity to do good must be present. The worldwide dispersal of the Jews will ensure this. They are present in almost every nation on earth, so the opportunity to act toward a Jew as one should act toward Christ will be present.

Second, the obligation to do good will be present. Every person on earth has the obligation to respond to the test God sets up as a proof of genuine faith. The days will be so dark and dreadful that to befriend a Jew will bespeak some kind of faith in that true and living God to whom the Jews will be a witness. Thus, in the context of this parable, "works" become the silent and shining evidence that the Gentiles designated "sheep" dared to believe God and

199

were righteous—even though they confess their personal ignorance of Christ. If they did not know Him, He certainly knew them. This is the background of this parable.

The first great factor in this parable is *the throne*. "When the Son of man shall come in his glory, and all the holy angels with him, then shall he sit upon the throne of his glory" (Matthew 25:31). Although the title "Son of man" is the title He employs for Himself in describing His relationship to the world, it is one that relates primarily to the nation of Israel. Jesus entered this world as a Jew, and as a Jew He will be the rightful claimant to the throne of David. He entered the world as a man, and as a man He will claim the throne of the world. The great assize now to take place determines who enters the millennial kingdom.

The "throne of his glory" is a literal throne. The Lord Jesus is yet to be seated in power on this planet, the scene of His rejection and crucifixion.

The parable focuses next on *the throngs* (Matthew 25:32-33). There are three distinct groups: those who are called "sheep," those who are called "goats," and those the Lord called "my brethren." We shall look first at the Hebrew people, the Lord's "brethren."

There are three circles of brotherhood in the New Testament. Some are the Lord's brethren because they have been born again. "He is not ashamed to call them brethren" (Hebrews 2:11). Some are His brethren because they were born into the same human family into which He was born (Matthew 12:47; 13:55-56). Some are His brethren on the grounds of national brotherhood, a tie that has always been strong among the Jewish people (Deuteronomy 17:15,18-20). Those in this third circle are described by the Lord in the parable as "the least of these my brethren"; that is, they were Jews. They belonged to the same nation as He.

Each November 11 the British observe Armistice Day, a day set aside to commemorate those who gave their lives in the first world war. One can stand by the side of the road and see, marching to the Cenotaph, a contingent of honored old men. Though their numbers get smaller every year, they lead the parade with heads held high, some of them hobbling on sticks. Who are these men? They are the "Old Contemptibles."

When the first world war broke out Britain, unready, sent an expeditionary force across the channel. It was ill-prepared and poorly equipped, but it was made up of the kind of men who had fought the French to a standstill at Agincourt and put an end to Napoleon's ambitions at Waterloo. The German kaiser was unimpressed. With a sneer he exclaimed, "This is a contemptible army!" Now those men, whose ranks are so thinned by the passing of time, are called "the Old Contemptibles." The name of shame became the name of fame. Those marching aged pensioners lift their heads high, because they halted the Hun as surely as their forebears outfought the French.

Now you may ask who are these Jews who take their stand there in the valley of Jehoshaphat. Well, during the great tribulation they were the filth and offscouring of the earth, objects of derision and shame, the world's contemptibles. But look at them now. They stand by the throne. The King, having come down from the sky in splendor, calls them "my brethren." They are His beloved "old contemptibles." They shared in His rejection, and the name of shame is now the name of fame. They are Jews; they are His brethren; they are His kinsmen according to the flesh.

Attention is next drawn to the heathen peoples. All who are left of the human race after the repeated horrors of the apocalypse will be there. From nearby lands and from distant corners of the globe they will be drawn to a valley outside Jerusalem to be judged by the King. They are summoned; then they are separated. "And before him shall be gathered all nations: and he shall separate them one from another, as a shepherd divideth his sheep from the goats: And he shall set the sheep on his right hand, but the goats on the left" (Matthew 25:32-33). A sheep is the emblem of gentleness, simplicity, patience, and usefulness. A goat is naturally quarrelsome, lascivious, evil-smelling (and, interestingly, identified with Satanism and witchcraft). The Lord with infallible judgment divides man from man, the sheep from the goats.

The sheep are made to stand on His right hand, the goats on His left. According to Joel 3:2,12 this judgment takes place in the valley of Jehoshaphat, the name given to the valley between Jerusalem and the mount of Olives, and which, in Jesus' day, was called the Kidron valley. Sitting on His throne the Lord will be in sight of Gethsemane and the city where He was crucified. The Lord's throne will be on Olivet. The Gentiles will be massed in the valley. Those on His right hand, therefore, will take up their significant stand by Jerusalem. Those made to stand on His left hand will take up their ominous stand by Tophet, the valley of the sons of Hinnom, where in olden times the garbage was burned.

The parable concentrates next on *the thrill* (Matthew 25:34-36). The King now speaks and He addresses first those who stand at His right hand. "Come, ye blessed of my Father, inherit the kingdom prepared for you from the foundation of the world: For I was an hungred, and ye gave me meat" (25:34-35). They have a standing in the blessing of both the Father and the Son.

An illustration of what takes place here is to be found in the story of Rahab. James told us that this pagan Gentile woman was saved "by works" (James 2:25). Paul told us she was justified "by faith" (Hebrews 11:31). She received the Lord's people into her home, hid them from their foes, told them of her fears, heard the way of salvation, and boldly acted on what she heard (Joshua 2:1-21). Her works and her faith were so closely knit it is impossible to separate one from the other. She was given a standing with the people of God because she took her stand for them.

That is in essence what will happen in the valley of Jehoshaphat. "Then shall *the righteous* answer him, saying, Lord, when saw we thee an hungred?" (Matthew 25:37, italics added) There it is. The *righteous* must have been believers, however faint and feeble their faith. "Abraham believed God, and it was counted unto him for righteousness" (Romans 4:3). It is the only way we can become righteous before God. These Gentiles will not know it at the time, but they will come under the full primal blessing of Abraham: "I will bless them that bless thee, and curse him that curseth thee: and in thee shall all families of the earth be blessed" (Genesis 12:3).

The Lord then states the principle on which He is accepting them into the kingdom. "Inasmuch as ye have done it unto one of the least of these my brethren, ye have done it unto me" (Matthew 25:40). The One who reads all hearts accepts what they had done for the Jews as though they had done it for Him. Theirs will be the thrill of happiness.

Attention is focused finally on those standing on the Lord's left hand. "Then shall he say also unto them on the left hand, Depart from me, ye cursed, into everlasting fire, prepared for the devil and his angels: For I was an hungred, and ye gave me no meat" (Matthew 25:41-42). The Lord can find nothing of value in their lives, not even token faith. They complain loudly at the sentence. "Lord, when saw we *thee* an hungred, or athirst, or a stranger, or naked, or sick, or in prison, and did not minister unto thee?" (25:44, italics added) They say, in effect, "If we had seen *you* we would certainly have flung open our doors to *you*." "Then shall he answer them, saying, Verily I say unto you, Inasmuch as ye did it not to one of the least of these, ye did it not to me. And these shall go away into everlasting punishment: but the righteous into life eternal" (25:45-46).

The villains in our literature are those who commit overt acts of wickedness. They kill, rape, steal, lie, and do other evil things. The villains of our Lord's parables are conspicuous not for what they do, but for what they fail to do. Their sins of omission alone are enough to send them to Hell. The Lord does not accuse these people standing before Him of the thousand and one sins that doubtless disgraced their lives. The one sin that damned them was a sin of omission: they failed to take Him into account. That ultimately is what sends people to Hell.

And there the Olivet discourse ends.

---

1. Phillips, *Exploring the World of the Jew*, pp. 87-102.
2. Other shortages are looming, too. The United States is almost wholly dependent on foreign countries for twenty-two of the twenty-six materials needed to feed its industrial complex—not to mention foreign oil. Items such as chromium, platinum, and cobalt are in critically short supply. Competition for strategic raw materials has increased dramatically in recent years, especially from Europe and Japan. The Russians have long foreseen this and have taken steps to ensure their own supplies. Most of America's strategic minerals are found in Russia or in a segment of Africa lying between South Africa and Zaire. It is obviously in the best interest of the United States to keep those areas free and to ensure the safety of the sea-lanes along which those minerals travel. The next world crisis could well erupt over competition for the dwindling natural resources of the planet.

9

Perilous Times
2 Timothy 3:1-9

Paul summed up the closing days of the church age in a passage pregnant with doom. He said they would be "perilous times." The word he used for "perilous" means "heavy, difficult, hard to bear, dangerous." The only other use of this word is in Matthew's account of the two demoniacs who met Christ when He visited the country of the Gergesenes. The demoniacs are described as being "exceeding fierce" (Matthew 8:28).

These perilous times have come. Paul linked their arrival with "the last days," an expression we have met before in our study. It is first used in Scripture by the dying Jacob. It is used fourteen times in the New Testament to describe both the course and the close of the church age.

Paul's list of end-time events can be summarized as follows. He saw a world controlled by:

I. People Without Character (2 Timothy 3:2-3)
   A. Their supreme concern (3:2)
      1. Love for self

   2. Lust for wealth
B. Their scornful contempt (3:2) (boastful, haughty, abusive)
C. Their sinful conduct (3:2-3)
   1. Toward parents (3:2) (disobedient, unthankful)
   2. Toward people (3:2-3)
      a. No reverence (3:2) (unholy or profane)
      b. No regard (3:3) (without natural affection, truce-breakers)
      c. No restraint (3:3) (slanderers, incontinent, fierce)
II. People Without Conviction (2 Timothy 3:3-5)
   A. Their false principles (3:3-4)
      1. Ruled by wickedness (3:3) (despisers of those that are good)
      2. Ruled by wiles (3:4) (traitors)
      3. Ruled by willfulness (3:4) (heady, high-minded)
   B. Their foremost passion (3:4) (lovers of pleasure)
   C. Their false profession (3:5) (having a form of godliness)
III. People Without Conscience (2 Timothy 3:6-9)
   A. Their vileness (3:6)
   B. Their victims (3:6-7)
   C. Their values (3:8)
   D. Their vanity (3:9)

These fierce times are upon us today. Illustrations can be found everywhere: in the unscrupulousness, ferocity, and planned wickedness of some nations; in the general godlessness of the once-great nations of Christendom; in organized crime; in the reappearance of the kinds of lawlessness and licentiousness that characterized the days of Noah and Lot.

Evil people have always plagued society, but for most of the last two thousand years the Christian ethic has acted as a measure of restraint. Today, however, Christian standards of morality and decency have been swept aside. Perversion flaunts itself unashamedly and boastfully. Courts, colleges, and communication media are showing increasing bias against the Christian moral code. We have arrived at "the last days."

PEOPLE WITHOUT CHARACTER (2 TIMOTHY 3:2-3)

Paul listed a dozen things to substantiate this aspect of the endtimes. He wrote down first that people would be "lovers of their own selves" (2 Timothy 3:2). Self-love, of course, is native to the human heart, something that shows itself in a child as soon as he can express himself. Nobody has to teach a baby how to throw a temper tantrum to get his own way. A healthy society, however, imposes restraints on selfishness. It recognizes the need to teach children respect for authority—their parents at home, their teachers at school, the law in society. A healthy society teaches children to be well-mannered and respectful of persons and the property of others.

But our society has institutionalized love for self. Children must not be punished lest they become inhibited. If they are flunking their lessons at school, the grading system must be adjusted lest their failure do them psychological harm. Criminals must be given their "rights," even though they have shown no respect for the rights of those they have robbed, murdered, and maimed. Recently a police chief summed up our generation by calling it "a lost generation," a generation that "thumbs its nose" at everything once held sacred. He described it as a generation addicted to drugs, given to self-indulgence, contemptuous of the law, and totally without regard for social values. In other words, he described the kind of end-time generation described by Paul.

The acquittal of John Hinckley, Jr., demonstrates how far we have gone in allowing human selfishness to go unchallenged in our society. This man put a bullet in the stomach of a secret service agent, a bullet in the neck of a police officer, a bullet in the brain of the president's press secretary, and a bullet in the body of President Reagan. Yet he was pronounced "not guilty" on all thirteen counts of assault, attempted murder, and weapons offenses. A Wyoming lawyer called the acquittal by reason of insanity proof that Americans are a people of "law and compassion." One juror thought Hinckley was "a sick white boy looking for someone to love him." Why did he do it? He wanted to prove his love for a movie star. It would be hard to think of a more callous act of selfishness.

Next, Paul said that "men shall be . . . covetous," or, as the New International Version renders that, "People will be . . . lovers of money" (2 Timothy 3:2).

Benjamin Franklin's dictum "It is better to go to bed supperless than to run into debt" sounds silly to our generation. The craving for "the good life" has lured millions of Americans hopelessly into debt. As a nation we are a people addicted to living beyond our means in order to gratify our wants. The old-fashioned idea of working and saving for what we want has been abandoned. Our love of money and the things that money can buy has saddled millions of Americans with a hopeless burden.

Love for self and love for money are born twins. Witness the increasing number of ordinary people sloughing off their debts by means of bankruptcy. The Bankruptcy Reform Act of 1978 has made the process almost painless. Bankruptcy is no longer considered a scandal but a shrewd way to shake off creditors. The bankruptcy laws of some states are even more liberal than those of the federal government. In California, for instance, the head of a household can keep up to $45,000 in the value of his home when filing for bankruptcy.

Paul said, too, that in the last days people would be "*boastful, proud, abusive*" (2 Timothy 3:2, NIV, italics added). Nowhere in our society is that better illustrated than in the popular music of this age. How a generation looks at life is reflected in its music. One generation gives birth to hymns, another to martial and patriotic songs, another to romantic melodies. Our generation has given birth to rock, hard rock, punk, and heavy metal. The music of today is filled with contempt toward human life and society. It is the music of a generation that is defiant, blasphemous, proud, yet at the same time gripped by despair.

The lyrics of today's popular music often glorify sin and rebellion. They scream in the face of God. The relentless beat hammers the message home to the depths of the human heart. The names taken by popular contemporary music groups also mirror arrogance and abuse. Such names as the Dictators, the Stranglers, and the Sex Pistols reflect clearly how these groups think.

The three words *boastful, proud, abusive* sum up much of the music of today, and the masses love it, invest millions of dollars in it, adulate its composers and performers, and listen to it by the hour. The words glorify sex, hate, and drugs; they attack patriotism, decency, and respect; and they assail moral purity. Yet these boastful, proud, and abusive words strike a deep chord of response in the soul of this generation.

Next, Paul said that in the endtimes people will be "disobedient to parents, unthankful" (2 Timothy 3:2). The apostle foresaw an ominous attack on the family unit and home life in the last days.

The roots of family indiscipline today are many and varied.

207

There is the soaring divorce rate, which has undermined the stability of the home and the authority of parents. Nearly half the marriages in this country end in divorce, one of the chief reasons being the easy accessibility of divorce nowadays. Most states have no-fault divorce laws, which encourage "throw-away" marriages. Advocates call these laws "an idea whose time has come." Conversely, millions of people don't bother getting married at all. They simply live together in disregard for the laws of God. With such lax attitudes toward responsibility displayed by adults, it is no wonder that children are growing up with little respect for authority.

Many parents are wringing their hands over the lifestyles chosen by their children, but often the parents themselves have turned on the TV set as a handy built-in babysitter for children and adolescents. Statistics indicate that most young people arrive at adolescence having been thoroughly conditioned by the largely unwholesome offerings of the networks. It is estimated that the average eighteen-year-old American has spent something like twenty-two thousand hours of those formative years watching TV. That's far more time than he spent in school. During those hours of TV brainwashing, he has been subconsciously conditioned to a life of fantasy, violence, sex, drink, and amusement. Is it any wonder that disobedience to parents has become a hallmark of our age?

Some years ago a mother wrote to a newspaper columnist bewailing the attitudes adopted by her seventeen-year-old son. He was drinking, experimenting with drugs, running with the wrong crowd, in trouble with the police, and resolutely refusing to listen to a word his mother had to say. The columnist advised: "Shrink him down to seventeen months and start all over again." Cold comfort, perhaps, but right on target. Millions of parents today, realizing they have lost all control over their children, are wringing their hands and saying, "Where did we go wrong?"

In fact, many people have simply given up on being parents at all. A book entitled *Love Plus* took France by storm and became a nationwide topic for discussion and debate. The book was written by a woman, a professor of philosophy at the Parise Ecole Polytecnique, the wife of a prominent lawyer, and the mother of three children. Her theme was "Is it natural to be a mother?" Her conclusion: The maternal instinct is a two-hundred-year-old myth invented to subjugate women. A considerable segment of the feminist movement would probably agree.

Even conscientious parents are finding it increasingly difficult to cope with the permissiveness tolerated by society and with the secular values taught in public schools. Schools across the country simply ignore parental objections to liberal teaching on homosexuality, abortion, birth control, sexual indulgence, and relative morality. And, of course, teaching the Bible is banned from classrooms. We can assign for reading and discussion any filthy book that comes off the press, we can study Karl Marx and George Bernard Shaw, we can invite witches, homosexuals, and anarchists into our classrooms to air their ideas—but we must not teach the Bible or have token prayers or Scripture readings in our schools. Is it any wonder that a quarter of all American fifteen-year-olds and a tenth of all thirteen-year-olds have experimented with sex?

We can come up with an equation. Add: liberal, secular educational philosophies; plus lack of classroom discipline; plus indifference to parental objections about certain books and items in the curriculum; plus the eroded teaching standards of many school systems. Multiply that sum by a large percentage of the public schools in this country, and the result equals disaster. It is no wonder that millions of youngsters leave school unprepared to meet the realities of life on the outside.

The courts seem to have joined in the overall attack on the home as the basic unit of society and on parental authority as the key to other authority. Juvenile courts in America have a reputation for inefficiency and leniency. Many offenders are acquitted on legal technicalities, even though they are known to the police as hardened offenders.

In 1977 Doubleday released a book entitled *The Children's Rights Movement*. The book was enthusiastically endorsed by UNICEF (which we support with our tax dollars) so that it could be offered at a discount to organizations and committees studying children's causes. The book declared that children should be allowed to leave home if they so desire and to live where they like. It said that children must be guaranteed full rights under the law and that they must be provided with advocates to espouse their cause in order to protect them from their parents. Is it any wonder that parental authority has been eroded almost to the point of extinction?

Some years ago a study of juvenile and youthful crime in America documented the fact that youngsters in many of our large cities rob, maim, and murder as casually as they would sit down to dinner. The observer documented incidents and spoke of "the mutant juvenile." He called the young criminals who roam many of the cities of America "a new remorseless generation" and said that there was "no more terrifying figure in America today." Much of the blame, the documentary stated, should be placed directly on the courts, which generally take the attitude that there is "no such thing as a bad boy."[1]

The apostle Paul next turned his attention to another ingredient in the recipe of ruin for the last days. He wrote that people would be "unholy," or profane (2 Timothy 3:2). There can be little doubt that we are witnessing widespread profanation. It reaches into every area of society; it is well financed, organized, and directed by forces that are hostile to our way of life. Our freedoms are being used to destroy us.

For instance, vice is encouraged at all levels of society because vice weakens; Rome rotted from within long before she was overthrown by barbarians from without. Vice saps a nation's moral fiber, promotes apathy, weakens character, destroys the will to resist. The enormous drug traffic in the United States and the western world and the wholesale promotion of sexual excess and perversion are all parts of a cleverly orchestrated plot to produce a decadent society, to demoralize youth, and to lure people into compromising situations so that they can then be exploited in the interests of a foreign power.

Along with this steady sapping of character in the western world, there has been a planned promotion and encouragement of everything that attacks the norm, undermines religion, weakens the family, destroys morality, and erodes patriotism. Help is given to all movements of protest, whether aimed at the military draft, nuclear strength, or societal ills. Peace movements, the gay-rights movement, and the feminist movement are all helped so long as their anti-establishment goals are in keeping with the master plot to undermine the stability of the western world and its ability to resist communist plans for world domination.

The communications media have been infiltrated so that news stories can be twisted and slanted in the interests of the enemy. Churches have been infiltrated, as is evident from the leftist causes espoused by the World Council of Churches and by certain segments of the Roman Catholic Church. Any drift toward unbelief, skepticism, and leftist ideology is helped.[2]

The results of thirty years of steady erosion are now evident in western society. Everything is profaned. Art forms have become decadent and puerile. The American flag is burned by protestors. Old-fashioned ideas of morality are ridiculed. National and international figures like the president of the United States, the queen of England, and even the pope are targets for assassins. Subjects that a few decades ago would have been considered off-limits for polite conversation are now aired, explored, touted, and publicized on radio and TV talk shows without any sense of shame or propriety. "In the last days, men shall be profane," Paul wrote (2 Timothy 3:2-3 paraphrased).

Paul also wrote that people would be "without natural affection, trucebreakers" (2 Timothy 3:3). The Greek scholar, Archbishop Richard C. Trench, said of the term *truce-breakers* that it does not seem to be used of truce-breakers as such; rather it refers to people who will make no truce. They are implacable and relentless. In other words, Paul foresaw a time when people would be callous and without either heart or principle.

Remembering the atrocities committed by the Nazis and the communists in their efforts to achieve supreme power evokes countless illustrations of the utter heartlessness of their regimes. The documentary evidence as well as the personal testimony at the Nuremberg trials of the Nazi war criminals added up to a tale of horror that outraged most of the world. It was almost unbelievable that one of the most gifted, enlightened, and cultured nations of Europe could have behaved with such calculated cruelty. The testimony told of horrible experiments on human guinea pigs, of people beaten and literally worked to death on a starvation diet, of mass murder on an unimaginable scale. Victims were forced into box cars to the point of suffocation and little children picked up bodily and tossed in on top of the mass of struggling, screaming humanity. Extermination camps brutally separated wife from husband, children from parents. The weaker and the useless were marched off at once to mass graves, to be gunned down in cold blood.

The epidemic of heartlessness that has so disgraced the twentieth century reaches into many of our cities' streets where gangs of thugs and hoodlums hold almost undisputed sway. Many of them are organized not just for financial gain, but to indulge sadistic tastes in crimes of senseless violence.

In Britain stories have been reported of gangs of girls who band together to commit mayhem on innocent and helpless victims. By day the girls are often friendly, ordinary young people, many from well-to-do homes. At night they are transformed into vicious animals who attack unsuspecting people in dark alleys and at lonely bus stops. Often their victims are the old, helpless, and infirm. One gang member cheerfully told a reporter that she had become tired of simply tagging along with the gang and had decided to branch out on her own. She described her specialty of beating up old women as "granny bashing."

Paul next said that the endtimes would see the rise of "false accusers," people who would be "incontinent, fierce" (2 Timothy 3:3). A number of interesting words appear here. *False accusers*, for example, comes from the Greek word *diabolos*, meaning "a slanderer" or "an adversary." The same word is used in the Bible as a name for the devil.

When the antichrist comes, he will "cause craft to prosper" (Daniel 8:25); and his coming will be "with all deceivableness" (2 Thessalonians 2:10). He will be *diabolos* incarnate. He will have imbibed to the full the spirit of Machiavelli, who advocated deceit as the proper basis for policy and power in a world ruler.

The shadow of this coming prince, this world dealer in deceit, already lies across our world. Hitler was a great believer in deceit as an instrument of policy. He wrote in *Mein Kampf* that the greater the lie, the more chance it had of being believed. Hitler's mantle has now fallen on the communists who believe that if you tell a lie big enough and often enough, people will believe it.

The word *incontinent* means "not having power or command over a thing." From its Latin equivalent we get our word *impotent*. As used in 2 Timothy 3:3, the word means to be without power or command over one's passions or desires; *unbridled* or *dissolute* would be the best synonyms. Some of the foul things we see in our society today could be associated with the word *incontinent*.

More than twenty years ago the *Intelligence Digest* warned that the Russians were preparing to wage subversive warfare on the world by means of trained and dedicated sodomites. It reported that Russia actually had a school for homosexuals, a place where people could be taught how to practice this perversion and to attract others to the vice.[3] Homosexuals do not reproduce; they recruit. The purpose of the school was to trap the unwary, especially high-placed officials, into compromising situations so that they could then be manipulated for subversive purposes. It is hard to believe that such deliberate wickedness could exist, but the credentials and reputation of the *Intelligence Digest* are beyond question.

The conspirators have succeeded. It is estimated that in the United States alone there are twenty-five million adults who are predominantly homosexual. They have picketed the White House, the State Department, and the Civil Service Commission. Scores of regional and national organizations fight on their behalf. People who practice this form of perversion once hid their behavior. Now they organize and march, heads held high, glorying in their shame, given a sense of boldness by their numbers and encouraged by the permissive attitudes of many in high places. A former mayor of Atlanta, for instance, gave them his moral support by endorsing a "Gay Pride Week" to honor them.

Society has surrendered to men of unprincipled, unbridled lust. It has been said that if God does not judge western society for tolerating these sins, He will have to apologize to Sodom and Gomorrah. Jesus foretold that the last days would be like those of Sodom, a city that has lent its name to this particular form of lust (Luke 17:28-30). The days predicted by Jesus and by Paul have arrived.

Society is becoming increasingly tolerant of perversion as a lifestyle. Homosexuals in New York state, for instance, now have the same rights as surviving husbands or wives to take over rent-stabilized apartments on the death of their partners. In 1989 Denmark became the first industrial nation to allow Sodomites to marry and be registered in the way husbands and wives are. A poll in the United States indicated that in 1989 about 23 percent of the population thought Sodomite marriages should be recognized by law, 54 percent thought homosexuals should be allowed to receive medical and life insurance benefits from their partners' policies, 65 percent thought homosexuals should be allowed to inherit their partners' property, and 17 percent (8 percent not sure) thought that practicing Sodomites should be allowed to adopt children.

The one institution in society that, above all others, should take a bold and uncompromising stand against sodomy is the church, but even there the walls are tumbling down. As perverts stage rallies, flaunt their shame, disrupt church services and demand endorsement of their abominations, some denominations are succumbing. In San Francisco, parishioners of St. Francis Lutheran Church voted overwhelmingly to call a pair of lesbians as assistant pastors. Both women are graduates of Luther Northwestern Seminary in Minnesota. Martin Luther would turn over in his grave. So far, the bishop of the synod has refused to endorse their appointment because they refuse to commit themselves to abstinence from practicing sodomy. Carter Heywood, a female priest and committed lesbian, teaches theology at the Episcopal Divinity School in Massachusetts. And so it goes on. A *Washington Post* article (September 1989) stated that a Baltimore therapist concluded, after a twenty-five-year study involving one thousand United States Roman Catholic priests, that 20 percent of them are gay. Another study set the figure higher. So far the Vatican has officially opposed any leaning toward sodomy, but its decrees are largely ignored.

Even secular authors are now commenting on the growing decadence of society. Historian and columnist Max Lerner, for example, in describing the sensuality of our society, called it "babylonian." Theaters and shows are packed with people watching salacious movies. Cable TV networks bring foul language, nudity, and every form of sex into thousands of American homes every day. Bookstores offer so-called "adult" books, which describe in lurid fashion the most obscene forms of immorality, homosexuality, and bestiality. American courts make it almost impossible to clean this kind of dissolute literature off the shelves of bookstores and drugstores. Books that would once have been outlawed in America are now placed within easy reach of children.

The Greek word translated "fierce" describes an aspect of the last days that needs scarcely any comment. We are living in days when fierce men terrorize whole segments of society. Who can doubt that international terrorism is on the rise? The Rand Corporation, which keeps an eye on the escalation of terror used to achieve otherwise unattainable objectives, claims that the number of acts of terror is increasing.

Studies have shown that a unified network of terror reaches from Havana, via Moscow, to the Middle East, Europe, and Japan.

The patron and ultimate beneficiary was the Soviet Union. Training camps have been known to operate in Cuba, the Middle East, and the Soviet Union. These camps have turned out terrorists by the thousands. Groups such as Italy's Red Brigade, Germany's Baader-Meinhoff Gang, the PLO, the Japanese Red Army, Uruguay's Tupamaros, and the Provisional IRA are all said to have received help from Russia in the past and to have contacts among themselves. One estimate is that there are as many as 140 such terrorist groups active in the world.

They are characterized by one thing, their fierceness. Terror is their weapon; a bomb or plastic explosive secreted in a car, school, hospital, church, bus, or airplane can influence millions who will see the results. The more extensive the newspaper and TV coverage, the better. A judge is killed; the editor of a newspaper is crippled; a statesman is kidnapped; a plane is hijacked; a group of school children are gunned down. The aim is to influence social and political decisions. These fierce people have no regard for their victims.

Terrorists are becoming better equipped. Their arsenals are known to include Soviet-made antitank guns, French air-to-ground missiles, and surface-to-air missiles. One such missile, properly handled, could easily shoot down a jumbo jet loaded with passengers. One rocket and the threat of more could paralyze the world's transportation system. And that is only the beginning. It is now technically possible for terrorists to manufacture atomic weapons. And what would happen if they acquired biochemical weapons? Just an ounce of anthrax, released into the ductwork of a single stadium, could claim an immediate seventy thousand victims.

PEOPLE WITHOUT CONVICTION (2 TIMOTHY 3:3-5)

Paul said that in the last days people would be "despisers of those that are good" or, as one translator rendered it, they will be "haters of good" (2 Timothy 3:3, NASB). The moral rot of our age has already penetrated deeply into western society. In Sweden, for instance, a royal commission some years ago heralded the arrival of "the contraceptive society" as though the achievement of free sex were a national moral goal. The commission announced that

93 percent of all Swedish people had a permissive attitude toward premarital sex and that some 33 percent of all Swedish brides were pregnant at their weddings. The commission added that the contraceptive society could no more be reversed than could the industrial revolution.

Jerry Falwell highlighted the open scorn of goodness in America. On August 13, 1981, he sent out a mailing that included a sealed envelope. The covering letter reminded his readers that some 250,000 homosexuals had marched through the streets of San Francisco while an additional 75,000 paraded in the streets of Los Angeles. He described how large groups of homosexuals come to his rallies constantly to demonstrate against him, shout obscenities, and wave banners bearing vulgar slogans.

The letter then drew attention to the sealed envelope and warned that it contained factual material and photographs that might be offensive to some. One picture showed a march of so-called gays waving their banners high. One banner read, "Bible-waving bigots are born-again hypocrites." Another proclaimed, "God is our Master, and He knows we are gay." In another picture a couple of parents were shown—the woman carrying a card reading, "Parents of Gays," and the man carrying a large placard announcing, "We Are Proud of Our Gay Children." Another picture showed men hugging and kissing each other. In another picture two men, one dressed like a woman, proudly displayed their marriage certificate. Another picture showed admitted homosexuals being sworn in as policemen in San Francisco. Another picture could have come right out of Sodom; it showed two men parading as women and wearing padded women's undergarments. The final picture showed two male homosexuals demonstrating against Dr. Falwell and carrying a banner between them proclaiming them to be "The Oral Majority." Such is the decadence of our age.

TV adds to the attack on goodness. Popular shows, for instance, occasionally present programs making sodomy a laughing matter. Nowhere is this attack on goodness more evident than in the sweeping acceptance by ordinary people of sodomy as an acceptable lifestyle.

How far we have gone in rejecting the Bible's code for moral goodness as a basis of behavior is illustrated in a cartoon in the *New Yorker* magazine. It depicted two women of the older generation talking. One was saying to the other, "No! No! It's Gloria and

Frank who are married but not living together; Judy and George are living together but not married."

Paul next told us that in the last days men will be "traitors" (2 Timothy 3:4). There have always been traitors; David had his Ahithophel and Jesus had His Judas. But in our day treachery has become epidemic. Movements such as fascism and communism have banded people together by the thousands for the sole purpose of betraying their homelands to foreign foes, whose ideologies they have been taught to embrace.

In 1936, during the Spanish Civil War, General Mola announced he would capture Madrid because he had four columns outside the city and a *fifth column* of sympathizers inside. The world pounced on the phrase because it expressed the dimensions of treason in our times. For a long time thereafter people who betrayed their countries were called "fifth columnists." But even that descriptive phrase has passed out of current usage now that we have the more ominous brand of communist-style treachery.

The parade of traitors' names in the news is endless. We think of Ethel and Julius Rosenberg and their accomplices, David Greenglass and the Soviet intelligence courier Harry Gold. They were members of a network of spies who handed over atomic secrets to Russia after World War II and made it possible for Russia to become an atomic power—and thus for the world to become an infinitely more dangerous place. Judge Kaufman, when he sentenced the Rosenbergs to death, declared, "Plain, deliberate, contemplated murder is dwarfed in magnitude by comparison with the crime you have committed."

We think of the names of Guy Burgess, Donald Maclean, and Kim Philby, men who systematically betrayed some of Britain's and America's most vital secrets to the Russians. Philby actually headed the Soviet section of British intelligence, was the head of all counterintelligence operations, and was also the liaison between American and British intelligence services as well as being the trusted friend of FBI director J. Edgar Hoover. It was Philby who tipped off the Soviets that Britain and America were raising a guerrilla force in Albania and thus enabled the Russians to foil the move and secure their hold on communist-dominated Eastern Europe. "He betrayed a whole generation" was one of Philby's colleague's comments when he heard of Philby's treachery.

Nobody has been able to assess the extent to which the

Russians have been able to penetrate the West nor the full extent of the treachery of our times. All we know is that Russian infiltration has been vast. NATO sources, years ago, estimated that the number of "legal" Soviet spies in the West (that is, agents using diplomatic, press, and trade passports) was about ten thousand. For every such Soviet spy legally in the West there has been an army of those who support him. The Russian KGB used to have an annual budget of about ten billion dollars. About 24 percent of all Soviet diplomats abroad were known to be KGB men. It is a mystery why the West put up with it. The Russians, in addition to their regular spying, have used such international agencies as the United Nations and its various departments as places in which to conceal more agents.

Stories surface continually. An Iranian major-general confessed to being a Soviet spy. A French spy-ring gave the Russians information about the advanced Mirage-2000 fighter plane and reveals some of the inner secrets of NATO defense strategy. A secretary in the office of a German chancellor was discovered to be a spy for East Germany. A Swiss general admitted that he had passed top defense secrets to Moscow agents. In a single clean-out, Britain expelled more than a hundred Russian diplomats on the charge of spying. Forty-six people were arrested in Israel as Syrian spies, four of them Jews and two of them elitist (native-born) *sabras*. A former CIA man sold technical manuals of crucial military and strategic importance to the Russians; but although he was convicted and sent to prison for forty years, nobody really knows for sure that he is the right man. The real traitor may still be at large, still in a position to do even more damage—and nobody knows how to assess the extent of the damage already done. Certainly Paul spoke the truth when he said that in the last days men would be traitors.

He also said they would be "heady [and] high-minded" (2 Timothy 3:4). The Greek word translated "heady" means "headlong, restless, precipitate." It carries the idea of falling down. The only other place where it is used in Scripture is in Acts 19:36 where it is rendered "rashly."

We do not have to look far for illustrations of people acting rashly. The drug scene alone gives us countless examples. It is estimated that in the United States alone people spend $140 billion annually on drugs. Dealers scoff at the law. It is nothing for one of them to post a million-dollar bond and then walk away laughing.

About fifteen million Americans smoke pot regularly. Some forty-five million Americans are said to have experimented with this drug. We are told that people are starting to try it at an earlier age than ever before and that they are smoking it more frequently and in much stronger doses. Teenagers think it smart to smoke pot. More money is spent on marijuana than on tobacco. Users consider marijuana a safe drug and scoff at stories that tell the opposite. Yet scientists warn that its habitual use damages the body's white blood cells, reducing one's ability to fight infection. It undermines the lungs, reproductive system, brain, and immune system. It is derived from the cannabis plant which yields more than a hundred known chemicals.

The best way to describe these drug users is with the King James version's old-fashioned word *heady*. Regrettably, they often have the sad example of their pot-smoking older brothers, sisters, and parents. Worse still, they receive confusing signals from officialdom. President Carter, for instance, supported the easing of federal laws against the use of marijuana.[4] Some government officials seem to feel that enforcing laws against marijuana is too expensive and difficult to be worthwhile.

Another popular drug is the highly dangerous PCP, sometimes called "angel dust." More expressive, perhaps, is another of its nicknames, *hog*. It is easy to make out of handy ingredients; it can be eaten, smoked, sniffed, or injected into the body's system. It is known to cause disorientation and, while it can give the user a high, it can also cause hallucinations, produce violent behavior, lead to comas, and end in death. According to one source, it is more prevalent on high school campuses than marijuana. It has been described as "a rattlesnake," yet kids, heady and high-minded, refuse to be told or warned, and pump the stuff into their systems.

Millions of professional people have their own drug, cocaine. Lawyers, politicians, businessmen, bankers, government officials, and solid middle-class citizens are all said to be users. They think it is safe. It is said to be a fast-acting drug which gives intense and vivid sensations by acting on the central nervous system as a powerful stimulant. Continued use, however, erodes the personality; its delusions and hallucinations are followed by deep depressions. Scientists say it can damage the liver and increase the danger of heart attacks. Yet these heady, high-minded people, who ought to know better, are scornful of the consequences and confident that no ill effects can happen to them.

The most deadly drug of all is heroin, the exotic export from the poppy fields of Iran, Iraq, Pakistan, and Afghanistan. It reaches the market via the syndicate that has its own processing plants and an army of distributors in the world's cities. The drug's route from the golden crescent to market has been dubbed "the godfather line."

Heroin gives a high that lasts up to ten hours as compared with the brief, hour-long, cocaine high. It is popular with poor, young, slum dwellers, because it offers a feeling of joy and relief from the tedium of poverty. Regular use leads to the most frightful addiction, so that addicts resort to crime to finance their habit rather than face the agonies of quitting. The number of heroin addicts is on the rise. Its use is said to be epidemic in New York City alone.

The abysmal folly of taking drugs should be clear to all, but despite the warnings millions start down this perilous road, heady, reckless, headstrong—just as Paul said—confident "it can't happen to me."

Along with all this, Paul said that in the last days people would be "lovers of pleasures more than lovers of God" (2 Timothy 3:4). There was once a time in this country when Sunday was "the Lord's day," publicly set aside for worship. Stores were closed, places of amusement were closed, taverns were closed, and public transportation operated on a reduced schedule. No more. Today Sunday is the big day for pleasure.

In this country, as in the western world in general, we have become a nation of pleasure-seekers. What someone has called "the pleasure explosion" has overtaken us so that in the United States alone the pleasure business has been growing at an average rate of about six billion dollars a year since 1965. Movie attendance alone takes in one billion dollars year. In most homes, TV sets are kept on about six hours a day. Thousands of people jam national parks on weekends. Americans drive an estimated 350 billion miles a year in the pursuit of pleasure.

Thrills and chills are available on demand. Popular amusement parks offer spectacular shows along with breathtaking rides. Six Flags in Atlanta, for instance, has its Great American Scream Machine and its Mind Bender, a gravity-defying roller-coaster that hurls its riders around three loops and down through underground tunnels. Six Flags in Texas has the Shock Wave, billed as "the largest, tallest, fastest, double-loop roller-coaster in the world." Riders are hauled up a steep incline to a height of 116 feet, suddenly dropped, and hurtled through vertical loops 70 feet tall. Then there is the Greased Lightnin' coaster at Astroworld. Riders are circled over 80 feet into the air, going almost straight up for the equivalent of about ten stories, and then orbited upside down at a force of six Gs. All for fun.

One of the latest comers to the pleasure market is the video game, which rivals even TV, itself one of the most pervasive sources of pleasure and amusement. One estimate is that five billion dollars are spent in a single year on video games and that during a single year people play them for the equivalent of seventy-five thousand *man-years*. Over and above that, something like a billion dollars are spent annually on games that can be plugged in and played on TV sets in the home.

People are getting hooked on them. One reporter found that children in the fifth grade think they need a minimum of three dollars just for one round of games in an amusement arcade, and some children said they spend as much as forty dollars a day to support the craze.[5] Not that children are the only addicts. In some cities playing with these sophisticated toys has become a lunch-hour pastime for many businessmen. Indeed, cases of "video epilepsy" have been reported, a syndrome brought on by overexposure to light patterns in certain games.

There can be little doubt that we have become a generation addicted to pleasure. That it is a generation addicted to pleasure *more* than to the things of God is evident too. The United States probably has the greatest percentage of people who go to church on a more or less regular basis. Yet the spending habits of the American public make it quite evident that token attendance to religious duties is in no way allowed to interfere with most people's pleasure.

One survey, taken some years ago, but probably still relatively valid, showed that in one year Americans spent $16 billion for amusements, $10.5 billion for alcohol, $5 billion for tobacco, $2 billion for travel, $325 million for cat and dog food, $304 million for chewing gum, and $76 million for lipstick. During the same period, the grand total reported to have been given for foreign missions by all the Protestant churches of the United States was said to be $145 million, less than half of what Americans spent on chewing gum. If those figures are only reasonably accurate, it is evident that people are lovers of pleasure more than lovers of God.

Along with this decline in interest in the things of God, Paul foresaw that in the last days people would have "a form of godliness, but denying the power thereof." He added, "From such turn away" (2 Timothy 3:5). The Greek word for power here is *dunamis*, the kind of power entrusted by the Holy Spirit to the church. It is the word used to describe the saving power of the gospel (Romans 1:16). Paul here described people who have perhaps been baptized and made a profession of faith, joined a church and become communicants. They support its programs and have even been ordained to its ministry, all without ever having known the life-transforming power of the gospel in their lives. They have "a form of godliness."

The word translated "form" is a rare one in the New Testament. It is used here and in Romans 2:20 where Paul accused his unsaved Jewish fellow countrymen of having a "form of knowledge." It was knowledge without substance, because it kept them from Christ. Paul saw the endtimes as a period when church attendance in itself would be deceptive; many religious people would be unsaved and going through an empty form of the Christian faith.

Paul warned true believers not to have fellowship with such. We are to put distance between ourselves and superficial professors of Christianity.

PEOPLE WITHOUT CONSCIENCE (2 TIMOTHY 3:6 - 9)

A day was coming when spiritual wickedness would masquerade successfully in religious disguise. The Bible often reserves its most scalding words for those who propagate false religion in the name of Christ.

"For of this sort are they which creep into houses, and lead captive silly women laden with sins, led away with divers lusts, Ever learning, and never able to come to the knowledge of the truth" (2 Timothy 3:6-7). J. B. Phillips's colorful rendering of the expression "creep into" is "worm their way into." The New English Bible is just as graphic. It renders the sentence, "They are the sort that insinuate themselves into private houses." These deceivers gain entrance by coming under cloak of the truth. Their favorite target is the woman of the house, so they frequently come at times when the man is away at work. They hope to get their feet in the door so that eventually they might subvert the entire household. Many modern cults specialize in this method of propagating their false teachings.

Some years ago I had a call from a woman who attended an evangelical church in town. She phoned to ask where she could get a polyglot Bible. I knew the woman and her family. She was a kindly woman but certainly no student. I asked her why she required a polyglot Bible (a Bible written in several languages). She said that the Bible could be better understood in Greek.

I guessed at once what was happening. She had been talking to some Jehovah's Witnesses. In fact, a brief conversation revealed that they had made considerable headway both with her and her husband. I asked her if she realized that Jehovah's Witnesses deny the deity of Christ, ridicule the trinity, deny Christ's bodily resurrection, deny the Biblical doctrine of Hell, and claim that only 144,000 people can be born again. She seemed dazed and agreed readily enough for myself and a friend to call on her and to meet her new teachers in her home.

When we arrived we found two or three Jehovah's Witness teachers already there; one of them was a traveling teacher for the movement. We laid down the ground rule that, in the coming discussion, the only book to be used was the Bible. My missionary friend, with the skill of a surgeon, dismembered Jehovah's Witness doctrine piece by piece. At one point he exposed a piece of trickery—the traveling teacher had concealed within the covers of his Bible a small book to which he referred from time to time. We asked him to lay it aside. In the end, late at night, they left. We stayed.

The woman and her husband seemed astonished that they had been so beguiled by the cult and had readily received such false teachings as gospel truth. The cult had wormed its way in. On a shelf the couple had a row of *Watchtower* materials as well as a copy of the Jehovah's Witness adulterated Bible. We advised them to burn the lot, and after some additional conversation and prayer we left.

But that was not the end. The woman refused to get rid of the books and the Jehovah's Witness Bible. They seemed to haunt her.

They had taken some kind of hold on her mind, and they held her in a grip from which nothing could pry her loose. She seemed far more attached to those publications than she ever had been to her Bible in all the years she had attended a fine Bible-teaching church.

Before long the inner struggle came to a head. Voices began to whisper to her that she was in danger of Armageddon. We showed the woman from the Scriptures that if she trusted Christ she would never see Armageddon and that the cult was using the threat of Armageddon to frighten her into submission. But still she refused to burn those books, and her husband did not oppose her wishes. Further visits from her Jehovah's Witness friends increased her mental confusion and the inner voices continued.

Finally she had to make a decision. She could not go on receiving visits from us and from the members of the cult. She asked us to stop coming. The last we heard of her she had been formally received into the Jehovah's Witness fold, had been baptized into their organization, and had begun to "witness" for them. It all began when a zealous ambassador of the cult came knocking at her door when her husband was away from home.

Paul, seeing these end-time dangers, seeing people "creep into houses," warned us to turn away from such. There are few things more underhanded than abusing hospitality in order to take over a home in the name of a Christ-denying religion.

Paul pointed out that "silly women, laden with sins" will be the primary targets of the end-time cults. The word translated "silly" is a diminutive of the word "women" and is used in a derogatory sense. One translator used the phrase *creatures of impulse* to render the expression; another said that the word *silly* comes from an Anglo-Saxon word meaning "inoffensive" or "harmless." Because such persons are looked on as an easy prey by scheming persons, the word *silly* has come to be used for those easily duped.

Dean Alford said of the phrase "laden with sins" that it means that these people are burdened by their wrongdoing; their consciences are oppressed with their sins, and in this morbid state they are an easy prey to religious teachers who promise them ease of conscience if they follow them. J. B. Phillips rendered the statement, "silly women with an exaggerated sense of sin and morbid cravings."

Paul added that these people are "ever learning." One translator rendered that as "curious to learn." That, of course, led to Eve's sin in the garden of Eden. She was curious to learn the forbidden secrets the serpent dangled alluringly before her, and that curiosity led her into rebellion against God's Word, into sin, and on to judgment. Paul foresaw, then, end-time cults making a special target of a certain kind of woman in order to further their own ends.

There is something else to add to the picture. "Now as Jannes and Jambres withstood Moses, so do these also resist the truth: men of corrupt minds, reprobate concerning the faith" (2 Timothy 3:8). Paul saw these false and subtle teachers as traitors to the faith.

The Old Testament incident to which he referred is recorded in Exodus 7. When Moses first appeared in Egypt as the liberator of the Hebrew people, Aaron was with him. God had two men in Egypt; Satan had two men in Egypt. At Moses' word, Aaron cast his rod on the ground before pharaoh and it became a serpent. At once the magicians of Egypt imitated the miracle. Moses turned the water of Egypt into blood, and again the magicians duplicated the miracle. Moses summoned frogs from the river, and the Egyptian magicians did the same. Their purpose was to oppose the truth of God and hold the pharaoh in bondage to error.

Paul held these two magicians up as examples of end-time false teachers who will likewise resist the truth of God and keep people enchained in deception. It is not that they do not know the truth, but that they deliberately oppose the truth. We would probably be astonished if we knew how many false teachers and apostate religious leaders there are who once knew God's Word in truth.

Take the case of Aleister Crowley, an English occultist who delved into the black arts, specializing in orgiastic black magic. He liked to call himself Beast 666 and to describe himself as "the wickedest man on earth." He claimed to be an incarnation of the infamous Borgia pope, Alexander VI. He had a burning lust for women and wore a special perfume he called Perfume of Immortality, which he claimed made him irresistible. He was also a homosexual. At one time he was a member of the Golden Dawn, an occult society from which the Nazis derived much of their inspiration. His unsavory reputation brought him into disfavor with other members of the society and he left to found his own lodge, the Astrum Argentinum, which he dedicated to the practice of black magic. He became an exponent of a brand of perverted and sadistic magic. At his funeral in 1947 he had recited an orgiastic poem in which he described himself as god and as one who raved, raped, and ripped "world without end."

This evil man was brought up among the Plymouth Brethren, a group of fundamentalist, evangelical, Bible-believing, Christ-honoring believers committed to the verbal inspiration of the Scriptures, to the cardinal doctrines of the Christian faith, to the new birth, and to godly living. Crowley was the kind of man referred to by Paul, a man of corrupt mind and reprobate concerning the faith. He is one of many more whose rebellion against the truth of God have led them into the paths of error.

Paul showed that eventually God draws the line with all such people and with the cults they establish and promote. "But they shall proceed no further: for their folly shall be manifest unto all men, as their's [Jannes and Jambres] also was" (2 Timothy 3:9). These people reckon without God. God permitted the Egyptian magicians to go just so far with their deceptions; then He stopped them in their tracks and exposed them. Just so, with these end-time false teachers, God will allow them their seeming successes. But in the end, in His own good time and way, He will expose them for what they are. In a coming day Satan's two men, the beast and the false prophet, will be the supreme examples of all such false deceivers.

The river of apostasy is rising today. The "perilous times" of which Paul wrote are on us. Soon the river will overflow its banks as all the tributaries of delusion and deception join the main stream. When it reaches flood level, that river itself will inundate the earth in the final apostasy: the enthronement of the devil's messiah as this world's god and king.

---

1. "The Youth Crime Plague," *Time* (July 11, 1977), pp. 18-20.
2. "The Attack," *Intelligence Digest* (August 1961, September 1961).
3. "Something Rotten," *Intelligence Digest* (May 1962).
4. "The Potshot that Backfired," *Time* (July 19, 1982), p. 79.
5. "Games that People Play," *Time* (January 18, 1982), p. 52.

10

Demonic Teaching in the Last Days
1 Timothy 4:1-3

The Bible clearly teaches that we can expect an invasion from the pit in the last days. People will be led astray by evil spirits and occult teachings. The shadows of these things are already darkening the world. Nothing but the restraining presence of God the Holy Spirit is holding back the flood-time of this evil. As we have seen elsewhere in this study, advanced spiritism was a mark of Noah's day; it is becoming an increasingly evident characteristic of the age in which we live.

It has long been known, for instance, that Adolph Hitler consulted horoscopes and that Nazi Germany had its Federal Commission for Occultism, the first time that a modern state officially recognized the existence of the occult and created a government department to oversee it.

People who had personal contact with Hitler often spoke of the strange hypnotic power he was able to exert. Hitler's former lawyer and his governor general for occupied Poland, Hans Frank, while sitting in his prison cell at Nuremberg, spoke of Hitler's disconcerting stare. He described it as "the stare of an insensitive psychopath." He confessed to the prison psychologist that in serving Hitler he had been "in league with the devil."[1]

The British government took Hitler's occultism seriously. Winston Churchill actually retained the services of a German occultist, Dr. Walter Stein, to keep him informed on what the astrologers were telling Hitler. Stein was an initiate into the occult mysteries, a clairvoyant medium, and a student of the same books that enslaved Hitler. (Stein was not really able to tell Churchill what German astrologers were telling Hitler, because horoscopes vary as widely as the people who cast them.)

Deitrich Eckart, one of the seven founders of the Nazi party, initiated Hitler into occultism. Hitler then became a member of the powerful Thule Group in Germany, an occult society that included judges, lawyers, doctors, university professors, industrialists, surgeons, military men, and members of the nobility. The members of this secret society were Satanists who practiced the black arts and communicated with demons. Eckart was the reigning high priest. Hitler was the promised messiah whose coming the mediums had foretold. Initiation into the deeper mysteries of this powerful and widespread fellowship of occultists included committing atrocities as part of the ritual magic. Horrible rites opened Hitler's soul to possession by powerful demons. The whole story has been told in a remarkable book, *The Spear of Destiny*, in which much about Hitler and the Nazis, usually left untouched by more conventional histories, is explained.[2]

The demons that controlled the demented soul of Adolph Hitler lured him and Germany into World War II and then abandoned both him and his country to their fate. Heinrich Himmler and many members of the dreaded SS also were initiates of Satanic cults. One of the secret aims of the Nazi leaders was to impose a new world religion on mankind once the war was won. In this religion the swastika would replace the cross, Hitler would be the messiah, and demons would guide the destinies of mankind.

Hitler and his fellow conspirators came close to succeeding. They failed because the time was not yet ripe in the counsels of God for the forces of Satan to triumph. However, the whole Nazi era was a dress rehearsal for the coming of the beast and the consequent baptism of unregenerate mankind into just such a religion.

In his first letter to his young convert and colleague, Timothy, the apostle Paul unveiled this aspect of the last days. He warned that the endtimes will be characterized by a massive invasion of human society by demonic cults and devilish philosophies. Men of the endtimes, despite their science and sophistication, despite their skill in engineering and technology, will become prey to occult forces. In this chapter we are going to examine what Paul had to say about demonic teaching in the endtimes. His comments are found in 1 Timothy 4:1-3.

I. Rebellion Against Divine Truth in the Last Days (1 Timothy 4:1)
II. Revival of Demonic Teaching in the Last Days (1 Timothy 4:1-3)
    A. Its propagators (4:1-2)
        1. Lying spirits (4:1)
        2. Lying sophists (4:2)
    B. Its prohibitions (4:3)
        1. Forbidding marriage
        2. Forbidding meats

A REBELLION AGAINST DIVINE TRUTH (1 TIMOTHY 4:1)

The apostle began by pointing out that before the occult world achieves success there must be a massive revolt against the truths of God. He wrote, "Now the Spirit speaketh expressly, that in the latter times some shall depart from the faith, giving heed to seducing spirits, and doctrines of devils."

The Greek word for "depart" means "to apostatize." It indicates a widespread turning away from the truth of God toward the end of the age. Paul foresaw that people would turn their backs on Christian faith and embrace religious teachings and secular philosophies secretly sponsored by lying spirits. The Christian ethic in society would be replaced by a general secularization of mankind, which in turn would give way to outright occultism.

The preparation of the world for the coming antichrist, the supreme occultist, is proceeding along both lines. The world is being secularized. Perhaps nothing has made this possible more than the publication of Charles Darwin's *On the Origin of Species*, the book that launched the theory of evolution. The theory was seized on by T. H. Huxley, who saw in it a way to vent his personal spite on the clergy. He became Darwin's bulldog, biting and barking away at the theologians.

Evolution has achieved its phenomenal success chiefly because it gives people a working hypothesis for atheism; the origin of the universe can be "explained" without having to face the fact of God. Professor Adam Sedgwick, a Cambridge geologist, saw right through Darwin's book as soon as it was published. He described it as "a dish of rank materialism cleverly cooked and served up merely to make us independent of a creator." He and Thomas Carlyle both shared the fear that if Darwin's theories were generally accepted the human race would inevitably be brutalized.[3] After two world wars and the global communist conspiracy we can see how right they were; Darwin's theory of the survival of the fittest underlies the political theories of both Nazism and communism. Karl Marx wrote, "Darwin's book is very important and serves me as a basis in natural science for the struggle of history."[4]

Darwin was by no means the hero his admirers make him out to be. He was a waster at school, improvident, and a constant disappointment to his father both while at Edinburgh University and at Cambridge. He once decided to go into the Christian ministry but when given the chance to go to sea on the staff of the *Beagle*, he decided to abandon theology.

While on board he began to collect evidence for the theory of evolution which had already been tentatively suggested by others. Even when his findings were in order, he vacillated for months before making them public because he was afraid he might fall between scientific scorn on one side and theological abuse on the other. It wasn't until he discovered that a rival was about to publish similar views that he took the plunge. In the end, Darwin flung his religious beliefs to the winds and became the tool of Huxley and his circle of God-haters. Evolutionary theory has triumphed so completely in the secular world of today that, despite its obvious flaws and inconsistencies, it is at the root of much of the thinking of our age.

Public opinion is being increasingly shaped by secular humanists who have wormed their way into our schools, courts, and government, where they exercise influence out of all proportion to their numbers. And they are becoming bolder. I noticed, for instance, one of the larger advertisements in the classified section of *Atlantic Monthly*. It offered a white cotton T-shirt with red silkscreen print depicting the SECULAR HUMANIST and the system's three favorite publications—*Das Kapital, Origin of Species*, and *Playboy* magazine. A free catalog was also offered.

Secular humanists have a fourfold goal. They want a world religion based on science in which man is his own god, in which the state is supreme, and in which the best of all religions is synthesized into a common faith. They want a new economic system based on socialism or communism. They want a new world order in which war and poverty are abolished and there are no social problems. They want a new race in which man takes charge of the destiny and evolution of the human race, using genetic engineering to breed a new kind of man. Education must serve the interests of this new order, which means that children must be indoctrinated from the age of two through college. The mass media, courts, educational system, churches, and government agencies must all be enlisted to speed up the process. They see Biblical Christianity as old-fashioned, and patriotism and traditional beliefs as obstacles that must be systematically attacked and uprooted.

A passing glance is all that is needed to see how far the secularists have already succeeded in forcing their views on society. Secular humanists recognize that man is a worshiping creature; but the emasculated religion they intend to put in the place of Christianity is so sterile, unspiritual, and nonsupernatural that it will never fill the God-shaped vacuum in the human soul. So the secularism these people have espoused will be overtaken by occult religion. The process is already underway as people are becoming increasingly influenced by eastern religions and by witchcraft, astrology, psychic phenomena, hauntings, ESP, and spiritism. These things are accepted by millions without question as being of divine origin. Paul's warning that the last days of the church age will coincide with massive demonic activity in society is carelessly ignored.

An increasing number of books, films, TV programs, and news articles deal with the occult. Take, for instance, the book and film *Rosemary's Baby*, both of which had phenomenal success. The book was the story of a woman who was made pregnant by the devil and who bore a son with the marks of the devil on him. *Rosemary's Baby* has been called "the greatest advertisement for satanism ever concocted." The promotion for the film bordered on the blasphemous. When it premiered on the west coast, newspaper advertisements pleaded, "Pray for Rosemary's Baby."

The producer was Roman Polanski, who made a number of horror movies and at one time enjoyed the reputation of having made the most horrifying ever filmed. He married Sharon Tate, who often acted in movies about devil worship and sacrificial murder. Ironically, Sharon Tate was one of the victims of the Satanist, dope-drenched, sex-saturated Manson cult. She was stabbed to death in her own home shortly before she was about to give birth to a baby of her own. She died pleading in vain for the life of the unborn Richard Paul Polanski.

Numerous other books and movies have also taken bookstores and box offices by storm. *The Exorcist,* which relates in lurid detail the demon possession of a twelve-year-old girl and the attempts made to expel the spirit that controlled her, drew phenomenal crowds. The suburban gothic chiller *Poltergeist* grossed $39.5 million in its first eight weeks.

Millions of people have read such books as *God from Outer Space* and *Chariots of the Gods.* Whole sections of bookstores are now devoted to the sale of occult books. Millions of people across the nation tune in to talk shows featuring psychics, witches, and soothsayers. Handbooks on witchcraft and spells are readily available. Astrology is experiencing a revival. The United States supports about twenty thousand astrologers in contrast with two thousand astronomers. We read in newspapers and magazines accounts of telepathy, levitation, UFOs, telekinesis, or some odd happening in the Bermuda Triangle. More and more the occult is intruding into our society.

Few people realize it, but occultism is at the root of Mormonism, one of the world's fastest-growing religious cults. The cult's leaders know the truth; the fact that Joseph Smith and other prominent founding fathers of Mormonism had recourse to the spirit world is too well documented to be denied. Dr. Walter Martin, who is probably as well versed in Mormon history and doctrine as anyone in this country, has exposed and documented the truth in his writings. He has a chapter on "The Occult Side of Mormonism" in his book, *The Maze of Mormonism.*[5]

He told us, for instance, that Joseph Smith was an occultist who used a special "peepstone" to help him translate his Bible. Wilford Woodruff, one of the early presidents of the Mormon cult, talked openly of his occult experiences. He claimed to have received visits from Joseph Smith, Brigham Young, and Heber C. Kimball on various occasions. These founders of Mormonism gave heed to "doctrines of demons." Paul warned of such and indicated that their teachings would be a feature of the last days. The fact that Mormonism puts on a respectable front for public consumption does not alter its murky past. Its antibiblical doctrines confirm the cult's source of inspiration. Nor do the present leaders of Mormonism repudiate the movement's founders. On the contrary, they glorify them and present carefully edited versions of their history to the public for mass consumption.

Occultism led Bishop James A. Pike of the American Episcopal Church to his death. Pike was a lawyer turned clergyman turned spiritist. He was already an apostate from the faith and under investigation by his church for heresy before he became the dupe of deceiving spirits. He was a rationalist and a disbeliever in the resurrection of Christ, even while holding high office in the church. He was lured into demonism after the death of his son, who committed suicide in New York City at the age of twenty, having become addicted to psychedelic drugs. The agnostic bishop had his boy's body cremated and the ashes scattered on the Pacific Ocean just beyond San Francisco's Golden Gate bridge.

The heartbroken father went to Cambridge, England, where he and his son had once spent some happy times together. It was a pilgrimage of remorse. He sought out the apartment where they had stayed, and there strange things began to happen. The evidence that these happenings were supernatural in character was overwhelming, and the distraught father became convinced that his dead son was trying to get in touch with him. He became so obsessed with this idea that he decided to consult a spiritist medium and sought out a certain Mrs. Twigg, reputed to be England's most distinguished and successful clairvoyant.

Sure enough, the medium professed to receive a message from the dead boy, and this was backed up with enough surface evidence to make it convincing. As part of the deception, the supposed ghost of Paul Tillich appeared. Tillich was a German-American theologian who had died some months before and who had been one of the apostate bishop's friends. The supposed spirit of Tillich thanked Pike for dedicating a book to him and also urged him to continue his campaign against orthodox Christian doctrine.

Bishop Pike returned to America, resigned his position in his church, and became a champion for the weird world of the occult.

In the end, the spirits lured him to his death in the desert that surrounds the Dead Sea. The story of Bishop Pike is another indication that Paul's words are true. "Some shall depart from the faith, giving heed to seducing spirits."

We can expect more and more departures from the faith as time goes on. The warnings of the Bible against any form of necromancy, spiritism, witchcraft, soothsaying, and astrology are brushed aside as more and more people are becoming a prey to the doctrines of demons. It all begins with a rebellion against divine truth, with people who think they know better than the Bible, who repudiate the Word of God and abandon the teachings of the Christian faith. Those who thus abandon the faith throw away the only armor that can protect them from lying spirits.

A REVIVAL OF DEMONIC TEACHING (1 TIMOTHY 4:1-3)

The falling away from the faith, Paul said, would be accompanied by increasing reliance on false teaching inspired by demons. In developing this area of his prophecy, Paul discussed first *the propagators* of the lies that will deceive mankind. The attack will be led by "seducing spirits," and people will believe "doctrines of demons."

The occult world has never been very far away. From time to time in human history it has broken through, as it did in the days before the flood and again in Canaan prior to the Hebrew invasion under Joshua. It broke through again in the time of Christ. It is interesting that the first miracle of Jesus recorded by Mark and the first recorded by Luke both concern an encounter with an evil spirit. The presence of Christ on earth and His resounding defeat of the devil in the wilderness aroused all Hell. The Lord Jesus' presence threw the underworld into confusion. The demons knew Him instantly. They had been scanning human faces for centuries. Their information, pooled and shared, ranged over all continents and oceans; and their knowledge embraced also that other world which lies beyond the reach of our senses. Their testimony to Christ blazed forth instantly. "Unclean spirits, when they saw him, fell down before him, and cried, saying, Thou art the Son of God" (Mark 3:11). The tormenting demon that possessed the soul of the demoniac in Mark's first recorded miracle cried, "I know thee who thou art, the Holy One of God" (Mark 1:24). "Jesus I know," cried the fearful spirit in Acts 19:15. So said they all.

It is interesting that Christ "suffered not the devils to speak, *because* they knew him" (Mark 1:34, italics added). He would not accept testimony from such a perjured source. A lying spirit is not to be relied on even when it speaks the truth.

Modern spiritism was founded in 1848 by the Fox sisters who lived in Hydesville, New York. Margaret was twelve and Kate was four when they first heard tapping on the wall of their home. They devised a system of raps in order to establish communication with the haunting spirit. The spirit claimed to be that of a peddler who had visited the house five years previously and had been murdered by the blacksmith who then owned it. The spirit said that its body had been buried by the blacksmith in the cellar below the house. Sure enough, when the basement was investigated, gruesome remains were found beneath a plank of wood buried five feet below the surface. This occurrence attracted a great deal of attention, especially when it became evident that an organized attempt was being made by beings from another world to communicate with mankind. The first message received from beyond by an official group of investigators said, "We are all your dear friends and relations."[6]

The new movement soon attracted some outstanding advocates, including the brilliant British scientist Sir Oliver Lodge and Sir Arthur Conan Doyle, renowned inventor of the fictional detective Sherlock Holmes.

Spiritism insists, as the case of Bishop Pike illustrates, that communication with the other world is possible. The seeker assumes that the medium has made contact with a loved one or with someone else who once lived on earth. But what if other hands should create the phenomena of the seance and other voices dictate the script? What proof is there that the medium has really conjured up the dead? The Bible denies that they do. All mediums have what they call "familiar spirits"—that is, spirits who are familiar with the lives of those who once walked this earth. The only seance recorded in Scripture was broken up by God, and King Saul, who ordered it, was then and there sentenced to death (1 Samuel 28). The medium involved was stricken with horror. She had been expecting her familiar to appear, but instead, God sent back the spirit of Samuel the prophet to pronounce the sentence of doom.

Even spiritism's ablest advocates are shocked at the incompetence and often brazen wickedness of the spirits they contact. They tell us of Homers who can not speak passable Greek, of Shakespeares who can not write Elizabethan English, of Sir Isaac Newtons who can not solve the simplest mathematical problems. They confess that most of the phenomena encountered—noises, movement of tables, raps and taps, and inane answers to questions—are usually puerile, vulgar, or ridiculous.[7]

Serious investigators for the Society for Psychical Research have amassed volumes of evidence that a spirit world does exist and that it is possible for people to have contact with that world. So the question of whether or not the inhabitants of that unseen world come and go has long since been resolved. The question is, Who are they? Nothing is more amazing than the credulity of the spiritists, a credulity that survives even their own complete exposure of the character of the spirit beings with whom they are in contact. The spirits contacted deny all the cardinal doctrines of the Christian faith and substitute the bland lies of the pit. These lies are readily swallowed. Even when the "messages" that come are confessedly vague, incomplete, false, childish, and often blasphemous, they are still gullibly accepted as truth.

Sir Oliver Lodge once said, "Occasionally there are direct impersonations."[8] He was driven to confess that "the only alternative [to the return of the dead] is to imagine a sort of supernormal mischievousness, so elaborately misleading that it would have to be stigmatized as vicious or even diabolical."[9]

Stainton Moses, a former Oxford clergyman turned apostate by his familiar spirits and one of the foremost spiritists of the nineteenth century, confessed that the spirits with whom he communed were

> without moral consciousness; some will say anything. . . . There is an organized plan on the part of the spirits who govern these manifestations to act on us and the religious thought of the age. The central dogmas of the Christian faith seem especially attacked; and it was this that startled me.[10]

Yet the man was too deluded to realize that Paul had described him nearly two thousand years before when warning that people

236

would give heed to "seducing spirits, and doctrines of devils" (1 Timothy 4:1).

Sir Arthur Conan Doyle confessed much the same thing. He wrote, "We have, unhappily, to deal with cold-blooded lying on the part of wicked intelligences."[11]

The evil spirits that haunt the seances of the spiritists are clever enough to know the craving of the human heart for assurance that there is a life of rest, peace, and happiness beyond the grave. They go to considerable lengths to keep their human victims enmeshed in the web of lies and deception they have woven for their souls. Therefore they occasionally produce convincing and startling phenomena, sufficient to snare the minds of men like Lodge, the English physicist and scholar whose discoveries did much to make modern radio possible, and Doyle, the medical doctor who turned to writing fiction with such success that he became the most highly paid short-story writer of his time. He abandoned this lucrative profession to devote himself to studying and lecturing on spiritism.

Doyle told us of the materialization of a spirit called Eva. He said:

> When Eva is at her best, there forms a complete figure; this figure is molded to resemble some deceased person; the cord which binds her to the medium is loosened; a personality which either is or pretends to be that of the dead takes possession of it; and the breath of life is breathed into the image so that it moves and talks and expresses the emotions of the spirit within.[12]

The propagators of the lies that will delude mankind will be lying spirits. Satan's demonic hordes lurk in the unseen world to prey on unsuspecting human beings through spiritism and occultism, through the false religions they inspire and energize, and through destructive philosophies aimed at uprooting Christianity and replacing it with soul-destroying ideologies. Their purpose is to pave the way for the coming of the antichrist and to prepare people's minds for the last great lie.

The renewed interest in occultism in our age is one of the multiplying signs of the times. The testimony of Charles D. Lamme is particularly significant, and its value is not diminished by the fact that it was given a number of years ago:

For many years prior to my conversion, I was a student and teacher of occult philosophies. . . . Because I was sincere in my search for truth after being "initiated" into the inner circle of Theosophy, doubts began to arise in my mind as to the dependability of the system of which I had become a part. I knew that a great supernatural power was at work and I knew that I had touched realms that were more than physical. . . . Not being a Christian believer, I did not believe in the personality of Satan. This made it doubly hard, for I had no adequate explanation concerning the source of evil. . . . My learning made me hostile to the Bible. . . .

Satan working through occultism seems strange and weird to those who lack spiritual discernment. . . . The average man does not know what one is talking about when he speaks of the "Masters" and "Elder Brothers" of the many false religions. These are beings I now know to be great demon intelligences. I once revered them as the controlling agencies of the various mystic orders. I have been far enough to know that they are real. I do not hesitate to say that I believe that occultism is helping to make preparations to have the False Prophet and the Antichrist received.

There is an expectancy spread throughout the world that a Great Teacher is coming very shortly. . . . The Satanic hosts are now engaged in the superphysical world in making preparations for the Man of Sin. The word has gone out from the unseen sources, coming from the so-called "Masters," and the teaching is now spread throughout the world. They are creating channels in the minds of men by manipulating psychic agencies for a great expectancy which is but a promise of swift realization.

I have heard such men as C. Jindarapodasa, a Buddhist, deliver messages containing secret information outlining the knowledge which had come to them from the unseen realms regarding the coming of a Great Leader. Certain Hindi seers say . . . a great World Teacher must come as the reincarnation of some "Master" of the remote past. . . . In Buddhism, the monks tell of the rise of a world Buddha who will be a holy and supremely enlightened One. The master minds of Buddhism claim to have come in contact with unseen beings who have sent out information that One is coming.

> The Antichrist . . . will meet the demands of the occultists of all shades of thought who are predicting that a God-emperor will manifest himself. . . . The method of his appearing is to take possession of a body chosen by himself and prepared for his use. In other words, the occultists are looking for a man whose spirit will incarnate itself in a human body.[13]

In other words, evil spirits are already spreading the word throughout the occult religious systems that the devil's messiah is on the way. The above testimony was given some sixty years ago, and we are a lot closer now than we were in Lamme's day to the coming of the antichrist.

Trevor Ravenscroft's studies of occult forces behind the Nazi movement in Germany give corroborative evidence. He told us that the inner initiates of the Thule Group, those most familiar with its deepest and darkest secrets, were expecting a German messiah and that in Hitler they saw the one for whom they were waiting. Once Hitler had a sufficient power base in Germany, he established contact with Tibetan occultists and even established a community of them in Germany so that he could keep in close contact with what they had to say. There seem to have been ties between the various occult orders, the Theosophists, the Tibetan mystics, and the Nazi system.[14]

The occult religions of the East are still at it. On Sunday, April 25, 1982, an arresting full-page advertisement appeared in the *New York Times*. Similar full-page advertisements have appeared in the daily newspapers of major cities throughout the world, including Amsterdam, London, Stockholm, Paris, Rome, Frankfurt, Zurich, Madrid, Cairo, Johannesburg, Mexico City, Sydney, New Delhi, and Los Angeles. Evidently the movement being advertised is well-financed. The advertisement proclaimed that "the Christ is now here." It identified him as "the World Teacher, Lord Maitreya," and said that although his location was known only to a few, he would reveal himself and speak to the world within the next two months. Along with the advertisement were given two addresses in the United States, one in Holland, and one in England to which interested people could write for further information.

I wrote and received in return a brochure that, among other things, identified the source of the new information on the advent of the Christ as one Benjamin Creme, described in the brochure as a Scottish artist and esotericist who has been trained as the Christ's herald for twenty years. According to Mr. Creme, Maitreya (as the brochure prefers to call this "Christ") entered "his point of focus" on July 19, 1977, in "a well-known country of the modern world" (identified now as a Pakistani community in southeast London). He is said to have assumed a fully adult physical body and to be gradually unfolding his plan of emergence. His plan is to reveal his actual identity by the late spring of 1982 (already past) at which time "every eye shall see him and every ear shall hear him." At the time of this unveiling, the "Christ," it was promised, would "mentally overshadow all humanity simultaneously," his words being heard inwardly by all peoples in their own language.

The brochure tells us that throughout history a select group of men and women have been sending forth their teachings and that their influence has been staggering. Known collectively to esotericists as the masters of wisdom, these individuals have perfected themselves over many lifetimes and, as a "Spiritual Hierarchy, guide the development of mankind." According to the brochure, in every new era a master appears as an avatar, or world teacher. The master *Maitreya*, the greatest of them all, has now evolved.

All this is linked with the usual mumbo-jumbo of occultism and with "the age of Aquarius," a period of interest to astrologers and others as the time when a new world is supposed to begin. According to astrology, the age of Aquarius is due to begin about the year 2000. Forecasters predict that since Aquarius is a "fixed Air sign," the coming age will be one of order, construction, and intelligence.

The sign of Aquarius is the water carrier, originally the woman-ish Ganymede who poured out nectar for the gods on mount Olympus. He was carried off by Zeus in the form of an eagle; hence the constellation of the eagle is near Aquarius in the sky. In astrology people who are born under the sign of Aquarius (January 20 to February 18) are supposed to be brilliant, inventive, and very anxious to help others (hence the water carrier) by pouring themselves out in the service of their fellow men. (They are prone to be struck by lightning!)

According to astrologers we are presently in the age of Pisces, an age which began about A.D. 1. Pisces is a "changeable sign," symbolized by the fish (which is why Jesus chose fishermen to be His disciples). In astrology opposites are supposed to attract; that accounts for the prominence of the virgin Mary, since Virgo is the sign opposite Pisces. The symbolism of Christ as a lamb and as a shepherd does not fit, so that is described as a hangover from the age of Aries (supposedly conspicuous for ram worship). All of that is so much solemn nonsense.

The brochure on the coming of this new "Christ," however, seizes on "the age of Aquarius" myth as being proof of the arrival of the Christ. The brochure points out that Christ sent two of His disciples into Jerusalem to meet a man with a pitcher of water in his hand; he would lead them to the upper room. That is supposed to be some kind of proof that the Christ has now come, for this "Christ" the brochure heralds will give mankind the "life-giving waters" of Aquarius. The brochure also says the last supper prefigured "the sharing by all humanity of the world's bounty" (of course, the Bible says it symbolized Christ's death). The brochure would also impress us with the fact that the promised fifth Buddha is expected under the name of Maitreya-Buddha and that somewhere there exists a statue of Maitreya-Buddha carrying a water jar on his shoulder. This Maitreya-Buddha is to be the world teacher in the Aquarian era.

The brochure also contains what is called "Message from Maitreya No. 81, September 12th, 1979." The message emphasizes sharing the world's wealth. It deplores the money spent on arms and defense and the waste of grain on livestock in the "wealthier countries." One wonders how much this program of advertisement cost, and one is sure the money could have been better spent on the poor.

The dangerous nature of this advertising campaign becomes evident after a more careful study of the theological implications of this brochure. In the first place, the "Message from Maitreya" uses capitalized pronouns to convey the impression that this teacher is God. This message states that "man is an emerging God," echoing the original lie of Satan to Eve: "Ye shall be as gods." In the message, man is urged to "manifest his divinity" by embracing the ideas of Justice, Sharing, and Love (capitalized).

In an attempt to disarm the suspicion that this heralded "Christ" might turn out to be some kind of antichrist, the brochure tells us that the antichrist is not a man who appears before the Christ, but an energy that becomes embodied at various times. Interestingly enough, it declares that this "energy" was embodied most of all in seven men in Nazi Germany (Hitler and six of his closest colleagues) and also in a group of Japanese militarists as well as in some people in Italy. Evidently the eastern oriental cultists are rankled at the kind of "Christ" Hitler turned out to be. The defeat of the Axis powers is supposed to have rid the world of the antichrist.

The brochure also says that the "forces of evil," incarnated in Hitler and his associates, are the "forces of matter." Here we have the old gnostic heresy that matter is essentially evil. In addition, "matter" is supposed to be a kind of by-product of the deity. The deity is said to produce pairs of opposites, spirit as opposed to matter. "They are not separate from God," the brochure says. "Everything is God." This is nothing but pantheism, and it makes God the author of evil. The bottom line of all this expensive advertising is that, according to Benjamin Creme, the antichrist has come and gone; so the path is now clear for the "Christ" he heralds to begin building the world anew.

It is not likely that this kind of thing will make much of an impression on pragmatic western society. It does reveal the fact that teachings from the occult world are now being broadcast by means of modern advertising and direct mail techniques.

A big part of the developing occult scene is the so-called New Age movement, a strange blend of Indian gurus, flying saucers, holistic medicine, tarot cards, superstition, astrology, and spiritism. The New Age movement is a large network of organizations and individuals held together by common ideas. The common vision is that a new age is coming, an age of peace and mass enlightenment, the age of Aquarius. No beliefs are universally held by New Agers, although certain Hindu concepts of God as an impersonal, infinite consciousness and power seem to be generally accepted. Most also hold to the Hindu doctrine of reincarnation. Also there is general belief in a spiritualized version of evolution. Along with all this is a rejection of orthodox Judeo-Christian beliefs.

The New Age movement is not just a fad. It comprises a mobilizing and vocal minority in our society. It has attracted some able advocates, including celebrities like Shirley MacLaine, who has piloted her side of the cultic coalition into a lucrative business.

New Agers profess great concern about the nuclear arms race and other threats to survival on this planet. They believe in the essential goodness of human nature. They hope to mobilize enough people to avert global disaster and to generate an evolutionary move towards a racial new world.

The New Age movement is antichristian, occult, and pagan. Politically the movement embraces the one-world philosophy of the highly dangerous Club of Rome. The New Age movement could be written off as a lot of nonsense were it not for the fact that this conglomeration of ideas is alluring a number of people from the world's intellectual elite. Its adherents are people who are attracted to mysticism and who see in New Age philosophies the spiritual dimension missing in their lives.

Some idea of the impact this movement is having is indicated by the fact that it made the cover of *Time* magazine (December 7, 1987). The cover story was entitled "New Age Harmonies" and the headline read, "A strange mix of spirituality and superstition is sweeping the country."

So then, Paul foretold the nature of the propagators of the delusions that will grip the minds of men in the last days. People will fall under the influence of deceiving spirits. Once the church is removed, there will be a tremendous acceleration of this process.

Paul next turned his attention to *the prohibitions* that will characterize occult teaching in the last days: "Forbidding to marry, and commanding to abstain from meats, which God hath created to be received with thanksgiving of them which believe and know the truth" (1 Timothy 4:3).

The demonic attack upon *marriage*, a divinely instituted ordinance, is well under way. In his classic on spiritism and occult religion, G. H. Pember spoke of the "strange doctrines" spiritists have "concerning elective affinities and spiritual alliances, which tend to an utter rejection of [marriage] as ordained by God."

> In spite of the Lord's express declaration to the contrary, Spiritualists of the school with which we have now to deal teach that the marriage of male and female is the great institution of the next life and that every person has an affinity who will be his or her spouse for eternity, but that in this present time there are frequent mistakes, and that, conse-

quently, those who are not spiritual affinities being joined together are unable to agree and live in union. This they affirm to be the cause of all misfortune in wedded life. . . . Many Spiritualists, however, go much further, and declare that marriage should last only so long as the contracting parties may be disposed to live together, in short that God's first ordinance, like every other restraint, is to be snapped asunder as soon as it becomes wearisome.[15]

Pember also quoted from a paper on "Matrimonial Relations and Social Reforms" read by Herbert Noyes before the London Dialectical Society. This paper was presented at a time when modern permissiveness was not even thought of.

After expressing his opinion that "divorce should be prompt and free whenever mutually desired" and obtainable under certain conditions and safeguards even when demanded by only one of the pair, Mr. Noyes remarks that the main obstacle to such a state of things "consists of untenable ecclesiastical fallacies." He continues "Of all the mischievous inventions blasphemously ascribed to the Almighty, and published as His Word, I doubt if there be one more mischievous and mistaken than the text which asserts that there is no marriage in heaven. . . . I am disposed to think that in a true marriage man and wife are not so much one flesh as virtually one spirit and one soul. . . . The adventitious sanctity of marriage derived from ecclesiastical ceremonies is doomed to be ignored by coming generations.[16]

Pember wrote his book near the end of the nineteenth century when spiritism was making its first inroads into western society. To what extent demonic forces have influenced secularist thought, it would be impossible to say, but certainly secularism has whole-heartedly espoused the demonic teachings concerning marriage.

The clear teaching of demons, as indicated by Paul and illustrated above, is that marriage is a thing of the spirit, not of the flesh; that there is marriage in the afterlife; and that human marriage is of little account and should be scrapped at will.

In concluding his summary of end-time demonic teachings, Paul indicated that there will be an attack on eating *meat*. The word he used for "meats" is the word regularly used for solid food. Dean Alford, the great Greek scholar, said:

> It does not appear here from what sort of food this abstinence would be enjoined: but probably the eating of flesh is alluded to. Eusebius quotes from Irenaeus . . . a description of men who called themselves Abstainers, or Temperance men, who preached celibacy and abstinence from eating flesh. These seem to be the persons here pointed at.[17]

The command of God that men should eat meat was given right after the flood. The antediluvians seem to have become adept in what the Bible calls "the deep things of Satan." They seemingly learned how to have intercourse with fallen angels so that they were able to produce a hybrid demon progeny on the earth. Pember said:

> It is not impossible that the permission to eat flesh, given as it was immediately after the angel-transgression, may have been intended to render man less capable of conscious, intelligent intercourse with supernatural beings, and consequently less exposed to their wiles. And, if so, the desire on the part of demons to withdraw it is easily understood.[18]

Trevor Ravenscroft, a modern writer well versed in occult matters, affirmed much the same. He told of Hitler's early experiments in transcendent consciousness and how Hitler accomplished it by means of drugs. The interesting fact is that Hitler, who was a vegetarian, was in a state of near-starvation at the time. Ravenscroft said that Hitler's physical condition was such that he had "little or no protection" from the influence of the hallucinogenic drugs he took. Hitler's experience really went far beyond a drug-related "trip," however. He achieved a monumental personal breakthrough into the demonic world, which led directly to his becoming possessed by a horrendous evil spirit. Ravenscroft gave his opinion that the human soul is "imprisoned" in its material environment and that man's material limitations "serve as a protection."[19] Abstinence from eating meat is essential to any real advance in spiritism and occultism.

Pember reminded us that abstinence from eating meat is "a

fundamental law of theosophy," an eastern-oriented and occult-oriented cult.

> Theories at first confined to physical evolution have been applied to the soul with the result that transmigration has become a common doctrine among the more intellectual Spiritualists. Thus a great barrier between Buddhism and Western ideas is swept away, and a horror is induced of any food that involves a sacrifice of animal life. For what man would devour the body of an existence destined, perhaps, ere long to be his own child? Or who would violently strip the spirit of a peccant and regressive ancestor?[20]

The oriental cults sweeping the western world are nearly all advocates of vegetarianism. Take, for instance, the testimony of Tal Brooke, who spent years of his life chasing the bubble of oriental mysticism. After first saturating himself with drugs while pursuing his quest in the United States, he wandered across India for three months, sampling the gurus and plunging into the morass of eastern soul-destroying cults. In India he first sought out the ashram of Maharishi Mahesh Yogi, whom he had seen on television in San Francisco. After seeking initiation into his cult, and pursuing its path for a while, he decided that its devotees were on some kind of endless yoga treadmill meaninglessly repeating a single word in the hope of arriving at godhood.

He told how he came in contact with Sai Baba who claimed to be Lord Krishna, Christ reborn, and the only true worker of miracles in India. Brooke became an initiate and an intimate of a man adored by five million in India—a man able to do some astonishing "miracles," which could not be readily explained; a man adored as the savior, enduring infinite torments in order to pay for the sins of others; and a man who in the end proved himself to be a fraud.

The path of Brooke's initiation led directly to a vegetarian diet. He ate food boiled for so long to rid it of amoebas and tapeworm eggs that it was nothing but tasteless mush. He ate no meat, no fish, no eggs, no milk—just rice and pepper-water with traces of vegetables. His revulsion when he discovered what kind of a "savior" he had been following was devastating. He felt he had been "tainted by something he did not understand."[21]

246

Throughout the western world today there is reaction against food additives. Capitalizing on this, many are saying that meat is harmful and that only organically-grown vegetables should be eaten. There is some nutritional truth in what is said. The danger comes when people drift from a quest for more wholesome food into vegetarianism and then into eastern mysticism. Near where I live, for instance, there is a small food market that specializes in health foods. People are invited to join cooperatively in the pursuit of good health. One part of this store is devoted to books on health and eastern religion. It is but a step from one to the other. We need to be on our guard, since Paul warned that the endtimes will be marked by an increasing emphasis on diet-related propaganda. We should beware of any trend toward vegetarianism, especially when the advocacy of this kind of diet has religious undercurrents connected with it.

The Lord Jesus was no vegetarian. He fed the five thousand with loaves and fishes. In the upper room, when He appeared before His disciples in His resurrection body, He ate fish and a honeycomb to prove the reality of His body. In one of His preincarnate appearances, when He visited Abraham prior to sending down His judgment on Sodom, He ate a meal of bread and meat.

There are cases when it is medically advisable to abstain from certain kinds of food; but apart from that, especially in these days when the occult world is closing in to prepare for the coming of the antichrist, we need to be wary of anything that has occult overtones. The Holy Spirit has so warned us, and we would do well to pay heed.

---

1. G. M. Gilbert, *Nuremberg Diary* (New York: New American Library, 1947), p. 25.
2. Trevor Ravenscroft, *The Spear of Destiny* (New York: Bantam, 1974).
3. R. E. D. Clark, *Darwin: Before and After* (Grand Rapids: Grand Rapids International Publications, 1958), pp. 91, 96.
4. Ibid., p. 113.
5. Walter Martin, *The Maze of Mormonism* (Santa Ana, CA: Vision House, 1978), pp. 211-236.
6. G. H. Pember, *Earth's Earliest Ages*, 13th ed. (London: Alfred Holness, n.d.), pp. 316-317.
7. "Spiritualism and the Churches," *Dawn* (January 15, 1943), p. 462.

8. Oliver Lodge, *Strand* (June 1917), cited in D. M. Panton, "Spiritualism—Its Origin and Character," *Present Day Pamphlets-I* (London: Thynne and Jarvis, 1923), p. 22.
9. Ibid., p. 23.
10. Stainton Moses, "Spirit Identity," pp. 30-31, cited in *Dawn* (October 15, 1928), pp. 295-296.
11. Sir Arthur Conan Doyle, *The New Revelation*, p. 123, cited in Panton, p. 22.
12. Doyle, *Strand* (November 1920), cited in Panton, p. 36.
13. Charles D. Lamme, "Spirit Expectancy," *Dawn* (September 15, 1933), pp. 261-263.
14. Ravenscroft, pp. 156, 164, 255.
15. Pember, pp. 382-383.
16. Ibid., pp. 383-384.
17. Henry Alford, *The New Testament for English Readers* (Chicago: Moody Press, n.d.), p. 1373.
18. Pember, p. 37.
19. Ravenscroft, pp. 80-81.
20. Pember, pp. 373-374.
21. Robert Taliaferro Brooke, *Lord of the Air* (Herts, England: Lion Publishing, 1976), pp. 97, 125, 171.

11

The Blessed Hope
1 Thessalonians 4:13–5:10

Paul called the rapture of the church a "blessed hope." Every true child of God anticipates not the grave, but the glory; not some ethereal kind of eternal life as a disembodied spirit or ghost, but a full-bodied life—real, deathless, tangible—an exciting climax to life here on earth.

Paul once described his own foretaste of this to his friends at Corinth.

> I knew a man in Christ above fourteen years ago, (whether in the body, I cannot tell; or whether out of the body, I cannot tell: God knoweth;) such an one caught up to the third heaven. And I knew such a man (whether in the body, or out of the body, I cannot tell: God knoweth;) How that he was caught up into paradise, and heard unspeakable words, which it is not lawful for a man to utter (2 Corinthians 12:2-4).

The word *paradise* denotes a pleasure garden, such as ancient oriental monarchs used to build around their royal residences.

The idea behind the word is a real, literal place of rest, beauty, refreshment, and delight, such as can be enjoyed in the body. On the occasion to which he referred, Paul did not know whether he was experiencing the delights of paradise in or out of the body. The inference is that the place to which he was caught away was one that he could thoroughly have enjoyed in a literal, physical sense. He made no attempt to describe the place. He simply said that what he experienced there was "unspeakable" or, as some have suggested, "untranslatable." There was no way he could convey in language its sounds, scenes, and sensations. It was life in a wholly different dimension, but not so different that he felt strange or out of place there.

All this confirms the words of our Lord Jesus: "In my Father's house are many mansions: if it were not so, I would have told you" (John 14:2). In other words, if we should find Heaven to be so different a place from what we know, love, and enjoy down here, so different that we should feel lost and ill at ease there, Jesus would have told us. But it is not like that at all. Heaven will be a familiar place to us, not so different from earth that we should feel strange and be startled there.

Paul's experience of paradise was so enthralling that God had to give him "a thorn in the flesh" to remind him that he was still on earth with duties and responsibilities to be fulfilled (2 Corinthians 12:7). Ever after that experience Paul had what he called "a desire to depart, and to be with Christ." His foretaste of the glory land had made it clear to him that what awaits us on the other side of Jordan "is far better" than anything we have down here (Philippians 1:23).

The great hope of the church is that Christ will come and rapture us to Heaven before death intervenes, but even if death comes first, we shall be resurrected and given glorified bodies like His (Philippians 3:21).

There are two comings of Christ in the future. First He is coming *for* us; then He is coming *with* us. The first of these comings is to the air, the second to the earth. The first we call the rapture, the second we call the return. The first has to do primarily with the church, the second with Israel and the world. What believers are looking for in this age is the rapture. Teaching on the rapture is found in 1 Thessalonians 4:13–5:10. Before we examine this important New Testament truth, let us analyze that passage:

250

I. Some Woeful Saints (1 Thessalonians 4:13-15)
II. Some Welcome Sounds (1 Thessalonians 4:16)
   A. Rapture! We're going up!
      The shout of Christ—to summon the saints to glory
   B. Ruin! They're going down!
      The voice of the archangel—to send the angels to war
   C. Revival! They're going in!
      The trump of God—to sound the alarm for Israel
III. Some Wondrous Sights (1 Thessalonians 4:16-18)
   A. Resurrection—those who are "asleep" (4:16)
   B. Rapture—those who are alive (4:17-18)
IV. Some Warning Signs (1 Thessalonians 5:1-7)
   A. Sudden destruction (5:1-3)
   B. Surrounding darkness (5:4-6)
   C. Sleeping drunkards (5:7)
V. Some Wise Suggestions (1 Thessalonians 5:8)
VI. Some Wanted Solace (1 Thessalonians 5:9-10)
   A. Saved from the wrath to come (5:9)
   B. Saved from the wrath by Christ (5:10)

Paul introduced his discussion of the rapture with comforting words to *some woeful saints* (1 Thessalonians 4:13-15). Some believers at Thessalonica had died; and believers in that infant church supposed that death had robbed these deceased loved ones of their hope of rapture. Paul told them they were not to mourn as those who have no hope. Death is indeed an enemy. It brings its dark shadows even into Christian homes. Its sorrows are real, as Jesus experienced when He wept at the graveside of Lazarus. But those who have laid believing loved ones in the grave do not have to grieve with the hopeless sorrow of the lost, who have no hope beyond the grave. The believer has a "blessed hope," the certainty that Jesus is coming again and that at His return He will bring with Him those who have "fallen asleep" in Him. Their souls are already with Him, and at His coming they will be united with their resurrection bodies.

From this general assurance, Paul launched into a full-length discussion of what we call "the rapture." Although that word is not found in Scripture, the truth of the rapture is not invalidated any more than the absence of the word *trinity* invalidates the concept that word embodies, or the absence of the word *millennium* invalidates its reality.

Paul began by drawing attention to *some welcome sounds.* "For the Lord himself shall descend from heaven with a shout, with the voice of the archangel, and with the trump of God" (1 Thessalonians 4:16). The voice is for the church, the shout is for the world, and the trump is for the nation of Israel. All three divisions of the human race are to be affected by the rapture.

First, the Lord will descend from Heaven with a shout; He will speak with the voice that awakens the dead. Three times in the New Testament the Lord raised His voice in a shout, and each time the result was resurrection. The first time was at the tomb of Lazarus when Jesus cried with a loud voice, "Lazarus, come forth." Instantly that dead man, decaying in his tomb, sprang back to life and, graveclothes and all, emerged triumphant to the light of day (John 11).

The second time Jesus shouted was on the cross. "Jesus, when he had cried again with a loud voice, yielded up the ghost. . . . And the graves were opened; and many bodies of the saints which slept arose, And came out of the graves after his resurrection, and went into the holy city, and appeared unto many" (Matthew 27:50-53).

The next time Jesus shouts will be at the rapture, and then a whole church will arise. This is the first welcome sound of the rapture, the shout of the Lord for His bride.

The word *shout* carries the idea of a word of command, a command that will force the grave to surrender its believing dead once and for all. Thus the "last enemy" will be forever defeated for the people of God (1 Corinthians 15:26). That command will throw back Satan's opposing forces in the air (Ephesians 2:2; cf. 1 Thessalonians 4:17), clearing the way through those demon-infested regions that surround our planet. The rising, glorious church, "terrible as an army with banners," (Song of Solomon 6:4) will burst upon those hellish hordes and, with the Lord at its head, will cleave the sky and rise in triumph to its home beyond the stars.

The shout of the Lord is accompanied by "the voice of the archangel." That voice will assemble the angels of God for the impending battles of the apocalypse. The book of Revelation is filled with angelic activity. In chapter 1 it is an angel who enables John to see the visions of the apocalypse. In chapters 2 and 3 angels stand in watchful silence beside the churches. In chapter 5 they add their voices to the worship around the throne of God. In chapter 7 they hold back the four winds of Heaven. In chapters 8 and 9 angels blow the trumpets of doom. In chapter 12 they cast Satan from the sky. In chapter 14 they issue words of warning. In chapter 18 angels herald the fall of Babylon. In chapter 19 they summon the carrion birds to Armageddon. In chapter 20 they lock up Satan in the abyss. Throughout the book they appear again and again to explain to John the significance of what is going on. The voice of the archangel, then, is to summon the angels to war.

The voice and the shout are accompanied by the trump of God. The trump is primarily for Israel. When Israel left Egypt, Moses made two silver trumpets to be used to direct the people on their march across the desert. The various corporate activities of Israel were heralded by the sound of these trumpets. They were blown to direct Israel's walk, warfare, and worship in the wilderness and to alert them that the time had come to be on the move again (Numbers 10:1-10).

One of Israel's annual feasts was the "feast of trumpets" (Leviticus 23:24). It is significantly placed in the series of feasts. There was a gap in the Jewish religious calendar after the feast of Pentecost. Then came three more feasts—trumpets, atonement, and tabernacles—all celebrated one after the other and designed to bring to an end the annual religious festivities of the Hebrew people. That gap symbolizes the historical gap between Pentecost and the endtimes. The waiting period is almost over. The trumpet will sound and Israel will once more be on the march as a nation; for when the church is raptured, God will take up with Israel just where He left off nearly two thousand years ago. The "trump of God," then, is primarily for Israel and will be used to gather increasing numbers of Jews back into the land. It also sounds the alarm for the world at large. The day of grace is over; the day of judgment has come; the great tribulation is on the way.

Paul wrote next of *some wondrous sights* (1 Thessalonians 4:16-18), the first of which is the resurrection of those who are asleep. "And the dead in Christ shall rise first." This is Paul's reference to what the Scripture calls "the first resurrection" (Revelation 20:5). The first resurrection is actually in three stages, corresponding to the stages of the Jewish harvest: (1)the first fruits were reaped and presented to God; then (2)the harvest was reaped; and (3)the gleanings were gathered in. The first fruits of the resurrection were gathered in at Christ's resurrection. The resurrection harvest will take place at the rapture, and the gleanings will be collected at various times during the great tribulation period.

We are not told just how God will gather together the scattered dust of the dead, reassemble that dust into their very own bodies so that the dead will be reconstituted physically. Since God is God we do not doubt for one moment His ability to do this. As Paul said to King Agrippa, "Why should it be thought a thing incredible with you, that God should raise the dead?" (Acts 26:8) When we think how astonishingly we are made in the first place, and when we consider the remarkable complexity of these bodies of ours, so mysteriously fashioned in the darkness of the womb, it is really no less credible that we should live *again* than that we should live *at all.* If God can bring forth a body from a womb, He can certainly bring back a body from a tomb.

God has written the resurrection story into the world of nature to illustrate His ability to raise the dead. Think, for instance, of the caterpillar. It begins life as an earthbound grub, circumscribed by the law of its being, a crawling thing lifting its head from some lowly leaf to stare toward the sky, but with no hope of ever soaring up into the blue. But then a change akin to death overtakes that worm. It weaves a coffin and a shroud, crawls inside and dies to this world and to the life it had known. Time comes and goes while the caterpillar sleeps on. Then, suddenly, comes a mysterious resurrection call, and the little creature rends its coffin apart. Forth it comes, into the blaze of the sun, a gorgeous butterfly. The same creature that went into that tomb comes forth, but it is a creature metamorphosed, changed. It spreads its splendid wings and soars to the sky.

That is what is going to happen to the dead in Christ. They lie in the grave; and there their bodies sleep as the ages come and go, as empires wax and wane, as kingdoms rise and fall. Their bodies return slowly to the dust; and the dust is blown across the face of the earth, forgotten by all except God. But one of these days the Lord will descend from Heaven with a shout, and the dead in Christ shall rise. Forth from their graves they will come—up from the sea, up from the sod—the same people who fell asleep in Jesus, but gloriously changed. They will rise to meet Him and their loved ones in the air. They will be wearing bodies made anew, bodies with some of the properties they had before, but bodies with glorious powers. After His resurrection, the Lord could sit at a table and eat a meal, but He could also come and go through stone walls, appear and disappear at will, and ascend through cloud and sky to His Father's home on high. Our resurrection bodies will be like His.

That will be the first of the wondrous sights, the rising of the dead in Christ. But there is another sight of which Paul wrote, the rapture of those who are alive. "Then we which are alive and remain shall be caught up together with them in the clouds, to meet the Lord in the air: and so shall we ever be with the Lord. Wherefore comfort one another with these words" (1 Thessalonians 4:17-18). We too shall be changed "in a moment, in the twinkling of an eye" (1 Corinthians 15:52). Our mortal bodies will put on immortality. The chains that bind us to this world will be loosed. We will feel the strong attractive power of the returning Christ, and we will leap skyward, fitted in an instant for the dimensions of eternity.

Again, God has given us an illustration, this time in the magnet. Take a mixture of metals—gold, silver, copper, iron, lead, and zinc. Scatter those metals on the ground, and bury some of them beneath the soil. Then take a powerful magnet, and pass it over that site. Immediately one kind of metal will leap skyward to meet that magnet in the air. The magnet will leave behind the silver, the gold, the copper, the lead, and the zinc. It will draw to itself just one kind of metal, the iron. Why does the magnet attract only the iron? Because the iron has the *same nature* as the magnet.

When Jesus comes at the rapture, He will draw to Himself only one kind of person—not necessarily the rich or the poor, the religious, the respectable, the moral, the church member, or the theologian—just those who have the same nature as Himself. That fact, of course, is what gives all the more point to the Lord's word to Nicodemus: "That which is born of the flesh is flesh; and that which is born of the Spirit is spirit. Marvel not that I say unto thee, Ye must be born again" (John 3:6-7). The all-important question I need to ask myself is this: Have I been born again?

Here, then, we see the essence of the rapture. It entails Christ's coming to the air (1 Thessalonians 4:17), His raising of all those who have died trusting in Him, and the home call of all born-again believers still alive and on earth when He comes.

At this point in our Bibles we have a chapter break that might prevent us from reading on. But Paul, by no means finished with this theme, set before us *some warning signs* (1 Thessalonians 5:1-7). He spoke about *sudden destruction.*

> But of the times and the seasons, brethren, ye have no need that I write unto you. For yourselves know perfectly that the day of the Lord so cometh as a thief in the night. For when they shall say, Peace and safety; then sudden destruction cometh upon them, as travail upon a woman with child; and they shall not escape (1 Thessalonians 5:1-3).

The rapture of the church will be the prelude to the coming of the day of the Lord, that terrible day when God will enter into judgment with this world over the rejection of His Son. The church will be gone; judgment will begin. To understand the verses now before us we must take into account the use of the personal pronouns *ye, we,* and *us,* which describe the believer, and the pronouns *they* and *them,* which describe those left behind at the rapture to face the coming wrath. These pronouns should be underlined in one's Bible. They unlock the whole passage and prove that the church will not be left here to face the coming day of wrath.

The sudden destruction Paul foresaw does not involve "us" but "them." Paul assured his readers that he had no need to rehearse truth concerning the day of the Lord for them or to remind them of that coming event. The church will be gone, and people will rush into the arms of the devil's messiah. He will usher in a brief span of prosperity and peace for the world, and people will think that earth's problems are solved. Then, like a fury out of Hell, he will mobilize the world against the Jews, and the great tribulation will begin. Paul, using the Lord's own figure of speech to describe this coming holocaust, said it will be like the sudden onslaught of birth pangs. A new golden age is about to be delivered, but not without travail and pain.

Next, Paul wrote of *surrounding darkness.*

> But ye, brethren, are not in darkness, that that day should overtake you as a thief. Ye are all the children of light, and the children of the day: we are not of the night , nor of darkness. Therefore let us not sleep, as do others; but let us watch and be sober (1 Thessalonians 5:4-6).

Paul deliberately contrasted believers, who are candidates for the rapture, with unbelievers, who are in the dark about spiritual things and what is coming on the world. We who have this inside information should be alert to what is happening. We should carefully guard our lives so that we shall not be ashamed before our Lord at His coming (1 John 2:28). The coming rapture of the church is kept before us in the New Testament as a purifying hope (1 John 3:3). The word *all* in 1 Thessalonians 5:5 is an inclusive word for the entire body of believers. None will be left behind at the rapture. The Lord is going to have a raptured church, not a ruptured church.

Paul added a warning about *sleeping drunkards*. "For they that sleep sleep in the night; and they that be drunken are drunken in the night" (1 Thessalonians 5:7). Again we note the use of the pronoun as Paul pointed away from believers to unbelievers, living their lives without regard for the coming of the Lord. All they can do, Paul said, is try to forget the kind of world in which they live, in sleep and drunken stupor. Millions are like that today. They are trying to wring some small bit of solace out of a world already filled with the nightmares of aggression, terrorism, war, and potential nuclear disaster.

Paul next had *some wise suggestions*. "But let us, who are of the day, be sober, putting on the breastplate of faith and love; and for an helmet, the hope of salvation" (1 Thessalonians 5:8). He told believers to guard their hearts with the breastplate of faith and love and their heads with the helmet of the hope of salvation. In other words, believers should be on their guard against the spirit of the age. There is a contrast here with the armor of Ephesians 6. There Paul spoke of "the helmet of salvation" (Ephesians 6:17); here it is the helmet of the *hope* of salvation. In this entire passage in Thessalonians, Paul was writing about the believer's "blessed hope" of the coming of Christ. The hope of salvation is the second coming of Christ to take us out of this world before the end-time horrors begin. The world is ripening fast for judgment, but we need not be worried.

Finally, Paul offered *some wanted solace* (1 Thessalonians 5:9-10). He reminded us, first, that we are saved from the wrath to come. "For God hath not appointed us to wrath, but to obtain salvation by our Lord Jesus Christ" (5:9). The "wrath" here is evidently the wrath to come of Revelation 16. The context here in

1 Thessalonians has to do with the second coming of Christ, particularly Christ's coming to the air to catch away His church before that time of wrath begins.

Two Old Testament examples of this timely removal of God's saints before the coming of wrath endorse the concept. One of these is in connection with Noah, the other in connection with Lot—both common illustrations in the New Testament for depicting end-time events (Matthew 24:37-40; Luke 17:28; 2 Peter 2:5-9; Jude 7). Noah went into the ark just seven days before the wrath of God fell on the antediluvian world. The angel, in urging Lot out of Sodom, testified, "I cannot do any thing till thou be come thither" (Genesis 19:22).

Paul had one more word of solace. He assured us that we are to be saved from the wrath to come because God does not appoint the church, the bride of Christ, to wrath. We are saved from the wrath by Christ, "who died for us, that, whether we wake or sleep, we should live together with him" (1 Thessalonians 5:10). The wrath, as far as we are concerned, has all been visited upon Christ. So whether we are among those who have died in Him or whether we are still alive at His coming, His substitution is all we need to escape God's wrath—no matter what form that wrath may take.

Paul told us that we are going to "live together with him." Christ is coming to take us to be with Him before the work of wrath ever begins. The Holy Spirit describes the coming wrath as "the wrath of the Lamb" (Revelation 6:16), a strange, terrible, and mysterious expression, and one we can certainly disassociate from "the bride of the Lamb" (Revelation 21:9, paraphrased).

12
The Days
of Noah

Just before He went to Calvary, the Lord Jesus gave us His blueprint for the end of the age (Matthew 24–25). Among other things, He said that when conditions on the earth paralleled conditions as they were in the days of Noah, then He was coming back (Matthew 24:37-39). The Biblical account of the days of Noah is found in Genesis 4–6. A comparison of our day with the time of Noah enables us to see quite clearly that we have now arrived at that point in time indicated by the Lord.

The days of Noah were days of spiritual decline, social dilemma, shameless depravity, scientific development, strong delusion, some devotion, and sudden destruction.

SPIRITUAL DECLINE

The faith that had been delivered to Adam, for which the martyr Abel had been prepared to shed his blood, and which had been distorted by Cain into "another gospel," had largely disappeared from the earth by the time of Noah. The Holy Spirit gives us a glimpse of this by setting before us two family trees. He lists names in the godless line of Cain and names in the godly line of Seth. These names tell a story.

In the line of Cain, several names contain the suffix *el*, an abbreviation of the divine name *Elohim*, the name of the true and living God, the God of creation. The name of God lingered at least nominally in the Cainite family for some generations. But it was a meaningless gesture and even this casual and flippant use of God's name eventually disappeared from Cain's genealogy and God was forgotten—with one exception. When we come to the name *Mehujael* we see that God's name is used, but in defiance. One meaning of the name is "Blot out that Jah is God." By then the name of God was only used in contempt and hate. That was Cain's line.

Seth's line shows the opposite. The knowledge and love of God remained strong among the Sethites. Father and son, generation after generation, the Sethites carried the torch of divine testimony in a world growing increasingly evil. In the line of Seth, godliness climaxed in Enoch, who was translated to Heaven by rapture, and in Noah, who took a handful of believers with him through the flood to a new world on the other side of judgment.

The Cainites, however, had little use for the testimony of the Sethites. All the action in that ancient world lay with the godless but enterprising Cainites. They were the city-builders, the inventors and innovators, the pioneers of an advancing civilization. World opinion was not shaped by the moral minority. Cainites set the fashions of society and controlled the dynamics of secular power. It was an age of spiritual decline.

So it is today. Pockets of residual spiritual strength, leftover from the Puritan era and from past revivals, can still be found, so that voices of protest can still be raised against the perversions and pollutions of our age. But the rot has gone too deep for much to be done. And in the world at large, for all practical purposes, we are already living in what has been called "the post-Christian era." The church has very little voice in public affairs and such voice as it has is weakened by the fact that many who speak for "the church" are left-wing liberals who would as soon espouse the cause of Karl Marx as that of Jesus Christ.

Some time ago a Gallup poll was taken in various countries to see what impact religion had on modern world opinion. The results were revealing. Less than 10 percent polled thought that religion should be important in life. Less than two-fifths of the people polled in France and West Germany said they believed in God. We are living in days of spiritual decline, just like the days of Noah.

In Noah's day the number of genuine believers was an ever-increasing minority relative to the total world population. By the time of the flood there were only eight people left who believed enough in God and His wrath to accept shelter in the ark. As we have seen, there was a tendency to refer to God as *Elohim* rather than *Jehovah*. In other words, where there was any public acknowledgment of God, it was in general and generic terms rather than personal terms; God was referred to as Creator rather than Redeemer. God had become less and less relevant in society. Other things crept in to fill the spiritual vacuum created by agnosticism and atheism. There was, for instance, an increasing emphasis on humanism, on man as the beginning and end of life. People at large felt no need for God. The pace was set by Cain, founding father of that civilization. Cain was infuriated because he could not manipulate God, so he decided to get along without God. Whereas Abel and Seth became "pilgrims and strangers" in this world, Cain became "a fugitive and a vagabond" on the earth.

There was an increasing emphasis on materialism, always a deadening influence on the spiritual. Cainite culture was a materialistic culture. The emphasis was on "marrying and giving in marriage," on eating and drinking, on big cities and cultural programs, on cattle and economic growth, on art and science, on pleasure and entertainment.

Along with all this there was an increasing emphasis on the occult. The Cainites, having turned their backs on God, groped after "the deep things of Satan." They developed occult techniques and were able not only to materialize powerful spirit beings but could also cohabit with them. More, they produced a hybrid demon progeny on this planet, the final outcome of apostasy in a decadent culture (as we learn both from Peter's Second Epistle and from the book of Jude).

The same thing happened after the flood, and explains the extraordinary wickedness of the Canaanites and God's demand that the race be exterminated by Joshua. It was the emergence of this race of giants in the antediluvian world that made so necessary God's intervention in judgment in human affairs.

Craving for occult experiences is a hallmark of our day. So-called "psychics" are regular guests on talk shows. We have spiritism, Satanism, witchcraft, New Age philosophies, and all the rest of it. Oriental cults, which have always been rooted in demonism, are making an increasing appeal in the morally and spiritually bankrupt West. The most culturally enlightened, scientifically oriented, literate, and educated society that has ever lived on earth has turned its back on God, on the Bible, and on the Judeo-Christian ethic, and has gone awhoring after ghosts and witches, demons and astrology, psychics and prophets, soothsayers and Hindu mystics.

SOCIAL DILEMMA

The social malaise of the antediluvian age had two basic ingredients. First, there was a tremendous increase in the world's *population*. The Holy Spirit says, "It came to pass, when men began to multiply . . . " (Genesis 6:1). In other words, multiplication, not mere addition, was the controlling factor in the demographics of the age. There was what we would call today a "population explosion." Moreover, the population of the world was becoming increasingly urban. God had placed man in a garden; Cain placed men in cities.

We do not need to look far for the present-day equivalent. On July 7, 1986, the world chalked up another record: its population passed the five billion mark. Every year about ninety million people are added to this planet—the increase of births over deaths. Every year we have to find room for the population-equivalent of another country the size of Mexico. One population expert put it like this: "Man, like a plague of locusts, has outstripped the capacity of his environment to sustain him."

Of the more than five billion people who now inhabit the globe, 78 percent live in the underdeveloped countries where famine, poverty, disease, and unemployment are endemic.

Taking the world as a whole, 45 percent of the world's total population now lives in cities. In the more developed countries that figure is much higher, around 72 percent. Cities like Calcutta,

Bombay, Mexico City, Rio de Janeiro, and Cairo have given up trying to cope with the squalor and desperation of major sections of their urban sprawl. Such cities, where the population is increasing even faster than the world norm, can not help but become jungles in which crime can not be kept under control, health standards can not be maintained, and people die on the streets as a matter of course.

Even in the United States, cities are encroaching on the suburbs; in some parts of the country, the suburbs of one city are spilling over into the suburbs of another city. In the East, the entire five-hundred-mile strip from Boston to Washington is becoming one vast, heavily-populated metropolis. Already it takes in forty-five contiguous communities. The area takes in only 1 percent of the land mass of the United States, yet about one of every five Americans lives there. It is swiftly becoming a city five hundred miles long.

Big cities are breeding grounds for crime and corruption. They foster drug addiction, mental illness, suicide, stress, and hostility.

And all this is only the beginning. The total world population is expected to *double* within the next fifty years. Every minute, 271 babies are born and only 95 people die. Therefore, every minute we have 176 more people on the planet.

There was not only an increase in the world's population in Noah's day; there was also a corresponding increase in *crime*. "The earth also was corrupt before God, and the earth was filled with violence" (Genesis 6:11).

The antediluvian world embraced the doctrine of permissiveness. As a result, crime went unpunished. Everyone "did his own thing." Society allowed free expression of whatever personal perversions and pollutions depraved people might wish to indulge. The doctrine of permissiveness was openly espoused by Lamech, the most powerful single individual of the age. Lamech (in the godless line of Cain) was the world's leading opinion-maker. He developed a wholly irregular lifestyle, forced his views on others, shook his fist in the face of God, and told God to stay out of his affairs.

Theologians sometimes refer to that age as the age of conscience, because the only thing Adam and Eve brought with them out of paradise was a conscience, the knowledge of right and wrong. But there seems to have been little exercise of conscience by the antediluvians. There were no restraints; everyone's lifestyle was accepted; crime and corruption went unpunished—even unnoted.

This characteristic of antediluvian society is a hallmark of our own. The twentieth century has put out of its mind, because it can no longer cope with the enormity of the statistics involved, the millions of people it has murdered, injured, tortured, maimed, or rendered homeless. Its record includes two major world wars, countless regional wars, and massacres and holocausts in various parts of the world. It has seen the development of international terror, not only as a means of gaining attention to arbitrary demands, but even as an instrument of national policy. It tolerates Mafia-type control of giant unions and major city governments. It puts up with alarming rates of crime in its inner cities, crime of such proportions that police forces can not begin to suppress it. Murders, rapes, assaults, and abortions are common, as are wife-beating and child abuse. Pornography is countenanced, and sodomy is "an alternative lifestyle." We are living in a society in which the courts often are more concerned about the "rights" of the criminal than they are about the rights of the victim and his family.

As it was in the days of Noah, so it is today. We are living in a world of violent crime. The crime clock in the United States, for instance, ticks ever faster. A murder is committed every twenty-four minutes, a woman is assaulted and raped every seven minutes, and a house is robbed every ten seconds. Young people commit most of the violent crimes in America, yet many judges refuse to admit that there is such a thing as a bad boy. Even when a youth is convicted, he may not be put away for months, sometimes not at all. Young criminals laugh at a justice system that treats them as socially deprived individuals, more to be pitied than punished, rather than as criminals.

S HAMELESS DEPRAVITY

"Every imagination of the thoughts of [men's] hearts was only evil continually" is the Holy Spirit's comment on the world of Noah's day (Genesis 6:5). Two contributing facts are set before us.

First, there was *polygamy*, an attack on the family. In Noah's day this took the form of a breakdown in the primeval law of marriage. It was Lamech who took the lead. He became the world's first polygamist, throwing convention to the wind and deciding he could do as he pleased.

Then, too, there was *pornography*, an attack on society. The vile imaginations of men were allowed full expression. The world wallowed in filth, so much so that the Lord declared that He was putting a time limit to His patience: "My Spirit shall not always strive with man, for that he also is flesh" (Genesis 6:3). He set a time limit of 120 years, beyond which He was not prepared to tolerate the vileness of the human race.

How much more must His patience be running out today. We are living in the age of the X-rated movie, available by cable for home viewing; the day of dial-a-porn, whereby children as well as adults can dial a phone number and have instant filth poured into their ears; the day of the marching sodomite, to whose vile views society is asked to bow; the day of rock music, glorifying sadism and illicit sex. In the face of all this, legislators and courts simply yawn. It is, after all, just an alternate lifestyle.

Scientific Development

The antediluvian world had discovered the art of smelting, a discovery that changed the face of that society as much as the industrial revolution changed the face of Victorian society, or the technology revolution has changed the face of ours. Driven out of paradise, men set about creating an artificial paradise based on science and technology. The Holy Spirit underlines three main areas of antediluvian development.

One area was *engineering*. Tubal-cain, a son of Lamech, discovered the secret of smelting iron and other metals. This enormously important discovery made possible whole new generations of farm implements and armaments, not to mention the development of a new industry. Tubal-cain had the secret of it and was an "instructor" in the art. Doubtless the new guilds were controlled by his family.

A second area of development was *economics*. Jabal, one of the great men of the age, another scion of the notorious Lamech family, developed a new and lucrative trade: the domestication of cattle and the more open nomadic way of life. No longer did men have to hunt; they could own cattle. And Jabal cornered the market on it; he was the "father" of all those who went in for that business.

A third area of development was *entertainment*. Still another son of Lamech, Jubal, invented stringed and wind instruments and gave the world its first orchestrated sound. He was the "father" of those who took up this line of things, suggesting that he headed up the entire entertainment business.

All these new advances were concentrated in the hands of the Lamech family. Lamech's name means "powerful." These were the things that made him powerful. He bestrode that ancient world like a colossus.

There was another Lamech in that ancient world, a godly man in the line of Seth. But his power was spiritual. The Cainite Lamech's power was secular. He appears on the page of antediluvian history as the first Biblical type of the antichrist.

The Holy Spirit gives us one illustration of the scientific and engineering achievements of Noah's day. The men of that day built the ark. True, God gave Noah the blueprints, but the vessel had to be built by human hands. The industrial skills for making this ship were available and ready. The ark had to be built to withstand the enormous stresses and strains that would be generated by the deluge. It had to endure wildly heaving seas and torrents of rain. It must not spring a leak or loosen a plank. It has been estimated that it was the size of a modern ocean-going liner, and it was built by the men of Noah's day.

There is scarcely any need to draw the parallel between Noah's day and ours when it comes to scientific development. There never was a time to compare with ours for technology and science. One example will suffice.

The space probe of the planet Saturn by the United States space vehicle *Voyager 2* will serve our purpose. This craft was loaded with instruments. It had cameras, radio receivers, cosmic ray detectors. It had detectors for infrared, ultraviolet and visible light. It had electric and magnetic-field probes. It raced toward Saturn at 54,000 miles per hour (twenty times the speed of a bullet) and traveled for four years across 1.24 billion miles. It arrived at its destination only 41 miles off target and only three seconds late! (One golf-minded scientist said that would be like sinking a 500-mile putt!) Then, coming within a hair of Saturn's stormy clouds, the space vehicle was hurled like a pebble in a great celestial slingshot on a new course toward the planet Uranus, propelled by the power of Saturn's gravity.

The people in Noah's day knew about art and science, music and metallurgy, agriculture and architecture. But they did not know God. They were as ignorant of God as a Russian communist or an American humanist.

STRONG DELUSION

Jesus said of the people of that day that they "knew not" (Matthew 24:39). Interestingly in His own description of Noah's day, Jesus ignored all their vileness and filth, all their scientific, economic, and cultural achievements, their humanistic views. He put His finger on their major folly, ignorance of God and of coming judgment. They were gripped by a strong delusion that manifested itself in two ways.

Their delusion took the form of *secularism*. They were materialists, living solely for this world, for "eating and drinking, marrying and giving in marriage" (Matthew 24:38). Note how the Lord underlines the legitimate things of life. But even legitimate things can become a sin when they crowd out God. The antediluvians were an intelligent race. They had the skill to transform the world and to build a secular paradise, but they were spiritual imbeciles. They were ignorant of the things in life that mattered most: the knowledge of sin, righteousness, and judgment to come.

Our society is much the same. We have legions of brilliant people who can speak with authority about physics, biochemistry, and computer science, but who are ignorant when it comes to the question of man's origin and destiny.

Along with secularism there was *supernaturalism*. As we have already seen, the world of Noah's day practiced advanced forms of demonism. Fallen angelic beings, in league with Satan, the prince of this world, had crossed a forbidden frontier. They had cultivated spiritist mediums until they were able to produce a hybrid race of giants on the earth. Memories of this are still preserved in Greek mythology and in the stories of the gods who peopled mount Olympus. Both Peter and Jude point to these things as a direct cause of the flood. By means of this invasion, Satan was able so to corrupt the human race that it was soon beyond redemption. Except for a diminishing handful of godly Sethites, who stood aloof from the sins and sciences of the age, the whole world lay supine in his lap.

The same kind of thing is about to happen again, as we discuss elsewhere in this book. Our world is becoming increasingly influenced by the occult. A walk through any major bookstore will reveal the extent to which such things as witchcraft, astrology, spiritism, psychic phenomena, demonic religion, and Satanism have penetrated our culture.

SOME DEVOTION

God never leaves Himself without a witness. It is a principle with God that the more degenerate the times, the more definite the testimony. God's witness to an apostate age invariably takes the form of faithful preaching on the one hand and fulfilled prophecy on the other hand. Both these things were present in apostate antediluvian society.

The faithful preaching was done by Noah, who is called "a preacher of righteousness" (2 Peter 2:5). He preached to his generation of coming judgment, as did Enoch before him. He warned of the nature of sin, the need for righteousness, and the nearness of judgment. So far as he was enlightened, he set before that wicked world the great truths later amplified and codified in the Epistle to the Romans. He was ignored.

The sign of the times was the ark. Day by day that mighty vessel grew. People either ignored it or mocked it. They certainly did not see it as a sign. That is what it was, though—a sign of judgment to come, judgment drawing nearer every day, judgment coming closer with every hammer blow, every pail of pitch. What must people have thought when the animals came to Noah and ascended the gangplank into the ark? No doubt it was the subject of more jokes.

The fulfilled prophecy of the age was the death of Methuselah. His father was Enoch, a prophet. When Methuselah was born, God evidently revealed the fact of coming judgment to this Old Testament saint, since the name he gave his son meant, "When he dies, it shall come." God lengthened out the days of Methuselah, but in the end he died. And with his death the stage was finally set for the flood to come. Similarly the signs of our times herald the imminence of the Lord's return.

SUDDEN DESTRUCTION

"The flood came, and took them all away" (Matthew 24:39). God warns. He woos. He witnesses. His grace is such that He will lengthen the day of grace for many a long year. Sometimes centuries pass until people convince themselves that Bible preaching on coming judgment is just another delusion of the evangelicals. Then, suddenly, with a crack of doom, the judgment comes.

It happened in Noah's day. It will happen in our own. The day of grace is still running its course, but it is running now swiftly toward its end. The mass of people ignore God's Word, abuse His people, and resist the Holy Ghost. All about us we hear faithful preaching and recognize fulfilled prophecy. The signs are abundant that the end is approaching. The time will come when God's patience with a Christ-rejecting world will be exhausted. As He translated Enoch to Heaven first, so He will translate the church. Then the fire of judgment will fall. Sudden destruction is on the way.

13

The Strong Delusion
2 Thessalonians 2:1-12

T he Thessalonian believers had been receiving false information about the day of the Lord, that final day when God would step into the arena of human affairs to deal directly with its wickedness. They were being told that the day of the Lord had already come. They had this information on what seemed to be excellent authority. It was confirmed to them by a spirit utterance, a prophetic word, and a letter supposedly signed by the apostle Paul (2 Thessalonians 2). They had been ensnared by a threefold deception; though the error had been confirmed by the required three witnesses (Matthew 18:16), the witnesses themselves were false. The day of the Lord had not come, and it still has not come. The Thessalonians had been victimized by wrong information.

The Thessalonian church was very young when Paul wrote to it. The two Thessalonian letters are believed to be the first inspired writings to come from Paul's pen and were written shortly after he had been driven out of Thessalonica by persecution. The believers there had eagerly received his preaching, as Paul admitted. "Ye received the word of God which ye heard of us, ye received it not as the word of men, but as it is in truth, the word of God" (1 Thessalonians 2:13). The problem was, they were just as willing to receive somebody else's word as well.

From Thessalonica, Paul went on to Berea. In the book of Acts the Bereans are contrasted with the Thessalonians; the Bereans would not take the word even of an apostle as from God without checking to see if it agreed with what had been revealed previously by God in His Word. Thus the Bereans "were more noble than those in Thessalonica, in that they received the word with all readiness of mind and searched the scriptures daily, whether those things were so" (Acts 17:11). The Thessalonians received the word gladly enough, but they failed to test all teaching by the Scriptures themselves—still a common mistake today. As a result they were easily deceived.

The message was plausible enough: the day of the Lord had already come. It was confirmed by a *spirit utterance*, for that is the force of the word *spirit* (2 Thessalonians 2:2). Someone, it seems, had stood up in their assembly and had declaimed under the influence of a lying spirit (possibly by means of tongues and interpretation) that the day of the Lord had come. The spirit utterance had not come from the Holy Spirit, but from a deceiving spirit. We are warned in Scripture not to accept such ecstatic utterances as being certainly from the Holy Spirit. It is possible to be deceived by supernatural phenomena, much of which originates from the enemy. We are to test the spirits to see whether they are from God.

The test of a spirit is whether or not it will confess that "Jesus Christ is come in the flesh" (1 John 4:1-4). Constantly throughout His public ministry the Lord Jesus silenced evil spirits when they sought to testify that He was the Christ. He wanted no confirmation of His person from such a source. Consequently, to this day a lying spirit is *unable* to make the confession that Jesus Christ is come in the flesh; all such spirits have been forever silenced on this subject. The Holy Spirit, however, can and will make the confession when asked. To accept untested utterances from the spirit world as being from the Holy Spirit (in a tongues meeting, for instance) is the height of folly. We can be deceived, and once deception takes root, it leads to further delusion.

In the early days of the modern tongues movement (Irvingism, as it was called in those days), certain instructed Bible teachers

271

made it their practice to attend tongues meetings simply to test the spirits. They would wait until a person broke into ecstatic utterance and then put the question. The question was not addressed to the believer who was speaking in tongues; he, often enough, was a sincere though deluded child of God. The question was always addressed to the spirit who was using the human tongue to convey a spirit utterance. "Spirit, do you confess that Jesus Christ is come in the flesh?" The reactions were startling, to say the least.

The investigators discovered that invariably the question was ignored at first, and the flow of words continued unabated. This, in itself, was proof that the spirit who was speaking was not of God, since God has pledged that His Spirit and spirits sent from Him *will* answer this question. The question being ignored, the questioners would put it a second time. This time the controlling spirit would make a statement about Christ that, although often true and sometimes magnificent, would not be an answer to the question but a deceptive evasion. Here was further proof that the controlling spirit was a deceiving spirit.

The question would be asked a third time. This time the deceiving spirit would release its control over the believer, whose tongue it had been using, *so that the believer himself* could answer the question.[1] Could deception be more crafty?

Well, the Thessalonians had received just such a spirit utterance and had taken it at face value. After all, if it came through a respected and well-loved fellow believer, how could it be false?

Along with the lying spirit utterance they had received what Paul calls a "word" (*logos*)—that is, a prophetic pronouncement. The gift of prophecy was still very much alive in the infant New Testament church at that time and was a necessary gift, because the New Testament had not yet been completed and circulated. The work of a New Testament prophet was to convey to a local gathering of believers, by direct Holy Spirit illumination, truth already apostolically revealed elsewhere but not yet in general circulation. This distinctive work of prophecy ceased once the New Testament became readily available because, like the gift of an apostle, the gift of a prophet in the early church was a foundation gift (1 Corinthians 13:8; Ephesians 2:20).

In 1 John 4:1-6, where he warned against lying spirits, John also warned against false prophets. Many such had already risen in his day to plague the church. The Thessalonians had been deceived by a man in their midst, supposedly speaking by direct Holy Ghost illumination, who had given them a pronouncement contrary to a considerable body of teaching in the Old Testament about the day of the Lord. In other words, they had been deceived by a false prophet, and had they known their Bibles, they would have detected the error at once.[2]

As if that were not enough, they had received a forged letter confirming the deception. The letter was supposedly from Paul, but he indignantly disassociated himself from it. He had sent them no such communication. He had indeed already written one letter to them (1 Thessalonians), and in that letter he had revealed new truth to them about the *day of Christ*. He had said also in that letter that he had no need to tell them about the *day of the Lord*, because they were already fully informed on that subject (5:2). Since the day of the Lord was the subject of considerable Old Testament revelation, he had not felt it necessary to go over all that ground again. But now they had received a letter, masquerading as a Pauline epistle, telling them that the day of the Lord, a day to be filled with signs and terrible judgments, had already come.

Faced with this threefold deception at Thessalonica, Paul first disassociated himself from false teaching, rebuked the Thessalonians for being so easily led astray, and turned the whole incident to good account. He used their situation as a springboard for unmasking Satan's secret plans for the endtimes. The "deep things of Satan" are now to be revealed and incorporated into Scripture, thus to be published and broadcast as far and wide as God's Word is read and loved. Satan's attack upon Paul's beloved Thessalonians had boomeranged.

We are now ready to examine the important eschatological passage found in 2 Thessalonians 2, but first let us look at the overall outline.

I. How the Man of Sin Is Revealed (2 Thessalonians 2:3)
   A. The climate of his coming
   B. The clue to his character
      1. As to his personality: the man of sin
      2. As to his person: the son of perdition
II. How the Mystery of Iniquity Is Restrained (2 Thessalonians 2:4-7)
   A. Satan's plan exposed by the Holy Spirit (2:4)
      1. He exalts his man to the highest pinnacle

2. He exhibits his man in the holiest place
   B. Satan's plan opposed by the Holy Spirit (2:5-7)
      1. The vigorous activity of Satan (2:5,7)
      2. The victorious activity of the Spirit (2:6-7)
III. How the Might of Satan Is Released (2 Thessalonians 2:8-12)
   A. God: Sovereign as ever He was (2:8)
   B. Satan: Subtle as ever he was (2:9)
   C. Man: Sinful as ever he was (2:10-12)

THE MAN OF SIN IS REVEALED (2 THESSALONIANS 2:3)

We are first given a description of how Satan's man is to be revealed, beginning with information about the nature of the times when he will come. We are forbidden in Scripture to set dates for the Lord's return, but we can test the moral climate of the age to see if it is like that depicted in the prophetic Word for the last days.

Paul began in the original Greek with a double negative. The King James translation reads, "Let no man deceive you by any means: for that day shall not come, except there come a falling away first" (2 Thessalonians 2:3). We do not use double negatives, because in English two negatives cancel each other and make a positive. If I say, "He does not want no more," I am really saying, "He does want more." In Greek, however, the double negative is used for emphasis; Paul was saying, "Let no man deceive you by no means." In other words, the coming deception will be so intense that we need to be doubly on our guard against it.

It will be heralded by a general "falling away." The word Paul used is *apostasia*, from which comes our English word *apostasy*. The only other time the word is used is in Acts 21:21.

Some think we can look for a worldwide spiritual awakening before the rapture of the church, but this passage indicates the opposite: a worldwide departure from the faith can be expected. God might indeed send a revival before He calls home the church, but the Scriptures do not prophesy one. There will be a revival *after* the rapture, because Israel is to experience a mighty moving of the Spirit that will spill over to all mankind (Revelation 7). This might well be a second Pentecost, since some of the things mentioned by Joel (Joel 2:28-31) and cited by Peter as evidence that God was at work (Acts 2:16-20) were not fulfilled on the original day of Pentecost.

As the dawning church age saw a mighty movement of the Holy Spirit, so the dawning kingdom age will see a great outpouring of the Holy Spirit. The church age will end in apostasy; the kingdom age will begin with revival. The church age will end with Laodicean lukewarmness, complacency, and rejection of Christ (Revelation 3:14-22); the approaching kingdom age will begin with the rekindling of revival fire.

Many of the marks of the coming apostasy are evident in the world today. As we have noted, the Lord directs us to the days of Noah (Matthew 24:37-39) and to the days of Lot (Luke 17:28) as illustrations of what the world will be like in the endtimes. The days of Noah were marked by a *permissive* society (Genesis 4–6); the days of Lot were marked by a *perverted* society (Genesis 19). The Epistles of Jude and 2 Peter were both written to deal with apostasy. Both add further details and confirm that permissiveness and perversion in society will mark the endtimes.

How *permissive* our society has become is indicated by the kinds of books people read, the kinds of movies they watch, and the kinds of indulgence tolerated everywhere with little or no protest. One of the most frightening indications is in our educational system, where fearful forms of wickedness are being openly advocated. One book suggested as a suitable text for young children is a book entitled *Show Me*. The cover describes this as "A Picture Book of Sex for Children and Parents." The cover picture is of a carefully posed but evidently naked little boy and girl. The boy wears a challenging expression on his face, and the girl is obviously pondering his suggestion to "show me."

One family therapist, who claimed that children have no vote in the matter of sex, said they have a right to express themselves sexually and claimed further that they have the right to have sexual contact with older people. Another prominent author argued that incest can sometimes be beneficial to children.[3] Such suggestions have their roots in human depravity and bring down the wrath of God on those who espouse them. Jesus said of such people that it would be better for them never to have been born, or better for them if a millstone were to be hanged around their necks and they be cast into the depths of the sea (Matthew 18:6; Mark 9:42; Luke 17:2).

How *perverted* our society has become is illustrated in the growing power and arrogance of those who practice sexual perversion and in the growing acceptance of sodomy as a "lifestyle." That society at large should tolerate such shameful sins is bad enough and proof of how far we have drifted from our moral moorings. But now people who openly practice the abominations that called down God's wrath in fire and brimstone on Sodom and Gomorrah are actually being ordained into the pulpits of some American churches. In 1979 the Episcopal church ordained a lesbian, Ellen Barrett, to the priesthood and in 1972 the United Church of Christ, heirs of the Puritans, ordained a homosexual clergyman. That is apostasy in its most blatant form. Such God-dishonoring, God-daring, and God-defying practices are openly accepted by some in our society, and those who oppose such practices are labeled intolerant and bigoted.

The first thing Paul underlined, then, was the moral climate of general apostasy that will mark the endtimes and will prepare the way for the coming of the devil's messiah. After this clue to the climate of his coming, Paul gave us a clue to the character of this epitome of evil. Paul described him as "the man of sin" and "the son of perdition."

As to his personality, he will be "the man of sin"—the embodiment, the incarnation, of sin itself. In fact, he will be the second person in a Satanic trinity; he will be the antichrist. As the Lord Jesus was the visible expression of the invisible God, so the antichrist will be the visible expression of the invisible devil. All the fullness of the godhead dwelt bodily in Jesus, so much so that He could tell people that if they had seen Him they had seen His Father (John 14:9). The beast will likewise be the bodily manifestation of Satan on earth. He will be the man of sin, glorying in sin, sponsoring sin, popularizing sin, enthroning sin, living in sin, embodying sin. Sinful men will be drawn to him as a needle to a magnet.

As to his person, he is "the son of perdition." Since Jesus described Judas Iscariot as "the son of perdition" (John 17:12), some grammarians say that the definite article (*the* son of perdition, not *a* son of perdition) identifies Judas with the antichrist. G. Campbell Morgan claimed that when Jesus said to His disciples, "One of you is a devil" (John 6:70), He not only referred to Judas but intimated that Judas was an incarnate demon and not a true human at all. Whether or not Judas is to reappear as the antichrist is a debated point. The idea, however, is contradicted by Revelation 17:9-11, which identifies the antichrist with a former world ruler.

Whoever he is, the antichrist, when he comes, will have his own unveiling. As Paul said here, he is to "be revealed" (2 Thessalonians 2:3). Paul used the word *apokalupto*, which means "to unveil so as to be visible to the eye." It is the word from which we get the word *Apocalypse* to describe the book of Revelation. As the Lord Jesus is going to be revealed to men in all His glory, so the antichrist will be revealed.

THE MYSTERY OF INIQUITY IS RESTRAINED (2 THESSALONIANS 2:4 -7)

Paul next explained how the mystery of iniquity is restrained, and it is here that the Holy Spirit unmasks Satan's secret plans. The goal is simple. Satan intends to have himself openly worshiped by all mankind. As the Lord Jesus is the One through whom we worship God, so the antichrist will be the one through whom people will worship Satan.

Satan will exalt his man to the highest pinnacle of worship so that all worship might be channeled through that one evil mediator to himself. The coming man of sin "opposeth and exalteth himself above all that is called God, or that is worshiped" (2 Thessalonians 2:4). Satan, far from opposing religion, is the secret source of inspiration and power behind all false religions. When the devil's "christ" is unveiled, he will be the false "christ" of the cults, the reincarnate Buddha of the Buddhists, the reborn Krishna of the Hindus, the fiery Mahdi of Islam, and the deceiving messiah of the Jews.

The antichrist will be an attractive and charismatic figure, a genius, a demon-controlled, devil-taught charmer of men. He will have answers to the horrendous problems of mankind. He will be all things to all men: a political statesman, a social lion, a financial wizard, an intellectual giant, a religious deceiver, a masterful orator, a gifted organizer. He will be Satan's masterpiece of deception, the world's false messiah. The masses will follow him with boundless enthusiasm and will readily enthrone him in their hearts as this world's savior and god.

Then Satan will exhibit his man in the holiest place of worship. He will sit "in the temple of God, shewing himself that he is God" (2

Thessalonians 2:4). The Jews will have rebuilt their temple in Jerusalem and restored the sacrificial system under his protection. But once the Jews have served his purpose, he will brush them contemptuously aside, garrison Jerusalem with his troops, and seize their temple. Satan intends to offer the final insult to God by enthroning his man of sin as God in God's temple. He intends also to put the beast's image in the temple as a further object of worship and as further provocation of the true God. This plan is here exposed by the Holy Spirit.

Satan's plan, however, is actively opposed by the Holy Spirit during this present age in which we live. For the time being, Satan is under restraint and can not bring his plans to fruition. He has tried over and over again throughout the course of history, but always he has been hindered by the mighty power of the Spirit of God.

Note what Paul said about the vigorous activity of Satan: "Remember ye not, that, when I was yet with you, I told you these things? And now ye know what withholdeth that he might be revealed in his time. For the mystery of iniquity doth already work" (2 Thessalonians 2:5-7). The word translated "work" is the word from which we derive our English word *energy*. It means "to work actively," "to work effectively," or "to be actively in operation." Paul used the word in 1 Thessalonians 2:13, where he spoke of the Word of God which "effectually worketh also in you that believe." The word is used in James 5:16 to describe "the *effectual* fervent prayer of a righteous man" (italics added).

Here in 2 Thessalonians Paul had in mind the active working of the leaven, which already permeated society in his day and which would continue to work energetically until all is corrupted. The only thing that will halt the action of Satan's leaven will be the fire of God's outpoured wrath. We can see the leavening process at work everywhere in today's society. So much of governmental legislation, attempts at moral reform, and efforts by well-meaning people to arrest the spreading corruption comes to naught. The leaven is preparing the loaf of human society for the final outburst of wickedness. We are witnessing the vigorous activity of Satan.

But we are also witnessing the victorious activity of the Holy Spirit. Paul said, "Ye know what withholdeth. . . . only he who now letteth [hinders, holds fast] will let [hinder, hold fast], until he be taken out of the way" (2 Thessalonians 2:6-7). The presence of the

Holy Spirit in the church is hindering Satan. On the day of Pentecost, the Spirit of God took up a new position in relation to this world. He began to baptize believers into the mystical body of Christ, the church (1 Corinthians 12:12-27). Through this unique body the Holy Spirit effectively restrains the full development of the mystery of iniquity in today's world. The Holy Spirit offsets Satan's "mystery" with God's "mystery" (Ephesians 5:32). At the rapture, the church will be removed from earth and the Holy Spirit will resume His former relationship with mankind; that is, He will revert to His Old Testament relationship and method of dealing with men.

The church age is a parenthesis in God's dealings with the world. The church, injected supernaturally into history at Pentecost, supernaturally maintained throughout this age by the baptizing, indwelling, and filling works of the Holy Spirit, will be supernaturally removed when this age is over. What is to be removed, then, is the Holy Spirit working in mighty power through the church. Until that happens, Satan can not bring his plans to a head. After the rapture of the church the Holy Spirit will continue His work in bringing people to salvation, but He will no longer baptize them into the mystical body of Christ, the church, nor will He actively hinder Satan from bringing his schemes to fruition. However, once Satan has achieved his centuries-long goal, Christ will return and demolish the whole thing.

We can trace the Holy Spirit's hindering process at work throughout history. More than once Satan has been ready to bring in his man and take over the planet, only to have his plans upset by a Holy Spirit revival. One page of history will suffice to illustrate this. Consider the Wesleyan revival which swept through Britain and which, the historian Lecky confessed, saved England from "bloody revolution." Conditions in England were as bad as they were in France, but France had revolution and Britain had revival. France had Robespierre, Marat, Danton, and Napoleon; Britain had John and Charles Wesley.

John Wesley barely escaped death at the age of six. Some of his father's parishioners, enraged at his fearless denunciation of their sins, tried to burn his house down. Little John, forgotten in the excitement, was stranded in the upstairs nursery. Nobody could reach him because the stairs had fallen in. The little fellow stood piteously at the window, and two courageous men, one standing on the shoulders of another, braved the flames to pluck him to safety. John Wesley often called himself "a brand plucked from the burning."

It was much the same with brother Charles. He was prematurely born and pronounced dead on delivery because he showed no signs of life, but his mother refused to believe it and wrapped him in wool for several days. At the time when he normally should have been born, he opened his eyes for the first time and cried and behaved like any normal newborn baby.

If ever there was a time when England needed a John Wesley to preach to its conscience and a Charles Wesley to sing to its heart, it was the 1700s. Historians tell us that the theater was decadent; the royal court and the castles of the nobility reeked with licentiousness. The common people were being swept into atheism by Hume, Gibbon, and Voltaire. Drunkenness was epidemic. In 1736, just three years before the Methodist revival, every sixth house in London was a tavern. These gin mills became headquarters for gangs of thieves who tortured, killed, and maimed.

The universities and colleges seethed with radical teachings. The priests of the established Anglican church were, for the most part, godless and worldly men. Augustus Toplady, who wrote the hymn "Rock of Ages," said that a converted Church of England minister was as rare as a comet. The bishop of Litchfield described the Lord's day as "the Devil's market day," given over to quarrels, murder, and sin. Immorality was championed and justified by society. Every kind of sin found someone to expound it, a publisher to print it, and a bookstall to sell it. Bishop Butler said it was taken for granted that Christianity was no longer worth discussing. Such was England on the eve of the Wesleyan revival; and such are Britain, America, and the world today.

John Wesley was his mother's pupil, and Epworth rectory was his school. For the first five years of his life, Susannah Wesley drilled him in Bible, laying such a foundation of Scripture in the lad's soul that all his subsequent ministry was based on it. When the time was ripe, the Holy Spirit sowed John and Charles Wesley into the English-speaking world; and a revival broke out that left its mark on the British isles for a generation. The devil's plans to seize England were thwarted, and a new generation of godly men and women arose to blaze new missionary trails around the world and bring an empire back to God.

So then, iniquity is currently being restrained and, bad as our world is becoming, will continue to be restrained as long as the Holy Spirit in the church remains to hold back the worst of it by His omnipotent power. The devil is no match for the Holy Ghost. After the rapture, however, this restraint will be removed; and Satan will be allowed to give his man his brief apocalypse.

THE MIGHT OF SATAN IS RELEASED (2 THESSALONIANS 2:8 -12)

Paul concluded this important prophecy by telling how, at last, the might of Satan will be released. He underlined three things in drawing the dreadful story to a close. First, God will be as sovereign as He ever was. "And *then* shall that Wicked [one] be revealed, whom the Lord shall consume with the spirit of his mouth, and shall destroy with the brightness of his coming" (2 Thessalonians 2:8, italics added). It will look as though Satan is having it all his own way, but that will not be so. A time note is underlined: "*then*," and not until then. Satan, for all his craft and cunning, for all his tremendous powers, will finally bring his plans to a head, not because he has outwitted the Spirit of God, but because God removes the restraint. A termination note is underlined as well. The beast, Satan's diabolical antichrist, will be destroyed at the second coming of Christ. In other words, God will be as sovereign as ever. He will be in control even during the fleeting days of Satan's seeming triumph.

Then, too, Satan will be as subtle as ever he was. Paul reminded us that the devil's man is to have a "coming." He used the word *parousia*, the same word used in the New Testament to describe the coming of Christ. Antichrist's "coming" will be "after the working of Satan with all power and signs and lying wonders" (2 Thessalonians 2:9).

Miracles are used only very sparingly by God. There are just five brief periods in Scripture when they are used. The first outbreak of miracles was during the Exodus and the conquest of Canaan. Moses and Joshua were leading God's people through a great period of transition in their earthly pilgrimage, and miracles paved the way. Those miracles stopped as suddenly as they began. In their place, God gave His people His written Word: the Pentateuch,

281

the early historical writings, some of the wisdom literature, and the Psalms of David.

A second outbreak of miracles occurred in the days of Elijah and Elisha, and those miracles likewise stopped as suddenly as they began. Again it was an age of transition. The miracles were designed to draw attention to the ministry of God's two witnesses, who were making a last-ditch attempt to bring the nation back to God. It was unavailing, however, so God prepared to hand the northern tribes over to the Assyrians. But first He replaced the miracles with His written Word: the later histories; the written prophecies of Isaiah, Jeremiah, and the early prophets; and more Psalms.

A third and brief outburst of miracles took place in Babylon in the days of Daniel and his friends. These, too, stopped almost at once and were replaced by additions to the Word of God: by the writings of the exilic prophets, the final historical books, the postexilic prophets, and a few more Psalms.

A fourth, and by far the most spectacular, period of miracles was associated with Christ and His apostles. This was yet another transition period when God first offered the kingdom to Israel, withdrew the offer when the King was rejected, and began to prepare the way for the church. This period of miracles, too, ceased as suddenly as it began, about the time of the destruction of the Jewish temple and the dispersal of the Hebrew people. It was replaced by the written New Testament.

Miracles are used by God only to get attention; then they cease and are followed by long periods of time devoid of spectacular miracles, because He would never have us rely on them. He would have us rely on His Word. We are to take His Word at face value and be content with that (Luke 16:27-31). When we put our trust in Christ through His Word, we do put our faith in the supernatural; because the Bible is itself a supernatural book, much more reliable than voices and visions (2 Peter 1:17-21). The fact of the matter is that miracles can be counterfeited.

There is only one other period in Scripture when miracles abound, and that is the period following the rapture of the church. God's two men (Revelation 11) will perform miracles, and Satan's two men will counter them with signs and lying wonders. The day is approaching—is already intruding on our credulous age—when people will be swept into the arms of Satan by all kinds of occult phenomena produced and promoted by the devil.

Finally, man will be as sinful as ever. Paul said that Satan's man will come

> with all deceivableness of unrighteousness in them that perish; because they received not the love of the truth, that they might be saved. And for this cause God shall send them strong delusion, that they should believe a lie: That they all might be damned who believed not the truth, but had pleasure in unrighteousness (2 Thessalonians 2:10-12).

Millions of people will be saved and swept into the kingdom after the rapture (Revelation 7), but those who have heard and rejected the gospel in this age will be excluded from their number. All such will believe the lie and be damned.

A threefold repudiation of truth is expressed in the solemn verses just quoted. The *heart* is involved because they "loved not the truth," the *mind* is involved because they "believed not the truth," and the *will* is involved because they "had pleasure in unrighteousness." Paul was describing no casual, accidental missing of the way, but rather a deliberate rejection of the truth as it is in Christ Jesus. At the rapture, all who have so slighted the gospel of God's grace will be handed over to Satan. Since they would not have the truth, then let them have the lie. They spurned His Holy Spirit, so let them become a prey to evil spirits. They wanted no part in Christ, so let them have their part in antichrist. Could anything be more just or more terrible?

---

1. See Panton, *Present Day Pamphlets.*
2. The "day of the Lord" is mentioned twenty times in the Old Testament (Isaiah 2:12; 13:6,9; Ezekiel 13:5; 30:3; Joel 1:15; 2:1,11; 3:14; Amos 5:18-20; Obadiah 15; Zephaniah 1:7,14; Zechariah 14:1; Malachi 4:5. It is mentioned four times in the New Testament (1 Thessalonians 5:2; 2 Thessalonians 2:2; 2 Peter 3:10; Revelation 1:10).
3. See "Cradle-to-Grave Intimacy," *Time* (September 7, 1981).

14
Peter and the Atomic Age
2Peter 3:10 -13

A TV program that held public interest for some time was entitled *That's Incredible*. It brought to the TV screen a series of remarkable feats, skills, coincidences, and beliefs.

But here is something that might seem even more incredible than anything seen on that show. An uneducated Galilean fisherman, living nearly two thousand years ago, wrote into the Bible an accurate description of the nuclear age. He also foretold how the nuclear age will end—with a big bang that will embrace both the terrestrial and the celestial spheres. But we need not worry. The holocaust is not going to dissolve our planet for some time yet. And when the disaster comes, God will unleash the holocaust, not some mogul in the Kremlin, some panic-stricken president in the White House, or some frantic red-eyed terrorist. That is not to say that there may not be nuclear exchange between the superpowers in the meantime. Such a possibility is suggested in various prophetic Scriptures. But the ultimate catastrophe can not take place for at least a thousand years, not until the end of the millennial age.

The atomic age was born at 3:36 p.m. on December 2, 1942,

under an abandoned and crumbling stadium at the University of Chicago's Stagg Field. It was there that scientists produced the world's first chain reaction. Neutrons split uranium-235 nuclei. Heat and more neutrons streamed from the resulting disintegration. As these neutrons spewed out of the uranium block they were slowed and split more uranium-235 nuclei. The first steps had been taken into the nuclear age. It was theoretically possible to manufacture an atomic bomb. The secret of the transmutation of elements had been learned, and this ability had given men a destructive capacity of apocalyptic proportions.

The war with Germany ended, and the fear in the West that Hitler might make an atomic bomb first was removed. As soon as the Anglo-American forces secured a firm foothold in Germany, physicists were sent in to see just how far Hitler had advanced with his own efforts. The German nuclear physicists had done surprisingly little. Hitler had long since chased the best brains out of his country in his mad persecution of the Jews.

The work on the project went on in the West; Japan was still far from beaten. The prospect of taking Japan, island by island, city by city, at a fearful cost in human lives spurred the Americans on.

The first atomic bomb was exploded at 5:20 a.m. on July 16, 1945. The place chosen for the experiment was an arid wilderness in New Mexico, fifty miles from Alamogordo. An enormous tower was built of ten-inch rails, weighing ninety pounds to the foot. When the bomb exploded, the tower vaporized and its debris was tossed seven miles into the sky. Where the tower had stood there was now a hole sixty feet deep and five thousand feet wide. For eighteen thousand feet in all directions, the ground was boiled, fused, or melted into glass.

Work on the bomb continued. But by now the nuclear scientists had become alarmed as the academic community whispered that the military intended to use the bomb on Japan, once it was ready. The scientists had opened a door, however, and it was now too late to close it. Einstein said afterward that there seemed to be a weird inevitability about it all. Work continued until two bombs were ready. They were not the same kind.

The first atomic bomb to be dropped on a city fell on Hiroshima at 8:15 a.m. on August 6, 1945. It was about fourteen feet long and five feet in diameter. It weighed under ten thousand pounds. It was a uranium-235 bomb. The people of the city saw a formation of planes fly overhead and then a cluster of three parachutes descend slowly toward the earth from one of those planes. It was the last thing many of them saw. At a height of eighteen hundred feet the bomb exploded. A city of 350,000 people was virtually leveled. Some 70,000 people were killed instantly, and as many more were severely injured. About two-thirds of the buildings were totally destroyed or damaged beyond repair. Many people died later of radiation sickness.

Three days later, after dropping warning leaflets on forty-seven Japanese cities, a second atomic bomb was dropped on Nagasaki, this time a plutonium bomb. The United States had totally exhausted its atomic-bomb arsenal, but *that* secret was well kept. Japan surrendered, but the atomic age went on. A door had been slammed irrevocably on the past. Life on this planet would never be the same again.

At 9:00 a.m. on July 1, 1946, the United States tested its atomic bombs against an experimental fleet assembled in a deserted lagoon at Bikini. Battleships, cruisers, aircraft carriers alike were sunk or badly damaged. Two miles away, a test ship burst into flames. Some ten million tons of water (the equivalent of the tonnage of the entire United States wartime fleet) were flung two miles into the sky.

In August 1949 the Russians exploded their first atomic bomb, and the United States decided to develop a hydrogen bomb. An atomic bomb is a fission bomb, made by splitting the atom. But the fission bomb was now to be used as a match to detonate the much greater hydrogen bomb. The sun, which gives off energy in changing hydrogen into helium, burns at some twenty million degrees centigrade. Since the A-bomb generates temperatures up to fifty million degrees centigrade, it could be used to produce a fusion reaction, like that of the sun, by igniting or fusing together two of the heavier isotopes of hydrogen.

On November 1, 1952, the United States tested the first hydrogen bomb near Eniwetok atoll in the Pacific ocean. It tore a one-mile island right out of the Pacific, leaving behind a hole in the ocean floor 175 feet deep, big enough to hold fourteen Pentagon buildings. That one bomb alone had more force than all the bombs dropped on Germany and Japan throughout World War II.

The effects of radiation from a hydrogen bomb bring the annihilation of all life on earth within the range of technical possibility. The explosion of a hydrogen bomb releases tremendous quantities of neutrons, which can enter any substance and make it radioactive. H-bombs can be designed in such a way that their explosion can spread into the air tremendous clouds of specially selected radioactive substances, which give off lethal radiation for a predetermined period of time.

Now we have the neutron bomb, the ultimate nuclear weapon. The neutron bomb has been developed to counter the threat of Russian tanks and armor rolling westward across the northern German plain. The purpose of the neutron bomb is to kill men on the battlefield, particularly those manning tanks and armored cars. Since there is very little residual radiation, once the enemy troops are dead, defending troops can quickly reclaim the invaded area. The weapon is technically known as the Enhanced Radiation Weapon. It is basically a fusion weapon. About 80 percent of its energy is released in the form of high-speed neutrons that penetrate steel and therefore render tanks and armored cars useless as protection for the crews inside. The remaining 20 percent of the bomb's energy is released in the form of heat and blast.

Ever since the threat of nuclear war became a possibility, the Atomic Energy Commission, the Pentagon, and top military strategists have been studying what would happen to the United States in the event of a nuclear attack. Here are the horrific findings if just *eighteen* of Russia's 100-megaton warheads were to land on strategic targets in this country.[1]

We can envision three such bombs incinerating the entire East Coast. Massachusetts, Rhode Island, and New Jersey would erupt in flames taking into oblivion with them New York City, Hartford, Philadelphia, Baltimore, and Washington, D.C. The area from Portland, Maine, to Norfolk, Virginia, would become a lake of fire.

Six more bombs might simultaneously explode in various selected regions. One might engulf the southern portions of Louisiana, Mississippi, and Alabama, enveloping 22,500 square miles in a 170-mile-wide sea of flames. Another bomb might baptize Detroit, Toledo, Cleveland, and half of Ohio in fire. Another might devastate sections of Wisconsin, Illinois, and Indiana in a fiery bath that would destroy everything from Milwaukee through Chicago and Gary to South Bend. On the Pacific coast another bomb might ignite everything between Portland and Seattle, another wipe San Francisco, Oakland, San Jose, Stockton, and Sacramento from the map of northern California. One more could send a belt of fire through southern California embracing everything from Oxnard, north of Los Angeles, to San Diego and the Mexican border.

Another eight warheads might explode over the ICBM complexes in the triangle from Arkansas to Montana, incinerating in the process Phoenix, Tucson, Little Rock, Wichita, Cheyenne, Kansas City, and many other population centers.

A final warhead might be exploded four thousand feet beneath the waters of the Pacific on the slopes of the Aleutian Deep. This would generate an enormous tidal wave, which would engulf vast areas of Alaska, Hawaii, and other Pacific coastal regions.

The resulting fire storms would rage throughout thirty-four of the fifty states. Even outside the actual areas of conflagration, the loss of life would be severe. Winds of hurricane force would be generated by air rushing in to feed the apocalyptic fires. So much oxygen would be used that people would actually die for want of air. About three-fifths of the population of the United States would die. The nation's industrial and military power would be gone.

American retaliation, however, would be already on the way. As soon as confirmation was received that missiles were launched, American missiles would head for Russia. Cold comfort for the American dead.

The United States has placed its reliance on smaller warheads than have the Russians. The number of weapons the United States has in its nuclear stockpile is a secret. One estimate is that there are some thirty thousand nuclear weapons available to the military, including about twelve thousand which could be landed on Russian territory. There is enough power in the American nuclear arsenal to annihilate the whole communist world in a single attack. The destruction of both Russia and the United States would take only about thirty minutes, and some four hundred million people would die. Facts like these make Russia hesitant about a final confrontation with the West.

There is really no defense against a nuclear attack. A group called Physicians for Social Responsibility has warned us what to expect. They call the aftermath of a nuclear exchange "the last epidemic." Apart from those who would die instantly, millions more would die of trauma, from burns, radiation sickness, and other injuries. Most hospitals and doctors would be gone, and probably very few of the doctors remaining would want to expose themselves to the certainty of radiation contamination. Much of the nation's communication and transportation systems would also be gone. Water would be contaminated. Epidemics would rage as a result of the putrefaction of countless unburied corpses. Many of those who did manage to survive all these horrors would die later from cancer and leukemia.

Miscalculation leading to a nuclear war is a fearful possibility in this crisis-ridden world. More and more nations are joining the atomic club, some of them highly unstable. When Israel sent its air force into Iraq and destroyed that country's nuclear potential in 1981, most people heaved a sigh of relief. Iraq's French-built Tammuz 1 nuclear reactor was located at El-Tuwaitha, about ten miles south of Baghdad. Half a dozen Israeli planes demolished the $260 million nuclear research reactor in a matter of minutes. It is generally conceded that the reactor could have turned out nuclear material for military use. Iraq angrily threatened to build a bigger and better reactor, and Israel promised to take out all the reactors Iraq wanted to build.

More than thirty major efforts have been made by the nations with nuclear know-how to curtail the proliferation of nuclear expertise. The Treaty of Nonproliferation of Nuclear Weapons was signed in 1968. The International Fuel Cycle Evaluation was launched in 1977. It was assigned the impossible task of dispensing the power of nuclear hardware but prohibiting its conversion to weaponry. The efforts have been fruitless. France, particularly, has exported nuclear know-how for cash. Canada gave India the power to build the bomb. West Germany exported the power to Brazil. The United States sells its technology almost everywhere.

The task of regulating the threat seems hopeless. A new nightmare has been added. What if terrorists get the bomb?

In 1975 a young man named John Aristotle Phillips transferred to Princeton. In his junior year he and some of his friends argued about the atomic danger from the hands of terrorists. Most of the students agreed that it was impossible for terrorists to make an atomic bomb. They didn't have the know-how, nor did they have access to the information. That was the general feeling.

Phillips decided to prove his friends wrong. He recorded his project with the physics office at school: "John Aristotle Phillips— Dr. Freeman Dyson, Advisor—'How to Build Your Own Atomic Bomb.'" He based his research on easily obtainable unclassified material made available by the United States Government Printing Office and came up with a plan for a crude but effective nuclear bomb. It would be two feet in diameter, weigh 125 pounds, and would fit into a car. It could flatten a quarter of Manhattan. To build this bomb a thief would need to steal only 21 pounds of plutonium. The full title of his paper was "The Fundamentals of Atomic Bomb Design—An Assessment in the Problems and Possibilities Confronting a Terrorist Group of Nonnuclear Nations Attempting to Design a Crude PU-239 Fission Bomb."

The threat of nuclear terrorism is so real that governments are taking it seriously. Any nuclear threat is at once given top priority by law enforcement agencies. Such a threat was leveled at New York City in July 1975. It read:

> We have successfully designed and built an atomic bomb. It is somewhere on Manhattan Island. We refer you to the accompanying drawing in 1/8 scale. We have enough plutonium and explosives for the bomb to function. This device will be used at 6:00 p.m. on July 10 unless our demands are met. Do not notify the public. This will result in hysteria and the use of the bomb.[2]

The FBI handles such threats and has organized a Nuclear Emergency Search Team to deal with them.

Even the peacetime use of nuclear energy has its problems. Atomic energy is being increasingly criticized in the United States, where it was once considered the solution to mounting energy problems. The disaster at Three Mile Island in 1979 shocked the nation. Optimistic predictions, which once saw as many as fifteen hundred reactors operating in the United States by the turn of the century, have vanished. Now an increasingly voluble minority would like to see an end to all reactors.

In 1986 at the Chernobyl nuclear plant in the Soviet Union there was a catastrophe. The Soviet Union's first reaction was to deny it, but as increasing proofs became available from western sources that a disaster of great dimensions had taken place and that contamination was not confined to the Soviet Union, Moscow belatedly admitted that something had happened.

It is now believed that the Soviets went to considerable lengths to deceive their own people. The meltdown took place April 26.

Although fully aware of the danger, the government delayed evacuating nearby towns and villages. On May 1 the annual May Day parade was allowed to continue in nearby Kiev, even though it was known that radiation had reached dangerous levels. It was not until May 2 that the decision was made to evacuate Chernobyl, and the last children did not leave nearby Narodichi until June 7. By that time they had been exposed to radiation for six weeks.

The most recent claim is that the Chernobyl nuclear disaster actually released at least twenty times more radiation than has been officially admitted, and that the Soviet nuclear authorities knew that the design of the reactor was unsafe.

One of the biggest problems facing the industry is what to do with nuclear waste. The world has never before known such dangerous material. A million-gallon tank of waste produced and stored according to current procedures contains 250 times the hazardous strontium 90 released by the Hiroshima bomb—even with 95 percent of the strontium removed. Enormous quantities of the deadly stuff are already stored in underground tanks in the United States alone. With some twenty-two nations now operating about 200 reactors and with another 150 reactors under construction around the world, the problem is becoming acute.

It is no wonder noisy voices are insisting that we halt nuclear development and, above all, ban the bomb. Only a decade after mass marches and turbulent demonstrations against the Vietnam war, the same voices were castigating the United States and attacking NATO in protest against nuclear weapons. Once again the communists showed how they could mobilize mass movements by playing on legitimate fears. It is hypocritical and dangerous to insist that the United States disarm itself of nuclear weapons without bringing equal pressure to bear on the Russians and the score of other nations that now have the bomb. As *Reader's Digest* put it in its June 1982 lead article, "Ban *Whose* Bomb?"

We can all sympathize with the demonstrator who carried a banner with the message "I'm Afraid." We can feel, too, for the young man who rose at a meeting in Massachusetts, where people from various professions were reciting the horrors of nuclear war, to say with passion, "No one should have the right to choose whether an entire generation gets to grow up or not." He should try preaching that on the steps of the Kremlin. Disarmament is a two-way street. There is nothing some would like more than for the

West to unilaterally disarm, leaving them free to plunder the world at will.

That is the background. We are now ready to see what the Holy Spirit revealed to Peter about the nuclear age. To put Peter's remarks into perspective, here is an outline of 2 Peter 3:1-18:

I. The Lord and His Delay (2 Peter 3:1-9)
  A. Ridicule on the part of the lost (3:1-7)
    1. Their insolence (3:3-4)
    2. Their ignorance (3:5-7)
      a. About the past: judgment by flood (3:5-6)
      b. About the future: judgment by fire (3:7)
  B. Restraint on the part of the Lord (3:8-9)
    1. God's mode of living transcends ours (3:8)
    2. God's method of loving transcends ours (3:9)
      a. He is remembering His promise
      b. He is revealing His patience
II. The Lord and His Day (2 Peter 3:10-18)
  A. Its implementation (3:10-13)
    1. A fiery conflagration (3:10-11)
      a. Its coming
      b. Its character
    2. A firm conviction (3:12)
    3. A future creation (3:13)
  B. Its implications (3:14-18)

It is evident from this passage that Peter's attention was focused on the last days. "There shall come in the last days scoffers, walking after their own lusts, And saying, Where is the promise of his coming?" (2 Peter 3:3-4) He anticipated a day when a renewed interest in the Lord's return would be matched by a rising tide of ridicule.

Such times have arrived. Renewed interest in the Lord's return was awakened in the Christian church by the preaching and writings of the early Plymouth Brethren about the middle of the nineteenth century. Men like John Nelson Darby, William Kelly, and Walter Scott rescued this truth from long neglect and proclaimed it with fresh conviction. Soon prophetic conferences sprang up on both sides of the Atlantic and interest widened. The birth of the Zionist movement and the rebirth of the state of Israel added to the interest.

This renewed interest has been matched, even in the church, by widespread opposition. Premillennial and dispensational teaching is vehemently attacked. A large segment of the professing Christian church espouses amillennial views. These views stem from covenant theology, which holds that the church is spiritual Israel and that the great promises and prophecies of the Old Testament about the nation of Israel are being fulfilled spiritually in the church. As a result many people see no divinely appointed future for Israel as a nation. They turn a blind theological eye on the rebirth of that nation. They persist with the view that the church *is* Israel and that the prophecies of the Old Testament have to be allegorized and spiritualized.

With such an entrenched attitude prevalent, it is no wonder that the world is plainly skeptical. Overly enthusiastic students of prophecy have not helped by naming Mussolini as the antichrist and fascist Italy as the revived Roman Empire; by declaring Henry Kissinger to be the beast of Revelation; by circulating rumors about the Jews importing stones from the United States in order to build their temple; by saying that vultures are multiplying near Megiddo; by finding the mystical number 666 in all kinds of strange places; by accusing giant American corporations of conducting their businesses in the interests of witchcraft; and by shortsightedly seeing the "fulfillment" of prophecy in every minor move that takes place in the Middle East.

There is widespread skepticism and considerable scoffing in the secular world about the impending fulfillment of prophecy. One example appeared in *Atlantic Monthly* (June 3, 1962) in a feature article written by William Martin. It is a sneering pseudoscholarly attack on those who believe in the second coming of Christ.

"The end is near," Martin said sarcastically, "because God has planned it that way for at least 1,900 years." He concluded, "But if Jesus keeps not coming, interest will eventually crest and recede to await the next promising configuration of signs." A four-color illustration, printed with the article itself, shows a man in a blue suit standing on a street corner, with a Bible securely tucked under his arm, pointing to his wrist watch. Bearing down on him is an army of giant green locusts. The whole article is a thinly-veiled attack on the truth of the second coming of Christ, and its author is a scoffer. The Lord's coming *was* to be delayed as He Himself taught and as the New Testament constantly proclaims.

Peter pointed out that the Lord's delay would be marked by divine restraint, rooted in God's kindness to mankind. When God next steps down into the arena of human affairs, it will be in wrath. The day of grace will be over, and the day of judgment will have come. Peter said that scoffers would be ignorant of the fact that God's method of keeping time is not the same as man's. "One day is with the Lord as a thousand years, and a thousand years as one day. The Lord is not slack concerning his promise, as some men count slackness" (2 Peter 3:8-9). The word *slack* means "to delay." The Lord does not delay His coming. He has flung the stars into space; He has orbited galaxies and planetary systems; He has done so with such mathematical precision that we check our measures of time by the systems of the sky. He has set His prophetic clock with equal precision. His long absence is not a mark of slowness or tardiness. It is a mark of the continuing love that has caused Him to lengthen the day of grace. He "is longsuffering . . . not willing that any should perish" (3:9).

Having set the stage, Peter then described how the day of the Lord *will* come, and in particular how it will climax and end. His vision was focused on what will happen at the end of Christ's millennial reign. Satan's final rebellion will mobilize the unregenerate of earth in one last crusade to dethrone God and His Christ.

Peter spoke of *a fiery conflagration*:

> But the day of the Lord will come as a thief in the night; in the which the heavens shall pass away with a great noise, and the elements shall melt with fervent heat, the earth also and the works that are therein shall be burned up. Seeing then that all these things shall be dissolved . . . (2 Peter 3:10-11).

There are a number of fascinating words in this remarkable prophecy. Take the word translated "elements," for instance. The ancient Greeks thought there were four elements (earth, air, fire, and water). They were wrong in both the nature and number of the elements. The English word *element* comes to us from the Latin *elementum*, which is a translation of the Greek word *stoicheion* used here by Peter. Philologists have attached several meanings to the word. It suggests the letters of the alphabet, a simple sound of speech, and also the letters of the alphabet as placed in order. Liddell and Scott in their *Greek-English Lexicon* claimed that in the field of physics *stoicheia* was defined as "the components into which matter is divided." It was therefore a suitable word for the Holy Spirit to use here in discussing the particles that make up matter. In today's English *stoicheia* would be expressed by the word *atoms*. As *stoicheia*, the letters of the alphabet, are the component parts of words, so *stoicheia*, the atoms, are the component parts of the elements.

The word translated "dissolved" is the Greek *luo*, which means to "break up," "destroy," or "melt." It is translated "unloose" in Mark 1:7, Luke 3:16, John 1:27, and Acts 13:25, in connection with John the Baptist's declaration that he was not worthy to untie the latchet on Christ's shoe. After raising Lazarus from the dead, Christ commanded that he was to be untied. "Loose him," He said (John 11:44). As the word is used in the New Testament, it conveys the thought of setting free something that has been bound.

The Holy Spirit is saying here that at the end of the age there will be a great conflagration of the heavens and earth. He employs language of the most precise kind. He says that the elemental particles of matter, which we now call atoms, will be dissolved, untied, released. Their energies, hitherto imprisoned, will be set free. This is the cause of the coming holocaust.

Peter, of course, could not possibly have realized the technical accuracy of his terms, but the Holy Spirit did. The principle of nuclear fission, which is at the base of the atomic bomb, is clearly implied in Peter's words.

The expression "a great noise" comes from a single Greek word found nowhere else in the New Testament: *rhoizedon*. It refers to the whizzing of an arrow rushing to its target. According to W. E. Vine's *Expository Dictionary of New Testament Words*, the word also signifies "with rushing sound as of roaring flames."

The phrase "fervent heat" is a translation of the Greek word *kausoo*, a medical term denoting a fever. Peter's use of it is said to be the only known application of the word to inanimate objects.

So then Peter accurately described the untying of the atom and the resulting rushing, fiery destruction that follows it. He did not envision this holocaust overtaking the world at the end of the church age. He placed the event at the end of the entire calendar of prophetic events, at the end of the millennial age. The fact that the atomic age has dawned, however, is another ominous sign heralding the approaching endtimes.

In Revelation 16:2 another prophetic ray of light is shed on the atomic age: "And there fell a noisome and grievous sore upon the men." At Hiroshima God allowed us a glimpse of what lies ahead for the world. About two weeks after the explosion, individuals who had been well previously, and seemingly free from injury, fell ill in large numbers. Their symptoms were extreme weakness, pallor, loss of hair. Hemorrhages appeared on the skin, and there was ulceration and bleeding from oral mucosa. The victims became feverish and succumbed to lung and throat infections. Examination of their blood revealed extremely low red cell and hemoglobin values and low white cell counts. Prolonged bleeding resulted from loss of the blood's clotting factor. The condition progressed to death.

It is possible (both from Revelation 16 and Ezekiel 38–39) that some kind of nuclear exchange will take place between Russia and the United States. The disaster that will overtake Russia will be catastrophic; virtually annihilated, the country will cease to exist as a world power. The strange silence of Scripture concerning a major power in the western hemisphere has led some to think that a similar (and unrecorded) disaster might overtake the United States. However, it is always risky to make predictions based on the silence of Scripture. It is possible, however, that Russia and the United States will be removed as world powers in the endtimes, so that the prophetic world of Europe and the Middle East can again fill the stage.

Be that as it may, the dawning of the atomic age is the handwriting on the wall. It proclaims the approaching end. Even some secular scientists think this is true.

Soon after the atomic bomb was created, some of the people involved began to publish a newsletter known as the *Bulletin of the Atomic Scientists*. They chose as their cover symbol a doomsday clock. They placed the hands at eight minutes before midnight. From time to time they have moved the hands. After the United States and Russia tested hydrogen bombs in 1953, they advanced the hands up to two minutes before midnight. After the test-ban treaty in 1963, they changed the hands back to twelve minutes. In January 1981 the hands were placed at four minutes before midnight to reflect the new surge of weapons-development by both superpowers and the demise of the SALT II treaty. In 1991 the hands were moved to seventeen minutes before midnight as tension between the United States and Russia relaxed.

There can be no doubt that we are approaching the end. Peter followed up his remarks with *a firm conviction*. "Seeing then that all these things shall be dissolved, what manner of persons ought ye to be in all holy conversation and godliness, Looking for and hasting unto the coming of the day of God" (2 Peter 3:11-12). Peter believed that this great sign of the end should induce holy living and earnest expectation in the hearts of the people of God. He was right. So it should.

---

1. In its original form this scenario was produced by Craig Hosmer in *U.S. News and World Report* (July 31, 1967) from basic data supplied by the Atomic Energy Commission's Release D-279 (43 v.), October 31, 1961, and by *The Effects of Nuclear Weapons*, Samuel Gladstone, ed., AEC, April 1962. At the time, Hosmer was a member of the Joint Commission on Atomic Energy and chairman of the House Republican Conference Committee on Nuclear Affairs.
2. Larry Collins, "Combating Nuclear Terrorism," *New York Times Magazine* (December 14, 1980), p. 37.

15

The Nation
of Israel

T he plight of the Jewish people in a Gentile world was summed
up succinctly by the poet Byron:

Tribes of the wandering foot, and weary breast,
    When shall ye fly away and be at rest!
The wild dove has her nest, the fox his cave,
    Mankind their country—Israel but a grave.

Time after time in their long and troubled history the Jews have
faced the possibility of extermination. In 1548 B.C. a new pharaoh
came to the throne of Egypt, Amenhotep I. It was he who launched
history's first attempt to exterminate the Jews. All newborn
Hebrew males, he decreed, were to be tossed into the Nile. But God
stepped in and instead of extermination the Jews experienced the
exodus.

In 722 B.C. the Assyrians culminated a three-year siege on the
northern tribes of Israel. They sacked Samaria, depopulated the
country, and marched their Hebrew captives by the thousands

into exile and oblivion. In 701 B.C. the Assyrian monarch Sennacherib, having devastated most of Judah, turned his attention to Jerusalem to uproot what was left of the Jewish people. Again God intervened. This time the armies of the invader were swept away in a divine visitation of judgment, and the humiliated Sennacherib returned home to face an assassin's knife.

In 586 B.C. it was the turn of the Babylonians. Having led two successful expeditions against Judea and Jerusalem, Nebuchadnezzar returned to make an end of them. He demolished Jerusalem, burned the temple, slaughtered Jews wholesale, and deported the remainder to Babylon. But there they prospered, outlived the empire that had enslaved them, and were repatriated by order of the Persian emperor Cyrus—as foretold both by Isaiah and Jeremiah.

In 473 B.C. Haman, chief minister of the Persian tyrant Xerxes, persuaded his royal master it would be to his benefit to rid his realm of Jews. Again God intervened, this time through a woman; and the plots of this rabid antisemite were foiled. In one of the ironies of history, Haman ended up on the gallows he had prepared for Mordecai—the Jew he hated the most.

In 169 B.C. a half-mad Syrian tyrant named Antiochus Epiphanes, heir to a segment of the dismembered Grecian empire, captured Jerusalem and put the Jews to the sword. He defiled their temple, issued idolatrous laws no conscientious Jew would think of obeying, and did his best to replace Jewish culture and religion with Hellenism. But Antiochus perished and the Jews lived on.

In A.D. 70, after a long and stubborn siege, Jerusalem fell to another imperial power, Rome. During that war, over a million Jews perished by the sword, starvation, crucifixion, internal strife, and disease. The Romans glutted the slave markets and arenas of the world with captured Jews. But once more the Jews survived, this time to lay firmer foundations for Judaism as a viable force in a hostile Gentile world, no matter where or how Jews might be forced to live.

In A.D. 135 the Romans crushed a third Jewish revolt, this time led by Bar Kochba, a pseudomessiah. The infuriated emperor Hadrian now made it a capital offense for anyone to practice Judaism, but Hadrian died and the Jews lived on.

In 339 Emperor Constantius II made it illegal for Jews to intermarry with Christians. In 438 Emperor Theodosius II banned

Jews from all high office in the Roman world. In 531 Justinian resurrected and enforced the prohibitions of Theodosius and, in his famous *Corpus Juris*, made it illegal for Jews to appear as witnesses against Christians. In 630 the Byzantine emperor Heraclius connived at the massacre of Jews who had reinfiltrated Palestine. In 722 Emperor Leo III ordered all Jews to become Christians. In time, the Roman empire passed away. New powers took the stage, but the fate of the Jews remained unchanged. They were unwanted aliens in a Gentile world.

In 1066 the Muslim rulers of Granada in Spain massacred four thousand Jews in a single day. In 1096 Pope Urban II proclaimed the first crusade to rid the Holy Land of the Muslims. The crusade was preached throughout Europe by Peter the Hermit, and medieval knights rallied to the cause.

On their way to fight the Paynims, the knights found settlements of Jews in the cities through which they passed. "Why fight the enemies of the cross in Palestine," they argued, "and leave *these* enemies untouched?" So they massacred Jews by the thousands, torturing them, burning them, forcing them to commit sacrilege; and then they marched on their way to war, feeling they had done God a favor.

As crusade followed crusade the Jews of Europe knew what to expect when the knights and their motley armies appeared. In many communities the Jews adopted what they called the *kiddush ha-Shem* (the tradition of sacrifice), namely mass suicide. At least they could die in peace and dignity.

In 1149 the Berbers, who controlled the greater part of Spain, gave Spanish Jews the usual choice: convert to Islam or get out.

In 1215 the fourth Lateran council of the Roman Catholic Church (the same council that formalized the dogma of transubstantiation) ordered all Jews to wear a badge to distinguish them from other people. The edict was known as "the law of the patch," and its purpose was to segregate and degrade the Jews.

In 1290 all Jews were ordered out of England by Edward I. In 1306 all Jews were ordered out of France by Philip IV. In 1475 all Jews in the Italian city of Trent were killed. Throughout Europe, Jews were accused of poisoning wells, raping Christian women, and stealing infants from Christian homes to use their blood in ritual sacrifice.

In 1371 Jews were massacred in Castile under the rule of Henry

II. In 1391 they were massacred in Seville. Those who survived were forced to convert to Christianity, and those who did were called *marranos* (the damned). And damned they were, for the church suspected them of secretly practicing Judaism and bided its time.

In 1479 Ferdinand and Isabella united Spain and cleared the country of Moors. A tidal wave of pride, patriotism, and religious prejudice swept Spain. The Catholic church introduced the Inquisition to root out heretics, especially Jews and *marranos*. A new chapter of horror began for all who disagreed with Rome, especially those of Jewish blood. In 1483 Torquemada arrived in Spain to be father-confessor to the queen and to make the Spanish Inquisition the most feared instrument of terror in the medieval world. One of its primary goals was to root out and massacre Jews. In 1492, by the Edict of Expulsion, 300,000 Jews were tossed out of Spain to set out on a dreadful journey to nowhere.

In 1506 many Spanish Jews, who had sought refuge in neighboring Portugal, were mobbed and massacred. In 1531 the Inquisition was imported into Portugal, and Portugal became another Spain.

In 1648 hundreds of thousands of Jews in Poland were massacred by the Cossacks.

In 1660 the Jews of Europe were accused of spreading the Black Death which was depopulating the continent and they were slaughtered in country after country by the panic-stricken populace.

And so it went. Ever since the Jewish people in Pilate's judgment hall pulled down on their heads the dreadful curse "His blood be on us and on our children," they have wandered from land to land, from one graveyard to the next.

The curse of their own law has come upon them too. According to Deuteronomy 27 and 28, both blessings and curses were part of the Mosaic law. The passage contains many threats and warnings. The Jews were warned that national apostasy would be divinely punished. God said that He would bring disease, drought, defeat, and deportation upon them, and that their doom in foreign lands would be terrible indeed.

> And it shall come to pass, that as the Lord rejoiced over you to do you good, and to multiply you; so the Lord will rejoice over you to destroy you, and to bring you to nought; and ye shall be plucked from off the land whither thou goest to

possess it. And the Lord shall scatter thee among all people, from the one end of the earth even unto the other; and there thou shalt serve other gods, which neither thou nor thy fathers have known. . . . And among these nations shalt thou find no ease, neither shall the sole of thy foot have rest: but the Lord shall give thee there a trembling heart, and failing of eyes, and sorrow of mind: And thy life shall hang in doubt before thee; and thou shalt fear day and night, and shalt have none assurance of thy life: In the morning thou shalt say, Would God it were even! and at even thou shalt say, Would God it were morning! for the fear of thine heart wherewith thou shalt fear, and for the sight of thine eyes which thou shalt see (Deuteronomy 28:63-67).

No wonder a rabbi once said to Ferdinand and Isabella, "You cannot curse us for there is a blessing on us, and you cannot bless us for there is a curse on us." The history of the Jewish people since Calvary has been one long commentary on the curses of Deuteronomy. Their fate has pursued them relentlessly down the ages, right into the twentieth century.

In 1897 a pampered, half-assimilated, wealthy Budapest Jew by the name of Theodore Herzl said to himself, "Enough is enough!" Herzl was a journalist. He had long puzzled over the worldwide problem of antisemitism, that strange disease afflicting the Gentiles, always endemic, sometimes epidemic. At one time he toyed with the idea of persuading the Jewish people to embrace Roman Catholicism. Perhaps then they could be totally assimilated and their strange fate come to an end. The Dreyfus affair cured him.

Alfred Dreyfus was an officer in the French army. He was a Jew. On October 15, 1894, Dreyfus was arrested and falsely accused of spying for Germany. Found guilty by a military court, he was stripped of his uniform and sentenced to life imprisonment on Devil's Island. Dreyfus maintained his innocence throughout the trial, and his testimony convinced at least one member of the general staff. When this officer tried to espouse Dreyfus's cause, however, he was bluntly told by his superiors to let the matter drop. Dreyfus was eventually given a second trial; but by then antisemitism was rife in the French army, and the second trial was a mockery. It was not until 1906 that the French high court reviewed the Dreyfus case, acquitted him, and ordered him to be reinstated in the army.

Herzl followed the case with increasing dismay. When he heard the French mob shouting, "Death to the Jews," he concluded, with startling foresight, that there was no future for the Jews in Europe. (That was long before anyone had ever heard of a corporal in the German army by the name of Adolph Hitler.) Herzl's new convictions led him to found the Zionist Organization in 1897. His goal was to find a national homeland for the Jewish people, a place where being a Jew would cease to be a problem. At first even the Jews thought he was mad.

Many Old Testament Scriptures foretell the rebirth of the state of Israel in the last days. Take Isaiah 11:11-12, for instance. Here mention is made of a *second* return of the Jewish people from captivity, one in which Jews would be regathered to the Holy Land from Assyria, Egypt, the islands of the sea, and the distant corners of the earth. At the time this prophecy was given, the Babylonian exile was a century in the future. Isaiah's vision, however, went far beyond the limited repatriation of the small Jewish remnant that eventually returned to the promised land after that captivity.

Isaiah also foretold in this prophecy that the ancient division of the nation into two kingdoms (Israel and Judah) would end and that Israel would be reborn as a single nation. He foresaw that, when the time came for this return, the reborn state would wage victorious war on its neighbors. He also foretold something that is still future today: God will "destroy the tongue of the Egyptian sea" (Isaiah 11:15). Evidently Egypt will be numbered again with Israel's foes and during some future war the waters of the Nile will be cut off. A well-placed atomic bomb, at the site of the Aswan Dam for instance, could do untold damage to Egypt by affecting the flow of the Nile. Without the Nile, Egypt can not exist. Numerous prophecies in Scripture suggest that Egypt will be on the side of Israel's foes in the last days.

In Isaiah 43:5-6 the prophet spoke again of a universal regathering of the Jewish people from east and west, from north and south, from the ends of the earth. He also foretold something that has not yet happened: the Jews will be called by the Lord's own name (43:7).

There is another remarkable prophecy in Isaiah 60:8-10 in which the prophet foretold that Jews would return to their land by air. This actually happened on a large scale in the case of the Yemenite Jews, and, of course, many modern Jews have returned to the reborn state by plane. Isaiah said that the Jews would "fly like doves" to their land. A dove has a strong homing instinct, which always causes it to return to its nesting place no matter where it may be. Just so, the Jewish people, the prophet said, would be instinctively drawn to their own homeland. And that is what has happened. When the British government, for instance, offered the Zionist an attractive stretch of territory in Uganda as a national home for the Jewish people, the offer was declined. The homing instinct of the Jews was not for Uganda, but for the land of Israel.

In this same prophecy Isaiah also foretold that a great western maritime power would lend its aid when the time came for this return. He named this country *Tarshish*. In its general *prophetic* setting *Tarshish* seems to be a term used to depict the western world; here it is probably a reference to Britain, at least initially. Isaiah said that the sons of strangers would build up the walls of the promised land and their kings would minister to the returning Jews. Although this prophecy will probably have a more complete fulfillment during the millennium, we can not help seeing that it has had an initial and partial fulfillment already. The "isles" did serve the Zionist cause. The kings and ministers of a great seafaring power did play a leading part in administering Palestine on behalf of the budding Jewish state. The fact that the British mandate ended in tragedy does not alter the fact that Britain did much to make the Zionist dream a reality, far more than any other country in the world.

Isaiah concluded this particular prophecy by predicting a future flow of wealth into the new state of Israel, the ultimate conversion of the Jewish people, and the downfall of nations that refuse aid to Israel.

Isaiah was by no means the only prophet to see these things. "In the mouth of two or three witnesses every word may be established" is God's principle (Matthew 18:16). Thus we find that Jeremiah, Ezekiel, and other prophets were equally farsighted.

In Jeremiah 16:14-16 the prophet foretold there would come a time when the Egyptian exodus would cease to be a wonder, because it would be eclipsed by a greater one. The exodus from Egypt has been commemorated by the Jews in their annual Passover feast for thousands of years. It is a recurring theme in the Psalms, and it was intended to be an unforgettable reminder to the

Jewish people of the sovereign greatness of God in human affairs. But that great event in the history of the Jewish nation would become as nothing, Jeremiah said, when compared with the even greater miracle of Israel's coming national rebirth. He saw Jews flocking back to the land, not just from Egypt but from the lands of the north and from all lands.

He also foretold that this return would not be entirely spontaneous and idealistic. There would arise "hunters" and "fishers" who would treat the Jewish people as so much game. The Jews would be sent fleeing to the land to save their lives. Hitler was one such hunter.

In Jeremiah 23:3 the prophet again spoke of a gathering of a Jewish remnant out of all countries. He saw to the very end when at long last this regathered people would become spiritually fruitful, when they would be converted, and when they would become "a righteous branch." That has not happened yet, but it will.

Jeremiah 29:14 also records again the end-time gathering of the Jewish exiles and the final end of the long exile of God's ancient people. The prophet saw his people being gathered from all nations and from all the places where they have been scattered.

Jeremiah was the prophet of the Babylonian captivity. It was he who actually specified the length of that captivity and foretold its end. But the visions and prophecies of Jeremiah mentioned above go far beyond the Babylonian captivity and far beyond the events connected with its termination. The return from Babylon was not universal in scope, and its dimensions did not eclipse the exodus from Egypt. When the Babylonian captivity ended and permission was given by Cyrus for the Jews to return to their ancient land, only a handful of Jews responded. The majority had settled down in Babylon and ignored the decree ending the captivity.

The exilic prophet Ezekiel also foresaw the end-time regathering of the Jews to their land. In Ezekiel 11:17-19 he likewise foretold that the Jews would come back home from all countries. He saw the land cleansed of its detestable abominations and idolatries, and he foresaw the coming conversion of the Jewish people.

In Ezekiel 34:11-24 he spoke of the Lord shepherding Israel as a flock back to the land. Thus, while wicked men might hunt them and fish them, God Himself would shepherd them. Like a shepherd He would gather them out of all countries and bring them back to their rightful fold. Looking even further into the future, Ezekiel described a coming day when David himself would rule over the Hebrew people as a shepherd king. Thus Ezekiel looked forward to the resurrection and the millennial age.

The prophet had more to say in Ezekiel 36:24-28. Again he foretold the regathering of the Jewish people from among the heathen and their return to their own land, and once again he spoke of their coming conversion when they would receive a new spirit and a new heart.

Probably the most famous of Ezekiel's prophecies about the rebirth of the state of Israel is found in Ezekiel 37. The chapter actually contains two visions. The first is the vision of the valley of dry bones, in which the prophet saw Israel scattered and dead as a nation, buried far and wide in Gentile lands. He was asked by God whether these bones could live. They were very many, and they were very dry. Could the impossible happen? He was then told in his vision to prophesy to the bones so that they would come together as skeletons. The skeletons were then clothed with muscle and sinew, and the corpses were then resurrected to life as a mighty army. He was expressly told that these bones represented the house of Israel—dismembered, scattered, and buried in Gentile lands. It was a vision of a miracle, the miracle of the rebirth of a nation, a miracle that has come to pass in our own days.

In the second vision Ezekiel saw two sticks becoming one stick. This pictured an end to the centuries-long division of the nation into two kingdoms, and it foretold the regathering of the Hebrew people as one nation in the endtimes. He saw this newly united nation abhorring idolatry. He also saw the time when David would rule over them.

What makes Ezekiel's prophecy so relevant is found in the next two chapters in which he foretold the rise and fall of Russia. The two events were to be contemporaneous. The rebirth of the state of Israel in the last days would coincide with the rise of a great northern power, which in turn would meet its end when it launched its armies against the reborn nation of Israel.

It seems incredible that with such a weight of evidence before us anyone could deny that Israel has a great national future and that the rebirth of the state of Israel is an event of great prophetic significance. Many do deny that, however, usually because they have decided to spiritualize prophecy and equate the church with

306

Israel. The rebirth of the state of Israel, nevertheless, is a fact. It vindicates the view that these Old Testament prophecies are to be taken literally.

It was Theodore Herzl who set the process in motion with his call for the rebirth of the state of Israel. Not that Herzl himself believed in the fulfillment of prophecy; he was an agnostic and had no faith whatsoever in the Bible. He was not motivated by religious convictions but by political considerations, as he said in his epochal work, *The Jewish State.* In this book he voiced his unbelief and scorned the idea that theocratic principles should have any part in the new state. On the contrary, he envisioned a state run by an "immoral band of Free Thinkers." His idea for an Israeli flag likewise scorned all idea of religion. He wanted a secular flag for a secular state, a flag with a white field embroidered with seven stars, the white background to symbolize a pure, new Jewish life and the seven stars to depict "the seven golden hours of our working day."[1]

Thus, unknown to himself, Herzl actually fulfilled another Biblical prophecy. The Lord Jesus, in His Olivet discourse, foretold that the end-time rebirth of the state of Israel would be in *unbelief.* He foretold this by comparing the rebirth of Israel to a fig tree covered with leaves. Just shortly before, He had cursed a literal fig tree for this very thing—bearing nothing but leaves (Matthew 24:32; cf. 21:19-20).

Herzl's dream took concrete form when Chaim Weizmann, a Jewish chemist in Great Britain, rendered unique service to the British government during World War I. Asked by Lord Balfour to name his own reward, Weizmann, an ardent Zionist, asked for British help in establishing a national home for the Jewish people in Palestine. The British government issued a famous document, known as the Balfour Declaration, in which it pledged itself to do all in its power to bring this about.

In 1917 General Lord Allenby liberated Palestine from the Turks, and in 1922 the League of Nations conferred a mandate on Britain to establish a Jewish national home in Palestine. One of Britain's first moves was to sever a sizable section from the country and create the state of Trans-Jordan as an Arab national home, separate from Palestine. Far from being satisfied by this gesture, the Arabs were enraged at the influx of Jews into the remainder of Palestine. The country erupted with violence. In

1939, with World War II imminent, with the Arabs in revolt, with Germany making friends in the area, and with vital oil resources to be considered, Britain betrayed its trust. Just at a time when Hitler was preparing to launch the Holocaust and the Jews of Europe desperately needed a place of refuge, the British issued a white paper that drastically curbed any more Jewish immigration into the country.

Enough was not enough after all. Antisemitism had not died. What Herzl foresaw came true in all its horror. Hitler applied "pest control" techniques against unwanted peoples in his growing domains. His goal was to exterminate about thirty million people including all the educated classes in Poland, a very large percentage of Slavs and, above all, every Jew in Europe. This was his "final solution to the Jewish question." After the war, when the horror camps of the Nazis were overrun and their atrocities shown to the world, civilized people could hardly believe the thoroughness with which the Nazis had pursued their cause.

Auschwitz is an example. At the end of the war the camp commandant was Rudolph Hess, age forty-six. He talked freely to those who interviewed him while awaiting transfer to Nuremberg. He showed no sense of guilt as he reviewed his activities. In a matter-of-fact way he estimated that probably 2.5 million Jews had perished under his personal direction. Even greater numbers could have been handled, he said. The killing had been easy; it was the disposal of the corpses that slowed things down. The killing, in fact, was so simple that guards weren't even necessary. People went into the gas chambers thinking they were going for showers. It wasn't until the doors clanged shut and the gas jets hissed that they realized what was happening. Then it was too late.

The order to exterminate the Jews had been given to him by Heinrich Himmler in person. "The Fuhrer has ordered the *Endlosung* [the final solution]," Hess was told. Auschwitz had been selected as the main site because it was isolated and accessible by rail. And he had been chosen to get the job done.

Auschwitz, located on marshy ground in southern Poland, covered eight thousand acres. It was surrounded by a high concrete wall, with watchtowers strategically placed around the perimeter. Two high electric fences also surrounded the camp. Twenty-eight two-story blocks of buildings housed the prisoners. Three miles farther on was another camp.

Initial methods of mass murder soon proved inadequate. Millions of French, Belgian, Dutch, Polish, Greek, and Italian Jews had to be killed; new crematoria were built to speed up the disposal of bodies. When Auschwitz was operating at full capacity in the spring of 1944, trains arrived in an endless flow. Sidings were built so that trains could pull in while others were being unloaded. Furnaces for burning the bodies were so overworked that their chimneys split; the system broke down. Corpses were then burned in the open until repairs could be made. Corpses awaiting burning were stacked like firewood. During those few weeks of spring, half a million people were murdered at this one camp alone. By then there was a sense of urgency, of unfinished business. The Russians were closing in.

The Russian prosecution at Nuremberg told what they had found: a camp where mass murder beyond anything that could be imagined was being performed and where experiments in sterilization and castration were carried out with coldblooded cruelty. They introduced documents telling of a doctor, for instance, who experimented with teenage girls. He used electrical currents and X-rays to destroy their hormones and make them prematurely old. The teenagers became old hags, hobbling on sticks, and looking as though they were seventy or eighty. What did it matter if they grew old in a hurry? They were going to die in a hurry anyway.

Auschwitz was only one example. Diabolical experiments were performed on women at Ravensbrueck and elsewhere. Inmates at Buchenwald were submitted to tests to determine the value of vaccines. They were injected with typhus, yellow fever, smallpox, cholera, and diphtheria. Himmler put hundreds of concentration camp prisoners at the disposal of the doctors whose experiments brought about slow, painful, frightful death. More and more camps were discovered by the Allies, and in each of them the story was the same: beatings, starvation, backbreaking work, torture, murder.

And it was profitable. When Auschwitz was overrun, its safes were found to contain over $40 million in currency taken from prisoners. In addition there were enormous piles of watches, jewelry, and precious stones. Dentures, shoes, clothing, artificial limbs, gold teeth, hair, tattooed skin, eyeglasses—all were salvaged. Gold extracted from teeth was melted down into ingots and shipped to the Reichsbank, tattooed skin was made into lampshades, and human hair was baled for commercial purposes. As Sir Hartley

Cross observed at Nuremberg, "Mass murder was becoming a state industry—with byproducts."

The fate of the Jews in Nazi-occupied Europe spurred the Zionists on. As soon as the war ended they chartered any vessel that would float, as long as it could make the Palestinian shore. They ran the British blockade and defied the gunboats sent out to intercept them. They smuggled hundreds of thousands of Jews into the country by night, hiding them in the kibbutzim, absorbing them smoothly and efficiently into Jewish life, preparing them for the struggle ahead and for statehood. Jewish terrorist organizations operated throughout the country, blowing up trains, bombing buildings, attacking British troops and the British-dominated Palestine police, raiding banks, murdering British soldiers by way of reprisal when their own men were tried and hung as terrorists by the British.

Britain was exhausted after World War II, virtually bankrupt, and controlled by a left-wing party that had as a major goal the dissolution of the British empire. Soured against the Jews by the ceaseless acts of sabotage and terrorism and anxious to placate the oil-rich Arab states, Britain handed the Palestine problem over to the United Nations.

In 1947 the United Nations General Assembly adopted the idea of a partitioned Palestine as a solution which, it hoped, would satisfy both Jews and Arabs. Although the boundaries drawn were unworkable, the United Nations pressed ahead with its plans. The vote was taken on Friday, November 29, 1947. The outcome swung in the balance to the very end, since the Jews needed a two-thirds majority to win and thirty-three votes just to offset the voting power of the Arab-Islamic members. In the end the Jews won partition. The Arabs had been able to muster only thirteen votes against it—those of their own Muslim bloc and two others— Greece, which voted against partition under heavy pressure and coercion, and Cuba, the only nation the Arabs had been able to persuade to take a stand against the Jews.

Arab reaction was predictable. "There are fifty million Arabs," cried Ibn Saud of Saudi Arabia. "What does it matter if we lose ten million people to kill all the Jews?" The head of the Muslim brotherhood vowed that the Muslim peoples would fill the sea with Jewish corpses. The Grand Mufti of Jerusalem called for a holy war and urged Muslims to murder Jews. The secretary general of the

Arab League called for a war of extermination and declared that what was needed was a massacre equal to those associated with the Mongols. The Arabs picked up the mantle dropped by Adolph Hitler.

Then came 1948. On May 14 Israel was proclaimed a state. On May 15 the last of the British forces withdrew, having deliberately left a number of strategic positions in Arab hands. Israel was immediately invaded by Arab armies from surrounding countries, and a fierce war of independence was waged. At the same time Jewish immigration into the country became a floodtide. The Arabs were defeated and called for a truce.

In 1949 Chaim Weizmann became the first president of Israel. That same year Israel was admitted to the United Nations, and the Jewish population in Israel reached a million.

In 1956 the Sinai War broke out; and Israel occupied Sinai and the Gaza Strip, relieving the country of oppressive Egyptian military pressure.

In 1967 war broke out again between the Arabs and Jews. Egypt moved her armored forces into the Sinai and Jordan; Iraq and Syria joined the assault. Other Arab nations joined in as the United Nations peace-keeping forces beat a hasty retreat, and Israel's friends in the western world hemmed and hawed. The Arabs suddenly realized they had a tremendous weapon in their hands— oil! The Jews discovered a forgotten weapon too—millions of Jews in other countries who could supply men and money and bring political pressure to bear in high places.

Again the tide turned against the Arabs as Israel stormed the Golan Heights and threw Syria back from her threatening position overlooking the fertile Israeli farms below. Jordan was pushed back across the river, and Jerusalem was seized by the Jews. When Israeli forces seized Sinai and threatened Egypt, the Arabs again called for a truce.

But the war of attrition went on. The Arabs wielded their new-found oil weapon to bully and blackmail the western powers and the needy nations of the Third World. Propaganda offensives were mounted in the West to make friends and influence people for the Arab cause. Jewish goods were boycotted, and nations having business ties with Israel were threatened with the loss of oil supplies. Acts of terrorism began to escalate.

Then in 1973 the Arabs decided to try again, and the Yom

Kippur war broke out. Egypt and Syria threw themselves fero-
ciously on Israel at a time when most Jews were celebrating the
holiest of their annual feasts and their guard was down. Egypt
fielded 700,000 men, 2,500 tanks, 650 planes and 150 antiaircraft
missile batteries. Syria brought up 300,000 men, 2,000 tanks, 330
planes, and 35 antitank missile batteries.

Israel had to oppose a million men equipped with modern
heavy weapons. Caught off guard, Israeli forces reeled back.
Nevertheless, within three days they had not only recovered, but
their army was within sight of Damascus. Two days later Israeli
forces crossed the Suez and took Egyptian defenses in the rear.
Had not the West intervened, Israel could have taken Damascus
and Egypt—and probably have dealt their old enemy Libya a
crushing blow as well.

Egypt began to have second thoughts about fighting Israel, and
Anwar Sadat made peace overtures. Negotiations began which led
to the signing of a peace treaty, and Israel handed the Sinai back to
Egypt.

The Palestinian Liberation Organization, based in Lebanon,
refused to learn any lessons from Arab wars with Israel. It kept up
its murderous terrorist attacks on Israeli citizens not only in Israel,
but around the world. In 1982 Israel struck back. They moved the
full weight of their armed forces into Lebanon to throw the Syrians
of the country out and make an end of the PLO as a guerilla force in
the Middle East. The Arab nations, while sending up howls of
outrage at this attack, seemed secretly pleased. The PLO discovered that it was not really very popular with most Arab states.
Certainly no Arab country wants to repeat the experience of
Lebanon, which offered asylum to the PLO only to be saddled with
a militant force able to intimidate and dominate its government.

The war in Lebanon went wrong. The country could not be
permanently occupied by Israel. The pressure of world opinion,
the erosion of support for the war in the army and at home, and the
high cost in lives and money led to a withdrawal. It was a war with
no clear beginning, no clear ending and no clear results. PLO terror
was replaced by Shiite terror. Syria occupied much of Lebanon,
bringing an eventual confrontation between Israel and its powerful
Soviet-backed northern neighbor that much closer. On the home
front, Israel became a house divided. In Lebanon, members of the
PLO, expelled at such cost, began to filter back.

In late 1987 a new threat raised its head—Palestinian Arabs in
the occupied territories of the West Bank and the Gaza Strip began

to riot. The confrontation became more serious when 740,000 Arabs holding Israeli citizenship joined their brethren in the occupied territories in a general strike, breaking a tradition of peaceful coexistence with Israeli Jews. The Jewish response was swift: a crackdown on rioters no matter who was hurt, and even deportation of ringleaders.

The majority of Israelis see the occupied territories as vital to their security. Without them, Israel is a strategically crippled country. Few thinking Jews can concede to allowing those areas to be returned to Arab military occupation. The combined Arab armies of the countries directly surrounding Israel number 1.2 million men as compared with Israel's regular army of only sixty thousand soldiers. It takes Israel forty-eight hours to mobilize fully. It can not afford ever again to return to the indefensible pre-1967 borders. Arab armies are now better trained than they used to be.

The outbreak of violence by Arabs inside Israel strengthens the hand of hard-liners in the Jewish state who bluntly label all Arabs in the country as enemies and who advocate driving them out. The debate is a hot one. Do Arabs in Israel have the right to full equality, eventually to outnumber Jews in the country, to seize on the democratic process to become the voting majority and turn the country into an Arab state? Many are saying no to that. Some are saying that the essence of Zionism is to have a land of Israel with a Jewish majority—a Jewish state, at all costs.

Thus Israel, reborn, has defended its national interests with courage and vigor. It is back in the land to stay, and the Arabs know now that any attack on Israel will be costly indeed. However, Russia looms in the background with long-range plans to take over the whole area in the interests of world conquest. And standing even further in the shadows, not yet summoned on stage, is the antichrist. His coming has long been foretold, and one day he will dominate affairs, not only in the Middle East, but in the whole world. And behind him looms the figure of the Christ, who will return in Israel's most desperate hour to rescue her from all her foes and make her the world's leading nation.

---

1. Wilbur M. Smith, *World Crisis and the Prophetic Scriptures* (Chicago: Moody Press, 1950), pp. 191-192.

16

Russia, Its Allies, and Its Adversaries

E zekiel lived during the tumultuous days of the fall of the Judean monarchy. He spent much of his life in Babylon as a captive. His prophecies embraced the impending fall of Jerusalem, included the Jews already in exile, and swept on to the last days. Two of his chapters foretold the rise and fall of a great antisemitic atheistic northern power and that nation's latter day invasion of the reborn state of Israel (Ezekiel 38–39). To aid us in our study of this fascinating prophecy we shall divide the subject into three major segments:

> I. The Background
>> A. The places involved
>> B. The period involved
> II. The Build-up
> III. The Battle

First let us examine *the places* involved in this prophecy. Long before Russia emerged as a world superpower, careful Bible teachers were identifying this prophecy with Russia and making the most astonishing statements. Take, for instance, the following from the pen of a thoughtful Bible scholar writing in 1888. At that time Russia was still ruled by the czars and was one of the most backward and ill-ruled nations of Europe.

> Russia is evidently destined to become the master of Asia. Her frontier line across Asia will be 5,000 miles in length. . . . It is well known that Russian policy is one of steady aggression, not only in Europe but in Asia. [She is] probably the most ambitious and grasping of modern kingdoms, the most faithless in public honor and treaty engagement, the character ascribed to her in the prophetic Scriptures. Coupled with her frequent outbreaks of undisguised and disastrous hostility to the things of God, and in the more awful future exhibits, Russia is in a most unfavorable light.
>
> Russia has for ages meditated on the conquest of Asia, and India and China. Great Britain and the United States stand face to face with this Russian power; and these two sides will come into one final, awful struggle. We judge that the tide of Russian conquest will flow on to the frontiers of China. The ascendence of Russia in the East and the revival of the old Roman Empire in the West necessitates the meeting of these two dominating, opposing powers; and the great Jewish question must be settled at Jerusalem, the city of the Great King, leading to millennial triumph in Israel and her headship over the nations of the world.
>
> We believe from the place assigned to Russia in the Word of God that her legions will sweep over the plains and mountains of Asia, and become the dominant power over all the east until she falls forever on the mountains of Judah. Thus she will command for a time the powers north of Palestine and east of the Euphrates.[1]

When Walter Scott wrote that astonishing statement, Jerusalem was of interest only to tourists and archaeologists, and Russia herself was looking westward. The communist revolution (which now seems to have run its course and appears to have been one of Satan's "dress rehearsals" for the real thing) was barely dreamed of. Men like Walter Scott, John Nelson Darby, and William Kelly were right on target. They had insight into prophetic truth far beyond any light available to them from world events of their day. They took the Bible at its face value, rightly divided the Word of Truth, and applied sound hermeneutical principles to the prophetic Scriptures. They were therefore able to speak with assurance on such seemingly outlandish themes as the rebirth of the state of Israel, the revival of the Roman empire, and the rise of Russia as Israel's great enemy of the last days. Some of these men were scoffed at by religious leaders of the day, especially by those who allegorized the prophetic Scriptures. Time has vindicated these discerners of God's truth, however, and shown that their principles of Bible interpretation were sound.

Some object to the view that Ezekiel 38 and 39 refer to Russia and to identifiable allies already lining up in its sphere of influence. H. L. Ellison, for instance, maintained that these chapters must be interpreted allegorically. He dismissed any attempt to identify Gog and Magog and the other nations in the prophecy ("We will not concern ourselves much with identification"). He referred "the curious" to G. H. Lang and to the *New Bible Commentary*. Even so, Ellison admitted that the peoples mentioned by Ezekiel have to be located in the outer fringes of the known world of Ezekiel's day.[2]

Similarly A. P. Fausset, in his section of the famous commentary, objected to the literal interpretation. He dismissed as "most unlikely" any coalition of nations that would include such places as distant from Israel as Persia and Libya.[3] Dr. Fausset wrote long before Russia had emerged as a world power with global strategic spheres of interest. The alliance, prophesied by Ezekiel and foreseen by those who interpreted the prophecies literally, is no longer "unlikely." We have seen how rapidly it can become a fact in spite of recent setbacks.

Even though he rejected the literal interpretation of Ezekiel 38, Dr. Fausset did try to identify the nations mentioned by the prophet. He referred to an invasion of Egypt by the dreaded Scythians, which had undoubtedly left an indelible mark on the minds of people in Ezekiel's time. Dr. Fausset included the Moschi and Tiberani (Meshech and Tubal) as part of this incursion of northern Asiatics into the Mediterranean world. He thought Ezekiel might have simply adopted these names, since they were familiar to the people of his day, and applied them to this anti-Christian invasion of the last days. He identified "the chief prince"

("Rosh" in the King James version and "Rhos" in the Septuagint) as the Scythian Tauri in the Crimea. He suggested that the modern Russians may have assumed the names of Moscow and Tobolsk from the names Meshech and Tubal. He said too that the Araxes river was called Rhos in ancient times. The Araxes is identified on modern maps as the river Araks which separates Armenia and Azerbaijan from Iran.

There can be little doubt that Ezekiel was identifying a coming alliance to be dominated by a power occupying territory in "the remote parts of the north" (Ezekiel 38:6, 15, ASV). This in itself firmly identifies the main nation in the alliance, and much of the rest of the identification given below is simply embroidery. All geographic references in Scripture are stated in terms of Israel. Only one country occupies a position in "the remote parts of the north" as far as Israel is concerned; and that nation is Russia, whose land mass stretches all the way from the Baltic to the Bering sea. The identification of Magog, Meshech, Tubal, and Rosh are therefore interesting and confirmatory, but not essential to the understanding of prophecy.

We shall begin with *Magog.* Josephus said of Magog that he founded a people who derived from him the name of Magogites but who were called Scythians by the Greeks.[4] The *Pulpit Commentary* agrees and identifies the Scythians with a people whose country lay on the borders of the sea of Azov in the Caucasus region.[5] According to *The New Schaff-Herzog Encyclopedia of Religious Knowledge*, Magog is to be located between Armenia and Media, possibly on the shores of the Araxes. This suggests that the people from this region migrated northward across the Caucasus mountains and thus filled Ezekiel's northern horizon. The encyclopedia supports this view by referring to Assyrian inscriptions.[6]

The name *Rosh*, because of a translator's preference, does not appear in the King James text, but it does appear in numerous other versions including the American Standard version which reads, "Son of man, set your face toward Gog of the land of Magog, the prince of Rosh, Meshech, and Tubal, and prophesy against him" (Ezekiel 38:2). William Kelly said that while the name *Rosh* can be taken as a title meaning "head" or "chief," such a rendering of the word here introduces unnecessary confusion. He insisted that in Ezekiel 38 and 39 *Rosh* must be taken as a proper name, the name not of a man but of a *race.* This rendering is strengthened by the names *Meshech* and *Tubal*, which precede and follow the word *Rosh*. Since these are names, then *Rosh* must be taken as a name, rather than a title.[7]

The 1991 collapse of the Soviet Union has directed our attention to the size and significance of Russia, by far the largest and most prosperous of the former republics. It is this country that seems to be what is indicated by *Rosh*, rather than either the old Soviet Union or the new Commonwealth.

The names *Meshech* and *Tubal* point directly to Russia. Both these names are linked with Gog and Magog by Ezekiel. Gesenius, whose Hebrew lexicon has never been surpassed, said that Gog is undoubtedly the Russians.[8] As has been noted, Meshech and Tubal have often been identified with Moscow, the capital of modern Russia, and Tobolsk in Asiatic Russia. Modern Tobolsk was founded in 1587 in western Siberia, and from there the Cossacks rode eastward to open up all of Siberia to Russian domination. Meshech and Tubal, then, are names that stand for Russia in Europe and Asia. L. Sale-Harrison corroborated this identification on linguistic grounds.[9]

Ezekiel went on to associate certain allies with this great northern power we now recognize as Russia. Although he named Russia's chief allies, he did not restrict Russia's sphere of influence to the countries he named. He said that she will have "many people" on her side (Ezekiel 38:9).

First, there is *Gomer.* According to various authorities Gomer is to be identified with the Cimmerians (the Cimarrai of the Assyrian inscriptions), located on the shores of the Black and Caspian seas.[10] The Cimmerians are well known to secular historians. The Scythians chased them across the Caucasus mountains into Asia Minor (Turkey). They made their way through that land, destroyed the Phrygian kingdom in the seventh or eighth century B.C., and in the fifth century raided the kingdom of Lydia. They kept all of southern and western Asia in turmoil for a century and a half. *The World Book Encyclopedia*[11] bluntly identifies them as the Gomer of the Bible, and the *Encyclopedia Britannica* has a similar comment.[12]

It is not so easy to identify Gomer with a modern nation. Harry Rimmer thought the name refers to a Balkan people. He appealed to Assyrian records to show that the original Gomer was a tribe of wild barbarians who crossed the Caucasus mountains from Russia. He agreed with others who say that they settled in Cappadocia. He concluded that from there they headed back north to settle in what we now call the Balkan states. He saw them as Russia's natural allies, since Russia was their original homeland.[13]

This view is suspect since the Balkans were part of the Roman empire and, therefore, from the prophetic standpoint belong with the revived Roman empire rather than with Russia. The collapse of the Warsaw Pact and the liberation of Eastern Europe seems to confirm this.

Others identify Gomer with Germany. A. C. Gaebelein said that the Talmud positively identifies Gomer with the Germans.[14] Genesis 10:2 shows Gomer, Magog, and Meshech as among the sons of Japheth, which indicates that the peoples descended from them have close blood ties. Verse 3 says Gomer had three sons, Ashkenaz, Riphath, and Togarmah. To this day we identify Ashkenazi Jews as German-speaking Jews. This at least helps to identify one of Gomer's tribes with Germany. The *Pulpit Commentary*, drawing on numerous sources, makes a similar identification.[15] Henry Morris, too, followed such ancient writers as Herodotus and Plutarch in identifying Gomer with the Cimmerians. He saw the name *Cimmeria* surviving in the word *Crimea*.[16]

From all this we conclude that Gomer, with ancient blood ties to the people who inhabited the land we now identify as Russia, is to be identified with Germany.

The reunification of Germany in recent times may be of considerable prophetic significance. It lends new significance to Ezekiel's words: "Gomer, *and all his bands*" (Ezekiel 38:6, italics added). United Germany may decide to go its own way in Europe once it has digested the economic and political costs of reunification. It could again turn antisemitic and militaristic. A united Germany allied to a revitalized and antisemitic Russia in an attack on Israel could be a formidable combination to face.

Togarmah is another country solidly lined up with Russia by Ezekiel. Togarmah was a son of Gomer, so the same blood ties are again in evidence (Genesis 10:3). Rimmer had no doubts that Togarmah is Armenia and cited certain Assyrian chronicles as well as Tacitus in support of his view. He said that the title *the House of Togarmah* is a common description for Armenia in Armenian literature.[17]

The land we now know as Armenia occupies part of northeast Turkey, spreads down from the Black Sea to the borders of Iran, and spills over into Russia where it used to be known as the Armenian Soviet Socialist Republic. The biblically important river, the Euphrates, has its source in the mountains of this area. Mount Ararat, where Noah's ark came to rest, is in Turkish Armenia. The land has been invaded and conquered many times; the history of its people is one of massacre, persecution, suffering, and exile.

While some commentators identify Togarmah with Armenia, others identify it with Turkey. Some see a possible etymological connection between the name *Togarmah* and the names *Turkey* and *Turkestan*.[18] Since Armenia is partly in Turkey and partly in the Commonwealth of Independent States, we can not rule out the possibility that Turkish Armenia might one day be absorbed into the Commonwealth. Certainly the Russians have long coveted Turkey. It is a strategically located country. Possession or control of Turkey would give the Russians control of the vital Dardanelles ports on the Mediterranean and the ability to outflank much of Europe. If we limit Togarmah to what used to be called Soviet Armenia we are on even surer ground, since in Ezekiel's day Togarmah seems to have been the name for several small nations living south of the Aral sea and between the Aral and the Caspian seas. Ezekiel identified Togarmah with "the uttermost parts of the north." Recent troubles in Armenia and in neighboring Azerbaijan have tended to push the Armenians closer to Moscow though there are some nationalist Armenian organizations that want total independence. Even so they might well look to Russia for protection.

Ezekiel, then, envisioned an alliance of northern powers which he named as Magog, Rosh, Meshech, and Tubal—all of which we identify with Russia. He saw allied with this mighty northern power two other northern peoples he called Gomer and Togarmah, nations we identify with Germany and Armenia (or possibly Turkey). What we have, then, is a group of nations all firmly identified with the country we now call Russia. Later in this chapter we shall take a closer look at Russia as it exists today, but first, let us identify the other allies of this northern power: Persia, Ethiopia, and Libya (Ezekiel 38:5).

We have no trouble identifying *Persia*, since the name has continued in history until today. It is the country we call Iran. Winston Churchill, during World War II, ordered that the country be called Persia in all war communiques to avoid possible error and confusion with Iraq. Iran, with its oil, its strategic location on the Persian gulf, and its access to the Arabian sea and the Indian ocean, is a prize imperialist Russia has long coveted.

Russia's next ally is *Ethiopia*, called "Cush" in some versions. Some identify Cush with northern Arabia since an Asiatic Cush is mentioned in the description of the garden of Eden (Genesis 2:13, NIV; Ethiopia, KJV).[19] But in the table of nations in Genesis, Cush is shown as a descendant of Ham, which would link him more directly with Africa than Arabia. Ethiopia and Egypt share the Nile (the Blue Nile rises in the Ethiopian highlands); and from earliest times Ethiopia was called *Kos*, evidently an etymological variant of *Cush*. Unger pointed out that in almost every passage where the name *Cush* appears, it may safely be regarded as referring to an African people. The one exception he made is in 2 Chronicles 21:16, and this reference may be to a people living in the southwest part of the Arabian peninsula adjacent to African Ethiopia.[20]

Shortly after World War II, I had a conversation with a missionary from Ethiopia (it was then called Abyssinia) and asked him if he had ever considered the possibility of Ethiopia's becoming a Russian satellite state. He seemed astonished and thought it most unlikely. "What would the Russians want with Abyssinia?" he asked. "There's nothing there!" We shall see later that Ethiopia has one thing above all else that the Soviet Union coveted in the heyday of its imperial ambitions: a strategic location from which to control the Red Sea and from which neighboring African countries such as the Sudan, Kenya, and Somalia can be effectively threatened.

Next comes *Libya*, or Put, as the country is called in some versions. Some have sought to identify Put as an Arabian country, but the King James text bluntly translates Put as Libya, and Unger agreed. He thought the name refers to the country of the Ludim (Genesis 10:13), which was to be located on the African coast between Egypt and Carthage. Cyrene was one of its cities.[21] If this is so, then of course Put is Libya. One of Russia's friends among the Arab Muslim states has been Libya, a country attracted to the Soviets by its hatred of Israel.

So then, Ezekiel 38 lists Russia's chief allies in the last days, but the same chapter mentions three nations that oppose, or at least challenge, the Russian invasion of Israel. These are "Sheba, and Dedan, and the merchants of Tarshish, with all the young lions thereof" (38:13).

Sheba is in Arabia and is often identified with the country of the

321

Biblical Sabeans, the country we now know as Yemen. Yemen is an oil-rich country facing onto the Red Sea and the gulf of Aden. Unger thought that the queen of Sheba came from here on her twelve-hundred-mile desert journey to visit Solomon.[22]

Dedan is the next country named. Two people are named Dedan in Scripture, one a son of Cush and therefore a Hamite (Genesis 10:7) and the other a descendant of Abraham through Keturah and hence a Semite (Genesis 25:3). Unger quoted various authorities and concluded that the descendants of the two Dedans intermarried. He believed that some of them eventually settled on the shores of the Persian gulf and others on the borders of Idumea (Edom), and that there was a thriving caravan trade between them linking the gulf with the land of Canaan.

Sheba and Dedan, then, in their prophetic context, appear to be countries in Arabia. The prophet saw them as part of an alliance that opposes the Russian invasion of Israel. Russian moves in Yemen and in Ethiopia and the Russian potential for control of Iran will give the oil-rich Arab sheikdoms of the Arabian peninsula cause for alarm. Right now they are blinded by their hatred of Israel. The western powers, too, have been complacent about Soviet intrigues in this area. But if Russia touches the oil-nerve of the gulf, the reaction might be different. Certainly once the beast has united Europe and the West, Russian moves in the Middle East will be promptly, efficiently, and decisively countered. Ezekiel's prophecy lines up Arabia solidly with the West prior to the Russian invasion of Israel.

The 1991 war with Iraq over its invasion of Kuwait amply illustrates the lightning response of which the West is capable when someone touches the sensitive and raw oil-nerve of the Middle East. Russia sat out "the Desert Storm," as the war with Iraq was called. Its time for trouble-making in the Middle East still lies ahead.

There remains *Tarshish.* As Magog, Rosh, Meshech, and Tubal were in "the uttermost parts of the north," so Tarshish occupied the uttermost parts of the west. It was to Tarshish that Jonah tried to flee in his desire to put the width of the world between himself and Nineveh (see Jonah 1:3).

Biblical Tarshish seems to be Tartessus, located in Spain not far from the strait of Gibraltar. It was a Phoenician colony, an important outpost in a string of colonies that extended as far north as the tin islands of Britain. Tin was used in making bronze and was worth a fortune in eastern markets. The Phoenicians had a virtual monopoly of the trade, and Tartessus was one of their important terminals for the shipment of the wealth of the world between east and west. Barry Fell of Harvard thought that the Phoenicians penetrated much farther west than Spain, that they crossed the Atlantic and left traces of their presence in the Americas.[23] Historical Tarshish, then, was a maritime center of great importance, linked with Palestine and with contacts as far west as the ancients went. This gives us some clues for identifying prophetic Tarshish.

Other Scripture references give us further help. Looking at the regathering of Israel in the last days, Isaiah said, "Surely the isles shall wait for me, and the ships of Tarshish first, to bring thy sons from far. . . . And the sons of strangers shall build up thy walls, and their kings shall minister unto thee" (Isaiah 60:9-10). It is a fact of history that the Zionist movement became a reality only when the government of the British Isles championed its cause. British kings first threw the weight of empire behind Theodore Herzl's lonely cry in the courts of Europe that the Jews be given a national home in Palestine. Britain's subsequent mandate over Palestine had many failings. Just the same, the British did much to rebuild the country, and prepare it for the day when the Jews, having won their independence, could give birth to the state of Israel.

Isaiah's prophecy is of interest, therefore, because it hints at the identity of prophetic Tarshish. Britain, and later the United States, first helped make the Zionist dream a reality. As historic Tarshish took in the mainland of Europe, reached to Britain and on to the new world, so prophetic Tarshish probably does the same. A further hint of this is found in the expression "Tarshish, with the young lions thereof," which points to Europe and her former colonies in the Americas. Since Ezekiel's prophecy comes to a head in the days when the beast will have successfully united Europe and brought the western hemisphere into a close alliance with himself, the name *Tarshish* is probably a prophetic reference to the western world as it will be in his day.

These, then, are the nations mentioned by Ezekiel. Now we shall trace the rise of Russia and her relationships with the countries mentioned by Ezekiel.

The Soviet Union

The giant conglomerate empire we have known as the Soviet

Union has now passed into history. However, a survey of that history will be most instructive.

The shadow of Russia's destiny fell on her after her disastrous defeat by the Germans in World War I. That defeat eroded what was left of czarist authority and opened the door to revolution.

When we think of the Soviet Union we think of Karl Marx. The philosophy of this atheistic Jew was preached to the Russian people for seventy-five years as the embodiment of the supreme wisdom of the age. Marx, however, was eclipsed in communist theory and practice by Lenin. While Marx was revered, Lenin was worshiped. No longer! Lenin's statues have been toppled and his terrible legacy assessed. Even the city named after him, Leningrad, has gone back to its old name of St. Petersburg.

In 1917 Lenin led the Bolsheviks to power in Russia, and the czar and his family were murdered. The Bolsheviks swiftly spread their rule from town to town, took over Russian industry, set up their secret police, and made peace with Germany.

By 1921, seven years of war, revolution, civil war, and invasion had left Russia exhausted. Lenin was left with a free hand to take what steps he would to improve the economy and to form the Union of Soviet Socialist Republics (USSR). The Union was gradually expanded until, at length, it took in all the far-flung outposts of the empire we came to recognize as the Soviet Union.

The instrument for power was the communist party, which Lenin adroitly fashioned as a political army. The Soviet Union was controlled by the politburo which, more often than not, was dominated by one man—Lenin, Stalin, Kruschev, Brezhnev, and for a while Gorbachev. Stalin kept the masses in line by terror. He presided over the extermination of at least twenty million people most of whom he classified as "enemies" and "traitors." His goals and those of his successors were served by a militarism unequaled in history.

Lenin died in 1924, after bringing a dreadful dictatorship into being. Countless people were killed to further his ambitions. The day he died he had enjoyed another triumph over a group of Roman Catholic priests in Moscow, but that night death came calling on *him*. Lenin's death has often been glossed over in the past, but the details of his brain disease were commonly reported in the press at the time. The story ran through Russia that the once all-powerful dictator spent his last days crawling around his room on all fours like an animal, apologizing to the furniture for his misdeeds and shouting repeatedly, "God save Russia and kill the Jews."[24]

This was soon forgotten, however, amid the carefully orchestrated adulation of Lenin which followed his death. A special mausoleum was built in Moscow's Red Square, and Lenin's body was embalmed and placed on permanent view. The faithful would line up, even in the sub-zero cold of a Russian winter, to wait their turn to enter and view the corpse. Lenin's mummified remains were often viewed with a reverence akin to worship, the kind of worship usually reserved for the founder of a religion.

For seventy-five years the driving force behind the Soviet Union *was* a religion, communism. The driving force behind communism was atheism—bitter, militant, intolerant atheism. It was Zenoviev, friend and colleague of Lenin, who voiced the nation's new hatred of God. He said, "We shall grapple with the Lord God in due season, we shall vanquish Him in His highest heaven, and wherever He seeks refuge, and we shall subdue Him forever."[25] God says: "Is that so!"

Communism was exported abroad by every possible means and with a fanaticism unparalleled in history. What Napoleon, Alexander, or Ghengis Khan ever enlisted the enthusiastic aid of millions of nationals in countries slated for destruction, imbued them with devotion for the policies of the enemy, and inspired them to work tirelessly at all levels of society for the success of the foe? This record belongs to the communists alone.

The record of the past seventy-five years of intensive global propaganda was certainly impressive. The communists overlooked nothing. Their dogma was spread by hours of broadcasting, by books, by attractive magazines, by pamphlets, by movies, by cultural exchanges, by arms, by technicians and other military advisers, by the diplomatic corps, and by the KGB. It was spread by popular fronts; by infiltration of the communications media of the free world; by highly placed agents in all segments of society; by schools and seminars; by slogans and marches; and by organized violence. Billions of dollars were invested annually to disseminate propaganda and to mobilize thousands of paid or volunteer activists and agents.

Lenin, Stalin, and their successors labored tirelessly to change the world in the name of Karl Marx in the interests of Soviet long-range foreign policy objectives. Marxism was really simply the camouflage for the Soviet Union's true nationalistic and global ambitions. Lenin, of course, was a revolutionary before he became a Marxist. Marxism was simply a convenient tool to further his own ends. It remains in China for instance, despite its obvious economic flaws, a useful tool for deceiving Third World countries. No one who has lived under communism, however, seems anxious to go back to its stifling embrace.

Up until the attempted coup on August 19, 1991, Gorbachev claimed that it was useless to deny "the enormous and unique contribution of Marx, Engels and Lenin to the history of social thought and to modern civilization as a whole." According to him dismantling Stalinism did not mean a retreat from socialism, but rather a move toward it. He declared, "I am now, just as I've always been, a convinced Communist."[26] The coup changed his mind.

"I think this experiment that was conducted on our soil was a tragedy for our people," said Yeltsin, the leader of the giant Russian republic in a live broadcast linked to the United States. "That model has failed," Gorbachev echoed.[27]

The Soviet Union occupied one-sixth of the world's land mass. It had an area of 8.6 million square miles, and stretched for more than 3,000 miles through two continents and eleven time zones. For a long time the Soviet Union was able to project to the world the image of a monolithic empire of some 289 million people. The dismal failure of communism as an economic system and the unraveling of the empire, however, unveiled the truth.

The Soviet Union was made up of about eighty-five ethnic groups, speaking a babel of languages, embracing a variety of religions, and cherishing different customs. Of these, twelve ethnic groups accounted for 89 percent of the population: Russians (51 percent), Ukrainians (15 percent), Uzbeks (6 percent), Belorussians (4 percent), Kazakhs (3 percent), Azerbaijanis (2 percent), Tartars (2 percent), Armenians (2 percent), Tadzhiks (1 percent), Georgians (1 percent), Moldavians (1 percent), and Lithuanians (1 percent). The other ethnic groups included Latvians, Jews, Poles, Estonians, Koreans, Greeks, Gypsies, Hungarians, Kurds, Romanians, Finns, Iranians, Czechs, Arabs, Chinese, Slovaks, Afghans, Serbs, Croatians, and others. The Russians themselves were always a minority in the Soviet Union.

Lenin's revolution would never have succeeded had he not enlisted the support of the nations that occupied the far reaches of Asia. Many of these former colonies of the czarist empire thought Lenin was going to liberate them. They exchanged one tyranny for another. However, communism never eradicated their yearning for independence.

With the breakaway from the Soviet Union of Russia's Eastern European satellites and with total economic collapse threatening the whole country, a new spirit of restiveness swept through the various republics, many of which demanded independence from the Union. In view of this, and in view of the increasing importance of the Russian republic, it will be helpful to summarize facts and figures about the fifteen republics.

1. Russia

This republic has 148 million people, half the population of what was once the Soviet Union. It is the real Rosh of Ezekiel 38–39.

Russia produces 63 percent of the electricity of what was once the Soviet Union, 91 percent of its oil, 75 percent of its natural gas, 55 percent of its coal, 58 percent of its steel, 50 percent of its meat, 48 percent of its wheat, 85 percent of its paper, and 60 percent of its cement. It has had to subsidize inefficient industries in the other republics; the region of Siberia supplies more than three times as much raw material as the rest of the country, but most of it has been shipped to other republics below the market price.[28]

Boris Yeltsin, Gorbachev's chief rival, capitalized on "Mother Russia's" resentment over this uneven treatment. In a dramatic move, even before the attempted coup, he quit the communist party and threatened to take this key republic out of the Soviet Union. In the following months Yeltsin's Russia played a key role in the breakup of the USSR and the formation of the new Commonwealth. We can expect Russia's significant influence to continue.

Russia is the Rosh of Ezekiel's prophecy. One of the predominant groups in this republic is the ultranationalistic Pamyat party that is openly antisemitic. The name *Pamyat* means "memory." The party evokes disturbing memories of the Nazi movement. Members wear black shirts and armbands. To become a member it is necessary to supply the organization with the names and addresses of four Jews. Its slogan is "Death to the Jews." We can well see, then, how eventually Russia will lead the anti-Israel and antisemitic coalition foretold by the prophet.

2. Ukraine

This is the largest non-Russian republic. Its population (73 percent Ukrainians, 22 percent Russians, 1 percent Jews, 1 percent

Belorussians) is 51.8 million. Even before the coup it was demanding autonomy, more democracy, and greater use of the Ukrainian language. Keen resentment is felt over the 1987 Chernobyl nuclear disaster. In 1991 the Ukraine voted for independence but agreed to partnership in a new eleven-republic Commonwealth.

The provinces of Uzbekistan, Kazakhstan, Tadzhikistan, Kirghizia, and Turkmenistan comprise what has been known as Soviet Central Asia. There is a strong possibility that once freed from the Soviet Union these countries will experience a wave of Muslim fundamentalism. They are poor, and even before the coup had signed an economic cooperation pact.

3. Uzbekistan

This republic has a population of 20.3 million. It was incorporated into the Soviet Union in 1925. One of its demands even before the coup was for the protection of the Uzbek language (spoken by 71 percent of the population). Another was Muslim religious freedom.

4. Kazakhstan

The population is 16.7 million (40 percent Kazakh, 38 percent Russian, 6 percent German, 5 percent Ukrainian). Established as a separate republic within the Union in 1936, Kazakhstan was the first to be swept by unrest after Gorbachev began his reforms.

5. Tadzhikistan

The population is 5.3 million. It is the smallest of the Central Asian republics. Relations with Moscow were strained even before the coup because of rumors that Armenian refugees from Azerbaijan would be given housing in preference to Tadzhiks. It is thought that Muslims have long been smuggling in arms from neighboring Afghanistan.

6. Kirghizia

This republic was established in 1936 and now has a population of 4.4 million. It too has aspired toward independence.

7. Turkmenistan

This republic, formed in 1925, has a population of 3.6 million and borders on Iran. Turkmenistan has been the most docile of the republics.

8. Belorussia

The population is 10.3 million. Belorussia became a republic in 1922. Like the Ukraine, Belorussia harbors ill-will because of the Chernobyl nuclear disaster.

9. Azerbaijan

This republic was incorporated into the Union in 1936 and now has a population of 7.1 million (83 percent Azerbaijanis, 6 percent Armenians, 6 percent Russians). Azerbaijanis long wanted to break away from the Union and form an independent state with ties to Iran. There are real fears that Shiite extremists will rise to power in this republic. Most Armenians and many Russians are leaving.

10. Georgia

Georgia has a population of 5.5 million. It became a republic in 1936, but the Soviets, even under Gorbachev, were never able to quell strong nationalistic fervor. Georgians cheered on the Baltic states in their efforts to secede, and up until this time have declined to be a part of the new Commonwealth of Independent States. Relations with Moscow always were strained.

11. Moldavia

Most of this republic was once part of Romania. Moldavia became a republic in 1940 and now has 4.4 million people. The Moldavian Popular Front had become a strong nationalist movement with possible aspirations to reunification with Romania even before the coup.

12. Armenia

Armenia was established as a separate Soviet republic in 1936, but was incorporated into the Russian empire in 1828. The population of 3.3 million is nominally Christian. The neighboring republic of Azerbaijan, which is mainly Muslim, has been feuding with the Armenians. Armenia fears its Muslim neighbors and its old enemy Turkey and tended to look to Moscow for protection. Before the coup it was becoming increasingly wary of Moscow, however, because of Gorbachev's favoritism toward Azerbaijan.

13. Lithuania

The population is 3.7 million. Like its neighboring Baltic states, Latvia and Estonia, it became a republic in 1940 as a result of Stalin's deal with Hitler. Lithuania led the Baltic states in their drive for independence. The separatist majority was actively looking for ways to quit the Soviet Union even before the coup. This state has now regained its independence. One of its first acts was to exonerate some one thousand Lithuanians convicted by Soviet courts of collaborating with the Nazis. That brought protests from Jewish organizations both in Israel and the United States.

14. Latvia

The population is 2.7 million. Ignoring a large Russian minority (33 percent), Latvia, long anxious to secede from the Soviet Union, achieved its independence after the coup.

15. Estonia

The smallest of the Baltic republics with a population of 1.6 million, Estonia was determined to quit the Soviet Union. Estonians were already developing their own economic and monetary systems before the coup. They now have their independence.

The first act of the new State Council, established to replace the old Soviet Union in September 1991, was to grant independence to all three Baltic republics.

The Russians tried to spread themselves more evenly over other areas of the Soviet Union, but did not succeed in making any appreciable difference. The former Kremlin policy of forcing Russians to colonize the republics means that they now reside where they are not wanted. Over the past few years many Russians have left the Central Asian republics rather than face growing local hostility.

Muslims make up one of the fastest-growing non-Russian minorities in the former Soviet republics. This has given the Russian leaders nightmares. They have been forced to think what a pan-Islamic movement could do if ever it took root in these republics. Communist ideology never did make much headway among Soviet Muslims.[29]

The situation in the various republics continues to change. The Soviet Union has now been broken up into fifteen independent countries. Eleven of these have formed themselves into a Commonwealth, but the area is still unstable and what kind of final alliance will emerge remains to be seen.

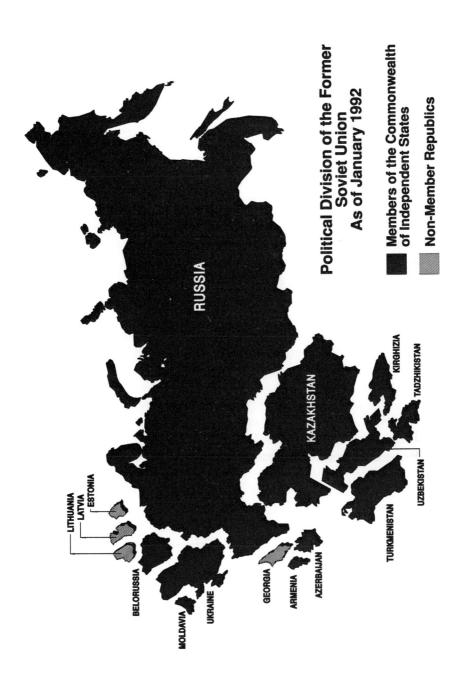

Political Division of the Former
Soviet Union
As of January 1992

■ Members of the Commonwealth
of Independent States

▨ Non-Member Republics

RUSSIA

KAZAKHSTAN

KIRGHIZIA

TADZHIKISTAN

UZBEKISTAN

TURKMENISTAN

GEORGIA

ARMENIA

AZERBAIJAN

MOLDAVIA

UKRAINE

BELORUSSIA

LITHUANIA

LATVIA

ESTONIA

Several other nightmares haunted the men in the Kremlin. They feared the dynamic economic success of the western world and Japan and the potential power of the European Economic Community. They long feared China. The Soviets shared a forty-five-hundred-mile common border with China, and across that border is a nation of a billion people. Little love has been lost between the two giants. The Soviets consoled themselves with their military, industrial, and technical superiority over the Chinese. They have viewed with apprehension any cooperation between China and the United States. Perhaps they remembered that Mao Tse-tung once said that he would be willing to start a third world war if it were in China's interests, and that he would sacrifice 300 million *Chinese* people if he thought it would further his strategic aims. The men in the Kremlin must often have bitterly regretted the shortsightedness of those who exported communism to their populous neighbor. And what would happen if one day the manpower of China were to be united to the economic might of Japan against Russia?

Indeed, thoughts of the sheer size of the territory the Russians would have to defend in the event of a world war must itself be a recurring nightmare. It is bigger than China, Europe and the United States combined.

Then too, the West has only had one potential foe, the Soviet Union and its allies and client states. Gorbachev realistically faced the folly of counting too much on the loyalty of the Warsaw Pact countries and dissolved the Pact. The Gulf War taught the Soviets another lesson: in the event of war with the West, the Soviet Union would quickly find itself outclassed by such powers as the United States, China, Britain, France, Sweden, and Japan. In addition to this, the economic plight and the ethnic unrest in the Soviet Union made it extremely vulnerable.

Ever since the days of Stalin, Moscow sought to build a protective buffer zone around the Soviet heartland. This is what prompted Russia to leave its armies in Poland and the Baltic states, in Hungary, Czechoslovakia, Bulgaria, Romania, and East Germany. While this tactic seemed to promise the Soviets security, it was seen as a threat by the western powers. It gave rise to the cold war, to NATO, to a continued United States military presence in Europe, and to an economically crippling arms race with the West.

Moreover, these European satellites, while forced into an alliance with Moscow and into the Warsaw Pact, proved to be an expensive and unaffordable luxury for the Soviets. Nor could many of them be regarded as wholly reliable. Whenever one or another of them showed signs of restiveness, the Soviet response was to send in tanks and troops.

Gorbachev redefined Soviet security needs even before the coup. It had become obvious to him that this collection of widely-differing satellites, arbitrarily fenced off from the rest of Europe and drilled into a sullen obedience by an unwelcome ideology, was unreliable at best. Under his revolutionary new policy of *glasnost*, one country after another took the quantum leap toward freedom. In the end the Warsaw Pact itself was dissolved.

With the coming of Mikhail Gorbachev, *perestroika*, and *glasnost*, a welcome pause occurred in what almost seemed to be a break-neck countdown to the holocaust described in Ezekiel 38–39. Events since the coup, culminating in the breakup of the Soviet Union, seem to have eliminated the possibility of a collision be-tween the Kremlin and the West, at least for the present. The Holy Spirit is working according to the divine timetable. The Ezekiel passage is a postrapture prophecy, and as long as the church remains on earth, we can expect Him to hinder the mad onrush of human affairs. This welcome pause is of great interest.

The demise of the Warsaw Pact, the independence of the former Soviet European satellites, and the reunification of Ger-many have changed the whole picture.

The Soviet military were dismayed by these revolutionary changes and tried to rein Gorbachev in. When Gorbachev visited Japan in April 1991, they successfully brought pressure to bear. The bone of contention between the Soviets and Japan has been the future of the four Kurile islands that the Soviets seized from Japan in the closing days of World War II. The Japanese want the islands back. The Soviets needed access to Japanese trade and technology. The two issues are tied together. In the midst of the Tokyo talks the commander of Soviet forces in the Far East sent a warning to Gorbachev. He warned that if the USSR gave back the islands "it could no longer call itself a great power."

The Soviet high command continued to smart over the loss of the Warsaw Pact countries. One Soviet official called that "the greatest geo-political defeat ever suffered by a nation that has not actually lost a war."[30]

As an economic system, communism does not work, but capitalism does. Given another ten years of communist economic blundering, the Soviet Union would have been reduced to the status of a Third World country in everything except military might. That failed to impress the army, the KGB, and the communist party.

For decades Russian shoppers have faced long lines and empty shelves, as well as shoddy merchandise. Of some 1,200 basic consumer items taken for granted in the West, nearly 1,000 have long been in chronic short supply in Russia. Of some 220 basic food items, about 200 are increasingly hard to get.

About 11 percent of the Soviet gross national product has traditionally gone to shore up inefficient factories. About 15 percent of the Soviet budget has been used to import food. About 20 percent of the grain harvest has gone to waste every year because of the lack of efficient transportation and storage facilities. Under communism, the supply and service areas of the Soviet system have fallen apart because of the priority given to the military and heavy industry, leaving little money to maintain these secondary areas.

Eventually Gorbachev found himself facing economic crises everywhere. His drive against drunkenness backfired. It resulted in a decline in income from the sale of vodka, a major item in the national budget, and a corresponding rise in the deficit. The deficit has been running at about 11 percent of the USSR gross domestic product (as compared with 3 percent in the United States). A major worry is inflation. The classic definition of inflation—"too much money chasing too few goods"—is all too true in the Soviet Union. One estimate is that the people have been hoarding $165 billion, which they would turn loose immediately if they only had something to buy. If the government were to deregulate prices, wild inflation would follow. One answer would have been to import consumer goods from the West and sell them at twenty times the official ruble exchange rate.

In January 1991 Gorbachev instituted draconian measures to try to rescue the practically worthless ruble from oblivion. He ordered all 50- and 100- ruble notes to be pulled from circulation. The immediate result was panic and a rush on the banks. According to the decree the Soviets were allowed to change their large bills for the equivalent of a month's salary, but no more than 1,000 rubles at that. Pensioners could only change 200 rubles. The decree also froze bank accounts, restricting withdrawals to no more than 500 rubles a month.

The measure was enormously unpopular. Moreover it could not succeed because it was not accompanied by economic reforms along with the creation of a market system. Gorbachev seemed unable to grasp the basic economic facts of life that there could be no halfway house between a command system and a free market, and that free enterprise can not flourish apart from private ownership.

The economy could not be divorced from the military. The Kremlin urgently needed to cut drastically its enormous military budget, one of the prime causes of the Soviet Union's economic woes. Yet any suggestion of such a move made the military establishment nervous. The military saw their country as being encircled by American bases and locked in between a dynamic Europe that is fast becoming a united economic power and a none-too-friendly China.

In addition to steep cuts in the military, the Soviet Union needed western capital, cooperation, and technology. Gorbachev, however, found himself hampered by a bureaucracy that was resistant to change. Moreover, most Soviet citizens found themselves so indoctrinated to distrust capitalism that they were uneasy about all the reforms inherent in *perestroika*. Indeed, they thought of the Brezhnev era, with its price fixing and cast-iron control, with a degree of nostalgia. One Soviet poll found that nearly 60 percent of the people were worried about the future. Nor did the fact that even in its initial stages *perestroika* cost millions of people their jobs reassure them.

Gorbachev, while inching toward some form of capitalism for the Soviet Union, found himself harried by the threats of his rival Boris Yeltsin, chairman of the Russian parliament and head of the major Russian republic. Yeltsin kept on demanding immediate and far-reaching moves to a market economy and threatened to set up a rival power center in Moscow if his demands were not heeded.

Many westerners thought Gorbachev was walking a tightrope. They speculated as to which would bring him down first—economic collapse or ethnic upheaval. Added to his political woes was the fact that his policy of *glasnost* had resulted in widespread unrest deep within the Soviet Union itself. There were at least thirty-five areas of conflict where territorial squabbles, strikes, and defiance of Moscow were a source of daily worry to the Kremlin.

At this time one observer said the only alternative to *perestroika*, the economic reform of the Soviet Union, was *war*. (War is the classic solution of dictatorships to internal problems; it distracts people from their troubles and unifies the nation in a common cause.) He said also that the only alternative to *glasnost*, the new freedoms, would be a return to the antisemitic, Jew-baiting society of old. (Finding a scapegoat is a classic solution used by dictatorships for shifting the blame for failure. What more convenient scapegoat could the Kremlin have than its large population of Jews?)

Indeed, Vitali Korotich, editor of the Soviet magazine *Ogonyok*, declared, "Should *glasnost* end, we will be left a hungry, stupid, terrible country with a big army—a very dangerous country."

Then came the Gulf War in early 1991, and the short-lived coup of August 19, 1991. The Gulf War horrified the Soviet military. They saw Gorbachev deliberately abandon Iraq, a strategic client state in the vital Middle East. Then they watched with unbelieving eyes the speed and efficiency with which the United States and its allies dismembered the Soviet-trained and equipped Iraqi military machine. They saw high technology at work and were stunned. Many were too stubborn to admit that much of their own defenses was now completely outdated and their equipment outclassed.

So in 1991 the army bosses joined forces with the communist party and the KGB and made their move. Gorbachev had just returned empty-handed from a visit to a meeting of The Group of Seven (the leading industrial democracies). He had hoped to get economic aid amounting to an astronomical $250 billion. Instead he encountered hard questions—Why should the West subsidize Moscow's continuing repression of the Baltic states? Or its continuing enormous investment in the military? (The fact that the Soviet defense budget had actually risen from 26 percent of the total budget in 1990 to a projected 36 percent in 1993 and the fact that more than half of all industrial production was still military were not unnoticed by the western powers). "Why," asked the United States secretary of state, "should the West give the Soviets more aid when they continue to send large amounts of aid to Cuba?"

The so-called Gang of Eight acted. They detained Gorbachev. However, they made the critical mistake of leaving Boris Yeltsin, president of the vast Russian republic, at large. The tanks and troops rolled into Moscow to seize the key installations, but this time there was a difference. Yeltsin stood on the steps of the Russian federation parliament building holding the old, pre-revolution Russian flag, rallied the people, and defied the hard-liners. The troops refused to fire on the people. The coup had failed. It lasted only three days.

There was an immediate revulsion throughout all the republics. Never again would the army, the communist party, and the KGB be allowed to act in concert again. A chastened Gorbachev returned to Moscow to help spearhead reform. The old guard in the military was ousted. Younger and more liberal officers replaced them. Steps were taken to reduce drastically and overhaul the dreaded KGB. The union treaty, designed by Gorbachev to hold the Soviet Union together, was scrapped. The communist party was disbanded after seventy-five years of domination.[31]

Immediately after the abortive coup, Boris Yeltsin called for a Russian republic national guard as a protection against any further army coups. This republic is so vast and has so much weight to throw around, it was bound to dominate any reshaping of the former Soviet Union.

In September 1991 the Congress of People's Deputies decided by an overwhelming vote to create a transitional government. The new government was comprised of three functioning bodies. First, there was the State Council made up of Gorbachev and the heads of the ten cooperating republics. This was to be the main body responsible for foreign affairs, the military, law enforcement, and national security. The two subsidiary bodies were the Supreme Soviet, a reconstructed two-chamber parliament, and an Inter-Republican Economic Committee, a panel to oversee the economy and economic reform. The first act of the new State Council was to grant independence belatedly to the Baltic republics.

The State Council was no sooner formed than doubts were being voiced as to whether it could check the disintegration of the Union and to what extent it could uphold the Soviet Union's treaty obligations, proceed with nuclear disarmament, or accomplish economic reform. It was no sooner formed than former Foreign Minister Eduard Shevardnadze was gloomily warning that the struggle between the new democrats and the old reactionaries was not yet over. Foreign observers were equally cautious. The United

States secretary of state warned that nationalism can turn into fascism and that a move towards fascism or a return to communism would be disastrous. The media was also reminding western optimists that Gorbachev still commanded some four million troops and an arsenal of thirty thousand nuclear weapons.

Changes have been continuous and swift. Early in December 1991 the Ukrainian republic voted to become independent of the Soviet Union and to create what would be the fifth most populous country in Europe. A state department official declared, "Russia can do without the Ukraine, the Ukraine can do without Russia, but the Soviet Union can not do without the Ukraine. It's over." Dire predictions were voiced of a new Russian empire that would absorb the other non-Ukrainian republics. Others envisioned a score or more squabbling republics, some armed with nuclear weapons.

What emerged was a new eleven-republic Commonwealth, a loose association of former Soviet republics, tied together by economic realities.

On December 16, Defense Minister Yevgeny Shaposhnikov aligned himself, and the military, with Boris Yeltsin, president of the giant Russian republic. The military, in other words, had chosen the new Commonwealth over the old Soviet Union. Soviet president Mikhail Gorbachev was left out in the cold. Yeltsin responded by giving the military a 90 percent pay raise and promising that a military man, not a politician, and certainly not Gorbachev, would be chosen to head up a unified military command of the new Commonwealth. All the republics, he declared, would become nuclear-free except Russia. Yeltsin also announced that Russia wanted the Soviet seat on the United Nations Security Council, along with its veto power.

From the standpoint of Bible prophecy all that happened between 1917 and 1991 in the Soviet Union should now be viewed as a massive dress rehearsal for the ultimate fulfillment of the still unchanged prophecies of Ezekiel. Russia will again emerge as a world power, able to challenge the West. It will again pursue its age-long goals in the Middle East. The antisemitic forces in Russia are still a force to be reckoned with.

Right after the aborted coup, Israeli Prime Minister Yitzhak Shamir began urging Russian Jews to flee the country. He urged them not to try to salvage anything but to get to Israel while it was still possible to do so. In Russia the Pamyat organization preaches Jew hate. It says that the Jews killed Christ, that they killed Czar Nicholas II, that they organized the Bolshevik revolution, and that they masterminded Stalin's reign of terror. Leon Trotsky, Iakov Sverdlov, Lev Kámenev, and Grigorii Zinoviev, it reminds the Russians, were all Jews. It says that the United States, along with the media of the whole world, is controlled by Jewish capitalists. Some Pamyat members oppose Jewish emigration. They say that Jews should be kept and tried for their crimes.

Now let us review in more detail the various countries specifically listed as Russia's end-time allies.

Gomer

Ezekiel mentioned "Gomer and all his bands." The likelihood is that this is a reference to Germany and the various German-speaking countries of Europe, countries Hitler was so eager to gather together under the unifying banners of the Third Reich.

One of the most astonishing things Gorbachev did was to allow the Berlin wall to be torn down and to allow the two Germanys, divided since World War II, to reunite.

West Germany has had to pay a stiff price for reunification. It agreed, in tough bargaining with Gorbachev, to give the Soviet Union bank credits amounting to three billion dollars. It promised to pay nearly a billion dollars a year for Soviet troops remaining in East Germany until such time as they can all be removed. They also promised to build houses in the Soviet Union for the retiring Russian army of occupation.

The cost of absorbing the East Germans is astronomical. For fifty years East Germans had job security in inefficient companies unable to compete with their western counterparts. One estimate is that up to 20 percent of all East German businesses are doomed. Unemployment is expected to soar to as high as 3 million.

The reunification of Germany, even within the fold of NATO, worries many thoughtful observers. Germany h⸱s had a history of looking eastward. Memories are being revived of the Brest-Litovsk treaty in 1918 which disengaged Russia from World War I; of the Rapallo treaty in 1922 under the terms of which Germany was able to train soldiers and pilots in the Soviet Union in defiance of the Versailles treaty; and the treacherous Molotov-Ribbentrop pact in 1939 which cleared the way for Hitler to launch World War II.

Singlehandedly, a united and greater Germany (Gomer and all his bands) came within a hair of winning World War II. The Nazis' attempt to achieve global power cost 35 million lives. On the battlefields 1 out of every 22 Russians was killed, 1 out of every 25 Germans, and 1 out of every 150 Britishers. In addition 2 out of every 3 European Jews were systematically exterminated. It took all the combined might of the British empire, the Soviet Union, and the United States to fight Germany to a standstill. What if a united and antisemitic Germany were to seek its future fortunes allied to an antisemitic Russia?

Persia

Like so many of the countries of the Middle East, Persia was brought into the modern world by the discovery of oil beneath its sands. Persia is the land that first saw roses bloom, where astronomy grew to a science, mathematics was born, and Eden's gorgeous glades once stood. Centuries before the Romans ventured on the stage, the Persians ruled an empire reaching from India to the gates of Greece. Persian kings were addressed as "King of kings, King of many races, King of the earth."

Persia's relationship with Russia in modern times originated during World War I when Iranian affairs were dominated by Russia and Britain. Both countries were determined to keep Persian oil fields out of German hands.

In the 1920s an illiterate infantryman soared to the rank of general in Iran's tiny army, seized power for himself, and five years later proclaimed himself the shah.

During World War II both Britain and Russia seized Iran again, determined to keep its vital oil fields out of German hands. The shah was deposed for his Nazi leanings and his son, Mohammed Reza Pahlavi, was installed in his place. At the end of the war the British pulled out as part of their policy of withdrawing from all bases in the East. The Russians, more pragmatic, were determined to stay and doubtless would have done so had not President Truman ordered them out. They left in 1946.

Meanwhile the young new shah lived a careless life of ease, disdainful of the welfare of his people. He was shaken out of his complacency in 1953 when Premier Mossadegh and the communist Tudeh party came within a hair of seizing power. Once again the Americans saved him when the Central Intelligence Agency brought about the swift downfall of Mossadegh and his friends. The time had not yet come for Iran to enter the Russian fold.

Secure again, the shah turned his attention to his country. Now he was determined to haul his backward nation headlong into the twentieth century. He became a reformer. He forced the feudal landlords to disgorge the land which had been consolidated in the hands of about a thousand families for centuries. He created a literacy corps to teach millions of peasants to read and write. He established tent schools to bring a measure of education to Iran's nomads. He began a program of land reclamation to restore Iran's deserts to their one-time fertile splendor. He spent billions of dollars pushing through social reforms, careless of the enemies he was making among the powerful conservative Muslim mullahs.

Above all else, the shah determined to make Iran the leading power in the Persian gulf and to give it the best equipped army in the Middle East. His ambition was to fill the power vacuum in the gulf left by the departure of the British. Also he wished to curb neighboring Iraq's ambitious plans to control the strategic strait of Hormuz, gateway to the incredible wealth of the whole area. A glance at the map will show the prize. The strait of Hormuz is located between Iran and Oman and is just forty miles wide at it narrowest point. Through this strait passes most of the oil on which the world's industrial nations depend. Whoever controls the strait controls the Middle East's oil and has a stranglehold on the world's throat. Russia's hands, of course, are itching to get a good grip on the strait of Hormuz.

For twenty-five years the shah ruled with an iron hand and, blind to the growing power of the forces of reaction and subversion in the country, imagined himself secure in the affections of his people. That there was some opposition he knew, and he quelled it with his notorious security police agency, Savak. Dissent was not allowed and political parties that might challenge him were banned, but the forces of reaction seethed beneath it all.

Iran's conservative Shiite Muslims were among the first to rebel. This Iranian brand of Islam split off from the main stem in the seventh century and is now predominant in Iran, Iraq, and Lebanon. The Shiite mullahs revolted because they saw the shah leading Iran away from Islam altogether. They wanted a country based on the Koran and ruled by strict Islamic law. They were horrified at western ways being imported by the forward-looking shah with little regard for their scruples. Along with the mullahs, the students rioted, fomented by Islamic Marxists; and the old nationalist front of dead and buried Premier Mossadegh came back to life. The shah found dissent hard to suppress because it came from so many, varied, and mutually antagonistic sources. The name of Ayatollah Khomeini began to be spoken throughout the land.

Khomeini (the title *Ayatollah* means "sign of God"), a philosopher-theologian and a shrewd politician, was in exile. He was born in central Iran. His father was shot to death while on a pilgrimage to Iraq, and rumor had it that the shah was behind the assassination. Khomeini himself was educated in the holy Muslim city of Qum. It did not take him long to become active in movements aimed at the shah. In the early 1960s he openly condemned the shah's social and economic policies and was banished in 1964. He settled in neighboring Iraq and continued to incite political action against the hated shah. The shah countered by putting pressure on Iraq to expel him, and in 1978 Khomeini took refuge in France.

Khomeini hated everything that the shah stood for. He and his fellow fundamentalists were deeply offended by the westernization of Iran: the emancipation of women, the liberalization of laws to permit the use of alcohol, and decadent western-style entertainment. Almost equal to his hatred for the shah was his hatred of Israel. He was far more than an Iranian nationalist, for he envisioned a pan-Islamic world united by the Koran. As an exile in Europe, he fomented dissent throughout Iran, and set his sights fixedly on one goal, the downfall of the shah.

Strikes and riots began to mount throughout Iran, and many western observers could see that the end of the road was in sight for the shah. The United States refused to believe it. The shah was their friend. He stood for stability in the gulf; he was their protégé; he could not fall. But he did.

The shah underestimated the strength of the forces ranged against him in his country. When finally he awoke to reality it was too late, and his hasty, last-minute efforts to liberalize his dictatorial political policies, to free imprisoned dissidents from the hands of his secret police, and to form a new civilian government were all in vain. The whole country was torn with riots, strikes, marches, and giant rallies fomented by students, Marxists, and the mullahs. It was all urged on by the strident, incendiary demands of Khomeini and all cleverly orchestrated by the communists.

The men in the Kremlin must have sat back and rubbed their hands. They briskly warned the United States that military intervention would be considered "a matter affecting the security interests of the USSR." To back their words, they declared a military alert along Russia's 1,350-mile frontier with Iran. This time the strategic context favored the Soviet Union. Any clash would give Russia the advantage of proximity, whereas American forces would have to be airlifted over half the circumference of the world. Moreover, the United States president was seemingly unable to make up his mind what to do.

In January 1979 the shah gave up. He announced his intention of taking a vacation and ignominiously left the country. The people of Iran went wild with joy. The shah's pictures were torn down and pictures of the Ayatollah Khomeini went up in their place. "God is great" was the Ayatollah's reported comment when the news was brought to him.

And so, after fifteen years of exile, Khomeini came home. He announced the formation of a new revolutionary council and prepared for another battle, this time against the leftists on one hand and the generals and other supporters of the shah on the other. Before long the tortured country was torn from end to end. Workers rioted over unemployment and the heavy-handed censorship and puritanical reforms imposed by the clergy. The Marxists and the leftists exploited the discontent, and some of the mullahs accused the Ayatollah of incompetence.

Then a group of Marxist-oriented students seized the American embassy in Tehran. The Americans in the embassy were made hostages, paraded by their captors before vengeful mobs, and used as pawns in a new game. The students demanded the return of the shah, then undergoing treatment for cancer in the United States, in exchange for the release of the captives. Their action was condoned by the Ayatollah Khomeini, a man who himself had once sought political asylum in the West. He denounced the United States as "the Great Satan," gave his blessing to the students, made

343

impossible and insulting demands on the United States for the release of the hostages, and treated the world to the spectacle of a government officially sanctioning international gangsterism. The United States retaliated by seizing some $12 billion in Iranian assets in the United States.

The seizure of the hostages distracted the attention of the Iranian people from the desperate economic, social, and political problems of their country for months. They were months fraught with peril. The hostages were eventually released, but not until President Carter had made one inept attempt to rescue them and not until a pending change in the administration in Washington made the Iranians think that they were about to deal with a tougher president.

In the meantime the chaos in Iran continued. President Bani-Sadr was ousted by the mullahs, because he was seen as an obstacle to their plans to convert Iran into a theocratic Muslim state. Khomeini sacrificed him, even though Bani-Sadr had been his protégé and had extended hospitality to him during his exile. But Bani-Sadr was by no means through. He was smuggled out of Iran by the powerful Mujahedeen party and their leftist guerrillas. From Paris their leader and the exiled Bani-Sadr stepped up a campaign of terror inside Iran. In one act alone they wiped out the Iranian president, the prime minister, and six other top government officials. Then they killed Khomeini's defense minister, his acting chief of staff, and two other high-ranking commanders. Not even the Ayatollah himself felt safe.

Khomeini's response to the perils confronting him from the Mujahedeen was startling. He called in the Soviets. With the backing of his ruling Islamic republic party, he welcomed into Iran a group of Soviet KGB agents and other communist advisers to help him create an efficient intelligence and security force. The communist Tudeh party in Iran seems to have been behind this move. Embattled from the far left and from mullahs on the extreme right, Khomeini evidently felt he could use any help available; but the appeal to the Russians only introduced a dangerous new factor into Iranian affairs.

The Russians were quick to respond and clever in their approach. The KGB agents they sent into Iran were handpicked, highly trained professionals. They were members of Russia's Central Asian population, able to speak the Iranian language as though it were their mother tongue, and schooled to behave like devout Muslims. They lost no time in getting down to business. One of their first moves was to take over the facilities of the shah's dreaded Savak headquarters and to recruit some of its former agents.

Nor was the arrival of the KGB the end. More and more Soviet advisers showed up in Tehran, some of whom turned their attention to rebuilding Iran's economy, reduced to ruins by war, riot, and upheaval. The Russian ambassador went to work on Khomeini's fears, assuring the Iranian leader that the United States had plans to launch a counterrevolution. What Russia wanted, and offered Iran, was a mutual cooperation pact under which the Russians would provide Iran with arms, technical advisers, and a firm alliance against all outside attack.

In 1980 war broke out between Iraq, a Soviet client state, and Iran, a country the Soviets wanted to dominate. The radical Islamic regime in Iran had been urging Iraq's Shiite Muslims to depose Saddam Hussein. Iraq responded by invading Iran. Thus began, in the strategic, oil-rich Persian gulf, a war that was enormously costly for both sides, not to mention all countries with shipping in the area and dependent on Middle East oil.

Iran's strategy was to try to overwhelm Iraq with human assault waves, turning the conflict into one of the costliest in the twentieth century. Around the Iraqi city of Basra alone, the Iranians lost some four hundred thousand soldiers, many of them boys. The entire death toll for Iran has been estimated at more than a million men. The boys were sent in ahead of the regular army. The dead were given martyr status. Recruits were promised eternal bliss if they died in battle. Sending fourteen-year-old boys into the teeth of machine guns appeared quite rational to Khomeini, who saw himself as a messiah sent to save Islam from idolatry.

Even though indiscriminate sinking of the world's tankers in the gulf prompted the United States and other nations to take protective measures, Iran took care not to provoke either of the two superpowers. Iran's real ambitions lie to the southwest. If she can once neutralize Iraq, she will face states too weak to offer much resistance.

Iraq's invasion of Kuwait in 1990 and the subsequent global reaction may give Iran pause. The United States has demonstrated how quickly it can react when a country vital to its security is threatened. It would have been suicidal for the West to allow Saudi Arabia to fall into the hands of an international blackmailer like Saddam Hussein. An Iran solidly backed by Russia, however, might be another matter at some time in the future.

Currently Iran is in a mess. Inflation and unemployment, the aftermath of years of western embargoes, plague the country. The Iran-Iraq war, which dragged on for eight years, cost Iran one trillion dollars. Even a surge in global oil prices would not pull Iran out of its economic mess for years. It is certainly in no position to tangle with the western powers. The allied military feat in Iraq has sent a sobering message to all the local troublemakers. The catalyst remains the nation of Israel. Iran, like all the other Muslim states, hates Israel. But it can do nothing about Israel so long as Israel is defended by the West. A lineup with Russia, however, backed by Germany, the Arabs, and Ethiopia might well offer Iran a fresh glimmer of hope.

What Iran really covets is complete hegemony over the gulf, over the oil, and over the holy places at Mecca and Medina. Iran also wants to extend Shiite fundamentalism over all Islam, recovering the unity and power Islam had in the middle ages. Russia might eventually make common cause with the Islamic southern republics in some overall "deal" involving the Middle East. The inclusion of Persia in Ezekiel's lineup of Russian allies seems to point to some future Russian deal with Islam.

There are some fifty-five million Muslims located in Azerbaijan and the five Central Asian republics, of which Tadzhikistan, bordering on Afghanistan, is probably the most vehemently Islamic. After the Russians sent troops into Azerbaijan to quell rioting, one prominent Soviet commentator on Muslim affairs reminded the Kremlin that "Iran has threatened the Soviet Union with an Islamic conflagration."[32] The Russians have yet to harness their Muslim population to their long-range imperialist goals. Doubtless the coming war with Israel foretold by Ezekiel will pull them in line.

In the meantime other Muslim states in the Middle East are encouraging Muslims in the Commonwealth to increase their Islamic awareness. Saudi Arabia, for instance, printed one million copies of the Koran for them. There was nothing surprising about that, but what was new was that the Soviet aeroflot agreed to deliver them. Even before the coup greater freedoms were evident everywhere. Mullahs were allowed to actively proselytize; Muslim

TV and radio programs were allowed; the number of mosques was increasing.

Although the Muslims made up only 19.2 percent of the Soviet population, they have accounted for 50 percent of the total population increase in the past ten years, and they are still increasing at five times the rate of the rest of the population of the former Soviet Union. They comprised the fifth largest Muslim community in the world. (It is tied for fifth place with Turkey, after Indonesia, Pakistan, Bangladesh, and India).

A firm Russian alliance with its Muslim neighboring republics and with Iran would give the Russians some immediate advantages. Russia would gain access to warm-water ports with direct lines of communication back to the Russian mainland. At present, when Russian missile-firing submarines leave their ports around Murmansk and Archangel, they have to take into account the frigid Arctic winters. The loss of the Baltic states cuts them off from the Baltic sea. Warm-water ports on the gulf would give Russia easy access to the Indian ocean and much greater security.

Then, too, with Iran firmly in hand, Russia would be in a position to threaten the strait of Hormuz and the vital but volatile sheikdoms of the Arabian peninsula.

In addition, the quickest way to Iraq from Russia is through Turkey or Iran. Iraq has been a client state of Moscow in the past, but its aggressive moves in the Middle East were premature for Soviet interests. Iraq may be a useful troublemaker in the Middle East, but Iran would be a far superior prize. In any case Iraq, the ancient Babylon, belongs prophetically in the sphere of the revived Roman empire rather than Russia. With Iran firmly in the Russian camp, Iraq's independence could be curbed. Also Iran would give Russia a future base from which to threaten Pakistan and India.

In 1987 the Iranians greatly threatened the security of the Middle East by instigating riots during the summer hajj (pilgrimage to Mecca). A massacre ensued in which a number of Iranians were killed. Khomeini called for an immediate end to Saudi custodianship of Islam's holy sites. He went so far as to declare that Iran would, under certain circumstances, fight for "the liberation of Mecca." He thus flung the gauntlet in the face of the ruling house of Saud by challenging the legitimacy of Saudi Arabia's custodianship. Khomeini wanted Mecca to become the arena for the propagation of his Shiite fundamentalist brand of Islam.

Saudi Arabia is a desert country. Its population is only about eleven million. Its security and stability are vital to the West. It is the world's largest oil producer. It is vulnerable to extremists, and potential Iranian belligerence is not something to take lightly. It would be a disaster if Saudi Arabia's present regime were to be overthrown and replaced by a radical, militant, fundamentalist anti-American regime. Such an event would change the entire balance of power in the vital Persian gulf. No wonder, during the Iran-Iraq war, the Saudis contributed heavily to Iraq's war chest. This policy proved to be a mistake as Iraq's subsequent invasion of Kuwait proved. Nothing but a United States and United Nations countermove to defend Saudi Arabia saved that country from an Iraqi takeover. A viable Russo-Iranian alliance could prove an even greater threat than that of Iraq.

The costly Iran-Iraq war finally terminated with Iran's economy disrupted, and Iran began to look toward the Soviet Union as a partner. In 1979 a high-ranking Soviet delegation visited Iran, at which time an agreement was signed for the Soviets to resume imports of Iranian natural gas. It was also agreed that the two countries would explore the joint production of steel and petro chemicals.

In 1987 the two countries began to negotiate plans to reopen oil pipelines and to build a second rail link from Iran to Soviet Central Asia. The Russians see Iran as a natural land bridge between the gulf and themselves on the north, the Turks on the west, and Afghanistan, Pakistan, and Asia on the east.

One tool of Iranian policy is the Hizballah (the party of God) terrorist organization whose members adulated Khomeini. This group operates under various names—the Islamic Jihad and the Revolutionary Justice Organization, for instance. It is suspected of holding most of the foreign hostages. As the Iran *contra* hearings in the United States revealed, President Reagan's arms deals were designed to secure the release of Americans from Hizballah prisons—confirming to Iran that international terrorism pays. Hizballah ties to Iran are evident. Khomeini is reported to have spent up to fifty million dollars a year to underwrite the group's activities.

The one constant factor in the entire Middle East equation is Arab and Muslim hatred of Israel. Sooner or later the Russians will see how best to exploit this constant to support a final bid to gain control of this vitally strategic area.

Ethiopia

Up until recently Ethiopia was a constitutional monarchy derived from an earlier kingdom. The last emperor was Haile Selassie, who was crowned on November 2, 1930, in a half-Christian, half-pagan ceremony. After five thousand cattle had been slaughtered to provide a feast of raw meat for the masses, a crown worth half a million dollars was placed on the emperor's head by the Coptic archbishop of Ethiopia. Haile Selassie then assumed the titles of Elect of God, Lion of the Tribe of Judah, Light of the World, and Power of the Trinity. Behind the throne were massed Coptic priests in vestments of scarlet, green, yellow, and purple, carrying gold and silver crosiers and golden censers.

Haile Selassie claimed, on the basis of an age-old tradition, that he was a direct descendant of King Solomon. Tradition, probably unfounded, states that the queen of Sheba gave birth to a son by Solomon after her arrival back home from Jerusalem. The son was named Menelik and, according to tradition, succeeded her on the throne after being crowned king of Ethiopia in Solomon's temple. After his coronation, Menelik is supposed to have returned to Ethiopia with a large retinue of the firstborn of Israel and Judah and a share in the divine blessings bestowed on the Jewish people.

Abyssinian Christianity was imported into Ethiopia by the Ethiopian eunuch who was led to Christ by the evangelist Philip. For seven or eight centuries, when all the world around was submerged in Islam, the Ethiopians preserved their variety of the Christian faith intact. Augustine's church in North Africa and the church of Athanasius in Egypt were swept away, but the Ethiopian church survived.

Haile Selassie set out to lift his country from barbarism into the twentieth century, but then came Mussolini with his storm troops and his ambition to resurrect the Roman empire. The backward Ethiopians were no match for his modern, well-equipped army. Their country was quickly crushed by the Italians, and Haile Selassie found political asylum in Britain. In March 1941 British troops drove out the Italians and restored Haile Selassie to his throne.

The emperor liked to think of himself as the 225th consecutive Solomonic ruler of his people. He was a professing Christian and a man open to change. Soon after his enthronement he began to think about giving his country a new constitution, which actually came into effect on November 4, 1955.

Before we examine the swift-paced events leading to the ignominious fall of Haile Selassie, we need to consider the resources and potential of Ethiopia.

The name *Ethiopia* is derived from two Greek words meaning "to burn" and "face"—the land of those with burnt faces. It is a country of spectacular scenery and breathtaking mountains that soar straight up from the burning sands below. The population of Ethiopia is a mixture of Semites, Hamites, Bantus, and others. Haile Selassie ruled a country where less than 10 percent of the people were literate; smallpox, typhus, and malaria raged; one of the lowest standards of living in the world prevailed; and cities were plagued by roving bands of beggars and thieves. It was a country with no free press. It was a land plagued by corruption in government and saddled with a powerful and feudal church. The emperor had his work cut out for him to bring this wild land into the modern world.

Yet the potential of the country is great. It is said to be rich in gold. Ancient Ophir, from which Solomon obtained much of the gold that flowed into his coffers, is believed by some to have been in Ethiopia. The country also has rich deposits of platinum and potash. It could become the produce market of the Middle East; its soil is abundant and fertile. But the people need incentive to work, modern farming technology to utilize the soil, and roads and railways to get goods to market. The population is over thirty-five million, ten times greater than that of its neighbor and rival, Somalia, a former Soviet client state.

For years Ethiopia was America's best friend in their part of the world. Haile Selassie ruled his country with a firm hand and with the sincere wish to lift his people, but he moved too slowly. As long ago as 1953, young Ethiopians and other Africans were being recruited in Addis Ababa for study at Lenin University, from whence they were sent to Prague for training as Soviet agents. Indoctrinated, they returned to their various African homelands to become the backbone of communism in Africa.[33]

For some years before his fall, Haile Selassie found himself fighting thousands of students rioting over the country's political and economic ills; these riots were fomented by a hard core of well-trained communists. Their initial goal was simple: drive out the

Americans, overthrow the monarchy, and destroy the existing structure of Ethiopian life.

The emperor's troubles were compounded by a rebel movement in neighboring Eritrea, a former colony of Italy turned over to Ethiopia by the United Nations in 1952. Eritrean rebels were receiving plentiful aid from radical Arab governments in Syria, Libya, and Iraq. Then, too, Ethiopia's old enemy Somalia (at that time a Russian client state) intensified its hostilities against Ethiopia, demanding the return of certain territories which they claimed belonged to them.

Haile Selassie's absolute monarchy suddenly collapsed in a welter of discontent brought on by food shortages, skyrocketing inflation, and mass poverty. Most of his troops joined with the dissidents. They occupied Addis Ababa and other cities and effectively isolated the emperor from his people. They accused him of betraying the country, dismantled his power structure, arrested most of the country's nobility and former leaders, and put the emperor under house arrest. As soon as the new junta had consolidated its power, it massacred fifty-nine members of the former ruling elite, including Haile Selassie's grandson. In August 1975 the emperor himself, then an old man in his eighties, was likewise killed.

The new regime lost no time in lining up with the Soviet Union. Americans were given four days to leave the country. Power was consolidated in the hands of Mengistu Haile Mariam, a Marxist with a taste for terror. He launched a deliberate campaign to liquidate all opposition and tighten his grip on the country.

The Soviet Union backed the new regime with tanks, guns, and other implements of modern war. The Kremlin realized that by doing this it was risking the loss of Somalia. For about fifteen years the Russians had armed and trained this coastal country. They had established ties of friendship with the Somalians and built an important naval base at the seaport of Berbera in order to command the approaches to the Red Sea. The Russians, while hoping to control both Ethiopia and Somalia despite the deep-seated hatred between the two countries, pragmatically evaluated Ethiopia as more important to their long-range goals. Control of the Ethiopian port of Massaua on the Red Sea would help offset the loss of Berbera. If it won, the Kremlin intended to turn Ethiopia into a Cuban-style satellite for exporting revolution to all of Africa.

In 1984, 1985, and again in 1987, terrible famines swept through Ethiopia. Enormous rescue efforts were mobilized by the West. The United States spent half a billion dollars in one year alone, trying to help the starving people. (The Russians gave the Ethiopians two planes.)

Ethiopia has earned the unenviable reputation of being the world's poorest country. According to the World Bank, average annual per capita income is $110. The infant mortality rate is 16.8 percent. Of the country's over thirty-five million population, about six million faced starvation in 1987.

Western philanthropy has been discouraged in the past by reports that the Marxist regime taxed relief shipments at the rate of fifty dollars per ton to help finance its army (the largest in black Africa). Moreover the anti-Marxist rebels attacked relief convoys to retaliate and to help support their cause.

No doubt drought has been a contributing factor, but much of the blame for Ethiopia's disaster lay at the door of the Marxist regime. Its policies included the mass relocation of 1.5 million people into Soviet-style collective farms, carried out in the Stalinist tradition of heartless cruelty and mindless inefficiency. Marxist policy forced farmers who had a surplus, to sell to the state at ruinous prices.

The Marxist regime, however, had to battle twenty-three rebel groups, the two strongest being in Tigre and Eritrea—the provinces most affected by the drought. The Marxist dictator Mengistu, sensing defeat, salted away a fortune in foreign banks against the day when he would have to skip the country. Then rebel forces from the Tigre People's Liberation Front and the Eritrean People's Liberation Front began to move closer to Addis Ababa. Ethiopians still in the capital feared a massacre once the rebel factions took the city.[34] It should be remembered that these rebel forces were Marxist.

Russian successes in Ethiopia alarmed the moderate Arab states. Saudi Arabia and some of the other wealthy sheikdoms in the area offered Somalia vast sums of money if it would expel the Russians. Somalia responded and gave Russia and her Cuban puppets a week's notice to get out of the country.

This only made Ethiopia more attractive to the Kremlin. It poured more than a billion dollars worth of war material into the country, along with all kinds of advisers, hoping to consolidate its hold on Ethiopia. That would have given Moscow a base from which to control the Red Sea and the Suez canal and to threaten western oil routes from the Middle East. Ethiopia would be a prime location from which Russia could threaten Saudi Arabia. From Ethiopia, Russia could export subversion into the Sudan, Kenya, and other African countries.

In the end the various rebel armies arrayed against Ethiopia's Mengistu regime won.

Mengistu Haile Mariam, the one-time lieutenant colonel who had ruled Ethiopia for fourteen horrifying years, fled to Zimbabwe in May 1991. Not that the unfortunate Ethiopians were much better off. The victors began to eye each other with suspicion. The Eritreans, for example, want independence, but without Eritrea, Ethiopia has no access to the sea. On the other hand, the Eritreans can not afford to antagonize the new government in Addis Ababa.

What will happen next nobody knows. Ethiopia is exhausted from the policies and terrorism of Mengistu, and from repeated famines. It needs massive infusions of foreign aid. But no matter what happens in the meantime, Ezekiel made it plain that Ethiopia and Russia will again hold hands and that they will be partners in an end-time attack on Israel.

Libya

For the most part Libya is a sea of sand, but beneath that sand is oil. Libya is about the size of Alaska and Oregon combined and has a population less than that of Detroit. Summer temperatures rise to a blistering 130 degrees in the shade. Choking dust storms frequently obliterate the landscape. When Libya gained its independence after World War II, there were only sixteen college graduates in the country; per capita income averaged about thirty dollars a year.

Between 1951 and 1968 Libya was a monarchy. Its importance lay in its key position on the North African coast—lying across the Mediterranean from the vital NATO countries of Europe—and in the fact that it was a country rich in oil.

The Russians were not slow to sense the sudden new importance of Libya. As soon as oil was discovered they began to court the country's Arab leaders, offering to buy a large percentage of the nation's exports and presenting young Libyans with scholarships to Russian universities. Technology and interest-free loans were also offered to help Libya develop its natural resources. Nevertheless, it was the United States and European oil companies that developed the Libyan oil fields.

In September 1968 the Libyan king was deposed by a group of army officers led by a belligerent and unstable bedouin named Muammar al-Qaddafi. Qaddafi, born in a goatskin tent in the Sahara, came from a tribe of nomads who stopped occasionally to scratch a meager crop from the reluctant soil before moving on again with their herds. Qaddafi idolized Egypt's Colonel Nasser, who had helped rid Egypt of King Farouk and turn the country into a republic. Qaddafi decided that the army offered the quickest way to power, so he enrolled in the Libyan Royal Academy. He wasted no time in organizing his fellow cadets into a group modeled on the one that brought Nasser to power in Egypt. He bided his time. Then, when the aged King Idris was vacationing in Greece, Qaddafi and his friends seized power.

One of his first acts after seizing power in Libya was to turn the social calendar back to the thirteenth century. Alcohol was banned, mixed dancing was prohibited, and women, because of their "biological defects," were to stay at home. He also took Libya on a new political course. He ordered Americans out of the strategic air force base on the outskirts of Tripoli, nationalized foreign-owned business without compensation, and redirected the flow of the country's growing oil revenues. He invested in hospitals, roads, houses, irrigation projects—and in international terrorism.

One of Qaddafi's dreams has been to create a federation with other Arab states. He has made several overtures to other Arab or Islamic countries such as Egypt, Syria, and the Sudan in hopes of forming such a federation, but his neighbors have always backed off, alarmed by Qaddafi's erratic ways. Anwar Sadat once called him "a madman." The Sudanese president once said, "Qaddafi has a split personality, both of them evil."

Qaddafi violently opposed Sadat's attempts to make peace with Israel. "We reject peace with Israel, we reject recognition of Israel, we reject negotiations with Israel": that was Qaddafi's stand.

Young Arabs have seen Qaddafi's brand of puritanical idealism as a refreshing change from the weakness, rivalries, and corruption of most Arab states. This has been an important factor, since most of Libya's population is under thirty.

After Sadat broke with the Soviet Union, Qaddafi began to court Moscow and also to orchestrate attacks on moderate Arab governments in various parts of Africa. Qaddafi views any friend of the United States as an enemy of Libya. In his opinion, countries willing to accept Russian and Cuban military aid are only protecting themselves against American aggression. For years Qaddafi had a standing offer of one million dollars for anyone who would assassinate Anwar Sadat.

Nor have his own countrymen been safe. At one time he ordered all Libyan dissidents living abroad to come home and sent his paid assassins after those who refused.

His troops have invaded neighboring countries such as Egypt, Tunisia, and Chad. He supported Uganda's murderous Idi Amin and gave him political asylum when his regime was overthrown.

Qaddafi must have come as a delightful surprise to the Kremlin. For years Moscow looked for a means to outflank Europe in the Mediterranean, and in Libya it found just the ally it wanted. In 1976 he signed a $120 billion arms agreement with the Soviets, and without delay the latest in weapons and equipment began to arrive—along with advisers. To accelerate the arrival of the massive arms shipments from the Soviet Union the Libyan leader built nine airstrips for Soviet cargo planes.

He has sent thousands of Libyans off to Russia for training, ignoring the fate of Ethiopia's Haile Selassie. Doubtless these young Libyans will come back thoroughly indoctrinated in Moscow's line.

Qaddafi's dangerous dreams include nuclear weapons. This is one reason why his soldiers invaded neighboring Chad—Qaddafi wanted control of Chad's uranium deposits. Qaddafi has already conspired with the Chinese and with Pakistan to achieve his goal of becoming a nuclear power. He has recruited Arab physicists to aid him in achieving that goal.

Qaddafi's image of himself as the last great hope of pan-Islam (creator of a great Arab nation stretching from the Persian gulf to the Atlantic), as the scourge of the West, as a modern "old man of the mountains," as the head of the society of assassins, and as the foe of Israel, received a sudden and severe check in 1986 when the United States sent its bombers in a strike against Libya. The raid struck at strategic targets and also at Qaddafi's home. He escaped, but one of his sons was killed.

It took the spark out of Qaddafi's revolution. The military significance of the raid was minimal, but its psychological effects were tremendous. Ever since, Qaddafi has been in retreat, and not only as the leader of world terrorism. His demoralized army, which had been lording it over Chad, probably the weakest country in Africa, was defeated and thrown out of the country.

In 1989 Libya joined with Morocco, Algeria, Tunisia and Mauritania to form the Arab *Maghreb Union*. This union is matched by the *Arab Cooperation Council* comprising Egypt, Iraq, Jordan, and the Yemen Arab Republic, and by the *Gulf Cooperation Council* made up of most of the states of the Arabian peninsula. Only the Sudan, Syria, and Yemen remain independent of a regional power block in the Arab world.

The most powerful regional block is the Egypt-Iraq block. The Saudi block is the richest. But the Libyan block is the most strategically placed since it controls most of the North African Mediterranean coastline, an area vital to European security.

Within the Libyan block the five cooperating states have lifted border restrictions, allowing free movement of its peoples. Feeling threatened economically by the expansion of the European community to include Spain and Portugal, the Arab Maghreb Union envisions the creation of a common market among member states for agricultural products and locally manufactured items. It hopes thus to become more independent of the West for its basic needs. Libya and Algeria have already formed a joint bank, the Arab Maghreb Bank for Investment and Trade. The other member states will be asked to join the venture.

Membership in the Arab Maghreb Union has strengthened Qadaffi's domestic position and given him new credibility in the Arab world. Libya, with the smallest debt and highest income in the union, is its most important member.

There will almost certainly be some ebb and flow in the events connected with Libya. But Ezekiel had no doubts: Libya will join with Russia as an enthusiastic member of an anti-Israel coalition.

The Timing of the Russian Invasion

We have examined the *places* involved in Ezekiel's end-time prophecy; now let us look at the *period* involved.

Note the context of this prophecy. The prophet put it between a discussion (chapter 37) of the physical rebirth of the nation of Israel and a long description (chapters 40-48) of Israel's spiritual rebirth. In other words, Russia's brief day of triumph lies somewhere between those two crucial events. As it happened, the same events that gave birth to the modern state of Israel also gave birth to Russia as a world superpower.

Ezekiel 37 forms the introduction to the two chapters that chronicle the rise and fall of this northern power. In that introduction Ezekiel described his vision of a valley of dry bones. The bones represented the dismembered and scattered nation of Israel, buried in the graves of Gentile nations around the world. In his vision the prophet witnessed a moving of the Spirit of God in bringing the nation of Israel back to life again. Elsewhere we have examined the miraculous twentieth-century rebirth of Israel as a nation. The prophet next described a coalition of various godless nations, united against the newborn Israeli state and headed by "Gog of the land of Magog." Ezekiel then described Israel and the temple in the millennial age. In other words, the prophet deliberately sandwiched Russia's "date with destiny" between Israel's political and spiritual rebirth.

Where we should actually place this prophecy in relation to various other end-time prophecies is not a simple question, as evidenced by the fact that commentators differ widely on the subject. By a process of elimination, however, we can arrive at what seems to be the period when the prophecy comes to fulfillment.

It has been suggested by some that the prophecy will be fulfilled *before the rapture of the church* (1 Thessalonians 4:13-18). This hardly seems likely. The rapture of the church is always presented to us in the New Testament as imminent. In all periods since the apostolic age, believers could reasonably anticipate the rapture happening in their lifetimes. The only exceptions to this general rule were Peter, who knew he was going to die (John 21:18; 2 Peter 1:13-14), and Paul, who also knew (at the time of his second imprisonment) that he was soon to die (2 Timothy 4:6-8). Apart from these two apostles, the coming of Christ for His church is presented in the New Testament as an event that could happen at any moment; but it could not possibly be regarded as imminent if it had to await the events described by Ezekiel.

It has only been in the latter half of the twentieth century that the fulfillment of this prophecy has seemed likely. Also, the prophet expressly stated that his prophecy refers to "the latter years" (Ezekiel 38:8). That expression alone automatically rules out the greater part of the church age. He added that the invasion by Gog and his allies will take place *after* Israel is "brought forth out of the nations." It has only been in recent times that the conditions existed for the prophecy to be fulfilled.

Another fact is that this is essentially an Old Testament prophecy and as such has no direct bearing on the church age, which is a parenthesis in God's dealings with mankind and something wholly unforeseen by Old Testament saints (Ephesians 3:5-10; Romans 16:25-26). Before the church age God's dealings with this earth were concerned solely with Israel and the nations. Once the church age is over, God's dealings with mankind will revert to direct dealings with Israel and the nations. The fact that this is an *Old Testament* rather than a New Testament prophecy points to a time for fulfillment when God is once more dealing with Israel and the nations, which rules out the probability of this prophecy's coming to a head at a time when the church is still on earth.

Some have thought that the prophecy relates to a time *immediately following the rapture*. Ezekiel told us, however, that the invasion will take place when the Jewish people are not only back in their land but when they are dwelling there in safety (Ezekiel 38:10-11). The immediate postrapture years will be a time of upheaval and danger for all mankind (Revelation 6), which makes unlikely the fulfillment of this prophecy during that period.

Similar considerations rule out the suggestion that the invasion might take place in *the middle of the great tribulation*. One could not describe "the time of Jacob's trouble" as a time when the Hebrew people are "at rest," a time when they "dwell safely" (Ezekiel 38:11).

Others have equated the Russian invasion of Israel with the *battle of Armageddon*. There are many reasons why this can not be. The invasion described by Ezekiel comes from the north and involves nations we have already identified as Russia, Persia, Libya, Ethiopia, and certain countries in Europe. The battle of Armageddon involves an invasion from the east, led by "the kings of the east" (Revelation 16:12-16). Israel is at peace and dwelling in security when Ezekiel's battle takes place; she is in the throes of the great tribulation when Armageddon takes place. Ezekiel's battle brings an end to the power of Russia; Armageddon brings an end to all Gentile world power. Russia is overthrown by a series of national and natural disasters precipitated by God; the battle of Armageddon ends with the personal, visible return of Christ with His saints (Revelation 20).

The Russian invasion of Israel is part of the pattern of the endtimes. It takes place in the period of end-time events, but it is not part of the battle of Armageddon. The following chart shows the major differences between the two battles.

Contrasts Between the Russian Invasion of Israel and Armageddon

	Key Events	Ezekiel 38,39 Gog/Magog	Revelation 19:11–21 16:12–16 Armageddon
1	Only certain nations are involved	●	
2	All nations are involved		●
3	Civil war breaks out in ranks of invading army	●	
4	Vultures bury the dead		●
5	The Jews bury the dead	●	
6	The beast and false prophet are taken		●
7	Satan is now imprisoned		●
8	The invasion is from the north	●	
9	The invasion is from the east		●
10	The invasion is stated to be incited by demons		●
11	The war is fought by the returning Christ		●
12	Israel is dwelling in safety	●	
13	The great tribulation is in progress		●
14	Israel has allies	●	

Some have suggested that the Russian invasion of Israel takes place *immediately after the return of Christ* to set up His kingdom. This view creates a host of problems. The beast—the devil's messiah, or antichrist, as he is popularly called—is eventually to rule the whole earth (Revelation 13:7). It is difficult to see how he could do this unless Russia is first removed as a world power; and if Russia is removed as a world power, then it can not exist as a threat to the setting up of the Lord's kingdom at the beginning of the millennial era.

Similarly, Daniel's prophecies and Revelation 17 show the beast reviving the Roman empire at one stage in his rise to world power, but the Roman empire included some of the countries Ezekiel saw as being in the Russian sphere of interest—notably the Balkans and Libya. Obviously both empires can not control the same areas at the same time, and since the future tides all flow toward the beast, then Russia's tide must run out first. If Russia's demise comes while the beast's fortunes are still waxing to their full extent, then obviously Russia can not threaten the fledgling millennial kingdom of Christ.

In any case, Armageddon seems to bring a decisive end to all Gentile world power and is followed at once by the great assize of the nations (Joel 3:1-3; Matthew 25:31-46) and the handing over of world empire to the Jewish people under Christ.

At the end of the millennial reign there is to be a final invasion of the land of Israel and Jerusalem by the foes of Christ (Revelation 20:7-9). Since John used the expression "Gog and Magog" when describing this final assault, some have placed Ezekiel's invasion at *the end of the millennium.* This can not be, however, because the invasion John envisioned ends with the detonation of the planet and the ushering in of eternity. Ezekiel, on the other hand, saw the Jewish people burying the Russian dead, marking out places where corpses have been located, living off the abandoned fuel supplies for seven years (Ezekiel 39:9-14), enjoying a spiritual revival, and then rebuilding their temple (39:29; 40).

Then why did John use the terms "Gog and Magog" when describing this last invasion of Israel, which is to terminate the millennial reign? An illustration will be helpful. In the year 1815 Napoleon escaped from Elba, rallied France behind him, and for the famous "one hundred days" made a final bid for world power. He was met and mastered by the armies of the duke of Wellington at Waterloo. His defeat was so conclusive that the name *Waterloo* passed into the English language as a synonym for a great defeat or disaster. In the same way Russia's overthrow will become a synonym for defeat at the hands of God. Ezekiel hinted that this will be the case (Ezekiel 38:23; 39:7), and it is in this sense that John used the expression "Gog and Magog" in Revelation 20.

When then does this Russian defeat take place? Only one period fits all the facts. When the beast first comes to power in Europe he will quickly unify the West, impose his totalitarian will on the nations under his control, and begin to prepare for world conquest. The major obstacle to his future plans will be a revitalized Russia. A massive war between the beast and Russia would be so mutually destructive as to leave little in the world either to rule or be ruled. Wearing Russia down with incendiary attacks throughout its vast hinterland would take more time than the beast has. How then can he get rid of this massive hindrance to his global plans?

The solution lies in Ezekiel 38 and 39. God has already promised that He Himself will wipe Russia off the map the moment she sends her forces into the land of Israel, and this will be the beast's cue. He will sign a seven-year pact with the nation of Israel in which he unconditionally guarantees Israel's security (Isaiah 28:18), thus bringing about the peaceful and safe conditions envisioned by Ezekiel. The Jewish people will be protected by the western world, headed by the iron-willed beast. Under the umbrella of this pact they will begin to rebuild their temple, which will infuriate the Muslim world.

Russia will seize what seems like the golden opportunity to gain decisive influence over the whole Middle East and step again on stage as a global super power. She will commit all her forces to an invasion of Israel and will meet the doom described by Ezekiel. The invasion, then, takes place *after* the rapture of the church, *after* the rise of the beast in the West, *after* the signing of the pact with Israel, and just *before* the beast takes over the world. Indeed, it is the collapse of Russia that makes his global empire possible.

This sequence fits well with the design for the endtimes in the book of Revelation. In that book it can best be placed at the blowing of the sixth trumpet.[35]

The Build-up

Soviet foreign policy dating from the end of World War II was to maintain the capacity at all times to launch a surprise attack against the NATO forces and reach the English channel before the western powers could bring in reinforcements. The Warsaw Pact and an iron-fisted control of the Eastern European puppet states was an essential part of that policy. The breakup of Moscow's control over Poland, East Germany, Czechoslovakia, and Hungary and the evident weakness of Romania and Bulgaria radically changed Russia's ability to launch a surprise attack on the West. The coup and the subsequent demise of the Soviet Union also changed the picture. Doubtless the Russians will eventually look toward the strategic and oil-rich Middle East as the best sphere for future expansion once the country has its own internal and economic woes under control.

Trying to assess Soviet military strengths and weaknesses as compared with the West has been a complex science. Those interested can consult publications sponsored by the United States Department of Defense, the Goddard Space Institute, and similar sources. The actual statistics change but the ability of Russia to wage war remains a potent factor in global politics. After all there are still some 27,000 nuclear warheads scattered around several of the republics, most of them in Russia itself.

Ever since the days of Stalin, military build-up received the highest priority in Soviet national and foreign policy. Everything was subordinated to the determination of the Kremlin to be able, at any moment, to wage a global war. Science and industry were used first and foremost for military purposes. In addition the Soviets stole vast amounts of high technology from the West.

The Soviets repeatedly demonstrated their willingness to defend themselves and project their power abroad. They did not hesitate to shoot down in cold blood a Korean civilian aircraft that strayed across Soviet borders. They stockpiled weapons in Lebanon and in Grenada, invaded Afghanistan, installed a puppet state in Cuba, and attempted to do the same in Nicaragua. Their adventures had to be curtailed and more carefully masked as a result of economic and ethnic woes within the Soviet Union, but we should not be lulled into thinking that Russia's long-range goals have been greatly changed. They continue to have client states in the Middle East and know how to play a clever waiting game. We must remember Ezekiel's words: "I will bring thee forth, and all thine army, horses and horsemen, all of them clothed with all sorts of armour, even a great company with bucklers and shields, all of them handling swords" (Ezekiel 38:4).

Some have taken this verse to mean that Russia will employ an old-fashioned horse cavalry when she attacks Israel. They see proof in stories about Russia breeding large numbers of horses. They also point out that the terrain over which Russia's armies would have to travel is more suitable for horses than anything else. It has been suggested also that some kind of deathray might be invented which would render modern armor obsolete, or that perhaps the world will run out of oil. Those are all speculations. We must not underestimate man's inventiveness, especially when it comes to war. Alternate energy sources might well be a reality by the time this attack is made, or Russia might have stockpiled enough oil to serve her purposes. Rather than try to turn the clock back hundreds of years, it is more realistic to think in terms of today's world. What Ezekiel pictured is a large, efficient, and highly mobile fighting force pouring into Israel, confident that nothing can stop it. The western world must not allow itself to be lulled into a false sense of security.

The Russian army still has tens of thousands of tanks, armored fighting vehicles, and pieces of artillery, and thousands of helicopters. It has sophisticated electronic systems able to limit, delay, or nullify a potential enemy's command and control systems. It has highly developed chemical warfare techniques and elite forces trained to wage unconventional warfare. The Russians learned the value of this kind of war when their country was invaded by the Germans during World War II; Russian partisans killed, wounded, or took prisoner thousands of German troops and derailed more than eighteen thousand trains. The Russians are not likely to forget another history lesson taught them by the Germans. Germany lost World War II partly because she never gained control of the sea. The Russians, therefore, have transformed their navy from a small coastal-defense force into an oceangoing fleet capable of defying the West.

The Russian navy includes carriers, hundreds of major surface ships, hundreds of submarines (many of them nuclear powered and armed), and a larger assortment of naval vessels than any other navy in the world. All this is supplemented by a merchant fleet numbering thousands of oceangoing vessels.

The navy is supported at sea by hundreds of twin-jet Badger

aircraft equipped with cruise missiles and armed with either heavy explosives or nuclear warheads. It is daily increasing its ability to sustain long-range operations against substantial opposition. Amphibious assault forces made it possible for the Soviet Union to project its power to distant theaters, especially to Third World countries. The West's traditional dominance of the open seas has been challenged. The Soviets learned the prime value of old-fashioned British gunboat diplomacy.

The Soviet Union outstripped the United States in its deployment of missiles and created the ability to destroy more than a thousand United States launchers using only part of its total missile capacity. The Soviet Union's nuclear forces included large numbers of ICBMs (intercontinental ballistic missiles) and nearly as many SLBMs (submarine-launched ballistic missiles). These systems, supported by large numbers of long-range bombers, can deliver thousands of nuclear warheads to enemy targets.

United States intelligence sources have repeatedly warned in the past that if the Russians were to decide that war was inevitable, they would seize the initiative by launching a preemptive strike against its principal foes. Even more ominous has been the fact that in addition to their enormous missile capacity the Russians could reload and refire missiles from many of their launchers after delivering the initial round.

The Russian missile program is backed by an enormous air force. Russia has hundreds of intermediate and long-range strike and support aircraft, and a highly effective Airborne Warning and Control System (AWACS).

Russian military might extends into outer space. The Soviets once had the only operational antisatellite system in the world, and the military has continually worked on improvements. Some have claimed that the Russians are far advanced in laser technology and in the ability to neutralize United States ballistic missiles.

The annual payload the Soviets have put into space in the past has been ten times that of the United States, and at least 70 percent of Russia's space program has had solely military significance. One report is that the Russians have been working on a large space booster supposed to have six to seven times the launch-weight capacity of America's space shuttle.

Every day, Russian Cosmos military satellites fly over the United States, spying on missile sites and naval bases, picking up phone conversations in the nation's capital, and monitoring weather conditions over important targets. Former United States Secretary of Defense Caspar Weinberger claimed the Soviets had been pursuing a space weapons ("Star Wars") program for twenty years and had a working satellite-killer system already operational.

To back up all this active preparation for war, the Soviets put increasing emphasis on science and technology. They have had as many as a million fulltime scientists and engineers working in research and development and they were rapidly decreasing what was once an impressive western lead in basic technology at the time of the coup. The Soviet Union also had the largest raw materials base in the world, with its own deposits of most of the minerals needed by a modern industrial society. Over twenty years ago, the Kremlin grasped the importance of organic materials to a modern society and determined to maintain maximum military preparedness. Since that time, Russia has been expanding its chemical industry and hoarding essential raw materials.

The Kremlin thoroughly understood the extent to which Europe and the United States are dependent on the import of vital strategic materials. The military has been working to deny the free world access to essentials like oil, uranium, bauxite, and copper. The Soviet goal was to isolate the free world from its sources of supply by such means as manipulating markets, dominating producing or neighboring states, weakening western ties with producers, increasing its own military presence in sensitive areas, inflaming differences between allies, undermining western goodwill with friendly countries, and sapping the economic health and political stability of the United States and the countries of Western Europe. How much this will be changed remains to be seen.

The Soviet Union also made full use of its diplomatic corps in all countries where they maintained diplomatic relations. Soviet embassies always were the center of espionage systems, and many of their diplomats were actually spies.

To some extent, Soviet economic woes were a limiting factor in these preparations. A revolutionary departure from the build-up of the postwar years was signaled in February 1986 when the twenty-seventh communist party congress adopted a policy of "sufficient defense." Previously avowed military policy was that an overwhelming offense was the best defense. How much of this was propaganda to deceive the West can be judged by the subsequent continuing military build-up.

Facing economic necessities realistically, Gorbachev announced in December 1988 his decision to cut half a million men from the military and to reduce his arsenal of tanks by ten thousand. He retired all the marshalls of the Soviet Union and announced a 14.2 percent reduction in the defense budget. He also announced a 19.5 percent drop in the production of military hardware and his plan to convert hundreds of defense plants to factories for the production of consumer goods. Some Soviet spokesmen argued that a conscript army is not only obsolete but also too expensive a luxury to be continued. What effect the failed coup will have on all this remains to be seen.

The American and allied military spectacular in Iraq seemed to catch the Soviet military by surprise. The same is true of the Chinese. Neither country could match the high-tech weapons and tactics displayed by the United States and its allies in their lightning war with Iraq. The Russians and the Chinese simply do not have anything to match the stealth fighter-bombers, precision-guided munitions, and electronic systems of the West. Nor will they be able to catch up with the United States in the foreseeable future. Some Soviet generals resorted to bluff and bluster after the Gulf War calling the American success a propaganda stunt. Be that as it may, the entire one-hundred-billion-dollar Soviet radar and missile defense system has been challenged, and will continue to be if the United States pursues its development of "star-wars" techniques in space. "Desert Storm" sent a message to Russia and China—their military doctrine, their hardware, and the structure of their armed forces are out of date.

The Battle

We are not told what Russia will be doing while the antichrist builds up his empire in the West. The country's economic woes may well hamper its ability to oppose it, or it might well be that the Russians will become embroiled in a border war with China, which will force them to divert an increasing amount of men and material to the East. Under the second and fourth seals and the early trumpets of the Apocalypse, global and local wars break out (Revelation 6, 8–9). No details are given as to where and why these wars are fought. Perhaps a Chinese-Russian conflict will erupt during this time. China will play only a minor role in world affairs, it seems, until the time comes for the battle of Armageddon to be fought. A Russian border war with China, followed by a preemptive strike by Russia against China's developing might, could account for this. Russian economic woes and preoccupation with China would give the beast ample time to unite the West. By the time the Russians can again concentrate on their age-long ambitions in the Middle East, they will be confronted by a formidable western alliance already consolidated by a supreme dictator, one who knows what he wants, where he is going, and how to get there.

For one reason or another, according to Ezekiel, the Soviet Union will decide that it must strike Israel to keep the goodwill of the Arabs and to control the Middle East once and for all. That such a move might provoke war with the West will be a calculated risk the Russians will be prepared to take.

Ezekiel told us that Russia will first mobilize its armies as well as those of its allied states (Ezekiel 38:4,7,9,15). He saw "a mighty army" coming "as a cloud" to cover the land (38:15-16).

The divisions of Russia and its allies will roll on until they penetrate Israel. All this long while, God will hold His hand. It will seem that the Russians will have it all their own way.

However, God says that it is *He* who has put the hooks into the jaws of this great atheistic northern power and that it is *He* who draws this nation down into Israel. Ultimately, Russian foreign policy is not to be decided in Moscow at all, but in Heaven. Russia has a Foe who is not intimidated by the size of the Russian army. The time will come when Russia will have to pay for its antisemitism.

The western world will issue a formal protest (Ezekiel 38:13). Tarshish (the allied West), Sheba, and Dedan (nations in the Arabian peninsula), alarmed at this Russian incursion into their part of the world, will demand an explanation. No answer will be given.

Then God will strike. The prophet listed four things that will combine to defeat this final act of Russian aggression. First, there is to be "a great shaking in the land" (Ezekiel 38:19). Israel lies on one of the major earthquake zones of the earth, and earthquakes are to be part of the general picture of disaster in the apocalyptic age to come. This earthquake will do great damage to Russia's land forces as well as seriously impair their lines of communication.

Then the enemies of Russia will mobilize. The prophet reported God's warning: "And I will call for a sword against him throughout all my mountains, saith the Lord God" (Ezekiel 38:21). The western allies, encouraged by the difficulties the Russians will be experiencing because of the earthquake, will move into Israel in support of their client who is a member of the western pact.

We must remember that Russia is still essentially a backward country made up largely of peasants. Despite its military sophistication, it is no match for the West when it comes to technology. In a short time, given the necessary scare, the United States, Europe, and Japan could leave the Russians far behind. Discrimination against Jews has already robbed Russia of a vast reservoir of intellectual power. The multiracial composition of the former Soviet republics (about eighty-five ethnic groups speaking some 130 languages) will always work against any lasting cohesion.

The Russians are well aware of the size and sophistication of the United States intelligence system. A sneak attack against the West, the nightmare of western analysts, probably would not succeed because the wholesale mobilization necessary would alert the West. Moreover it would totally disrupt the Russian economy, farming, and industry.

Quite apart from the West's land-based missile defense, probably not so vulnerable as sometimes portrayed, the United States Navy's nuclear-armed submarines each carry enough warheads to annihilate every Russian city with a population of a million or more.

The growing Russian navy is only a fraction of the size of the total naval might of the West. The USSR marine force is not the world's second largest; it is only the world's fifth largest. Moreover the Russians lack warm-water seaports, as we have already noted.

The Soviet military machine has always been handicapped in other ways. The armed forces have been plagued by crime, drunkenness, racism, discrimination, bullying (based on a caste system in which length of service outweighs rank), mistrust, and hate. In the opinion voiced by one Soviet ranking military man some years ago: "If combat action began, one half of the company might shoot the other." (This is just what Ezekiel said in 38:21.) In addition, a large percentage of the Russian population is so backward as to be ineligible as first-class military material. Moreover a vast gulf exists between officers and men, and mutual mistrust and suspicion has always existed between junior officers and those in the higher echelons.

Russian obsession with secrecy has produced tremendous inhibition in industry, where it has handicapped research and the free sharing of technology. This kind of secrecy has existed in the army also. Maps, for instance, have been traditionally treated as state secrets, ordinary soldiers not being allowed to see them.

Numbers alone do not guarantee success. Many Russian weapons have been poorly designed, inefficient, and subject to frequent breakdowns. They are often handled by men who have little education and no technological sophistication. Moreover, military training is limited in both quantity and quality as compared with the West.

Even if they dared to launch a preemptive strike against American missile silos, the Russians would have no guarantee that they could totally eliminate the West's ability to retaliate. Too many factors are involved. A massive missile strike against the United States would be more the counsel of desperation than an option to be taken in cold blood.

The prophet Ezekiel has already foretold Russia's failure and doom. All the above are factors in an equation that help explain it.

Another reason why Russia's invasion of Israel will fail is that war will break out in the ranks of the invading army itself: "Every man's sword shall be against his brother" (Ezekiel 38:21). The Russian leaders will underestimate the hatred nursed by many ethnic groups against the Russians themselves. Also Russia's allies, though motivated by a common hatred of Israel, will probably have had more than enough of Russian arrogance and dominance. In any case, a long-smoldering revolt will break out and the invaders will turn on each other.

Then God will unloose His arsenals against the invader. He says, "And I will plead against him with pestilence and with blood; and I will rain upon him, and upon his bands, and upon the many people that are with him, and overflowing rain, and great hailstones, fire, and brimstone" (Ezekiel 38:22). Although this may sound like a nuclear holocaust, it may be that God will simply use the forces of nature to overwhelm the Russian army. This would be poetic justice, since for seventy-five years Russia championed the cause of atheism and was in the forefront of every movement directed against God.

Finally, the Russian mainland will be overwhelmed as will be "the isles." It is not certain whether this latter expression refers to

369

coastlands under Russian control or to the coastlands of the western world. In any case, God says, "And I will send a fire on Magog, and among them that dwell carelessly in the isles" (39:6). The Russian heartland will be visited with such devastation as the world has never seen.

The overthrow of the invaders will be so complete that five-sixths of the invasion force will be wiped out (Ezekiel 39:2). Moreover, it will take the Jews seven months to bury the dead. Indeed, cleansing the land of the rotting corpses will be a fulltime job for men specially assigned to the task (39:12-15). The Jewish people will be able to use the abandoned fuel supplies from this invasion force for seven years (39:9-10), and the abandoned war equipment will supply them with natural resources for a similar period.

Finally, so astounding and so complete will be the collapse of Russia that people will be forced to acknowledge God's hand in the whole affair (Ezekiel 38:23; 39:21-23).

What should be our attitude to this? It is natural for us to heave a sigh of relief as we realize that God Himself intends to annihilate the Russian military machine and desolate the Russian mainland. Most of us are like Jonah when he learned of the impending overthrow of godless and ruthless Nineveh. That seemed to Jonah to be the best of news, something to be anticipated with satisfaction, with a sense of relief, and with an outburst of national pride (Jonah 3:10–4:1).

But how unlike the attitude of Jesus our reaction is! As He gazed on Jerusalem, a city soon to be the scene of His murder, and foresaw its coming destruction at the hands of the Romans, He grieved (Matthew 23:37-38). Jerusalem had a cross for Him, but He could see the day when the Romans would crucify the people of Jerusalem by the countless hundreds. It broke His heart.

As we today think of all the peoples who make up Russia, and as we think of what that nation has in store, surely we should weep. And we should pray that the Lord of the harvest might be pleased to visit that land with a spiritual awakening before the darkness finally descends.

The rapid and astonishing changes have taught us to be more cautious about trying to predict events. There may well be more surprises ahead. However, the Bible prophecies stand unchanged and will all be literally fulfilled when God's time comes.

1. Walter Scott, *The Prophetic News and Israel's Watch*, June 1888. Cited by Smith, pp. 288-289.
2. H. L. Ellison, *Ezekiel: The Man and His Message* (Exeter: Paternoster Press, 1967), p. 134.
3. Robert Jamieson, A. P. Fausset, and David Brown, *Commentary Critical and Explanatory on the Whole Bible*, one vol. ed., (Grand Rapids: Zondervan, n.d.), p. 611.
4. Flavius Josephus, *Antiquities of the Jews* in *The Life and Works of Flavius Josephus*, trans. William Whiston (Philadelphia: Josh. C. Winston Co., n.d.), p. 40.
5. E. H. Plumptre and T. Whitlaw, *Ezekiel*, vol. 12 of *The Pulpit Commentary*, H. D. M. Spence and Joseph S. Exell, eds., 23 vols. (Grand Rapids: Eerdmans, 1950), pp. 284-285.
6. J. F. McCurdy, "Gog and Magog," *the New Schaff-Herzog Encyclopedia of Religious Knowledge*, C. C. Shermon, ed. vol. 5 (Grand Rapids: Baker, 1977), p. 14.
7. William Kelly, *Notes on Ezekiel* (London: Geo. Morrish Co., 1876), pp. 191-193.
8. S. P. Tregelles, *Gesenius' Hebrew and Chaldee Lexicon* (Grand Rapids: Eerdmans, 1957), p. 752.
9. L. Sale-Harrison, *The Coming Great Northern Confederacy* (Wheaton, IL: Van Kampen Press, 1933), pp. 19-20.
10. See *The Pulpit Commentary*, p. 285.
11. *World Book Encyclopedia*, s.v. "Cimmerian."
12. *Encyclopedia Britannica,* 1967 ed., vol. 5, p. 773.
13. Harry Rimmer, *Shadow of Coming Events* (Grand Rapids: Eerdmans, 1950), pp. 108-110.
14. Arno C. Gaebelein, *The Prophet Ezekiel* (Neptune, NJ: Loizeaux, 1972), p. 259.
15. "Genesis," *The Pulpit Commentary*, vol. 1, pp. 156-157.
16. Henry M. Morris, *The Genesis Record,* (Grand Rapids: Baker, 1976), p. 247.
17. Rimmer, pp. 110-111.
18. Morris, p. 247.
19. See J. Dwight Pentecost, *Prophecy Today* (Grand Rapids: Zondervan, 1961), p. 108. Pentecost thought it unlikely that Moses married an African (Numbers 12:1), identified the woman criticized by Aaron and Miriam with Zipporah, and concluded that she was a Semitic Ethiopian. If Numbers 12:1 does refer to Zipporah, one wonders why Aaron and Miriam took so long to voice their criticism. They must have met her a considerable time before, probably when Jethro brought her and her two sons to Moses at Horeb (Exodus 18:1-5). Why should they wait until they were well on their way to Kadesh-barnea before

criticizing Moses for marrying an Ethiopian? It could well be that the woman they criticized was a second wife of Moses. African Ethiopia is only a few miles by sea from the southeastern rim of the Arabian peninsula.

20. Merrill F. Unger, *Unger's Bible Dictionary* (Chicago: Moody Press, 1957), p. 327.

21. Ibid., p. 660.

22. Ibid., pp. 941-942, 1006.

23. Barry Fell, "America B.C.," *Reader's Digest* (February 1977).

24. *The Daily Mail* (February 1, 1924).

25. The London *Times* (December 24, 1924).

26. "I Am an Optimist," *Time* (June 4, 1990).

27. *Time* (September 16, 1991).

28. *Time* (March 12, 1922), p. 35.

29. Helene Carrere d'Encausse, *Decline of an Empire,* trans. Martin Sokolinsky and Henry A. LaFarge (New York: Newsweek Books, 1979), pp. 47-90.

30. *Time* (April 29, 1991).

31. It embraced fifteen million rank and file members. It supervised everything from kindergarten to nuclear rocket forces. It controlled all promotions in politics, industry, the army, and education. It owned 5,254 administration buildings, 3,583 newspapers, and assets valued at 4.5 billion rubles.

32. *Time* (March 12, 1990).

33. *Intelligence Digest* (May 1953).

34. *Insight* (April 15, 1991).

35. See chapter 4; also Phillips, *Exploring Revelation,* pp. 139-144.

17

Drawing in the Threads

During the long hours my wife and I spend in a car driving from city to city, she likes to crochet afghans. From time to time I look to see how she's getting along. It never ceases to amaze me—the sight of those long strands of yarn, often of many different colors, passing under her dexterous needle and emerging in patterns and designs, all according to plan. Sometimes the patterns and colors repeat themselves, and there are always loose ends. After using a color for a while, she will snip off the thread to take up another, leaving a length of the previous thread dangling from her work. When she has finished the whole, however, she will go back and carefully weave in all those loose ends.

That is what we are going to do in this chapter. In pursuing our study through the prophetic Scriptures, we have noticed that the same patterns keep coming up. Prophetic truth has tended to repeat itself. Part of God's plan is to confirm what He has to say by using the testimony of two or three witnesses. In our study, we have left loose ends here and there as a strand of Scripture has been introduced and then dropped. Now we must try to weave in those loose ends and show the finished picture of prophetic truth as best we can at this point in time.

We shall look at four general themes for a glimpse of the overall pattern of prophetic truth.

1. THE RAPTURE OF THE CHURCH

The church is a latecomer in God's historical dealings with mankind. For the first several thousand years following creation, God dealt with mankind in general, with what we now call "the Gentiles." From the time of Abraham and for the next two thousand years, He concentrated on the Hebrew or Jewish people. For the last two thousand years He has been speaking to mankind through the church. Outwardly the church age has been marked by opposition, failure, and limitation. Despite it all, however, God has been pursuing His sovereign purpose and has been gathering out of the nations a people for His name.

The New Testament teaches us to look for widespread apostasy toward the end of the church age and to expect a massive turning away from Christian faith. Jesus Himself taught that the last days would witness the coming of false messiahs and false prophets, that deceptions would increase, and that it would be hard to find faith on the earth. Paul predicted, too, that people would become selfish, materialistic, addicted to pleasure, and given over to treachery, violence, and lawless behavior. Occultism, he said, would creep back on stage from the distant wings to which it had long been banished by a virile Christianity. Matthew 24 and Revelation 6 also tell us to look for a marked increase in the occurrence and extent of war and for increasing proliferation of disease, disaster, persecution, vice, and violence. The world is to take on the features that marked the days of Enoch, Noah, and Lot.

These coming events have begun to cast their shadows on the days in which we live. Some believers hopefully look for revival. Yet although we acknowledge the absolute sovereignty of the Holy Spirit, His persistent and age-long activity in resisting the coming of the antichrist, and His faithfulness in bringing people to a saving knowledge of Christ, there are no signs of genuine worldwide revival. Instead, every sign points to the rapture as the hope of the church in this age.

The rapture is the next item on God's prophetic program. The true church is going home! The Lord is to step into the sky, the dead in Christ are to rise, and the living saints on earth are to be caught up with them to meet the Lord in the air. Then will follow the judgment seat of Christ so that we may all receive rebuke and reward and have our lives reviewed in the light of the coming kingdom.

Dead Christendom will be left behind. Organized systems of religion professing to be Christian, but Christian only in name and claim, will be left behind for judgment. This truth is taught repeatedly in the New Testament. It is illustrated in the mystery parables and in the picture we have in Revelation 17 of the scarlet woman, as well as in what the Lord says to the church at Laodicea in Revelation 3.

There is to be a great ecumenical movement in the last days, a drawing together of the denominations of Christendom, and even of the cults and false religious systems. The movement has already begun, and it will gather momentum and force after the rapture. Many denominations have united in the World Council of Churches, a thoroughly liberal and leftist organization. After the removal of the true church, there will be a general move of the emasculated churches toward Rome. Throughout the world the various cults and religions will draw toward a common center. They will see in the antichrist the messiah they have long expected to appear.

2. THE REBIRTH OF ISRAEL

Woven into many an Old Testament prophecy is the insistent theme that Israel as a nation is to be reborn in the last days and the scattered Jewish people are to be gathered back to their ancestral home. Jesus foretold that the Jewish nation would be reconstituted in the last days in unbelief. What the prophets foretold has happened. The prophetic clock, stopped for centuries, has been rewound and is ticking again. Soon it will start chiming out the closing hours of man's unregenerate day upon earth.

Old dying Jacob caught glimpses of the scattering and regathering of his people. The Gentile prophet Balaam foretold it, as well as the glories to follow. The Hebrew writing prophets repeatedly turned to the theme.

The Jews have defied thousands of years of persecution, endemic and epidemic antisemitism, bloodbaths, and holocausts. They have defied, too, the trend toward assimilation and absorption into other nations. They have retained their racial purity, outlived the nations that persecuted them, and returned in our times to the land of their fathers.

Two kinds of Jews have been repatriated by the newborn state of Israel. From the lands of the West have come the enlightened, educated, sophisticated Jews—the lawyers, the doctors, the professors, the industrialists. From the lands of the East have come the deeply religious, orthodox Jews, passionately devoted to building Zion into an exclusive religious state. Both kinds will see a promised messiah in the antichrist. Secular Jews will hail him because he will offer them a peace treaty that will guarantee their frontiers against attack. Religious Jews will embrace him because he will permit them to rebuild their temple under his protection.

Many times in the past people have thought that the return of Christ was at hand. When the Christian era reached its one thousandth year, many thought that Christ must appear. When Islam swept like a raging fury across the Middle East, Africa, and Europe, it seemed that the end was at hand. When the French revolution steeped a nation in blood and then elevated a military genius by the name of Napoleon, it seemed again as though the final actors had taken the stage. In more recent times, when Mussolini tried to reconstitute the Roman empire, many thought he was the antichrist. But no matter what configuration of world events seemed to come together in times past, one vital factor was always missing. Israel had not been reborn as a nation. Now it has been. That is the difference between the shadows of the past and the substance of today. The fact that Israel is back in the land adds a new urgency to our conviction; end-time events *can* now take their ultimate shape.

3. THE REALIGNMENT OF THE NATIONS

The major realignment of nations since World War II also points in the direction of things to come. The British empire, which once embraced a quarter of the world, is gone. The French empire is gone. Scores of new nations have emerged, have been enrolled in the United Nations, and have gravitated together as members of the so-called Third World. Russia came on stage with its satellites as the leader of a global conspiracy determined to enthrone atheism in men's hearts and communism on the world's throne. It felt its way into the Middle East and planned for an eventual assault on Israel. The European nations have made their first moves toward a federal government, reviving speculation that the Roman empire is about to re-form. These are all shadows of coming events.

After the rapture of the church things will move more rapidly. The breaking of the seals, the removal of restraint, and the stepping aside, as it were, of the Holy Spirit will result in global upheavals that will cause men to long for some superman able to take the reins and bring order out of chaos. He will suddenly be unveiled. He may already be here on earth, unknown and unrecognized, waiting for his cue to take the leading role in the drama of the endtimes. He will arise, in all probability, out of one of the nations that once comprised the old Roman empire, probably from Italy itself. Rome will be his capital and he will be in league with the heads of ten European nations, three of whom he will overthrow on his way to supreme power.

The religious system at Rome will ally itself with the antichrist in hopes, no doubt, of regaining its waning influence in the world through him. He will use this system until he is firmly in control of the West. Then he will cynically turn on it and hand it over to his allies to be dismembered and plundered.

Once firmly in control of the West, with its enormous economic, industrial, and military potential, he will sign a defense pact with Israel, under the umbrella of which the Jews will rebuild their temple. The infuriated Muslim world will doubtless look to Russia for help; and the Russians will be trapped in an all-out attack on Israel which, of course, will involve risking a war with the West. Russia will be spectacularly overthrown overnight. Its demise will enable the antichrist to take over all Russia's former spheres of interest and force the rest of the world into his now global empire. It will then be Israel's turn to be attacked by the antichrist, and the nation's hour of greatest peril will have arrived.

At some point during this series of events the beast, or antichrist, will be killed and brought back to life as "the beast that ascendeth out of the bottomless pit" (Revelation 11:7). His resurrection will so awe the world that it will be easy for him to claim worship for himself. He will seize the rebuilt Jewish temple in Jerusalem; his associate, the false prophet, will set up an image to the beast in that temple. A new form of universal caesar-worship having been announced, the false prophet will force compliance by making it mandatory for everyone on earth to be branded with the beast's mark. To refuse will single one out as a traitor, and will bring isolation from the rest of mankind by a totally enforced economic boycott. Then will begin a time of persecution unparalleled in history. It is spoken of in Scripture as the great tribulation; and it will be aimed not only at those who have refused the beast's mark, but at the Jewish people in particular.

God's judgments will then be poured out on the power structure of the beast, greatly weakening his hold on his empire. The eastern nations will break away in revolt and will mobilize against him, marching back across the Euphrates to meet him at Megiddo. Then will begin those maneuverings mentioned by Daniel and by Balaam as heralding the approaching end. The antichrist will lash out at his enemies, those who have rebelled against him in the Middle East, and will rush to Megiddo to confront his rivals from the East.

4. The Return of Christ

At this juncture in world affairs the plight of the Jew will be desperate. Many will already have been massacred, along with all those who have heard and believed the gospel of the kingdom so faithfully preached by the 144,000 witnesses. As events move rapidly to the close, the Lord's sign will be blazoned in the sky. The nations drawn up at Megiddo will conclude a hasty armistice and will join forces to repel the invasion from outer space led by the returning Son of God. They will be deluded by Satan into believing they can actually fight against Christ and win. One word from the Lord, however, and earth's massed armies will be swept into oblivion.

The Lord's feet will touch the mount of Olives, which will instantly split asunder. Satan will be seized and incarcerated in the abyss, and the beast and false prophet will be thrown alive into the lake of fire. The surviving peoples of the earth will be summoned to the valley of Jehoshaphat, just outside Jerusalem, for judgment. The Lord will divide believer from unbeliever as easily as a shepherd divides his sheep from his goats. The condemned will follow the beast and the false prophet into a lost eternity, and a small remnant of Jews and Gentiles will enter into the millennial kingdom.

Scores of Old Testament prophecies that foretell the future grandeur of Israel will then be fulfilled. The saints of the church age will reign with Christ from the heavenlies, and the Jewish people will become the earthly administrators of the millennial kingdom. Jerusalem will become the world's capital, a new temple will be built, and annual pilgrimages will be made to the Holy Land so that the presence of the Lord on earth may be a living reality to all. The knowledge of God will inundate the earth as the waters now cover the sea. Peace and prosperity will be universal, and Edenic conditions will prevail everywhere under the benevolent but firm monarchy of Jesus.

As time wears on and as thousands of people are born, voices of protest will begin to whisper against the rule of Christ. More and more people will be born who will refuse the opportunity to be born again. These unregenerate ones will resent the iron rule of Christ, the government of mankind according to the principles of the sermon on the mount, and the swift and certain punishment of evildoers. These people will be ready fuel for Satan's fires when, at the end of the thousand-year reign of Christ, he is released to test the nations for the last time. Millions will flock to his standard, mobilize against Christ, and march on Jerusalem.

At this point the eruption foretold by Peter will take place. The Bible does not explain how believers living on earth will be preserved at this final dissolution of the planet in a nuclear holocaust. Presumably they will be transferred to the heavenly Jerusalem and removed into an eternal dimension away from it all. The earth and the entire universe with all its countless galaxies will explode in a fiery conflagration. Time will be no more.

The wicked dead will be summoned from their graves, will be made to stand before God in all His blazing holiness, and will face eternal retribution for their sins. The dread destiny in the lake of fire is the subject of many a solemn warning in the Word of God.

The Lord will then create a new heaven and a new earth and the eternal state will begin, an eternity of anguish and remorse for the unregenerate and of endless bliss for the redeemed. With such a prospect of Heaven or Hell so clearly foretold in the Scriptures, and with so many evidences before us that the Bible is dependable as a book that foretells the future, surely it makes good sense to have one's name written in the Lamb's book of life.

"For God so loved the world, that he gave his only begotten Son, that whosoever believeth in him should not perish, but have everlasting life" (John 3:16).

18

Personal Destiny

David Nelson was a physician who was an infidel for many years. After his conversion to Christ he wrote a book entitled *The Cause and Cure of Infidelity* in which he devoted several chapters to one of the major considerations that eventually led him to Christ—his observations at the deathbeds of his patients. He first became interested in death scenes while attending lectures in Philadelphia:

> I heard from the lady with whom I boarded an account of certain individuals who were dead, to all appearance, during the prevalence of the yellow fever in that city, and yet recovered. The fact that they saw, or fancied they saw, things in the world of spirits, awakened my curiosity.

He pondered the stories and discounted them on medical grounds, but his curiosity remained when it became his business year after year to watch people die. His observations, extending over twenty years, led him to some interesting conclusions. One

case he recorded was that of a woman dying from uterine hemor-
rhage.

> When recovered from the first condition of syncope, she
> appeared as unconscious, or as destitute of activity of spirit,
> as others usually do. She sunk again and revived; it was still
> the same. She fainted more profoundly still; and, when awake
> again, she appeared as others usually do who have no thoughts
> which they can recall. At length, she appeared entirely gone.
> It seemed as though the struggle was forever past . . . but,
> unexpectedly, she awakened once more and, glancing her
> eyes on one who sat near, exclaimed, "Oh, Sarah, I was at an
> entirely new place!" and then sunk to remain insensible to this
> world.

Dr. Nelson wondered why this woman, like others he had
observed, had no thoughts she could recall when simply fainting.
He said, "Why her greatest activity of mind appeared to happen
during her nearest approach to the future world, while so near that
stage from which scarcely any return who once reach it, seemed
perplexing to me." He recalled the experience of the apostle Paul,
who said he was so near death that he could not tell whether he was
out of the body or not; but in that condition he was given an
indescribable vision.

Dr. Nelson described other experiences. There was a woman
richly endowed with spiritual grace. "It was after some kind of
spasm," wrote the doctor, "that was strong enough to have been
the death struggle, that she said in a whisper, being unable to speak
aloud, to her young pastor, 'I have had a sight of home, and I saw
my Savior!'" But there were others who, after wading as far as what
seemed to be the middle of the river of death, returned thinking
they had seen a totally different world. They had been given a
foreglimpse of Hell.

The doctor was continually surprised to find that the condition
of mind of those who only *thought* themselves dying differed very
widely from those who actually were dying.

> I had supposed that the joy or the grief of death originated
> from the fancy of the patient, one supposing himself very near
> to great happiness, and the other expecting speedy suffering.

My discoveries seemed to overturn this theory. . . . During twenty years of observation, I found the state of soul belonging to the dying was uniformly and materially unlike those who only *supposed* themselves departing.

There was a man who believed himself converted, and his friends, judging from his walk, hoped with him. He was seized with disease and believed himself within a few paces of the gate of the future. He felt no joy, his mind was dark, and his soul clouded. His exercises were painful, and the opposite of every enjoyment. He was not dying. He recovered. He had not been in the deathstream. After this he was taken again. He believed himself dying, and he was not mistaken. All was peace, serenity, hope, triumph.

There was a man who mocked at holy things. He became seriously diseased, and supposed himself sinking into the death-slumber. He was not frightened. His fortitude and composure were his pride, and the boast of his friends. . . . It was a mistake. He was not in the condition of dissolution. His soul never had been on the line between two worlds. After this he was taken ill again. He supposed as before that he was entering the next state, and he really was; but his soul seemed to feel a different atmosphere. The horrors of these scenes have often been described, and are often seen. I need not endeavor to picture such a departure here.

What impressed the doctor most, exerting a powerful influence on his mind and turning him away from unbelief, was that the things seen and heard at death by the servants of this world differed so singularly from the things seen and heard by departing Christians.[1]

The Bible explains the difference. Those who die trusting Christ as their Savior prove the reality of Paul's words, "To me to live is Christ, and to die is gain" (Philippians 1:21). When death finally comes, they are "absent from the body," and are "present with the Lord" (2 Corinthians 5:8). Those who die without Christ learn that "there remaineth no more sacrifice for sins, But a certain fearful looking for of judgment and fiery indignation" (Hebrews 10:26-27).

In this chapter we are going to examine what the Bible has to say about our personal and eternal future. We are more concerned with divine revelation than with human speculation, which is practically worthless. We can not be much impressed by the atheist who says that death ends everything, when Voltaire, one of the most renowned atheists, died with such shrieks and blasphemies on his lips that his nurses fled from his room. Voltaire knew perfectly well, at the last, that death did not end everything. The reason we do not have such horrifying deathbed scenes these days is that most people die under heavy sedation.

We can not be much impressed, either, with Hinduism's theories of reincarnation. "Death," says the Hindu, "is but an incident on the road to other births." Time is a revolving cycle. A good life leads to a better one at reincarnation, and a bad life results in rebirth at a lower order. Such doctrines stand condemned by their fruits: caste systems that excuse social injustice and stifle change; asceticism that seeks oblivion to sensation and withdraws from the real world; superstition that forbids feeding a nation's hungry millions with meat, forbids the killing of even a disease-carrying fly, and which allows rats and vermin to multiply because such creatures might be one's ancestors working out their destiny in the endless cycle of time.

Nor can we be much impressed by the Christian Science answer that "death is an illusion." Mary Baker Eddy, founder of the movement, wrote, "Man is incapable of sin, sickness, and death." Then senile decay overtook her, and she herself fell a victim to this "illusion," died, and was buried in Mount Auburn Cemetery in Cambridge, Massachusetts.

The Bible is the only book that speaks with authority about future events. Jesus, the Son of God, believed in both Heaven and Hell; His teaching about these places is sprinkled throughout the Gospels. It surprises some people to learn that Jesus spoke more about Hell than He did about Heaven. The four Gospels show He referred to the destiny of the damned nearly twice as often as He did to the destiny of the blessed.

The most complete record of His public teaching is found in Matthew's Gospel. In that Gospel, for every verse in which Jesus mentions the destiny of the blessed there are three verses in which He mentions the destiny of the damned.

See Appendix for references in the Gospels to Christ's teaching regarding Heaven, Hell, and related themes.

Because Jesus was God incarnate, He can speak with absolute

authority on the afterlife. If anyone should know what lies beyond the grave, He should.

THE GREAT WHITE THRONE (REVELATION 20:11-15)

Joseph Stalin ruled the Soviet Union for twenty-five terror-filled years. Genghis Khan and Ivan the Terrible were novices compared with Stalin. He was probably the greatest tyrant the world has ever seen. He exterminated more people in wars, and planned more famines, purges, mass deportations, and campaigns of terror than any other despot who ever lived. He was anti-western, anti-European, and anti-Semitic.

It is estimated that Stalin killed ten million peasants in his drive to collectivize the farms of Russia. An additional ten million Ukrainians vanished; another five million died of famine. Stalin's secret police shot and hanged whole villages. Millions were forced into slave-labor camps to build roads and canals, cut down forests, open mines, and gather harvests.

Stalin killed at least a million members of his own communist party and purged the leading generals and thirty thousand officers from the leadership of the Russian army. All Red Army officers who had gained experience in the Spanish civil war were brought home and shot.

Stalin banished his wife's sister to a concentration camp for writing her memoirs. During and after World War II he supervised the disappearance of some three million Jews in Russia, the Baltic states, and Soviet-controlled Poland. At the time of his death he was planning the systematic extermination of every Jew in the Soviet Union.

And he died in bed. He died with difficulty, it is true, slowly suffocating; but even if he had been tortured for a hundred years, mankind's sense of outrage at the wickedness of this man's life would not have been satisfied. There is no way we can calculate the aggregate of human suffering and misery he caused. Our instinct for what is right and wrong cries out for his punishment. Christian charity, it is true, hopes for his forgiveness; but for that he never asked. The conscience of the race demands that there must be a time and a place where men like him are brought to justice. There has to be a Hell. Even if the Bible did not reveal the existence of such a place, we would have to invent one.

Or take the case of Sally, who was just fourteen, with her whole life before her, when this incident took place. Her parents were missionaries to Latin America, home on furlough. Sally was almost a stranger to the United States. She had just entered junior high and had been in school here only a few days. Then something went wrong with her. She was confined to her bed where she lay screaming, perspiration soaking her body, her small frame twisting and contorting in agony, and her eyes rolling. Her neck jerked with such violence that her mother seemed to feel the terrible pain. Sally was rushed to the hospital where she fell into an incoherent state for four days, her body writhing constantly. She babbled nonsense by the yard: "I'm Noah's ark!" "I'm Jesus!" "I'm an atomic bomb!" She had to be locked up. Then the doctors diagnosed the trouble. Sally was experiencing the worst kind of withdrawal from a terrible trip. Someone at school had slipped LSD into her soft drink.

Unless the young criminal confesses, nobody will ever know who did it. He or she has merged into the anonymous background of the dope-taking crowd. But God knows who did it; and as sure as He is holy, just, and good, if that young person does not repent and seek the forgiveness that only Christ can give, there is a day of reckoning ahead at the great white throne.

Two thousand years ago God's own beloved Son, the Creator of the universe, stepped out of eternity into time and was incarnated at Bethlehem. He came to offer men salvation from sin, abundant life, and a place in the family of God. He went about doing good. His life proved He was all He claimed to be, God manifest in the flesh. But the people turned against Him, gave Him a mock trial, scourged His flesh, crowned Him with thorns, spiked Him to a cross, and gathered around to mock Him while He died.

For two thousand years, God in matchless love has been holding back His wrath and offering men peace through the blood of that cross. He has been offering forgiveness and eternal life to all who will repent and believe in His Son. The majority could not care less.

Eventually the day of God's patience will be replaced by the day of His wrath. The lost of all ages will be summoned to the great white throne to face judgment at the hands of His Son, the One they despised and rejected. We are now going to focus on that coming great assize, the facts of which are outlined in Revelation 20.

I. The Setting (Revelation 20:11-12)
  A. The background
    1. A terrible fact
    2. A terrible figure
    3. A terrible fear
    4. A terrible fellowship
  B. The books
II. The Summons (Revelation 20:13)
III. The Sentence (Revelation 20:14-15)

John said: "And I saw a great white throne, and him that sat on it, from whose face the earth and the heaven fled away; and there was found no place for them. And I saw the dead, small and great, stand before God; and the books were opened" (Revelation 20:11-12). This scene is set in eternity.

In the background there is *a terrible fact,* a great white throne of awesome majesty. It is ablaze with light—pure, holy, dreadful. The whiteness of that throne symbolizes the holiness of a God before whose presence even the sinless sons of light seek a hiding place. They take shelter behind their wings and cry, "Holy, holy, holy" (Isaiah 6:1-3).

There will be no hiding place, however, for guilty human beings summoned to stand before that throne. Forth from their tombs they will come, naked bodies reunited with naked souls, people face to face at last with the day of judgment. Their sophistries and bravado will be gone. We have heard them say a thousand times: "There is no God." "Death ends everything." "There is no judgment." "Sin is an error of mortal mind." "God is too loving to judge people." "There is no Hell." Those false philosophies end at the tomb. The blusterings of Voltaire, the God-hate of Karl Marx, the indifference of millions—all vanish in a flash before the terrible fact of that great white throne.

Then too there is *a terrible figure.* Men will recognize instantly the One who sits on that throne, even though they have never seen Him before. They will know Him by the nail prints in His hands, by the marks of Calvary in His feet, by the gaping wound in His side. He who is to sit on that throne bears the marks of man's brutality, the legacy of hammer and nail, spear and lash, and crown of thorns still printed in His flesh.

Once He lived on earth and was the kindest, most approachable of men. Women came to Him with their woes and brought their little ones for Him to bless. Strong men left their business to follow Him through torture and torment. He loved all people, healed their sick, raised their dead, and fed them by the thousands at picnics by the sea. He taught us a new name for God. God had been known as Jehovah, Adonai, Elohim, and El Shaddai. Jesus taught us that God is a Father, His Father, wanting to become our Father too. But all that will be over when the day of grace is past and the day of judgment has come.

The figure will awaken memories from the past. Some will say, "I used His name as a curse word." Others will say, "I heard about Him at mother's knee and in Sunday school, but I left Him out of my life." "I sold Him for a godless marriage" or "for a few short years of sin." "I never gave Him the time of day, never seriously considered His claims. I yawned in His face and wrote Him off as a myth." But there He will sit—real, solid, living, omniscient, terrible to behold, with eyes that flash like a flame of fire and burn into the consciences of men.

There is also *a terrible fear.* The sight of His face will evoke that fear. For the believer, the sight of that face will be the beginning of Heaven, but for the unbeliever it will be the foretaste of Hell. Heaven and earth have fled from that face, dissolved in an instant into primeval atoms and violent heat.

The lost of all ages will look at that face. Men spat on it once; they punched it and tore its beard out by the roots. He whose face they marred will be their judge. His face will haunt them forever.

Nothing familiar will remain in which the lost can take comfort. The earth with its rivers, seas, and shores will be gone. No clouds, no sun, and no stars will be left—just an appalling emptiness, a throne of dazzling white, a figure, a face, and a cramping fear. Again and again the Bible warns us to fear Him. "The fear of the Lord is the beginning of wisdom" (Psalm 111:10). Too late the lost will stand in fear of Him, with no place to hide.

There is also *a terrible fellowship.* "The dead, small and great, stand before God" (Revelation 20:12). Dead souls and dead bodies, the living dead, the dead newly arrived from the tomb, will stand before God's judgment throne. Petty men and women will be there—people whose lives were filled with nasty little sins, with snappishness, selfishness, mean thoughts, sordid acts; people who never amounted to anything; people whose sins were drab, dowdy, groveling, and vulgar. The great will be there—people who sinned with a high hand, with dash and courage; people who went in for wickedness on a grand scale; people who lived flagrantly and with arrogant flourish—dead now and on the way to being damned.

That is the background. The Holy Spirit sketches it in with broad, general strokes of the pen.

Then, too, there are the *books*. God is a great bookkeeper. He writes everywhere, on everything. He writes all the time.

Take, for instance, a tree. A fallen giant of the forest carries the record of its life in the fibers of its being. Its rings tell a skilled woodsman how old it is, how it was nourished by the soil, the way the prevailing winds have blown, which years were too dry, and which years were blessed by abundance of rain. It is all written down by a voluminous writer.

Take an old bone to an anthropologist. He measures it, weighs it, and tells you its history: the age, weight, sex, and health of the person to whom it once belonged. It is all written down.

Psychologists tell us that everything we have said or thought, felt or imagined, done or desired, is written into the mysterious codes of the subconscious mind. All that is needed is for the right stimulus to bring it back. God keeps books, and He keeps them for the day of judgment.

One book that God keeps is the record of each man's works: "The dead were judged out of those things which were written in the books, according to their works" (Revelation 20:12). In the Bible, salvation is according to *faith* and judgment is according to *works*. God, who knows our works, assesses even our "righteousness as filthy rags" (Isaiah 64:6). If that is what God thinks of our righteousness, our noblest aspirations, our best efforts, our most generous impulses, whatever does He think of our sins?

The common plea is "I'm doing the best I can." But nobody has ever done his best. Where is the donation that could not have been larger? The sacrifice that could not have been greater? The neighborly deed that might not have been repeated oftener? Those who claim they are doing their best are condemned by their own religion. The standard to which people will be compared is not some accommodating human standard, but the absolute standard of the sermon on the mount as exemplified in the perfect life of Christ.

That is why God offers us the choice between a fair trial and a free pardon. Those who elect a fair trial are condemned already, because nobody can produce the kind of life that God's infinite holiness demands. The only course is to plead guilty and accept the free pardon that is offered in Christ.

At the great white throne the records all people have kept of their lives will be opened with terrible consequences for them. If we could sit for a few minutes in the presence of God and read our own records, we would come under such conviction of sin that we would hurry to be saved. The book that will be opened at the great white throne is the accusing documentary of our thoughts, words, and deeds recorded in our souls and confirmed by a quickened memory.

But there is another book, "the book of life" (Revelation 20:12), and into that book God writes the names of those who put their faith and trust in Christ.

When Richard Nixon was president of the United States, he kept a taped record of conversations and transactions that took place in the oval office. If he had taken a magnet and passed it over those tapes, he might have served out his full term as president. However, he could never quite bring himself to do that; so, at last, the damning record became public: his secret conversations, cursing, lying, and duplicity. It ruined him as a politician.

The record each of us is keeping is far more thorough than the Nixon tapes. It is the record of thoughts and aspirations, secret lusts, vile imaginations, as well as things actually said and done. God will tap those records at the great white throne. People desperately need to come to Christ and have their records expunged. God has promised that by coming to Christ we can have our records blotted out once and for all. "Their sins and their iniquities will I remember no more" (Hebrews 8:12). "The blood of Jesus Christ his son cleanses us from all sin" (1 John 1:7). Those who come to Him for cleansing and forgiveness find "he is faithful and just to forgive us our sins, and to cleanse us from all unrighteousness" (1 John 1:9). The damning records against our souls are erased. Our names are written in the Lamb's book of life, and all whose names are written in that glorious book will never be summoned to this last assize. The great white throne judgment is convened only for the wicked dead, for those who die in their sins, unrepentant, unforgiven, unsaved, and lost.

Scripture tells not only of the setting, but also of the summons:

"And the sea gave up the dead which were in it; and death and hell delivered up the dead which were in them: and they were judged every man according to their works" (Revelation 20:13). There will be no place to hide.

The Bible begins with God asking two questions. He asked, "Where art thou?" (Genesis 3:9) and Adam and Eve came forth from behind the trees arrayed in the damning fig leaves with which they tried to cover their sin. God is going to ask that question again—"Where art thou?"—and the dead will come from the depths of the sea, from the dust of the earth, from the remotest plains and poles. The dust of the ages will be sorted out, every speck of it known by an omniscient God. Bone will be knit to bone; flesh, muscles, nerves, and sinews will be renewed as the dead are reshaped. Those who died but yesterday, still lying in satin-lined coffins in funeral homes, and those who died when the world was young, in the dawn of time—God knows them all and where they lie. He will call and, as crystals dissolved in a liquid re-form when the conditions are right, the dead will be re-formed, down to the very last man, woman, boy, or girl who has ever lived.

"What is this that thou hast done?" (Genesis 3:13) That is the second great question in the Bible. When God has reassembled the dead He will ask this question again. Memory will leap to life and long-forgotten sins will live again: childhood sins, sins of youth; sins committed at home, school, work, play; sins committed in broad daylight and sins committed under shade and cover of the night.

Finally, the Holy Spirit records the sentence: "And death and hell were cast into the lake of fire. This is the second death. And whosoever was not found written in the book of life was cast into the lake of fire" (Revelation 20:14-15). Could any words be more final, more solemn?

The great word of the gospel is "Come!" God can not end the book of Revelation without writing it down over and over again. Those who will not come will hear that other word: "Depart!" "I never knew you: depart from me" (Matthew 7:23).

Nobody needs to experience a lost eternity. Salvation in Christ, salvation full and free, salvation for ever and ever, is available for all, here and now.

Here is a man with a serious disease. He goes to the doctor who prescribes some medicine and assures the patient, "Take this and you will live." The man, for one reason or another, neglects to take the medicine. Who can tell why? Perhaps he doesn't like the doctor's personality, perhaps the medicine has a nasty taste, perhaps he doesn't believe the diagnosis or have faith in the cure, or perhaps he is too busy to bother. But for one foolish reason or another, the medicine lies neglected by his bed. The man dies and has nobody to blame but himself. The remedy was within reach, but he would not take it.

Men go to the lake of fire not because they are sinners, but because they refuse the remedy, the salvation God offers in the person of His Son. Who knows what excuse keeps a person from Christ? He doesn't like the preacher, perhaps, or he doesn't like the dogmatic terms of the gospel, or he thinks he's not nearly so bad as the Bible makes out. But he dies in his sins, and as surely as there is a God in Heaven, he will arrive at the great white throne and end up in the lake of fire.

THE RICH MAN IN HELL (LUKE 16:19 -31)

Different words are used in Scripture to denote the abode of the dead. There is the Hebrew word *sheol*, which occurs sixty-five times in the Old Testament and is variously translated as "the grave," "the pit," and "Hell." When translated "grave," it is to be distinguished from *keber*, the ordinary Hebrew word for a grave or burying place. The corresponding Greek word in the New Testament is *Hades*, used by the Greeks to denote the unseen world. The Holy Spirit equates *Hades* with *sheol* (Acts 2:27,31; Psalm 16:10). *Hades* occurs eleven times in the New Testament, and in every case except one it is translated "Hell." The English word "Hell" comes to us from the Anglo-Saxon *helle*, signifying a hidden place.

The words *sheol* and *Hades* are used to denote a downward direction in the earth; a place associated with mourning, sorrow, fright, terror, silence, and punishment, from which there is no escape apart from resurrection.

Two other words are used in the New Testament to designate the unseen world. One of these is *gehenna*, which is a transliteration of the Hebrew *Ge' Hinnom* (the valley of Hinnom). The corresponding Old Testament word is *Tophet*, which was a place in this notable valley. The valley of Hinnom was cursed because the fires of Molech were kept burning there, and it was there that the apostate Hebrews sacrificed their children (2 Chronicles 33:6). Here, too, the refuse of Jerusalem was burned in undying flames (Jeremiah 7:31-33; 2 Kings 23:10; Isaiah 66:24). The valley of Hinnom was used in this way in the Lord's times. The association of ideas made it a fit synonym for the place of judgment fire. The word *geenna*, the usual form of the word in the New Testament, occurs twelve times and is always rendered "Hell." It is the word that best embodies the thought of that lake of fire to which the lost are finally consigned.

One other word, *tartarus*, is used in 2 Peter 2:4 to depict the place where God has imprisoned certain angels whose sin was similar to that of the Sodomites. They went after "strange flesh."

In Luke 16:19-31 the Lord Jesus drew aside the veil to show us what happens after death. He told the story of a rich man and a beggar named Lazarus and recounted their experiences beyond the boundaries of time. The word Jesus used to describe the underworld was *Hades,* and the description He gave is that of Hades as it was prior to His own death, burial, and resurrection. Changes effected by His resurrection and ascension seem to relate to the believing dead and the transference of the "paradise" section of Hades to a new location. The conditions of torment and of bliss described by the Lord are virtually unchanged, so we can take this story at its face value as describing the condition of the saved and the lost in the next life.

This story does not seem to be a parable, but an actual incident known to Jesus. In our Lord's parables the people are unnamed. In this account both Lazarus and Abraham are named, suggesting that this is no mere parable but a sober statement of historical fact.

We have set before us:

I. Two Families
II. Two Funerals
III. Two Futures
    A. One of Great Happiness
    B. One of Great Horror

The rich man had five brothers, all of whom were as careless and as lost as he was. He was wealthy, clothed in purple and fine linen, the garments of royalty. The word for *clothed* literally means

"habitually clothed," the imperfect tense suggesting that he anticipated no end to his good fortune. Moreover, he "fared sumptuously every day," the word *sumptuously* meaning "in splendor." A
similar word is used of the robe Herod mockingly put on Christ at
His trial, a "gorgeous" robe (Luke 23:11). The man lived like a lord.

It does not take much imagination to reconstruct the kind of
conversation that would be common around the table in that rich
man's home, especially when he entertained his brothers. It would
turn naturally to business, and scorn would be poured on the
statement of the Lord Jesus "Ye cannot serve God and mammon"
(Luke 16:13). The conversation would turn no doubt to politics,
and all would agree that Christ's claim to be the king of the Jews was
ridiculous. "Love your enemies, indeed!" The conversation would
turn to religion, and it would soon be decided that nobody of any
importance believed in Jesus. He attracted fishermen, peasants,
Galileans, and people like that wretched Lazarus who plagued the
rich man's gate with his detestable presence. "I never give him a
thing," the rich man might say, "yet he sits there. Wish I knew how
to get rid of him." That was one family.

The family of Lazarus seemed to consist, for the most part, of
the dogs that roamed the streets, who showed him more kindness
than ever he received from Dives, as the wealthy man is sometimes
called.

Jesus said of Lazarus that he was full of sores, an eloquent
testimony to the neglect in which he lived. He was "laid" at the gate
of the rich man, the word meaning "cast down," suggesting that he
was just dumped there. Nobody wanted him or cared whether he
lived or died. And he was "desiring" to be fed with the crumbs that
fell from the rich man's table. The word means "eagerly desiring,"
and the implication is that he desired in vain, just as the prodigal
son "would fain" have filled his gnawing stomach with what the
pigs ate (Luke 15:16). Not even leftovers from the kitchen came out
to the gate to stave off the pangs of hunger that were the lot of
Lazarus.

Then came the two funerals. The Lord gave us a tender touch
in describing the funeral of Lazarus. His emaciated, disease-ridden
corpse was doubtless hauled away in disgust by the city scaven-
gers and, for all we know, was unceremoniously dumped into the
fires of gehenna along with the rest of the city refuse. But Lazarus
himself was not there. He was "carried by the angels into Abraham's

bosom." That in itself suggests that Lazarus was a genuine believer. The Scripture says of the angels, "Are they not all ministering spirits, sent forth to minister for them who shall be heirs of salvation?" (Hebrews 1:14). Those angels had hovered over this destitute man during his lifetime. They had carried back to the throne of God their detailed reports of the callous neglect with which he was treated, the contempt with which he was viewed. That ominous word "inasmuch" had been written alongside the rich man's name in the book that is kept on high (Matthew 25:41-46).

So the angels carried the soul of Lazarus into "Abraham's bosom." The Pharisees taught that there were three places to which the blessed dead were conducted. They were taken to Abraham's bosom, to a place "under the throne of glory," and to "the garden of Eden" (paradise). Speaking of death they would say, "This day he sits in Abraham's bosom." The Old Testament saints at death were said to be "gathered" to their "fathers" or "gathered to [their] people" (Genesis 25:8; 2 Kings 22:20). The idea is that they went to a place of rest and peace and to the fellowship of those who loved the Lord.

In contrast, the Lord Jesus passed over the funeral of the rich man with barely a word: "The rich man also died, and was buried" (Luke 16:22). No doubt he had a magnificent funeral, with mourners hired to lament his death, and eulogies read at his graveside. Great interest was probably taken in his will, in the size of his estate, and in his heirs and beneficiaries. No doubt his brothers came in for their share, since this rich man seems to have had genuine regard for them. Perhaps, like Joseph of Arimathea, this rich man had prepared a costly sepulcher for his bones in Jerusalem. Perhaps, like Nicodemus who brought a fortune in spices for the burying of Jesus, this rich man had made provision to be suitably embalmed, wrapped in the fine linen to which he had grown accustomed, and saturated with aromatic spices to offset the stench of the grave. He "died, and was buried." That was all Jesus had to say about it. Some ancient versions give us a slightly different rendering: "Died and was buried in hell."

The real teaching of the story is that there are two possible futures. One is a future of great happiness. For Lazarus it was bliss such as he had never known on earth; it was good company and fellowship from which his wretched estate on earth had excluded him; it was "joy unspeakable and full of glory." No details are given. All we know is that he was "comforted." In life he had received "evil things" (the word used being *kakos*, meaning "depraved, bad in nature, vicious disposition and desires"). He had been the recipient of that kind of treatment, but now he rested in Abraham's bosom.

The other future is one of great horror. The rich man went to a place of torment. He was fully conscious, possessed of all his faculties. He could see, hear, talk, think, remember, and feel. He knew he deserved to be there; although he wailed out his anguish, he never once suggested that injustice had been done to him. He spoke of being "tormented in this flame." Whether or not that is to be taken literally is open to question. If literally, we know of nothing that creates worse pain than a severe burn. If the flames of a lost eternity are to be taken figuratively, they nonetheless suggest excruciating anguish.

Two facts emerge from the conversation between the rich man and Abraham. We notice at once that the lost man in Hades became a sudden believer in prayer. But he prayed too late, to the wrong person, for the wrong things, and without any appeal to the one glorious name that makes prayer effective, the name of Jesus.

He prayed first that Lazarus might be sent down to where he was with a drop of water to cool his tongue; his anguish was so great that even a moment's relief seemed like a priceless treasure. He would have given all his wealth for a brief respite, but that wealth had been left behind on earth. Now *he* was the beggar.

He was told some of the facts of the life he had lived on earth. "Son, remember . . ." added Abraham, and those two ominous words awoke a million memories. Many years ago my father often quoted a verse that makes the point well:

> Memory like an adder stingeth
> All the wasted past upbringeth,
> If I could the viper strangle
> Half my misery would be o'er;
> But around my heart it coileth
> 'Tis the worm that never dieth
> Gnawing at my bosom's door.
> Will he leave me nevermore?
> Echo answers: "Never more."

The flames of a lost eternity will be made all the hotter by the memory of wasted opportunities, of times when the Holy Spirit convicted of sin and Christ came knocking at the door of the heart, only to be turned away. Memory will recall the time when Christ was rejected for a godless friendship, a promotion at work, a false religious belief, a game of golf on Sunday, some sinful indulgence of the flesh, or fear of the sneers of the world.

Then the rich man was told the facts of eternity: "Between us and you there is a great gulf fixed" (Luke 16:26). The word *gulf* is *chasma,* from which we get our English word *chasm.* It is a medical word for an open wound, perhaps containing a veiled reference to Lazarus's running sores which had so disgusted the rich man and which he had done nothing to help or to heal.

The rich man also learned the horrifying fact that his condition was permanent. There is a road that runs from earth to Heaven, a road Lazarus found, a road that now runs by way of the cross. There is also a road that runs from earth to Hell, the road the rich man had trod flamboyantly and carelessly (Matthew 7:13-14). But no road runs from Hades to Heaven. One's destination is forever fixed at death. The Roman Catholic idea of purgatory is without any foundation in fact.

The rich man had never been particularly impressed by preaching when he lived on earth, but in a lost eternity he became a sudden believer in preaching as well as prayer. He said, "I pray thee therefore, father, that thou wouldest send him [Lazarus] to my father's house: For I have five brethren . . . lest they also come into this place of torment" (Luke 16:27-28). He had the idea that some mighty miracle might awaken his brothers to their peril; but he was quickly disillusioned, for Abraham replied, "They have Moses and the prophets; let them hear them" (16:29). His brothers had the Bible. That is all they needed. God has told us all we need to know in His Word. Miracles are superfluous.

At once the rich man began to argue. "Nay, father Abraham: but if one went unto them from the dead, they will repent" (Luke 16:30). Repentance, indeed, is what they needed, and the rich man's pathetic hope was pinned on some startling miracle that might awaken his brothers. If Lazarus came back and could tell them what awaited them beyond the grave, perhaps they would repent. He was cut short: "If they hear not Moses and the prophets, neither will they be persuaded [much less repent], though one rose from the dead" (16:31). If a person will not believe the Bible, then he will not believe anything else God might say or do.

The truth of the Lord's words was soon evident; the very next person the Lord Jesus raised from the dead was a man named Lazarus. So great was the hardness of the unbelievers' hearts, they had immediate plans to put him back in his tomb (John 12:10). Nor did the Lord's own resurrection persuade them (Matthew 28:11-13). On the contrary, the obdurate leaders of Israel bribed the soldiers with large sums of money to spread the rumor that the disciples had stolen the body of Christ.

And there the veil falls back over the unseen world. We are left with the rich man silenced, his doom forever sealed, his unsaved loved ones still on earth rejecting the Word of God. That is where the Spirit of God leaves the unbeliever today—face to face with the Scriptures, which he can either disbelieve to his eternal peril or take at face value to his eternal joy.

Heaven (Revelation 21:1–22:5)

Just before He went to Calvary, the Lord Jesus took His disciples aside and told them He was going away: "In my Father's house are many mansions: if it were not so, I would have told you. I go to prepare a place for you. And if I go and prepare a place for you, I will come again, and receive you unto myself; that where I am, there ye may be also" (John 14:2-3).

The Lord's heart was hungry for home. He had been here for over thirty-three years. Gethsemane, Gabbatha, Golgotha, and the grave lay ahead, and after that—glory. He wanted His friends to know that although He would soon be leaving them, it would only be for a while; in the meantime, He would be getting things ready for them on the other side. Heaven is a prepared place for a prepared people. It is what someone has called "my favorite country."

Three things about this country will occupy our attention in this chapter. First, it is *a hidden country*. Paul said, "Eye hath not seen, nor ear heard, neither have entered into the heart of man, the things which God hath prepared for them that love him" (1 Corinthians 2:9). While this statement may have primary application to spiritual verities, it has application also to eternal verities. Heaven is a hidden country beyond the normal reach of our senses.

Just because Heaven exists beyond the realm of our senses does not mean that it is unsubstantial or unreal. Many things in the physical world are beyond the range of human senses but are within the range of measurement of specialized instruments. Just because we can not see or hear something does not mean that it is not there.

The eye, for instance, requires light in order to see. Light is an electromagnetic radiation. The electromagnetic spectrum has frequencies as low as those associated with electrical power transmission (sixty cycles per second) to frequencies as high as cosmic rays (about six sextillion—6×10^{21}—cycles per second). In between are radio waves, heat waves, light waves, ultraviolet rays, X-rays, and gamma rays. Between the heat rays and the ultraviolet rays is that narrow segment of the vast electromagnetic spectrum to which our eyes are sensitive. If we were to try to depict the electromagnetic spectrum on a lineal scale by drawing a line to show all the points on the scale between the low frequencies of electrical power and the high frequencies of the cosmic rays, we would need to draw a line 300 billion miles long. The visible spectrum, the part of the line that represents the utmost limits of man's ability to see, would be represented on that line by one inch. That is how little of what exists we can actually *see.*

The same is true of hearing. In the laboratory, scientists use a high-powered whistle known as the Galton whistle. The sound in the beam under the reflector is intense enough to hold cork ships in suspension and is actually louder than a thunderclap, but we hear nothing. We have developed instruments called barium titanate ceramic transducers, which can produce sound of such intensity that it will splash water all over the place or shake grease and dirt from instrument parts at a million cycles or more, but nothing is heard. At the lower end of this spectrum there are sounds we can feel but can not hear; and still further down, there are sounds so deep that they can not even be felt. Scientists have discovered, for instance, that the earth rings like a bell after heavy earthquake shocks, but it does so with a tone about sixteen octaves below the lowest note a man can hear. So, just because we can not see something or hear something does not mean that it is not there. It simply means that we are not tuned in to it.

Heaven is a hidden place. Heaven, for all we know, may simply be a place, just like our own world, operating at a different frequency or in a different time-space dimension.

The fastest thing known to man is the speed of light, which travels at some 186,000 miles per second, an almost inconceivable six trillion miles a year. Light speeds across the void of sidereal space at the highest velocity anything can attain. We have detected objects in space that are estimated to be some fifteen billion light years away from the earth. Suppose Heaven were out there, beyond the farthest stars in space. Traveling at the speed of light, it would take us billions of years to get there.

But *is* light the fastest thing known to man? In actual fact there is something that travels so much faster than light, that light by comparison is a lumbering ox wagon. The fastest thing known to man is the speed of thought.

When I was in the British army I went once into the Church of the Holy Sepulchre in Jerusalem, and for the first time in my young life, I smelled incense. Its peculiar pungent odor left its mark on my memory. Years later I walked into a dime store in Chicago at Christmastime, and for the second time in my life I smelled incense. The store was selling miniature manger scenes and, along with them, small incense burners. The moment that unforgettable fragrance touched my senses I was transported back some thirty years in time and over some six thousand miles in space, and—in thought—instantaneously I stood again in the Church of the Holy Sepulchre in Jerusalem. That is the speed of thought.

When a believer dies, Paul said he is "absent from the body . . . present with the Lord" (2 Corinthians 5:8). The transfer from one realm to the other is instantaneous. When we receive our resurrection bodies, we shall have bodies with remarkable new powers:

> There is one glory of the sun, and another glory of the moon, and another glory of the stars: for one star differeth from another star in glory. So also is the resurrection of the dead. It [the body] is sown in corruption; it is raised in incorruption: It is sown in dishonor; it is raised in glory: it is sown in weakness; it is raised in power: It is sown a natural body; it is raised a spiritual body. There is a natural body, and there is a spiritual body (1 Corinthians 15:41-44).

The physical will be present in that resurrection body, but it will be subordinated to the spiritual. Physical properties will exist but higher spiritual properties will control. The word Paul used

400

here for the "spiritual" body is *pneumatikos*, and it is applied to things in the spiritual sphere as well as to things presently in Satan's realm (Ephesians 6:12). In Paul's great resurrection passage the word is deliberately put in contrast with what is natural (1 Corinthians 15). It is used in 1 Corinthians 10:3-4 to describe the kind of food eaten by the Israelites during their wilderness wanderings; the word *supernatural* would best express the meaning there. It occurs twenty-six times in the New Testament. It is always translated "spiritual" and is the only word so rendered, except in 1 Corinthians 14:12 where the expression "spiritual gifts" is literally "spirituals."

From all this we gather that our spiritual body is to have spirit properties. It is to be a supernatural body, able to do things of which we are incapable in our present natural bodies. It is to be a body in which the spirit predominates. We speak of ourselves as consisting of body, soul, and spirit. The Holy Spirit puts it the other way around: "spirit and soul and body" (1 Thessalonians 5:23). That was the original order and that will be the new order. The spirit will control soul and body so that the properties of the spirit will rule the intellectual, the emotional, the volitional, and also the physical.

So then, even though Heaven may be billions of light years away, that will make no difference to us; with our spiritual bodies, space will be annihilated by thought. We shall be able to travel the vast distances of space at the speed of thought, taking our new bodies with us wherever we wish to go. Heaven, then, is a hidden place, but it is not far, far away. It is near to us, closer than the house next door.

Also, Heaven is *a happy place*. Most religions envision Heaven as an ideal place in which to spend eternity. The ancient Norsemen, with their love of battle, thought of Valhalla as a place for warriors. The Romans depicted Heaven as Elysian fields. Muslims envision the place as a perfumed paradise where men lie on soft couches quaffing cups of wine handed to them by maidens of exotic beauty, who exist solely to bring carnal pleasure to the faithful. At the other end of the pagan scale is the Heaven of the eastern religions such as nirvana, the ethical state that makes further births unnecessary, a state in which the spirit is no longer encumbered with a body, a state of passionless peace in which the flame of desire has been extinguished—a state that hardly involves "living" in any ordinary sense and scarcely seems worth bothering to attain. "The wick is finished, the oil is dry, the dewdrop slips into the shining sea." The curse from which the Buddhist longs to escape is life itself. The Biblical Heaven avoids the sensuality of the Muslim Heaven and the arid nothingness of the Buddhist.

We come closest to understanding Heaven when we look at the celestial city described in Revelation 21 and 22. In the first place this city seems to be a literal city—a real, actual, tangible city for real people. It is the place which Jesus says He has gone to prepare for us. The fact that John described the place in symbolic language does not make it any the less a literal reality. The symbolism is doubtless necessary, because of our inability to grasp data outside the realm of our present experience. If a nuclear physicist were attempting to explain to a five-year-old the difference between nuclear fission and nuclear fusion, he would try to accommodate his language to the vocabulary and comprehension of a child. He would have to resort to pictures and analogies. John did that in describing the celestial city.

It is very much like an earthly city, yet at the same time very much unlike an earthly city. It will come down out of Heaven from God and will be brought out of eternity into time. It is a perfect cube measuring twelve thousand furlongs in each direction (probably about fifteen hundred miles). The height of the city is staggering, unless we envision it as a celestial satellite brought into time-space dimensions. During the millennial age this city is to have a direct relation to earth, but it is essentially heavenly in character and composition (Revelation 21:2).

We can learn much about Heaven by studying the details of this city. That it is a happy place is evident from what is *not* in that city. In the first place, there is no sin. Sin has wrecked and ruined this world, but God is determined that it shall not wreck and ruin the world to come. All unregenerate people will be eternally banished from Heaven. Their destination is Hell, which is just as real a place as Heaven.

> But the fearful, and unbelieving, and the abominable, and murderers, and whoremongers, and sorcerers, and idolaters, and all liars, shall have their part in the lake which burneth with fire (Revelation 21:8).

> And there shall in no wise enter into it [the celestial city]

anything that defileth, neither whatsoever worketh abomination, or maketh a lie: but they which are written in the Lamb's book of life (Revelation 21:27).

There is no sea connected with that city, which suggests that life in Heaven will be different in some ways from life as we know it today. Or perhaps, as so often in Scripture, the sea is symbolic of the restless nations. Heaven is a place where all that is symbolized by the sea—the heaving, storm-tossed sea—will be absent. No restlessness, no strife, will ever enter there.

There is no more sorrow; all tears are wiped away. Heaven has no funeral homes, no insane asylums, no hospitals, no prisons, no armies, no wars. The tragedies that plow through human homes and break human hearts are unknown there.

There is no more sun. The light of that city comes from within, not from without. "And there shall be no night there; and they need no candle, neither light of sun; for the Lord God giveth them light" (Revelation 22:5). Everything that we associate with the dark, with shadows and gloom, with the terrors of the night, will be missing from Heaven.

There is no sanctuary there, no temple. People will need no mere building to remind them to worship. "The Lord God Almighty and the Lamb are the temple of it" (Revelation 21:22). Worship will be the instinctive desire, the irrepressible response, of every heart.

But if Heaven is notable for what is prohibited there, it is nonetheless notable for what is present there. Our believing relatives will be there; after all, so much of our happiness is related to people. Heaven will be filled with wonderful people, with the salt of the earth, the saints of all ages, the aristocracy of the human race. And every one of them will be just like Jesus. Imagine a world where every single person, man and woman, boy and girl, is just like Jesus; where every thought, word, deed, every moment in each and every place, is Christlike! John said, "We shall be like him; for we shall see him as he is" (1 John 3:2).

Some are troubled by the thought that in Heaven they will be haunted by the memory of lost loved ones. Not so. Nor for a single moment will God allow the thoughts of His own to be held ransom by those in Hell. C. S. Lewis gave us the best explanation of what will happen when we reach the other shore. In his book *The Great Divorce* he pictured a person dying and arriving in the lower regions, in a gray city where everything is drab, dilapidated, and dull, where the sky is overcast and threatening rain. In the background, too, is the impending horror that one day it will grow permanently dark, that the world will be gripped by blackness forever. The people in that city are not pleasant. They are quarrelsome, selfish, peevish people.

Some of them get a chance to visit the outskirts of Heaven. They take a bus ride up the face of an enormous chasm and at last arrive at their destination. Shining ones from "deep heaven" come to meet them. But the visitors do not like even the remotest fringes of Heaven. The grass hurts their ghostly feet, the sun dazzles their eyes, and the sound of falling water dins discordantly in their ears. C. S. Lewis imagined various conversations carried on between the bright ones and the ghost people from the underworld. In one of the conversations the question of lost loved ones comes up, and the shining one explains why such thoughts have no room in "deep heaven." He reminds the ghost to whom he is speaking of the journey up from the underworld, and the ghost sees again that chasm which it had taken so long to climb and which had appeared to him to be so enormous. Stooping down, the shining one hunts among the cracks in the soil and, pointing to one, says, "This is the one up which you came."

In other words, in Heaven we have such a tremendous sense of reality that thoughts of the lost will be but a crack in the soil— nothing. Not worth a second thought. Our perspective in Heaven will be so wholly God's perspective that things which loom so large and important to us now will be absorbed into a new dimension of living that will make such things inconsequential. Certainly God will not allow us to be haunted by thoughts of our lost loved ones. No sad thought will ever find a place in Heaven.

Then, too, our blessed Redeemer will be there. In describing the celestial city John, like his Master, kept the best wine till last. "And they shall see his face," he said (Revelation 22:4). That will be the crowning bliss of Heaven. No wonder Fanny Crosby, blind, but with her spiritual vision quickened, could write words like these in her hymn "When My Life Work Is Ended":

> Oh, the soul-thrilling rapture
> when I view His blessed face,
> And the luster of His kindly beaming eye;

> How my full heart will praise Him
> for the mercy, love, and grace,
> That prepare for me a mansion in the sky.

Heaven is a hidden place, a happy place, and *a holy place.* Not everybody will be in Heaven. The dirty, the degraded, and the deceitful will be banned from Heaven. Lust, lewdness, and lying disqualify a person from entering there.

Only those who are washed in the blood of the Lamb will enter through Heaven's gates. The celestial city has towering walls of adamantine jasper and gates of pearl. Those gates of pearl symbolize the sufferings of Christ that made access to the city possible.

When the Lord Jesus told His disciples that He was going away to prepare a place for them, they naturally wanted to know how they could be sure of finding their way to that place. He said, "I am the way . . . no man cometh unto the Father, but by me" (John 14:6). There are many ways to Christ, but there is only one way to Heaven. Jesus alone is that way. To get to Heaven we must first come to Christ.

In the old days in the South, a landowner had a slave who was a Christian. When the master died, folks told him he had gone to Heaven. "Oh, no," said the slave, "Master has not gone to Heaven." They asked him how he could be so sure. "Well," he replied, "when Master went North or took a long journey he talked about it for a long time, and he prepared himself for the journey. I never heard him talk about going to Heaven, and I never saw him get ready to go."

Heaven is a prepared place for a prepared people. It is a holy place. One gets there only by coming to Christ as a lost sinner and accepting Him as personal Savior.

Years ago I was invited to come to the United States to take up a position on the staff of the Moody Bible Institute in Chicago. My wife and I were Canadian citizens, and coming to the United States to live meant that adequate preparations had to be made. We could not just walk over the Canadian-United States border and move to Chicago. We had to make application to the United States Department of Immigration for permission to enter the country as permanent residents. We had to go through a period of thorough examination, answer scores of questions, be fingerprinted, and take a trip to Vancouver for a personal interview with immigration officials. We had to pledge our allegiance to the United States; and I had to state my willingness, if necessary, to serve in the armed forces. We had to have passports. Those passports, with the accompanying documents, had to be presented to the immigration officials at the American border and be properly inspected, verified, and endorsed. Only then were we allowed to take up residence in the United States. To enjoy the privileges and protection of the country, we had to enter it legally.

In the same way, many years before, we both made application to go to Heaven. The Lord said to us in His Word what He says to everybody: "You can only enter Heaven on my terms." When my wife and I made application to come to the United States someone had to vouch for us. Just so, when we made application for Heaven, God said, "And who will vouch for you?" We needed a citizen of Heaven to take up our cause. We found that person in Jesus, Son of the living God, the One who sits at God's right hand. He vouches for all those who come to God by Him (Hebrews 7:25).

It has been my privilege to travel to many countries around the world in the course of my ministry. Every country into which I have sought entrance has filed me through its immigration barrier. Some countries have treated me with much greater ease than others. Since I have a Canadian passport, I have rarely had more than a passing nod from the officials of countries in the British Commonwealth. Some countries are much tougher than others.

The toughest country of all to enter is Heaven; for Heaven is a holy place, and God will keep out all who have no right to be there. To get into Heaven you have to be more than a citizen, you have to be a son. Jesus said, "Except a man be born again, he cannot see the kingdom of God" (John 3:3).

There are no illegal immigrants in Heaven. Everyone must have a passport. Happily, it is the easiest thing in the world to obtain a passport to Heaven. Jesus is all the passport we need, and He says, "Him that cometh to me I will in no wise cast out" (John 6:37).

---

1. David Nelson, *The Cause and Cure of Infidelity* (American Tract Society, 1841), pp. 299-313.

Appendix

Bible prophecies deal with the rise and fall of EMPIRES, such as,

Egypt (Isaiah 19:1–20:6; 30:1-17; 31:1-9; Jeremiah
    43:7-13; 44:1-30; 46:1-28; Ezekiel 29:1-21; 32:32)
Assyria (Isaiah 10:5-34; 20:1-6; 30:31; 31:8-9; Nahum;
    Zephaniah 2:13-15)
Babylon (Isaiah 13:1-22; 14:4-23; 47:1-15; Jeremiah 25:9-14; 27:1-
    22; 50:1–51:64; Habakkuk 1:6-11)
Persia (Daniel 8:3-7,20; 11:2)
Greece (Daniel 8:3-27; 11:2-4)
Rome (Daniel 2:33,40; 7:7-11,19-28)

Bible prophecies deal with the fortunes of lesser NATIONS,
such as,

Israel (Genesis 15:13-14; 49:1-28; Numbers 23:7-10, 18-24; 24:3-
    9,14-24; Deuteronomy 28:1-68; 33:1-29; Isaiah 9:8-21; 28:1-
    29; Hosea 9:1-17; 11:1-12; Amos 2:6; 3:11-15; 5:27; 7:8-9; 8:11-
    12; 9:1-10; Micah 1:6-9)
Judah (Isaiah 37:6-7,33-35; 39:5-7; Jeremiah 4:5-31; 5:14-19; 7:32-
    34; 19:6-9; 20:4-6; 21:3-10; 24:8-10; 25:8-11; 29:10; 32:26-29;
    42:7-22; Ezekiel 6:1-14; 7:1-27; 12:1-16; 14:12-23; Amos 2:4-5;
    Micah 4:9-13; Zephaniah 1:1-13)
Ammon (2 Kings 8:8-13; Jeremiah 49:1-6; Ezekiel 21:28-32; 25:
    1-7)
Edom (Isaiah 21:11-12; 34:5-6; Jeremiah 49:7-22; Ezekiel 25:12-
    14; 35:1-15; Joel 3:19; Obadiah)
Elam (Jeremiah 49:34-39)

Moab (Isaiah 15:1–16:14; Jeremiah 48; Ezekiel 25:8-11; Amos 2:1-3; Zephaniah 2:8-11)
Philistia (Jeremiah 47; Amos 1:6-8)

Bible prophecies concern themselves with CITIES, such as,

Jerusalem (Isaiah 29:1-24; Jeremiah 9:11; 25:15-18; 34:1-7; 37:8-10; Matthew 23:37; 24:1-2)
Tyre (Isaiah 23; Jeremiah 25:22; 47:4; Ezekiel 26–28; Joel 3:4; Amos 1:9-10)
Sidon (Ezekiel 28:21-24)
Damascus (Jeremiah 49:23-27; Amos 1:3-5)
Nineveh (Nahum)
Capernaum (Matthew 11:23)

Prophecies in the Bible are sometimes directed toward INDI-VIDUALS, such as,

Jezebel (1 Kings 21:23)
Josiah (1 Kings 13:1-3)
Jehoiakim (Jeremiah 36:29-30)
Zedekiah (Jeremiah 32:1-5)
Nebuchadnezzar (Daniel 4)
Cyrus (Isaiah 44:28–45:6)
Judas Iscariot (Psalm 41:9; John 6:64; 13:18,21)

Prophecies concern themselves with various EVENTS, such as,

famines (Genesis 41:1-36)
floods (Genesis 6)
wars (2 Chronicles 16:9; Jeremiah 50:21-29; Zechariah 14:2)
revolution (1 Kings 11:11-13; 14:7-11)
intrigues (Daniel 11:24-27)
births (Genesis 18:10; 25:23; Judges 13:1-5; Luke 1:13,31-37)
marriages (Daniel 11:6,17)
deaths (2 Samuel 12:14; 1 Kings 14:12; 2 Kings 6:24–7:20)

A vast body of prophecy has to do with the FIRST COMING OF CHRIST.

He was to be born
of the seed of Abraham (Genesis 21:12; Galatians 3:16)

of the tribe of Judah (Genesis 49:8-10; Revelation 5:5)
of the line of David (2 Samuel 7:12-13; Jeremiah 23:5; Acts 13:23; Romans 1:3-4)
of a virgin (Isaiah 7:14; Matthew 1:18-21)
in Bethlehem (Micah 5:2; Matthew 2:1)

He was *to sojourn in Egypt* (Hosea 11:1; Matthew 2:13-15).

He was to be
announced by a herald (Malachi 4:5-6; Mark 1:1-8; Matthew 11:13-14)
anointed with the Holy Spirit (Psalm 45:7; Isaiah 11:2; 61:1; Matthew 3:16; Luke 4:18-19)

His ministry was to commence in *Galilee* (Isaiah 9:1; Matthew 4:12-13,16,23).

He was to *preach the gospel* (Isaiah 61:1-2; Luke 4:16-19).

His ministry was to be accompanied by *tenderness, compassion, and transparency* (Isaiah 40:11; 42:3; 53:9; Matthew 12:18-21; 1 Peter 2:21-23).

He was to be *rejected*
by His relatives (Psalm 69:8; John 7:2-5)
by His nation (Psalm 69:4; 118:22; Matthew 21:42-46)

He was to *ride in triumph into Jerusalem* (Zechariah 9:9; Matthew 21:1-11).

He was to be *betrayed*
for thirty pieces of silver (Zechariah 11:12; Matthew 26:14-16) and the blood money subsequently used to *buy a potter's field* (Zechariah 11:13; Matthew 27:3-10)
at the hands of a friend (Psalm 41:9; John 13:18-21); in fact *all His friends would forsake Him* (Zechariah 13:7; Matthew 26:56)

After His death, He was to

be buried with the rich (Isaiah 53:9; John 19:38-42)
be raised from the dead (Psalm 16:10; Acts 2:23-32)

ascend into Heaven (Psalm 68:18; Luke 24:51)
take His place at God's right hand in Heaven (Psalm 110:1; Hebrews 1:3)
exercise a priestly office in Heaven (Zechariah 6:13; Romans 8:34)

In addition to the many Scriptures that foretold the Lord's first coming, all of which were literally and actually fulfilled, there are many that foretell HIS SECOND COMING (John 14:1-3; Acts 1:11; 1 Corinthians 15). Some of these seem to be having an initial fulfillment today, as coming events cast their shadows on our times.

The Lord's second coming will be preceded

by *perilous times* (2 Timothy 3:1-9; Matthew 24)
by a tremendous *knowledge explosion* (Daniel 12:4)
by *labor strife* (James 5:1-7)
by the *rebirth of the state of Israel* (Isaiah 11:10-16; 43:5-6; 60:8-10; 61:4-6; Jeremiah 16:14-16; 23:3; Ezekiel 11:17-20; 37:1-28; Matthew 24:31)
by the rise of *Russia and her satellites* (Ezekiel 38–39)
by *the apostasy of the professing church* (2 Timothy 4:1-4; Jude; 2 Peter 2:1-22; Revelation 17:1-6,15-18)

It will be marked

by a repetition of times such as characterized *the days of Noah* (Matthew 24:37-39; Genesis 4–6)
by the dawn of *the nuclear age* (2 Peter 3:1-13)
by *the rapture of the church to Heaven* (1 Thessalonians 4:13-18; 1:10; 5:9; 1 Corinthians 15)
by *the coming of the antichrist* (2 Thessalonians 2:1-12; Revelation 13; 17:7-18)
by *the day of the Lord,* with its accompanying sorrows, including the great tribulation and judgment of earth (Isaiah 2:12,19; 13:6-11; 26:20-21; 34:1,2,8; 66:15-16; Jeremiah 46:10; 61:2; Ezekiel 13:5; 30:1-3; Joel 1:15; 2:1-2,11,30-32; Obadiah 15; Zechariah 12:2-3,9; 14:1-9; Amos 24:21-22; Zephaniah 1:7,14,17; Malachi 4:1,5; 1 Thessalonians 5:2; 2 Thessalonians 2:2; 2 Peter 3:10; Matthew 24:21-22; Revelation 6:7,12-16; 7:3-4;

11:8,13,18; 14:10-20; 15:1; 12:6,13-17; 16:1,8-9,19; 17:15; 18:8,12; 19:11,14-16)

It will be accompanied

by *the judgment seat of Christ* for believers (Matthew 12:36; 16:27; Luke 14:14; Romans 14:10; 1 Corinthians 3:11-15; 4:5; 2 Corinthians 5:10; Galatians 6:7; Ephesians 6:8; Colossians 3:24; 2 Timothy 4:8; Revelation 22:12)

by *the millennial reign of Christ* (Psalm 72:1-20; Isaiah 60:1-22; 62:1-12; 65:17-25; 66:10-14; Ezekiel 37:21-28; Revelation 20:1-6)

by *the imprisonment and doom of Satan* (Revelation 20:7-10)

by *the judgment of the nations* (Matthew 25:31-46)

by *the judgment of the wicked dead* (Revelation 20:11-15)

by *the eternal bliss of the redeemed* (Revelation 21–22)

Scripture references to *Christ's teaching regarding Heaven,* eternal life, "Abraham's bosom," and similar themes include

Matthew 5:12,19-20; 6:20; 7:14; 19:17,21; 25:46
Mark 10:21,30
Luke 6:23; 10:20; 12:33; 16:22,25; 18:22
John 3:13; 4:14,36; 5:24,29,39; 6:27,40,47,54; 10:28; 12:25; 14:2-3; 17:2-3

Scripture references to *Christ's teaching regarding Hell,* judgment, destruction, outer darkness, and related themes include

Matthew 5:22,29-30; 7:13; 8:12; 10:15,28; 11:22-24; 12:36,41-42; 13:40,42,50; 16:18; 18:8-9; 22:13; 23:15,33; 25:30,41,46
Mark 3:29; 9:43,45,47; 12:40
Luke 10:14-15; 11:31-32; 12:5; 16:23-25,28; 20:47
John 5:22,24,27,29-30; 9:39; 12:31; 16:8,11; 17:12[1]

---

1. David F. Siemens, Jr., *Exploring Christianity* (Chicago: Moody Press, 1969), pp. 95-96.

About the Author

D r. John Phillips is a native of Britain where he received some of his Bible teaching from the well-known Stephen F. Olford.

Dr. Phillips served as assistant director of the Moody Correspondence School and director of the Emmaus Correspondence School, one of the largest Bible correspondence ministries in the world. He also served as an instructor in the Moody Evening School and as a teacher on the Institute's radio network; he was a fulltime member of the Extension Department for thirteen years.

John Phillips holds a D.Min. degree from Luther Rice Seminary. Although retired from the Moody faculty, he remains active with his written ministry, and preaching in churches and Bible conferences both in North America and overseas. He and his wife Jean reside in Raleigh, North Carolina.